Y0-CBA-406

Structured BASIC Programming

Structured BASIC Programming

John G. Kemeny

Thomas E. Kurtz
Dartmouth College

John Wiley & Sons
New York Chichester Brisbane Toronto Singapore

Library of Congress Cataloging in Publication Data:

Kemeny, John G.
Structured BASIC programming.

Includes index.
1. BASIC (Computer program language) 2. Structured
programming. I. Kurtz, Thomas E. II. Title.
QA76.73.B3K46 1987 005.13'3 86-28275
ISBN 0-471-81087-8 (pbk.)

Printed in the United States of America

10 9 8 7 6 5 4 3 2 1

Preface

There are at least three reasons for students to learn programming. First, and perhaps the least important, a small percentage of them will become professional programmers. Second, a computer program is undoubtedly the most effective way to represent and study algorithms, whether they be in computer science, mathematics, or any other subject. Third, the discipline of organizing, designing, and writing computer programs is problem-solving personified. The experience of writing large computer programs provides the student with problem-solving skills that can carry over into other fields.

This book addresses the second and third reasons. After introducing the ideas of programming in the first eleven chapters, the book describes many algorithms and programs from a number of fields—simulation, modeling, business, mathematics, music, and so on. The student can thus see how the algorithmic processes from those fields can be successfully transcribed into computer programs. And this book teaches the writing of large programs as an aspect of problem-solving by concentrating on the notion of a subroutine and on collections of external subroutines called *libraries* as well as on the notion of a leveled design sometimes referred to as a *top-down* design.

For students outside the computer sciences, the best of the computer languages available for this purpose is a well-structured BASIC, which is the most widely used computer language in the world. With the addition of the constructs of structured programming and the libraries of external subroutines, BASIC becomes an excellent environment for writing a wide range of programs and applications, from the very small to the fairly large.

The version of BASIC used in this book is True BASIC,* a structured version based on the American National Standard for the Programming Language Full BASIC (X3.113-1987, ANSI, 1430 Broadway, New York, N.Y.). True BASIC provides the traditional constructs of BASIC (such as the GOTO and IF–THEN–GOTO statements) but also provides a range of struc-

---

* True BASIC is a registered ® trademark of True Basic, Incorporated.

tured constructs (such as the DO–LOOP and the SELECT–CASE). In addition, it provides internal and external-named subroutines, with parameters. Last but not least, BASIC provides pixel-independent graphics.

It is impossible to learn programming without significant hands-on experience. The students must have access to a personal computer and to the language True BASIC. A disk containing the programs from this book is available for any computer on which True BASIC runs.

As the student reads each chapter, students should call up and try the programs, experiment with modifications of them and write similar programs of their own. Several exercises should be assigned from each chapter. These are computer exercises that must be written and tried on a computer.

This book is not designed to teach about hardware. Only minimal knowledge of hardware is necessary: how to load a disk, how to type a program and make corrections, and how to run a program. True BASIC is a hardware-independent language; the same BASIC programs will run on a variety of computers. Teaching too much about the peculiarities of a particular computer will only confuse the purpose of the book.

The content of the book is divided into four parts:

Part One	**Introduction to Programming**
Part Two	**Text Applications**
Part Three	**Mathematical Applications**
Part Four	**Other Applications**

Each part is divided into several chapters. Part One is designed to be studied sequentially and in its entirety. The chapters in Parts Two through Four are designed to stand alone, depending only on Part One.

The book stresses throughout the importance of subroutines. Several libraries of external subroutines are referred to and are included in the accompanying diskette. Good structure and style is also stressed, however, in the interests of brevity, the programs themselves are only minimally commented.

This book is not intended to be a complete course in BASIC, per se, although no prior knowledge of BASIC is assumed. Only those details of BASIC that are used are discussed. The student and instructor should therefore have access to a reference manual for the version of BASIC being used. However, some experience with high school algebra is assumed.

The eleven chapters of Part One ("Introduction to Programming") take the reader from the most elementary and short BASIC programs up through, in Chapter 11 ("How to Program"), general advice on how to design, code, test, and debug large BASIC programs. In between, the reader learns the rudiments of the various structured constructs, the defined functions and subroutines, both of the internal and external variety. Lists and tables for both numbers and strings are covered, with examples, as well as the convenient MAT instructions for inputting and printing them. A brief introduction to files is included, as are simple graphics such as plotting points, lines, and text.

In Part One, we occasionally include facts in the chapter summaries that would be disruptive if included in the preceding text. For instance, the rules for legal variable names are presented in a summary, as are the rules for parentheses and the precedence of arithmetic operators.

Part Two deals with text applications. Its four chapters, starting with Chapter 12, illustrate string operations in more detail along with their use in typical applications. Chapter 13 describes several file applications, all of which deal at least in part with strings. Chapter 14 discusses searching and sorting algorithms. For each, both a simple and an efficient algorithm is presented. They lead into an indexing application, as preparing an index of a book. The culmination of Part Two is a miniature data base retrieval system, which appears as Chapter 15. This application illustrates many of the principles of good program design and is a useful application in its own right.

Part Three is concerned with mathematical applications. Chapter 16 deals with the elementary mathematical ideas of trigonometry, roots of equations, prime numbers, and the powerful MAT matrix manipulation instructions. Chapter 17 is concerned with stochastic simulation models. Simple coin flipping, dice rolling, and card dealing lead into a realistic simulation of a baseball team at bat and a study of the behavior of a particular storage management system for a personal computer. Chapter 18 addresses nonstochastic computer modeling. After treating a classic model from ecology, this chapter discusses population models based on cohorts and then describes a model of a small college with a complicated feedback mechanism.

Part Four, starting with Chapter 19, is devoted to business applications, such as budget projections, compound interest, and critical path analysis. Chapter 20 treats games such as tic–tac–toe and nim. Chapter 21 continues and amplifies the discussion of graphics begun in Chapter 7 and includes pictures with transformations and animation. The book ends, in Chapter 22, with a treatment of sound and music; it shows how to generate sound, demonstrates the use of the graphics of Chapter 21 to draw musical scores, and describes a computer program for creating musical harmony.

We wish to express our deep appreciation to the many persons who have contributed to the development of a well-structured version of BASIC and to many of the ideas found in this text. We especially appreciate the efforts of two former colleagues who made major contributions to the language. Arthur W. Luehrmann developed an approach to device-independent graphics at Dartmouth College in the early 1970s. Stephen J. Garland developed the first structured version of BASIC at Dartmouth College around 1974 and served as vice chair on the ANSI X3J2 committee responsible for developing Standard BASIC.

John G. Kemeny

Thomas E. Kurtz
January 1987

Contents

Structured BASIC Programming

PART ONE

INTRODUCTION TO PROGRAMMING

CHAPTER 1

BASIC BEGINNINGS

1.1 INTRODUCTION

A *program* is a set of instructions to the computer to carry out a specific task. A variety of languages exist to write programs. BASIC is an easy-to-learn and yet powerful language for computer programming.

Programs in BASIC consist of *statements*, with each statement occupying one line. The statement starts with a *keyword*, indicating to the computer what kind of statement it is. We will capitalize such keywords for easy identification of the type of statement (although BASIC does not care whether you use capital or lowercase letters).

In this chapter we introduce five of the most common keywords: `LET`, `PRINT`, `END`, `REM`, and `INPUT`. A surprising number of programs can be written with such a limited vocabulary.

These concepts are explained through simple examples. A description of how variables may be named, and what numbers may occur in a program, is included in the Summary.

1.2 A VERY SIMPLE EXAMPLE

We start with a program so simple that we hope it is self-explanatory. Indeed, it is so simple that it would be much faster to do it on a pocket calculator. But it serves to introduce three types of BASIC statements. We call it by the name `DIVIDE`.

The program DIVIDE follows.

```
LET n = 147
LET d = 69
LET q = n/d
PRINT q
END
```

If the program is run, we find that the quotient of 147 and 69 is

```
2.13043
```

The **LET** statement is the work-horse of BASIC. The first two lines are *assignments*; they assign numerical values to the variables `n` (for numerator) and `d` (for denominator). In the third statement **LET** is used to carry out a computation. It carries out the division and assigns the answer to `q` (for quotient). Notice that the sign for division is "/". A **LET** statement always evaluates the right side first, then it assigns the computed value to the variable on the left. Because the right side may contain a long and complicated formula, **LET** can do a lot of work for you.

The **PRINT** statement is an instruction to the computer to show the value of `q` (the answer) on the computer screen. If this statement were omitted (a common programming error) then the computer would know what the answer is, but it wouldn't tell you!

The **END** statement plays a double role. It marks the physical end of your program. And when the computer reaches **END**, it stops. In this simple program the computer will start at the first line, execute each line once, and then stop. We will need more sophisticated *structures* to take advantage of the power of a modern computer.

DIVIDE is the name of the program, and hence the name of the file on the disk that contains the program.

The choice of variable names is up to the programmer. We could have used `numerator` in place of `n`, `denominator` in place of `d`, and `quotient` in place of `q`. Indeed, consider the following variant:

The program DIVIDE2 follows.

```
LET cat = 147
LET dog = 69
LET horse = cat/dog
PRINT horse
END
```

It looks funny, but it will produce exactly the same result as the program **DIVIDE**. The computer does not understand a word like `numerator` or `cat`. It only understands that it is the name of a variable to which it is to assign the value 147.

Even simpler programs can accomplish the same purpose. For example, consider the following:

```
LET q = 147/69
PRINT q
END
```

Or even:

```
PRINT 147/69
END
```

The trouble with these programs is that no matter how many times they are run, they always solve the same problem. Let us make the program a little more interesting.

1.3 ASK ME

One way of making the program useful is to let the user specify what numbers are to be divided. As the PRINT statement is the *tell me* statement, INPUT is the *ask me* statement. When BASIC comes to an INPUT statement, it prints a question mark and waits until you supply the requested information.

The program DIVIDE3 follows.

```
INPUT n, d
LET q = n/d
PRINT q
END
```

We will show two runs of the program DIVIDE3. The numbers after the question mark were, in each run, typed by us. Note that the two numbers must be separated by a comma. The first becomes the value of n, the second the value of d.

```
run

? 147, 69
 2.13043

run

? 1001, 32
 31.2812
```

Let us turn to a more interesting example, a program to convert from the Celsius scale to Fahrenheit.

The program CELSIUS follows.

```
REM  Convert from Celsius to Fahrenheit

INPUT c
LET f = 9/5*c + 32
PRINT f

END
```

We note a REM statement at the beginning of the program. What does it do? Absolutely nothing! REM stands for "remark" or "reminder" and is there purely for the convenience of the programmer. BASIC ignores it. It is good style to start a program with one or more REM statements to describe what the program is supposed to do. We also note some blank lines. These also are ignored by BASIC. They serve here to set off the main part of the program–very much as we leave a blank line after a paragraph in typing a paper.

The rest is self-explanatory. At least it is if you know how to convert from the Celsius scale. If you do not, the computer can't help you. You, or someone else who knows, must write such a program before the computer knows how to make the conversion.

We show two runs. The first shows the origin of 98.6 as the normal body temperature of a human—it is an integer in Celsius. The other shows the only value that is the same in both scales.

```
run

? 37
 98.6

run

? -40
-40
```

Although we now have a more useful example, it is a nuisance to have to rerun the program for every conversion. This will be corrected in Chapter 2.

1.4 MORE ON PRINT

So far we have used `PRINT` just to print numbers. We can also print words, phrases, etc. The statement

```
PRINT "This is a good program."
```

will print the sentence. Note that verbal information must be enclosed in quotes. If `n` is one of our variables then

```
PRINT "n"
```

will print the letter "n", while

```
PRINT n
```

will print a number, the current value of the variable `n`.

If there are several `PRINT` statements in the program and no special punctuation is used, each item is printed on a separate line. But if we put a semicolon after the `PRINT` statement, then the next item is printed right after the present one. These options are illustrated in `CELSIUS1`.

The program CELSIUS1 follows.

```
REM  Convert from Celsius to Fahrenheit

PRINT "Temperature converter."
PRINT "Degrees Celsius";
INPUT c
LET f = 9/5*c + 32
PRINT "Degrees Fahrenheit = "; f

END
```

The first `PRINT` prints a heading for the output. It is not followed by punctuation, hence a new line is started. The second is a *prompt* to remind the user what should be INPUT. It is followed by a semicolon, so the next output is on the same line. The next output is the question mark produced by INPUT, hence the prompt comes out as

```
Degrees Celsius?
```

The final PRINT produces a labelled answer. It prints a label and immediately follows it by the numeric answer. The result is

```
Temperature converter.
Degrees Celsius? 37
Degrees Fahrenheit =  98.6
```

There are additional options in BASIC for formatting the output. These will be considered in later chapters.

1.5 SUMMARY

We have seen that a BASIC program consists of lines. Most of the lines are statements that contain commands to be carried out by the computer. The statements that we have seen so far are

REM to remind or explain; has no effect on computation
LET to assign a value to a variable or carry out a computation and assign answer to a variable
PRINT to print values or words on the screen
INPUT to ask the user for values during a run
END to end the program

For esthetic reasons, we use uppercase (capital) letters for keywords, but lowercase or mixed case may also be used.

Programs work with numbers and numeric variables. (Later we shall see examples of programs that deal with strings of characters.) Numbers are represented in the usual way, using digits, possibly a decimal point, and possibly a sign. It is a rule that there must be no spaces within a number. For example, each of the following is acceptable:

```
12345   .12345   -123.45   +.00012345
```

In addition, numbers may be represented in so-called *scientific* notation. An e6 at the end of the number would mean that it should be mutiplied by 10 to the 6th power, an e-6 that it should be multiplied by 10 to the -6th power. Thus,

1.2345e3 = 1234.5
1.2345e-3 = .0012345

Variable names in BASIC can consist of up to 31 characters. They must start with a letter and may contain letters or digits. All of the following are legal variable names.

```
meters   METERS   Meters   case1   case2   A12x7
```

The first three refer to the same variable; that is, uppercase and lowercase letters are equivalent in variable names, just as they are in the keywords of BASIC statements.

BASIC also allows "hyphenated" names, except that one cannot use an ordinary hyphen. The combination `first-name` would tell BASIC to take the value of the variable `first` and subtract from it the value of `name`. So an underline is used as a hyphen. Thus, `first_name` is a legal variable name.

Some keywords may not serve as variable names because of possible ambiguity. Examples are `REM` and `PRINT`. (For a complete list see your Reference Manual.)

EXERCISES

1. Write a program to calculate the area of a rectangle given the length and width. Use `INPUT` to supply numbers to the program and `PRINT` to display the result.

2. Write a program to calculate the circumference and area of a circle given its radius. (The value of π is stored in a special BASIC variable named `pi`.)

3. Write a program to convert from Fahrenheit to Celsius degrees.

4. Use `DIVIDE3` to explore what happens if the user makes one of the following mistakes:

a. Types only one number.
b. Types three numbers.
c. Supplies 0 for *d* (the denominator).

5. Write a program to convert from feet and inches to centimeters. (Hint: Convert feet to inches first, then inches to centimeters; there are 2.54 centimeters in an inch.)

6. Which of the following are legal variable names in BASIC? If not legal, state why.

```
A       b     aB        z23      24D case_1
case_b _case 2nd_case illegal x.y zzzzz
```

7. Which of the following are legal numbers in BASIC? If not legal, state why.

```
123.4567e7 123.4567e-3 -0.00001 321 e-4
e2            -147          0E0       1.2e2.3
```

8. Improve the program of Exercise 5 by printing the number of meters and number of centimeters. (There are 100 centimeters in a meter.) You need to know that `int(x)` equals the whole number part of `x`. Thus `int(12.34)` = 12.

CHAPTER 2

LOOPS

2.1 INTRODUCTION

In each of the programs in Chapter 1 the computer started at the beginning, and executed each instruction once until it reached **END.** One cannot take full advantage of the power of computers by such ''straight line'' programs.

Due to the fact that computers can carry out thousands, or even millions of operations, we want blocks of statements executed many times. A structure that allows cycling through a block of instructions many times is called a *loop*. We will first consider the simplest type of loop, which starts with DO and ends with LOOP.

2.2 THE SIMPLE LOOP

The program CELSIUS requires a new run for each conversion. If we wish to do several conversions in one run of the program, we modify CELSIUS as follows:

The program CELSIUS2 follows.

```
REM  Convert from Celsius to Fahrenheit

DO
   INPUT c
   LET f = 9/5*c + 32
   PRINT f
LOOP

END
```

The DO statement marks the beginning of a loop and LOOP marks the end of it. Unless otherwise instructed, BASIC will keep executing the statements inbetween. That is, it will do an indefinite number of conversions.

We have indented the lines between DO and LOOP. This makes no difference for BASIC, but helps us to see the structure of our program. The indented lines are the ones that are repeated.

We show a run that does several conversions.

```
run

? 37
 98.6
? -40
-40
? 100
 212
?
Program stopped.
```

The trouble with this program is that it loops forever. We stopped it by pressing the "break" key. Although effective, it is a poor program that can only be stopped with such a drastic measure!

There are several ways of telling BASIC when to terminate a loop. We will illustrate one common method, telling it to loop until something happens. For example, in the following program, the conversion of 100 degrees Celsius signals the end of the looping and, consequently, the end of the program. There is therefore no need to employ the break key to stop the program.

The program CELSIUS3 follows.

```
REM  Convert from Celsius to Fahrenheit

DO
   INPUT c
   LET f = 9/5*c + 32
   PRINT f
LOOP until c=100

END
```

2.3 TAKING SQUARE ROOTS

As a more interesting example we will now consider how calculators or computers find the square root of a number. There is a well-known simple algorithm for finding square roots. It is based on the following observations.

Let $n = 16$, the number whose square root we wish to find. We take a guess, and then divide n by the guess. If we make the correct guess, namely 4, then

```
guess = 4   ratio = 4   newguess = (guess + ratio)/2 = 4
```

If your computer does not have a break key, it might have a STOP or BREAK menu selection; consult your User Manual about how to stop a program.

and we know that we have found the exact square root. But suppose that we guessed 2.

```
guess = 2    ratio = 8    newguess = (guess + ratio)/2 = 5
```

Although the guess was poor, as we see from the fact that the ratio is far from our guess, the average of the guess and the ratio is closer to the right answer. We now take this average as our next guess.

```
guess = 5   ratio = 3.2   newguess = (guess + ratio)/2 = 4.1
```

Now we have a good approximation to the square root. And we can repeat the process until the answer is as accurate as desired.

This is a case where the computer program, which follows, is shorter than the verbal description.

The program SQR follows.

```
REM  Take square root of n

PRINT "Number";
INPUT n

LET guess = 1
DO
    LET ratio = n/guess
    LET guess = (guess + ratio)/2
LOOP until abs(guess-ratio) < .00001

PRINT "Square root ="; guess

END
```

The program asks the user for the number whose square root is to be found. The user is first *prompted* by printing the word "Number". Note the semicolon at the end of the line; this is a signal that the next character printed should follow immediately. The next character will be the question mark printed by `INPUT`. Hence, the user actually sees "Number?".

The program starts with a guess of 1. It repeatedly carries out the computation of `ratio`, and arrives at a new value for `guess`. For the statement

```
LET guess = (guess + ratio)/2
```

it is important to remember that the right side is evaluated first, and the answer is assigned to the variable on the left. Thus, the old value of `guess` is averaged with the value of `ratio`, and this average is assigned as the new value of `guess`.

How long should the loop continue? Suppose that we want to have the answer to at least five decimal places. If the distance between `guess` and `ratio` is less than .00001, then we must have the answer to the desired accuracy. In BASIC, `abs(x)` is the absolute value of `x`, hence `abs(guess-ratio)` is the distance between the two numbers.

We show three runs. The algorithm is so fast that we obtain answers instantaneously, even for a six-digit number—when the guess of 1 is a very poor guess!

```
run

Number? 16
Square root = 4.

run

Number? 123
Square root = 11.0905

run

Number? 123456
Square root = 351.363
```

The most commonly used computer algorithm for computing square roots is like `SQR`, but it takes a more sophisticated initial guess. (See Exercise 5 as an example.) For such a program one may be curious to see how rapidly the answer is approached. We accomplish this by printing each new guess. The insertion of a `PRINT` statement before `LOOP` will achieve this.

The program SQR2 follows.

```
REM  Take square root of n

PRINT "Number";
INPUT n

LET guess = 1
DO
    LET ratio = n/guess
    LET guess = (guess + ratio)/2
    PRINT guess
LOOP until abs(guess-ratio) < .00001

PRINT "Square root ="; guess

END
```

Note that the statement `PRINT guess` is inside the loop, and is thus executed many times. The first and the final `PRINT` are each outside the loop, and are thus executed only once.

```
run

Number? 123
 62
 31.9919
 17.9183
 12.3914
```

```
 11.1588
 11.0907
 11.0905
 11.0905
Square root = 11.0905
```

This trick, inserting a **PRINT** statement in a loop, is useful when we are testing a program—or "debugging" it. If we made a mistake, the more detailed output may show us where we made an error. And, after we are sure that the algorithm is correct, we can remove the inserted **PRINT** statement.

2.4 NESTED LOOPS

It would be very convenient if we could take several square roots during a single run. And, in fact, nothing could be simpler. We just enclose our program in a DO loop, so that now one loop is inside the other one. We refer to these as *nested loops*.

We need some convention to stop the outside (main) loop. We agree that asking for the square root of 1 is a signal for stopping.

The program SQR3 follows.

```
REM  Take square root of n

DO                                 ! Allow several examples
   PRINT "Number";
   INPUT n                         ! To take root of

   LET guess = 1                   ! Crude guess
   DO                              ! Square root algorithm
       LET ratio = n/guess
       LET guess = (guess + ratio)/2     ! Better guess
   LOOP until abs(guess-ratio) < .00001  ! To 5 decimals

   PRINT "Square root ="; guess
LOOP until n=1                     ! Next example

END
```

We have used this example to illustrate how to make a program more readable. Besides having a **REM** at the beginning, we added comments at the ends of lines. A comment is separated from the statement by an exclamation point, and is ignored by BASIC. Such comments would help someone else who wished to read our program. It also helps the author of the program to modify it later, when he or she might have forgotten how it works.

```
run

Number? 1024
Square root = 32.
Number? 123
Square root = 11.0905
Number? .56789
```

```
Square root = .753585
Number? 1
Square root = 1
```

There is a small improvement needed for SQR3. Typing the number "1" is the signal to quit. At that point, the program computes the square root of 1 and then quits. We would prefer to get out of the loop as soon as we typed "1" and to avoid doing the calculation. This will be accomplished in the next chapter.

2.5 SUMMARY

The simplest loop has the form

```
DO
   -----
   -----
   -----
LOOP
```

The statements inside the loop are repeated indefinitely. To terminate a loop we may employ a statement of the form

```
LOOP until .....
```

where "....." stands for a relation that is usually false for the first few iterations but eventually becomes true.

Loops may be nested. That is, one loop may be contained within another loop.

EXERCISES

1. Modify DIVIDE3 to allow several divisions. Pick a reasonable condition for terminating the loop.
2. Write a program that allows several conversions from Fahrenheit to Celsius.
3. Write a program to compute and print the successive powers of 2 (2, 4, 8, 16, ...) until the result is larger then 1e6 (one million). Before you run the program, guess how many numbers will be printed.
4. Modify SQR to print the number of different times we had to go through the loop. You will need a variable count, which is set to 0 originally and increased by one each time the inside loop is completed.
5. Use the previous program to show that for n>100, an initial guess of 10 is more efficient than starting with 1.
6. Write a program that prints the numbers from 1 to 10 as well as their squares and cubes. You will need a variable n that is set to 0 originally and is increased by one inside the loop.
7. Write a program to find the smallest integer whose cube is greater than 5,000.

8. Modify `SQR` to compute cube roots as follows:
    1. Ratio is n divided by the square of the guess.
    2. The new guess is 2/3 of the old one plus 1/3 of the ratio.

    Print the cube of the answer to verify that the program does indeed find cube roots.
9. Take a guess as to how the previous program should be modified to take 4th roots, 5th roots, and so forth. Try out your programs.
10. Modify the program of Exercise 8 to print out how often it goes through the loop. (See Exercise 4.) Use this to verify that the algorithm is more efficient than if we took the average of the old guess and the ratio as the new guess.

CHAPTER 3

CHOICES

3.1 INTRODUCTION

A second important structure is one that allows *branching*, i.e., taking different paths depending on the results. For example, if a given number is positive we take one route, if it is negative then another, and if it is 0 then we take a third route. In BASIC the simplest branching structure starts with the keyword **IF** and ends with **END IF**. In this chapter we will explore several variants of this structure. An even more powerful branching structure, **SELECT CASE**, will be introduced later.

The rules for the **IF** structure and for writing formulas in BASIC are detailed in the Summary.

3.2 IF

The simplest example of branching is one in which the type of computation needed depends on the information supplied by the user.

Take, for example, a case in which a salesperson works for a 5% commission. But, if in any month the total sales generated by the salesperson are over \$100,000, the commission on the excess is 7%. Thus, in the latter case, the commission is \$5000 on the \$100,000 plus 7% of the amount above \$100,000.

We ask for the amount of the sales and then need to carry out either one or the other of two calculations, depending on whether the sales are under or over \$100,000. The following program shows how easily this is accomplished with the **IF** structure.

The program PERCENT follows.

```
REM  Sales commission

PRINT "Sales";
INPUT sales

IF sales < 100000 then
   LET commission = .05 * sales
ELSE
   LET commission = 5000 + .07*(sales - 100000)
END IF

PRINT "Commission ="; commission

END


run

Sales? 60000
Commission = 3000.

run

Sales? 90000
Commission = 4500.

run

Sales? 120000
Commission = 6400

run

Sales? 150000
Commission = 8500
```

The **IF** structure always starts with

```
IF ..... then
```

where the "....." stands for a condition in BASIC that may be true or false. The structure must end with

```
END IF
```

In the simplest case, as in our program **PERCENT**, if the condition turns out to be true, i.e. sales are less than (<) $100,000, then the statement following **IF** is carried out. Otherwise, the statement following **ELSE** is carried out.

The symbol "<" is called a *relational operator*. These operators are listed in the Summary.

Several statements could follow both the **IF** and **ELSE**. Depending on the truth of the condition, one of these sets of statements would be executed.

If there are more than two branches, additional cases may be added by inserting statements of the form

```
ELSEIF ..... then
```

The rule that only one case is executed still applies. Let us examine such an example.

Midlands College has a complicated set of rules to determine how honors are awarded upon graduation. Indeed, the faculty has made the rules so complicated that it is simplest to explain them as a computer program. The type of honor awarded (if any) depends on the student's overall gradepoint average and on the average in the major subject.

The program HONORS follows.

```
REM  Rules for awarding honors

PRINT "Overall average, Average in major";
INPUT average, major

IF average>=3.5 and major>=3.75 then
   PRINT "Highest honors"
ELSEIF average>=3.25 and major>=3.5 then
   PRINT "High honors"
ELSEIF average>=3.2 or major>=3.3 then
   PRINT "Honors"
ELSE
   PRINT "No honors"
END IF

END
```

The four cases are handled by inserting two `ELSEIF` statements between `IF` and `ELSE`. We also note that we may have *compound conditions*. Highest and high honors are awarded only if two conditions are both satisfied (hence, we use the keyword `and`.) But, ordinary honors may be earned if one or the other of two conditions is satisfied (hence, we use the keyword `or`.) We show a run illustrating all four cases.

```
run

Overall average, Average in major? 3.3, 3.6
High honors

run

Overall average, Average in major? 3.0, 3.2
No honors

run

Overall average, Average in major? 3.8, 3.8
Highest honors

run

Overall average, Average in major? 2.7, 3.3
Honors
```

It should be noted that the conditions are not mutually exclusive. Indeed, any student who meets the requirements for highest honors also meets the requirements for high honors and honors. But, if the condition in the **IF** statement is satisfied, the program will print "Highest honors" and ignore the other cases. An **ELSEIF** statement is executed only if the previous conditions fail, and the **ELSE** only if all the other conditions were false. This is in agreement with ordinary usage of *else if* and *else* in English.

There is an abbreviated version of the **IF** structure. When there is only one statement between **IF** and **END IF**, a single-line condensation is allowed. Thus, the structure

```
IF x<0 then
   PRINT "negative"
END IF
```

may be abbreviated to the single line **IF** statement

```
IF x<0 then PRINT "negative"
```

3.3 QUADRATIC EQUATIONS

A standard topic in high school algebra is the solution of the quadratic equation, as follows:

$$ax^2 + bx + c = 0$$

Its "solution" is the formula

$$x = \frac{-b \pm \sqrt{b^2 - 4ac}}{2a}$$

This topic often causes difficulties because what one should do when confronted by an actual equation is not obvious from the formula. We need a precise recipe, called an *algorithm*, to find the solutions (if any). A computer program is often the clearest and simplest way to present an algorithm.

The nature of the solution depends on the quantity under the square root sign, called the *discriminant*. In our program we will

```
LET discr = b^2 - 4*a*c
```

The symbol "^" denotes raising to a power. Thus `b^2` is *b*-squared. (For a discussion of how formulas are written in BASIC see the Summary.)

If **discr** is negative, its square root is *imaginary*. For some scientific problems these solutions are very important, but for most applications one only cares about real number solutions. Testing whether **discr** is negative is therefore a key step in the algorithm.

In **QUAD** we ask the user for the coefficients and compute **discr**. Then we use an **IF** structure. If the discriminant is negative, we inform the user that there are no real roots. Otherwise, (the **ELSE** part) we compute the square root and print the two roots.

The program QUAD follows.

```
REM  Quadratic equation

PRINT "Coefficients";                    ! Ask user for a,b,c
INPUT a, b, c

LET discr = b^2 - 4*a*c                  ! Discriminant
IF discr<0 then                          ! No real roots
   PRINT "No real roots"
ELSE                                     ! Real roots
   LET s = sqr(discr)
   LET r1 = (-b + s)/(2*a)               ! From quadratic formula
   LET r2 = (-b - s)/(2*a)
   PRINT "The roots are: "; r1; r2
END IF

END
```

It is essential that we test `discr` for being negative before we attempt to take a square root. Otherwise we would get a terminal error message from BASIC for attempting to take a square root of a negative number!

```
run

Coefficients? 1, 4, 5
No real roots

run

Coefficients? 1, 4, 3
The roots are: -1 -3

run

Coefficients? 1, 4, 4
The roots are: -2 -2
```

The runs appear to be satisfactory until we examine the last one. It tells us that there are two roots (solutions), but both of them are -2. This is technically known as a *double root*. But, in reality, there is only one root in this case. If we compute `discr` we find that it is 0.

We therefore decide that there are not two but three cases. And, we arrive at a better version, as follows.

The program QUAD2 follows.

```
REM  Quadratic equation

PRINT "Coefficients";                    ! Ask user for a,b,c
INPUT a, b, c

LET discr = b^2 - 4*a*c                  ! Discriminant
IF discr<0 then                          ! No real roots
   PRINT "No real roots"
```

```
ELSEIF discr=0 then                    ! Single root
   PRINT "The root is: "; -b/(2*a)
ELSE                                   ! Two real roots
   LET s = sqr(discr)
   LET r1 = (-b + s)/(2*a)
   LET r2 = (-b - s)/(2*a)
   PRINT "The roots are: "; r1; r2
END IF

END


run

Coefficients? 1, 4, 5
No real roots

run

Coefficients? 1, 4, 3
The roots are: -1 -3

run

Coefficients? 1, 4, 4
The root is: -2
```

Now the runs are completely satisfactory.

3.4 A GUESSING GAME

Let us now write a program for a game. The computer will "think of" an integer from 1 to 100, and we will try to guess it. If we guess wrong, as will be the case the first few times, it will give us a hint as to whether we guessed too low or too high.

The only feature of the program that we have not yet covered is how one picks an integer at random. Random numbers will be discussed in detail in Chapter 17, which covers simulation. For the moment we need only two simple facts. Near the beginning of our program we should have the statement

```
RANDOMIZE
```

and later on the expression

```
int(100*rnd + 1)
```

which picks an integer from 1 to 100. The rest of `GUESS` is quite straightforward.

The program GUESS follows.

```
REM  Number guessing game

RANDOMIZE
LET number = int(100*rnd +1)        ! Pick number to guess
LET count = 0                       ! Number of guesses

DO                                  ! Guessing loop
    PRINT "Your guess";
    INPUT guess
    LET count = count + 1           ! One more guess
    IF guess>number then            ! Give hint
       PRINT "Too high"
    ELSEIF guess<number then
       PRINT "Too low"
    ELSE                            ! Must be right guess
       PRINT "That's right!"
       PRINT "You needed"; count; "guesses."
    END IF
LOOP until guess=number             ! Until guess is right

END
```

From the following runs one might estimate that the average number of guesses needed is about seven. (See the Exercises.)

```
run

Your guess? 50
Too low
Your guess? 70
Too high
Your guess? 60
Too low
Your guess? 65
Too low
Your guess? 67
That's right!
You needed 5 guesses.

run

Your guess? 50
Too low
Your guess? 80
Too high
Your guess? 65
Too low
Your guess? 70
Too low
Your guess? 73
Too low
Your guess? 77
Too high
Your guess? 75
Too high
```

```
Your guess? 74
That's right!
You needed 8 guesses.

run

Your guess? 30
Too high
Your guess? 20
Too high
Your guess? 10
Too low
Your guess? 15
Too low
Your guess? 18
Too high
Your guess? 17
Too high
Your guess? 16
That's right!
You needed 7 guesses.
```

3.5 LEAVING A LOOP

We can now solve the problem we noted with SQR3 at the end of the last chapter. One can leave a DO loop *in the middle* by means of the statement

```
IF ..... then EXIT DO
```

and can modify SQR3, as follows.

The program SQR4 follows.

```
REM  Take square root of n

DO                                ! Allow several examples
   PRINT "Number";
   INPUT n                        ! To take root of n
   IF n=1 then EXIT DO            ! Convention to stop

   LET guess = 1                  ! Crude guess
   DO                             ! Square root algorithm
       LET ratio = n/guess
       LET guess = (guess + ratio)/2      ! Better guess
   LOOP until abs(guess-ratio) < .00001   ! To 5 decimals

   PRINT "Square root ="; guess
LOOP                              ! Next example

END
```

The runs of SQR4 will be almost identical to those of SQR3, but the program will stop as soon as we INPUT a 1. It gets out of the loop before computing the square root, and then executes the END statement and, hence, stops.

Let us modify QUAD2 to allow the user to specify several quadratic equations. We will use a=0 as the condition to exit the loop. (See Exercise 10.)

The program QUAD3 follows.

```
REM  Quadratic equation

DO
   PRINT "Coefficients";
   INPUT a, b, c                         ! a*x^2 + b*x + c = 0
   IF a=0 then EXIT DO                   ! Convention for stopping

   LET discr = b^2 - 4*a*c               ! Discriminant
   IF discr<0 then                       ! Complex roots
      PRINT "No real roots"
   ELSEIF discr=0 then                   ! Single root
      PRINT "The root is: "; -b/(2*a)
   ELSE                                  ! Two roots
      LET s = sqr(discr)
      LET r1 = (-b + s)/(2*a)
      LET r2 = (-b - s)/(2*a)
      PRINT "The roots are: "; r1; r2
   END IF
LOOP                                     ! Get next example

END


run

Coefficients? 2, -3, 1
The roots are:  1  .5
Coefficients? 2, -4, 2
The root is:  1
Coefficients? 2, -2, 1
No real roots
Coefficients? 0, 0, 0
```

3.6 SUMMARY

Choices may be made in BASIC by means of the IF structure. Its commonest form is

```
IF ..... then
   ----------
   ----------
   ----------
ELSE
   ----------
   ----------
END IF
```

If the condition represented by "....." is true, then the statements immediately following are carried out. If the condition is false, the statements after ELSE are carried out. The closing statement END IF is necessary for BASIC to know where the structure ends.

More complicated choices may be made by inserting one or more segements of the form

```
ELSEIF ..... then
          ----------
          ----------
```

And, in the very simplest case, the abbreviated form

```
IF ..... then ---------
```

is allowed.

A `DO` loop may be exited *in the middle* by using

```
IF ..... then EXIT DO
```

BASIC follows the usual rules of algebra for formulas (which are often called *expressions*). These formulas use numbers and variables connected with arithmetic operators, which are as follows:

Operator	Interpretation
+	plus or add
−	minus or subtract
*	multiply
/	divide or divide by
^	raise to the power

Because it is hard to type superscripts on most computers, we use "^" to denote raising to a power. Thus

`x^2` means the same as x^2

Examples of formulas in BASIC follow.

Formula in BASIC	Interpretation
`a + b*c`	perform multiply first, then add
`a*b + c`	ditto
`a * b+c`	ditto!

Spaces are not needed in formulas, but can and should be used to make them easier to read. The second and third formulas (above) give exactly the same result, despite the fact that the spacing is different.

Sometimes, parentheses are needed, as shown in these examples:

`a - (b - c)`	calculate b-c first, then subtract from a
`a/(b+c)`	divide a by the quantity b+c
`a/b*c`	same as `(a/b)*c` or `(a*c)/b` or `a*c/b` and NOT as `a/(b*c)`

This last example is important, as it illustrates a common error. The formula in **QUAD**,

```
(-b + s)/(2*a)
```

is often *incorrectly* written in BASIC as `(-b + s)/2*a`.

In the **IF** statement we saw a comparison `discr<0`. Such a comparison is called a *relational expression*, or *relation* for short, and is either true or false. The symbol "<" is called a *relational operator*. The relational operators are shown in the following table.

Relational Operator	Interpretation
<	is less than
<=	is less than or equal to
=	is equal to
>	is greater than
>=	is greater than or equal to
<>	is not equal to

In general, then, a relation consists of an arithmetic expression, which may be as simple as a number or variable, followed by a relational operator, followed by another arithmetic expression.

EXERCISES

1. In Midville, purchases under $10 are exempt from tax but there is a sales tax of 5% on the amount above $10. Write a program to compute and print the sales tax in Midville.
2. Midville adds a luxury tax of 3% on the amount above $100. Modify the program of Exercise 1 to add this tax.
3. A store offers a discount of 5% on items costing $100 or more, a discount of 8% on items costing $250 or more, and a discount of 12% on items priced at $500 or more. Write a program that converts the price of an item to the discounted price.
4. Use **QUAD3** to find the roots for the following quadratic equations:

   $a = 1$ $b = -16$ $c = 64$

   $a = 13$ $b = 26$ $c = 13$

   $a = 13$ $b = 25$ $c = 13$

   $a = 10$ $b = 11$ $c = -6$
5. Modify **SQR** to print an error message if a negative `n` is entered.
6. Write a program that asks the user for a number `n` and tells whether `n^2` is *greater*, *equal*, or *less* than `n`. It should allow several numbers to be entered. The run should illustrate all three cases.
7. Modify **CELSIUS2** so that the program stops if a value of 1000 is entered for `c`. (Use **EXIT DO**.)
8. Run the game **GUESS** several times to estimate how many guesses you need on the average.
9. Modify **GUESS** to guess numbers up to 200. Repeat the experiment of Exercise 8. Why does it not require twice as many guesses?
10. What would go wrong if in **QUAD3** we used `LOOP until a=0` in place of the **EXIT DO**?

CHAPTER 4

THE FOR LOOP

4.1 INTRODUCTION

Any loop can be programmed using `DO` and `LOOP`. The `DO` loop continues until some condition is met as a result of our computations. But there are many cases where this structure is inconvenient. Suppose, for example, that we wish to print our name 10 times. BASIC provides a second looping structure for cases when the number of times through a loop is predetermined.

The new structure starts with the keyword `FOR`, followed by a *loop variable*, and a range for the variable, such as in

```
FOR n = 1 to 10
```

It is closed by a `NEXT` statement containing the same variable. There are a number of options on the `FOR` statement. These will be illustrated in this chapter.

4.2 THE SIMPLEST CASE

We wish to use our computer to print a birthday card that contains the same two-line greeting 10 times. We could achieve this by using 20 `PRINT` statements. But it is much simpler to tell the computer to print the two lines 10 times.

The program FOR1 follows.

```
REM  FOR/NEXT Loop

FOR n = 1 to 10
    PRINT "Happy birthday!"
    PRINT "And many happy returns."
NEXT n

END
```

In this simple case the *loop variable* n just counts to 10 and, when the instructions between FOR and NEXT have been carried out 10 times, the program exits from the loop.

```
run

Happy birthday!
And many happy returns.
Happy birthday!
And many happy returns.
Happy birthday!
And many happy returns.
Happy birthday!
And many happy returns.
Happy birthday!
And many happy returns.
Happy birthday!
And many happy returns.
Happy birthday!
And many happy returns.
Happy birthday!
And many happy returns.
Happy birthday!
And many happy returns.
Happy birthday!
And many happy returns.
```

The first time through the loop n will equal 1, then 2, and so on. One can take advantage of this by using n within the loop. The following is a very easy example.

The program FOR2 follows.

```
REM  FOR/NEXT Loop

FOR n = 1 to 5
    PRINT n; n^2
NEXT n

END
```

In this example n takes on the values from 1 to 5 successively, and we print the number and the square of the number. Thus we have constructed a table of squares. Had we wanted a larger table, we would only change the number after the keyword to. This would not increase the length of the program, only the length of the output.

```
run

 1   1
 2   4
 3   9
 4   16
 5   25
```

Next we'll write a program to add the integers from 1 to 100. We will need two variables: `number` will be our loop variable, running through the integers, while `sum` will keep track of the current sum.

The program SUM follows.

```
REM  Sum of integers

LET sum = 0                          ! Initialize sum
FOR number = 1 to 100
    LET sum = sum + number           ! Add number to sum
NEXT number
PRINT "The sum is"; sum              ! Answer

END
```

The key statement is

```
LET sum = sum + number
```

One must remember that in a `LET` statement the right side is computed first. Thus, the computer takes the previous value of `sum` and adds to it the value of `number`. Then it assigns this sum as the new value of `sum`. Suppose that we have already added the integers 1, 2, 3, and 4. Then `sum` = 10. Next, `number` takes on the value 5, and the new value of `sum` is 10 + 5 = 15.

The run shows that the sum of the first 100 integers is 5050.

```
run

The sum is 5050
```

4.3 MORE ADVANCED OPTIONS

So far the *`from`* and *`to`* in our `FOR` statements were constants, i.e. numbers specified in the program. But they could be variables or even formulas. In our next example we use variables, and ask the user to specify the *`from`* and *`to`*.

The program SUM2 follows.

```
REM  Sum of integers

PRINT "From, to";                    ! Ask user
INPUT a, b
```

```
LET sum = 0                                 ! Initialize sum
FOR number = a to b
    LET sum = sum + number                  ! Add number to sum
NEXT number
PRINT "The sum is"; sum                     ! Answer

END


run

From, to? 1, 100
The sum is 5050

run

From, to? 10, 50
The sum is 1230

run

From, to? 20, 20
The sum is 20

run

From, to? 20, 10
The sum is 0
```

We show four runs. The first repeats our initial example. The second computes the sum of integers from 10 to 50. The third example asks the computer to go from 20 to 20. There is only one integer in that range, namely 20. Thus the program goes through the loop only once (with `number` = 20), and the sum is, of course, 20.

In the last example we asked the computer to loop from 20 to 10. To be more precise, the loop is supposed to go through the integers greater than or equal to 20 and less than or equal to 10. Because there are no such integers, BASIC skips over the loop, and `sum` = 0. This convention is very important for several mathematical algorithms to work correctly. (See Exercises 1 and 3.)

An even more powerful option is the ability to specify the `step` size. When `step` is not specified, as it has not been so far, the loop variable increases by one each time we go through the loop. But suppose we want to go up by 2, or by a fraction. What can we do?

Let us write a program using this option to compute the sum of the odd integers from 1 to a number specified by the user.

The program SUM3 follows.

```
REM  Sum of odd integers

PRINT "To";                                 ! Ask user how far
INPUT b
```

```
LET sum = 0                          ! Initialize sum
FOR number = 1 to b step 2           ! Odd numbers only
    LET sum = sum + number           ! Add number to sum
NEXT number
PRINT "The sum is"; sum              ! Answer

END
```

This program is quite similar to SUM2, but we go in steps of 2. Thus, `number` takes on the values 1, 3, 5, and so forth. We show two runs.

```
run

To? 9
The sum is 25

run

To? 99
The sum is 2500
```

Next we show a program for a table of square roots, in which the step size is a fraction.

The program FOR3 follows.

```
REM  Table of square roots

PRINT "Number", "Square root"
FOR x = 1 to 2 step 1/8
    PRINT x, sqr(x)                  ! In two zones
NEXT x

END

run

Number         Square root
 1              1
 1.125          1.06066
 1.25           1.11803
 1.375          1.1726
 1.5            1.22474
 1.625          1.27475
 1.75           1.32288
 1.875          1.36931
 2              1.41421
```

This program also illustrates an additional `PRINT` option. So far we have used semicolons in `PRINT` statements, so that answers would be printed close together on the same line. When the item to be printed is followed by a comma, it is a signal to BASIC to go to the next *zone*. This makes it easy to line up columns of output, as demonstrated in the run.

Normally a zone has a *zonewidth* of 16 characters, so that a screen that has 80 columns consists of five equal zones. But such conventions can be overruled by a `SET` statement, as in the program `FOR4`.

The program FOR4 follows.

```
REM   Table of square roots

SET zonewidth 10
PRINT "Number", "Square root"
FOR x = 1 to 2 step 1/8
    PRINT x, sqr(x)                     ! In two zones
NEXT x

END
```

```
run

Number    Square root
 1         1
 1.125     1.06066
 1.25      1.11803
 1.375     1.1726
 1.5       1.22474
 1.625     1.27475
 1.75      1.32288
 1.875     1.36931
 2         1.41421
```

We now see a more attractive output.

In Section 3.5 we saw that a `DO` loop can be exited in the middle through the use of an `EXIT DO` statement. Similarly, a `FOR` loop can be exited before its completion through the use of an `EXIT FOR` statement. To demonstrate, let us find the smallest integer whose cube is bigger than 5000. A natural way to proceed is to try consecutive integers until we find one that is big enough. The first one we find will then be the smallest one.

The program CUBE follows.

```
REM  Find the first integer
REM  whose cube is > 5000

FOR n = 1 to 100                       ! High enough
    IF n^3 > 5000 then EXIT FOR        ! Found it
NEXT n
PRINT "The number is "; n
PRINT "The cube is   "; n^3

END
```

The key to understanding the program `CUBE` is that it leaves the loop as soon as we find an integer whose cube is greater than 5000. How did we know that `n` should go to 100? Well $10^3 = 1000$ is too small, while 100^3 is a million, too large. All we care about is that the number after the keyword `to` be large enough. Due to the fact that the program quits when the right integer is found, it would take no longer to run the program if we had used

```
FOR n = 1 to 1000
```

The following run shows that 18 is the smallest integer whose cube is above 5000.

```
run

The number is  18
The cube is    5832
```

4.4 NESTED LOOPS

It is permissible to have one loop inside (*nested in*) another loop. For example, if in `SUM2` we wish to allow the user to specify several examples, we enclose the program in a `DO` loop. Thus, we have a `FOR` loop nested inside a `DO` loop. We then need an exit condition for the `DO` loop; our convention is to quit when the user chooses 0 for `b`.

The program SUM2DO follows.

```
REM  Sum of integers

DO                                ! Allow several examples
   PRINT "From, to";              ! Ask user
   INPUT a, b
   IF b=0 then EXIT DO

   LET sum = 0                    ! Initialize sum
   FOR number = a to b
       LET sum = sum + number ! Add number to sum
   NEXT number
   PRINT "The sum is"; sum      ! Answer
LOOP

END
```

We will not show a run of `SUM2DO`, because the results would be identical to those of `SUM2`. The only difference is that we do not have to keep rerunning the program.

We may also have one `FOR` loop inside another one. As an example we will print a table in which, for a sequence of numbers, we wish to print the number, its square, cube and fourth power. The first or outside loop runs through the numbers (from 1 to 3 in steps of 1/4). The second or inside loop is carried out for each number. It computes and prints the first through fourth powers of the current number.

The program POWERS follows.

```
REM  Powers

SET zonewidth 10
PRINT "Number", "Square", "Cube", "Fourth power"

FOR x = 1 to 3 step 1/4                ! Outer loop
    FOR p = 1 to 4                     ! Inner loop
        PRINT x^p,
    NEXT p
    PRINT                              ! New line
NEXT x

END
```

This example also shows that indenting helps to display the structure of the program. This is even more important in a longer program.

In **POWERS** we also see two new features of the **PRINT** statement. The first **PRINT** statement ends with a comma. The effect, as we move through the inner loop, is that each power is placed into a new zone, thus lining up columns. But when we finish the loop we want to start a new line. A **PRINT** statement with nothing after **PRINT** accomplishes this.

```
run

Number         Square         Cube           Fourth power
 1              1              1              1
 1.25           1.5625         1.95312        2.44141
 1.5            2.25           3.375          5.0625
 1.75           3.0625         5.35937        9.37891
 2              4              8              16
 2.25           5.0625         11.3906        25.6289
 2.5            6.25           15.625         39.0625
 2.75           7.5625         20.7969        57.1914
 3              9              27             81
```

There is one more option that we would like to illustrate. Suppose that we wish to see the same table, but have the numbers run from the largest to the smallest (from 3 to 1). An attempt to use

```
FOR x = 3 to 1 step 1/4
```

will produce an empty loop, and nothing will be printed. But, we can specify a negative step size, as follows:

```
FOR x = 3 to 1 step -1/4
```

x starts with the value 3, then a **step** of -1/4 is added, so that **x** = 2 3/4, then **x** = 2 1/2, and so on until **x** = 1.

The program POWERS2 follows.

```
REM  Powers in reverse order

SET zonewidth 10
PRINT "Number", "Square", "Cube", "Fourth power"

FOR x = 3 to 1 step -1/4              ! Negative step
    FOR p = 1 to 4
        PRINT x^p,
    NEXT p
    PRINT
NEXT x

END

run

Number        Square        Cube          Fourth power
 3             9             27            81
 2.75          7.5625        20.7969       57.1914
 2.5           6.25          15.625        39.0625
 2.25          5.0625        11.3906       25.6289
 2             4             8             16
 1.75          3.0625        5.35937       9.37891
 1.5           2.25          3.375         5.0625
 1.25          1.5625        1.95312       2.44141
 1             1             1             1
```

4.5 SUMMARY

We have examined a second looping structure, whose form is

```
FOR n = a to b step c
    ----------
    ----------
    ----------
NEXT n
```

The *loop variable* is initially assigned the value a. After each execution of the statements between FOR and NEXT, c is added to the value. When the value is greater than b, the loop is exited. If c is chosen to be negative, then the values of the loop variable keep decreasing until a value smaller than b is reached.

In place of a, b, and c we may have numbers, variables, or formulas. If step c is omitted, the step size is taken to be 1.

If there are no possible values for n, the loop is *empty* and the computer skips over it. This happens when (1) c is positive and b<a, or (2) c is negative and b>a.

Loops may be nested, and either loop may be of the DO or FOR type.

We also noted some new PRINT options. If an item to be printed is followed by a comma, the computer moves to the next *zone*. Zones normally are 16 characters wide, but this may be changed by SET zonewidth. In addition, a PRINT statement with nothing after PRINT starts a new line. Such a statement may also be used to leave an empty line in the output.

1. Run `SUM3` with `b` = 0. Do you agree that the sum of *no* numbers is 0?
2. Write a program to compute the product of the integers from 1 to `n` (known as *n!* or *n factorial*). Be careful how you initialize the product.
3. Run the program of Exercise 2 with `n` = 0. The correct answer is 0! = 1.
4. Print the odd integers between 77 and 99 in decreasing order.
5. Run several examples of `SUM3`. There is a simple formula for the sum of the first n odd integers. Can you find it?
6. Find the sum of the integers 2, 5, 8, 11, ... , 302.
7. Write a program that repeatedly asks for an integer and then prints your name that many times.
8. Find the largest integer whose fourth power is less than one million.
9. Print the multiplication table (from 1 × 1 to 10 × 10). Use a narrow zonewidth so that you have room for 10 zones.
10. Write a program that asks for an integer *n* and then prints a triangle of asterisks of *n* rows. For *n* = 4, it should print:

    ```
    *
    * *
    * * *
    * * * *
    ```

11. Modify Exercise 10 to print the triangle upside down.
12. Rewrite `FOR2` using a `DO` loop.

CHAPTER 5

LISTS AND DATA

5.1 INTRODUCTION

We have seen that loops allow us to call for many computations by means of relatively short programs. We will now consider how a program can handle a great deal of information.

So far we have been able to represent our numbers by a small number of variables. But what if we want the computer to remember 100 numbers? It would be inconvenient to have to invent 100 variable names, and most inconvenient to use them. A *list* is a collection of related items all of which are referred to by the same *list variable*. We will show through examples how the use of lists makes many tasks much easier.

Secondly, we will consider how numerical data may be furnished for a program. If the same numbers need to be typed in every time the program is run, `INPUT` is a poor way to accomplish the goal. A better way to do this is through BASIC's `DATA` statements, which serve as a storage area for information needed by the program. `READ` statements then pull information out of the `DATA` storage area.

Thirdly, we will consider some examples of the `MAT` statement. This statement allows us to input, read, or print an entire list by means of a single statement. More powerful examples of `MAT` statements will be discussed later in the book (Section 16.5).

5.2 LISTS OF NUMBERS

Let us write a program that asks the user to furnish five numbers and then picks out the smallest one. The program `SMALL`, which does this, is quite simple. It first asks for the five numbers. Then it starts by assuming that the first number is the smallest one, and tests each of the others to see if they are smaller than the smallest one seen so far.

The program SMALL follows.

```
REM  Smallest number

PRINT "Five numbers";              ! Ask user
INPUT  a, b, c, d, e

LET small = a                      ! Assume first is smallest
IF b < small then LET small = b     ! Try the others
IF c < small then LET small = c
IF d < small then LET small = d
IF e < small then LET small = e
PRINT "The smallest number is "; small

END

run

Five numbers? 11, 5, 100, 2, 20
The smallest number is  2
```

There is nothing wrong with this program. But if we wanted a much longer list of numbers, we would encounter the problems mentioned in the Introduction. To counter these problems, we introduce a new type of variable, one that stands for an entire list of numbers. In the next program `x` will be such a variable. We must first tell BASIC that this is a list variable (because the same name could have been used for an ordinary variable). This requires the `DIM` statement

```
DIM x(5)
```

This statement tells BASIC that `x` stands for a list and that the list consists of five numbers, the components of the list. The first component will be referred to as `x(1)`, the second as `x(2)`, and so forth. The resulting program, `SMALL2`, differs from `SMALL` only in the names of the variables.

The program SMALL2 follows.

```
REM  Smallest number

DIM x(5)                             ! Must declare list
PRINT "Five numbers";                ! Ask user
INPUT  x(1), x(2), x(3), x(4), x(5)

LET small = x(1)                     ! Assume first is smallest
IF x(2) < small then LET small = x(2)   ! Try the others
IF x(3) < small then LET small = x(3)
IF x(4) < small then LET small = x(4)
IF x(5) < small then LET small = x(5)
PRINT "The smallest number is "; small

END
```

We do not seem to have made much progress! But now we can make significant improvements by taking advantage of the fact that we are dealing with a list. First, the statement

```
MAT INPUT x
```

allows us to ask for the entire list. The keyword `MAT` will always signal that the statement refers to an entire list (or table). Secondly, the repetitive testing of other components can be replaced by a loop. The result is shown in `SMALL3`.

The program SMALL3 follows.

```
REM  Smallest number

DIM x(5)                        ! Must declare list
PRINT "Five numbers";           ! Ask user
MAT INPUT x                     ! Input entire list

LET small = x(1)                ! Assume first is smallest
FOR i = 2 to 5                  ! Try the others
    IF x(i) < small then LET small = x(i)
NEXT i
PRINT "The smallest number is "; small

END
```

To appreciate how much progress we have made, consider changing the program so that it asks for 17 numbers. In `SMALL` this would require 17 variables and 16 statements for testing numbers. It would be a mess! In `SMALL3` we need only change the 5 to 17 in the `DIM` and `FOR` statements.

Can we take one more step and have a program that would work for various length lists? The answer is ''yes'', because we can let the user tell us how many numbers are to be supplied. If `n` numbers are asked for, we use the statement

```
MAT INPUT x(n)
```

specifying that our list `x` will have `n` components. But what happens to the `DIM` statement?

Let us be more precise about the role of `DIM`. It declares a variable as a list variable. It also tells BASIC what the maximum number of components can be. This is needed so that BASIC can allocate room for that many numbers. But in any given run the list may be shorter. So the number in `DIM` needs only to be large enough for whatever may be needed. In the following program we assume that the user will not want to type in more than 20 numbers.

The program SMALL4 follows.

```
REM  Smallest number

DIM x(20)                       ! Save room
PRINT "How many";               ! User specifies
INPUT n
PRINT "Enter them:"
```

```
MAT INPUT x(n)                     ! Input n numbers

LET small = x(1)                   ! Assume first is smallest
FOR i = 2 to n                     ! Try the others
    IF x(i) < small then LET small = x(i)
NEXT i
PRINT "The smallest number is "; small

END

run

How many? 8
Enter them:
? 10, 23, 55, 2, -3, 100, 77, 0
The smallest number is -3
```

Let us add one more feature to the program. We want to know not only what the smallest number is, but what its position is in the list (what component number). We introduce the additional variable `place`, which always equals the position of the smallest number seen so far.

The program SMALL5 follows.

```
REM  Smallest number

DIM x(20)                          ! Save room
PRINT "How many";                  ! User specifies
INPUT n
PRINT "Enter them:"
MAT INPUT x(n)                     ! Input n numbers

LET small = x(1)                   ! Assume first is smallest
LET place = 1                      ! Where found
FOR i = 2 to n                     ! Try the others
    IF x(i) < small then
       LET small = x(i)
       LET place = i
    END IF
NEXT i
PRINT "The smallest number is "; small
PRINT "It is in position"; place

END
```

We see three changes in this program. The variable `place` starts out equal to 1, because we asssume that the first number is the smallest. Every time we find a smaller component we need to change both `small` and `place`; thus, we need a multiline `IF` structure. Finally, we print both `small` and `place`.

```
run

How many? 8
Enter them:
? 10, 23, 55, 2, -3, 100, 77, 0
The smallest number is -3
It is in position 5
```

This is an important example because it can easily be expanded into a program that *sorts* the list (arranges the components in increasing order). Sorting will be discussed in detail in Part II.

5.3 READ AND DATA

It is often convenient to store data for a program right within the program. The one or more `DATA` statements serve as a storage area. For example,

```
DATA 3, 4.5, -11, 17
```

stores four numbers for use during the run of the program. The statement

```
READ a
```

will pick off the next available number from this `DATA` statement and assign it to `a`. `READ` is similar to `INPUT`, except that it gets its information from the stored `DATA` rather than from the user.

The simple program we are about to show reads two numbers at a time and prints them. It tries to do so three times.

The program READ follows.

```
REM  Illustrate READ and DATA

FOR n = 1 to 3                          ! Do 3 times
    READ a, b
    PRINT a; b
NEXT n

DATA 10, 9, 8, 7                        ! 4 numbers available

END


run

 10  9
 8  7
Reading past end of data.
```

The first time through the loop the first two numbers are assigned to `a` and `b`; thus, `a` = 10 and `b` = 9. They are then printed. The second time through the next two numbers are assigned and printed. The third time there aren't any numbers left in `DATA`; hence, an error message "Reading past end of data" is printed and the program stops.

Just as `MAT INPUT` will ask for an entire list, `MAT READ` will read an entire list. We illustrate this with a program that computes the average of a list of numbers.

The program SUM4 follows.

```
REM  Average of numbers

DIM number(20)                              ! Up to 20 numbers
READ n                                      ! How many numbers
MAT READ number(n)                          ! Read list

LET sum = 0                                 ! Add them up
FOR i = 1 to n
    LET sum = sum + number(i)
NEXT i
LET aver = sum/n                            ! Average
PRINT "The average = "; aver

DATA 6
DATA 100, -25, 77, 22, 0, -9

END
```

Because the program's **DIM** statement tells us that it is designed to work with any list of up to 20 components, we must first find out how many numbers there are. The **DATA** statements give us that information. The first **DATA** item is the number of components, and the second provides the components themselves. (This separation into two **DATA** statements is not mandatory, as we shall soon learn.) We first read `n` and then do a **MAT READ** `number(n)`, reading the entire `number` list. Then we add up the numbers (similar to **SUM**). Finally, we divide the sum by `n` to obtain the average. The result is as follows:

```
run

The average =  27.5
```

The advantage of this design is that all we have to change is the **DATA** block if we want to reuse the program but with different numbers. We can have a different list of numbers, or even a list of different length (up to 20) without having to change the main portion of the program.

The fact that we arranged the **DATA** on two lines is for our convenience. It makes it easier to understand the program. We could have had it all on one line, or put each item on a separate **DATA** line. Only the order of the numbers matters because **READ** always picks up the next available data item.

The placement of the **DATA** statements is immaterial. A **DATA** statement doesn't do anything during the run of the program. It is only a storage area. (See Exercise 8.)

5.4 MORE EXAMPLES

A small store carries five items. A customer orders some of each item. We wish to compute the total purchase price. The program **BUY** is designed to perform this computation.

The program BUY follows.

```
REM  Purchase price

DIM price(20), number(20)            ! Lists
READ n                               ! How many
MAT READ price(n)                    ! Read prices
MAT READ number(n)                   ! Numbers purchased

LET sum = 0
FOR i = 1 to n
    LET sum = sum + number(i)*price(i)
NEXT i
PRINT "Total sale = $"; sum

DATA 5                               ! Five goods
DATA .25, 1.35, 2.99, .35, 1.49      ! Prices
DATA 4, 2, 1, 10, 3                  ! Purchased

END
```

We need two separate lists, `price` for the price of each item and `number` for the number purchased of each item. We first read `n`, the number of items, then we read the two lists, and finally we carry out the computation. (See Exercise 7.)

```
run

Total sale = $ 14.66
```

We can make the program more useful by assuming that several customers send in orders. We must then enclose our computation in a loop, with one set of computations for each customer.

The program BUY2 follows.

```
REM  Purchase price

DIM price(20), item(20)              ! Lists
READ n                               ! How many
MAT READ price(n)                    ! Read prices

READ cust                            ! Customers
FOR c = 1 to cust                    ! By customer
    MAT READ item(n)                 ! Numbers purchased
    LET sum = 0
    FOR i = 1 to n
        LET sum = sum + item(i)*price(i)
    NEXT i
    PRINT "Customer"; c; "sale = $"; sum
NEXT c

DATA 5                               ! Five goods
DATA .25, 1.35, 2.99, .35, 1.49      ! Prices
DATA 3                               ! Customers
```

```
DATA 4, 2, 1, 10, 3                    ! Purchased
DATA 10, 0, 9, 1, 0
DATA 0, 0, 3, 4, 2

END
```

Note that the `price` list is read before the loop; i.e. it is read only once because the same prices apply to all customers. But new values for `number` are read each time we go through the loop, because different customers order different numbers of items.

```
run

Customer 1 sale = $ 14.66
Customer 2 sale = $ 29.76
Customer 3 sale = $ 13.35
```

5.5 SUMMARY

Variables may be used to represent an entire list. Such *list variables* must be declared by a `DIM` statement. For example, the statement

```
DIM  price(22)
```

declares `price` to be a list variable and saves space for up to 22 components for the list.

Individual components are referred to by putting a number in parentheses after the list variable. Thus, `price(7)` is the seventh price. In place of a number we may also use a variable, such as `price(i)`, which allows one to loop through the components.

Data that will be used by the program may be stored in `DATA` statements. These serve only as storage areas, hence their placement within the program is irrelevant. The program makes use of this data by `READ` statements that pick up the next available data item. Only the order of the numbers matters, for their arrangement into one or more `DATA` statements is purely for the convenience of the programmer.

`MAT` statements allow us to input, read, and print an entire list, as follows:

`MAT INPUT x`	Input list `x` as per `DIM`
`MAT INPUT x(n)`	Input `n` components into `x`
`MAT READ x`	Read list `x` as per `DIM`
`MAT READ x(n)`	Read `n` components into `x`
`MAT PRINT x`	Print the entire list `x`

We have seen uses of the first four. The exercises will explore the use of `MAT PRINT`.

EXERCISES

1. Write a program that asks the user for a list of numbers and then prints
   (a) every second number, and
   (b) the entire list in reverse order.
   Use a **FOR** loop with an appropriate step for printing.
2. Modify Exercise 1 to read the list from **DATA**.
3. Write a program that asks the user for a list of numbers and then prints the average of the numbers.
4. Write a program to read a list of numbers and print those numbers that are greater than 50.
5. Write a program to read a list of numbers and print their product.
6. Modify **SMALLS** to print the largest number and its position.
7. Step through the loop in **BUY** (by hand) to verify the computation of the sales price.
8. Rearrange the data in **BUY2**. Combine and divide **DATA** lines, and move some to another part of the program (but keep the order of the numbers the same). Verify that the program still works.
9. Use **MAT READ** to read a list of 12 numbers. Print them by means of **MAT PRINT**. Observe the output. Now add a semicolon at the end of the **MAT PRINT** statement. How does the output change?
10. Read a list and replace every second number with a 0. Use **MAT PRINT** to display the result.
11. Construct a list of 12 numbers as follows: The first two components are 1. The others (starting with the third) are the sum of the two previous numbers. Print the list. (These are called *Fibonacci numbers*.)

CHAPTER 6

STRINGS

6.1 INTRODUCTION

To this point, all of our examples have been numeric, using numeric constants (e.g. `125`) and numeric variables (e.g. `small`), but BASIC can work equally well with textual information. To that end, this chapter introduces the concept of a *string*, which allows us to work with any non-numeric information.

A *string* is an arbitrary combination of characters. It may be a word in English, or in French, or a phrase or sentence, or completely meaningless, such as "x!y&/z". We have already used string constants in `PRINT` statements: a string constant is any collection of characters enclosed in quotes.

BASIC also provides string variables, that is, variables that can *hold* strings. Their names look like numeric variable names except that the final character is a dollar sign `$`. It also allows string lists, whose names must end in `$`.

BASIC can perform a number of operations on strings. We will consider the simplest ones in this chapter. More advanced manipulation of strings and of textual information will be the subject of Part II.

6.2 STRING VARIABLES

BASIC can deal with strings just as easily as with numbers. To allow this, it provides for string variables and string constants. String variable names follow the same rules as numeric variable names, except that the final character must be a dollar sign `$`. String constants are just about any sequence of characters contained within quote marks. The following examples illustrate the similarities and differences.

Numeric variables:	x, k9, next_value
Numeric constants:	10, 1e-10, -17.24
String variables:	x$, k9$, first_name$
String constants:	"Jones", "12345", "siR41[<];;:"

We have already seen programs where string constants appear in `PRINT` statements. We illustrate the use of string variables in the very simple program `STRING`.

The program STRING follows.

```
REM  String INPUT, PRINT

PRINT "Two words";
INPUT a$, b$

PRINT a$, b$                                   ! In zones
PRINT b$, a$                                   ! Reverse order
PRINT a$; b$                                   ! Close together

END
```

The program asks the user for two words. They are printed (in zones—note the comma), then printed in reverse order. Finally, they are printed with the ";" convention of `PRINT`. Strings are always printed precisely as they are, without any extra spaces. The run shows that with the ";" convention the two words run together as if they were one word.

```
run

Two words? dog, house
dog            house
house          dog
doghouse
```

A more interesting example constructs a form letter from information supplied by the user. This program is too simple to be realistic, but it shows how string constants and variables can be combined to produce individualized letters.

The program LETTER follows.

```
REM  Letter writer

PRINT "College, relation";              ! User supplied
INPUT coll$, rel$

PRINT coll$; " is a very fine school."       ! Form letter
PRINT "I hope that your "; rel$;
PRINT " will go to "; coll$; "."

END
```

Note that the string constants have leading and/or trailing spaces to assure that there is a space before and after the values of the variables, as shown in the following run.

```
run

College, relation? Dartmouth, daughter
Dartmouth is a very fine school.
I hope that your daughter will go to Dartmouth.

run

College, relation? Knox College, son
Knox College is a very fine school.
I hope that your son will go to Knox College.
```

In the first run, the string variable `coll$` receives the value "Dartmouth" through the `INPUT` statement. And the string variable `rel$` receives the value "daughter". In the subsequent `PRINT` statements, printing the variable `coll$` causes the string "Dartmouth" to appear, and so on.

The `INPUT` statement allows a string constant to be entered without the enclosing quote marks, provided there are no commas within the string constant. Also, leading and trailing spaces are *stripped*. If the string you wish to enter has leading or trailing spaces that are important, or contains commas, then the string must be enclosed in quote marks.

6.3 STRING OPERATIONS

BASIC provides a number of tools for manipulating strings. We will consider some of the simplest ones, as follows:

`len(x$)`	Number of characters in the string
`x$ & y$`	Concatenated string
`ucase$(x$)`	All letters in uppercase
`lcase$(x$)`	All letters in lowercase
`x$[3:6]`	Substring of `x$`

Concatenation means that the two strings are "glued" together. Thus, if `x$` = `"abc"` and `y$` = `"de"` then `x$ & y$` = `"abcde"`. The following illustrates the first four tools.

The program STRING2 follows.

```
REM  String operations

PRINT "Word";
INPUT a$                        ! User's word
PRINT a$, len(a$)

LET b$ = "(" & a$ & ")"         ! In parentheses
PRINT b$, len(b$)

PRINT ucase$(a$), lcase$(a$)    ! Uppercase and
                                !     lowercase

END
```

The program asks the user for a string `a$`. The string and its length (number of characters) are printed. Then a new string `b$` is constructed by glueing "(" to the beginning and ")" to the end. That is, we enclose the given string in parentheses. Again the new string and its length are printed. Finally we show the given string in both uppercase and lowercase.

```
run

Word? House
House            5
(House)          7
HOUSE           house

run

Word? A small dog.
A small dog.     12
(A small dog.)   14
A SMALL DOG.    a small dog.
```

The second run is shown to emphasize that although we asked the user for a word, the concept of *word* is not one that BASIC understands. The program looks for a string to be input, and a sentence is a perfectly good string. Note also that `len` counts all characters, including spaces and the period.

The next operation we consider is extracting a *substring* from a string. For any string `x$`, `x$[3:6]` will be that portion of the string starting with character number 3 and ending with character number 6. This will usually be a four-character string, but it will be shorter if `x$` has fewer than six characters.

The program STRING3 follows.

```
REM  Substrings

FOR n = 1 to 3                            ! Three examples
    PRINT "Word";
    INPUT w$
    PRINT w$[2:4]                         ! Two substrings
    PRINT w$[5:9]
NEXT n
PRINT "Done"

END
```

This program asks for a word and prints two of its substrings. We loop through three examples so that we may illustrate various cases:

```
run

Word? Dartmouth
art
mouth
```

```
Word? Harvard
arv
ard
Word? Yale
ale

Done
```

For the string "Dartmouth", the result is self-explanatory. But "Harvard" has only seven characters, hence `w$[5:9]` pulls out characters 5 through 7. And "Yale" has only four characters, hence the second substring is the *empty string*. Note the blank line just before "Done".

As a more interesting example we present a program that reverses the characters in a string. The approach is quite straightforward. We pick off substrings of one character, starting at the end, and print them using the ";" convention. We encourage you to pick a value for `w$` and step through the `FOR` loop by hand.

The program REVERSE follows.

```
REM  Reverse a word

FOR n = 1 to 3                              ! Three examples
    PRINT "Word";
    INPUT w$
    LET ln = len(w$)                        ! Number of characters
    FOR c = ln to 1 step -1                 ! Reverse order
        PRINT w$[c:c];                      ! One character
    NEXT c
    PRINT                                   ! New line
NEXT n

END


run

Word? house
esuoh
Word? madam
madam
Word? A small cat.
.tac llams A
```

The second example uses a word that is the same forwards and backwards. The third example shows what our program does to a sentence. The characters are indeed printed in reverse order. One must remember that the spaces and the period are also characters in the string!

Although arithmetic operations are meaningless for strings, BASIC does provide for comparisons. The relation "<" is interpreted as, roughly, *earlier in alphabetic order*. The program `STRING4` shows which of two words is *earlier* according to "<".

The program STRING4 follows.

```
REM  Order strings

PRINT "Two words";
INPUT w1$, w2$

IF w1$<w2$ then                     ! Earlier alphabetically
   PRINT w1$
ELSE
   PRINT w2$
END IF

END


run

Two words? table, house
house

run

Two words? TABLE, house
TABLE
```

The second example shows why this program offers only roughly alphabetic order. On computers capital and lowercase letters are different characters, and in the ordering all capital letters come before all lowercase ones. Thus "TABLE" or even "Table" comes before "house".

To achieve true alphabetic order, we must compare the words when they are both in uppercase or lowercase.

The program STRING5 follows.

```
REM  Order strings

PRINT "Two words";
INPUT w1$, w2$

IF ucase$(w1$) < ucase$(w2$) then      ! Same case
   PRINT w1$
ELSE
   PRINT w2$
END IF

END


run

Two words? table, house
house
```

```
run

Two words? TABLE, house
house
```

6.4 STRING LISTS

Just as we can have numeric lists, we can have string lists. The only difference is that the name of the list must end with a dollar sign **$**. A nice illustration is to make a simple modification in **SMALLS**, the program that finds the smallest number in a list and the place where it occurred. We change the numeric list variable **x** to the string list variable **x$**, and change `small` to **first$**. We then have a program that will select the word earliest in alphabetic order and the place where it was found.

The program ALPHA follows.

```
REM  Alphabetic order

DIM x$(20)                              ! Save room
PRINT "How many";                       ! User specifies
INPUT n
PRINT "Enter them:"
MAT INPUT x$(n)                         ! Input n strings

LET first$ = x$(1)                      ! Assume first is first
LET place = 1                           ! Where found
FOR i = 2 to n                          ! Try the others
    IF x$(i) < first$ then
       LET first$ = x$(i)
       LET place = i
    END IF
NEXT i
PRINT "Earliest alphabetically: "; first$
PRINT "It is in position"; place

END
```

```
run

How many? 5
Enter them:
? pear, apple, banana, peach, cherry
Earliest alphabetically: apple
It is in position 2

run

How many? 5
Enter them:
? pear, apple, banana, Peach, cherry
Earliest alphabetically: Peach
It is in position 4
```

The first run works as expected. The second shows the problem that results when we compare uppercase and lowercase letters. (See Exercise 6.)

An interesting variant is to pick out the longest word in a list. The program that accomplishes this, `LONG`, should be self-explanatory.

The program LONG follows.

```
REM  Find longest word

DIM word$(20)                          ! Save room
PRINT "How many";                      ! User specifies
INPUT n
PRINT "Enter them:"
MAT INPUT word$(n)                     ! Input n words

LET long = len(word$(1))               ! Assume first is
                                         longest
LET place = 1                          ! Where found
FOR i = 2 to n                         ! Try the others
    LET ln = len(word$(i))
    IF ln>long then
       LET long = ln
       LET place = i
    END IF
NEXT i
PRINT "The longest word is: "; word$(place)
PRINT "Number of characters:"; long

END


run

How many? 7
Enter them:
? cat, mouse, elephant, dog, fox, cow, tiger
The longest word is: elephant
Number of characters: 8

run

How many? 5
Enter them:
? house, xxxxxx, table, a$#>*!!?b, chair
The longest word is: a$#>*!!?b
Number of characters: 9
```

We include the second run as a reminder, once more, that nonsense sequences of characters are perfectly legal strings. The program correctly picked the longest string, even though it is not a *word*.

We close by presenting a computer drill program. Although it is very simple, it contains the key idea of such drills.

The program DRILL follows.

```
REM  Drill program

DIM query$(100), answer$(100)
RANDOMIZE

READ question$                     ! Text of question
READ nq                            ! Number of questions
READ n                             ! Items
MAT READ query$(n), answer$(n) ! Topical information

FOR question = 1 to nq             ! Ask nq questions
    LET i = int(n*rnd + 1)         ! Pick at random, from 1 to n

    LET s$ = query$(i)
    LET c$ = answer$(i)
    PRINT question$; " "; s$;
    INPUT reply$
    IF ucase$(reply$) = ucase$(c$) then
       PRINT "That is correct"
    ELSE
       PRINT "No.  It is "; c$
    END IF
    PRINT
NEXT question

DATA  What is the capital of       ! Question
DATA  5                            ! Number of questions
DATA  12                           ! Number of items
DATA  Alabama, Delaware, Florida, Hawaii     ! States
DATA  Kansas, Maine, New Hampshire, New York
DATA  Ohio, Oregon, Tennessee, Utah
DATA  Montgomery, Dover, Tallahassee, Honolulu ! Capitals
DATA  Topeka, Augusta, Concord, Albany
DATA  Columbus, Salem, Nashville, Salt Lake City

END
```

The general instruction is first read into the variable `question$`. The program then reads the questions into one string list, and the answers into another. Next, the programs picks a question at random, and compares the reply of the user with the official answer (note the use of `ucase$` to allow answers in any case); it either tells the user that the answer is correct, or gives the correct answer.

The content of the drill is contained in the **DATA**. It starts with the general question (“What is the capital of”), then specifies how many questions should be asked and how many possible questions there are. Next come the items for the questions (names of states) and the answers (names of capitals). A longer drill program or one on a completely different subject can be prepared by changing only the **DATA**. (See Exercise 7.)

Picking an item at random is accomplished by

```
LET i = int(n*rnd + 1)
```

The statement picks an integer from 1 to n. The use of random processes in BASIC will be explained in Chapter 17.

```
run

What is the capital of Utah? Salt Lake City
That is correct

What is the capital of Delaware? Wilmington
No.  It is Dover

What is the capital of Florida? tallahassee
That is correct

What is the capital of Maine? Portland
No.  It is Augusta

What is the capital of Tennessee? NASHVILLE
That is correct
```

6.5 SUMMARY

A *string* is an arbitrary collection of characters. It may be a word, a sentence, or a meaningless assortment of characters. Constant strings are represented in BASIC by enclosing them in quotation marks. A dollar sign at the end of string variables distinguishes them from numerical variables.

Values of string variables may be `INPUT` or `READ`, similar to the way numbers are handled. In replying to an `INPUT`, the user need not enclose the string in quotes. Quotes are required only if the string starts or ends with a space, or contains a comma. The same convention applies to strings in `DATA` statements.

When a string is printed, no extra spaces are added. Therefore, care must be taken when using the semicolon convention for `PRINT`. Spaces to separate words must be explicitly provided.

BASIC provides for both numeric and string lists. The latter have names that end with `$`. The conventions for `DIM` and `MAT` statements are the same as for numeric lists.

We considered several string operations. For any string `x$`, `len(x$)` equals the number of characters in the string, `ucase$(x$)` is the string entirely in uppercase, and `lcase$(x$)` in lowercase. Substrings may be extracted, e.g. `x$[3:7]` consists of characters 3 through 7 of the original string (or fewer characters if `x$` had fewer than seven characters.)

If `x$` and `y$` are any two strings, then `x$ & y$` is the concatenated string—the second string attached to the first. The relation `x$` < `y$` is true if the first string is earlier in alphabetic order. At least, this is true if they are in the same case; otherwise capital letters come *earlier* than lowercase ones. Therefore, it is best to use `ucase$` (or `lcase$`) when comparing two strings.

EXERCISES

1. Change `STRING3` to use `READ` instead of `INPUT`.

2. Make up a more interesting letter writing program than `LETTER`.

3. Write a program that inputs a string and prints it as a *header*: it should change all letters to uppercase, and leave a blank between characters.
4. Write a program that inputs a string and prints the last three characters.
5. Use concatenation (in a loop) to form a string that consists of 10 copies of a given string.
6. Fix **ALPHA** so that it works whether the words are in upper or lowercase or any mixture of cases.
7. Choose your own subject matter for a drill program. Change only the **DATA** in **DRILL**.
8. Think up some features to add to **DRILL** to make the program more interesting.

CHAPTER 7

GRAPHICS

7.1 INTRODUCTION

One reason for the great popularity of personal computers is their ability to draw pictures. With BASIC it is easy to write such graphics programs.

Most pictures can be drawn as a combination of points and line segments. The **PLOT POINTS** and **PLOT LINES** statements accomplish these tasks. A graph can be labeled by means of **PLOT TEXT**.

BASIC allows the user to specify the coordinate system. One need not count *pixels* (dots on screen), but can simply specifiy the coordinate system by means of a **SET WINDOW** statement. This allows you to run your graphics program on a different computer without changing it.

Instead of using the full screen to plot a graphics picture, the user may specify a portion of it, called a *window*, by using an **OPEN** statement. A given program may use several windows for different purposes. The **CLEAR** statement empties (erases) a given window.

If color graphics are available on the computer, **SET COLOR** specifies the color to be used next. And, **FLOOD** allows the user to fill in an enclosed region with the specified color. **FLOOD** may also be used in black and white.

These simple statements allow us to do a wide variety of graphic applications. BASIC also provides much more powerful tools for sophisticated graphics, and these will be considered in Chapter 21.

7.2 POINTS AND LINES

The following program will draw three points, as specified by the x-y coordinates.

The program GRAPH1 follows.

```
REM Plots three points

PLOT POINTS: .3,.3
PLOT POINTS: .7,.3
PLOT POINTS: .3,.7

END
```

To draw the triangle with these vertices, we use `PLOT LINES` in place of `PLOT POINTS`.

The program GRAPH2A follows.

```
REM Plots triangle

PLOT LINES: .3,.3;
PLOT LINES: .7,.3;
PLOT LINES: .3,.7;
PLOT LINES: .3,.3

END
```

Alternatively, we could, more simply and naturally, use a single `PLOT LINES` statement.

The program GRAPH2 follows.

```
REM Plots triangle

PLOT LINES: .3,.3; .7,.3; .3,.7; .3,.3

END
```

Why did we have to specify four points in this? We asked the computer to draw the first point (.3,.3), to connect it by a line segment to the second point (.7,.3), to connect the second to the third (.3,.7), and connect it back to the first point, thus completing the triangle. The outputs of these programs are in Figures 7.1 and 7.2.

7.3 COORDINATE SYSTEM

The conventions for drawing in x-y coordinates are those of ordinary mathematics. But whether we draw on graph paper or the computer draws on a screen, only a small portion of the plane can be displayed. We specify the boundaries for the visible portion of the plane by a `SET WINDOW` statement. For example,

---

True BASIC allows the use of `PLOT` in place of either `PLOT POINTS:` or `PLOT LINES:`. If the coordinates of a point are followed by a semicolon, that point will be connected to the next point specified. Thus, `GRAPH1` and `GRAPH2` would work equally well with simple `PLOT` statements.

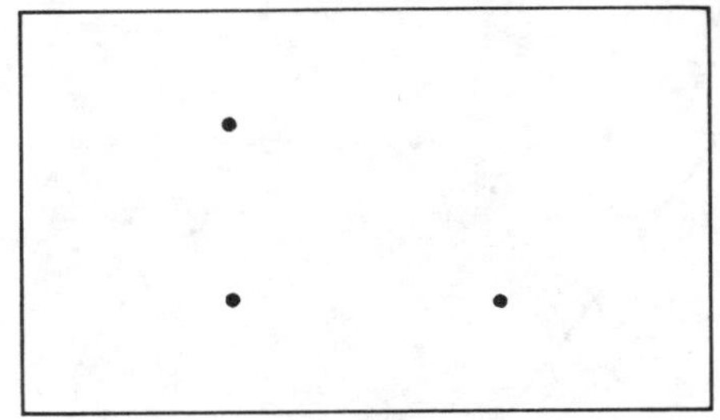

FIGURE 7.1 Output of the program GRAPH1.

```
SET WINDOW -3, 5, 0, 10
```

specifies that x goes from -3 to 5, while y has the range 0 to 10.

If no SET WINDOW statement is given, BASIC provides *default* boundaries, with both x and y having the range 0 to 1. The graphs of Section 7.2 were drawn in this coordinate system. (See Figures 7.1 and 7.2.) If we had tried to draw a larger triangle, as in the next example, only a portion of the triangle would have been displayed.

Let us next draw a larger triangle, specifying a coordinate system in which all of it is visible.

The program GRAPH3 follows.

```
REM Plots triangle

SET WINDOW 0, 10, 0, 5               ! Coordinate system
PLOT LINES: 1,1; 4,1; 1,4; 1,1

END
```

Figure 7.3 shows that because the x-boundaries are 0 and 10, and the triangle ranges from 1 to 4, the triangle is located in the left half of the window.

Let us now turn to drawing the graph of a function. We wish to draw a graph of the square root function sqr. Do we need a separate PLOT statement for every point? Of course not, because this is a perfect application of the FOR loop.

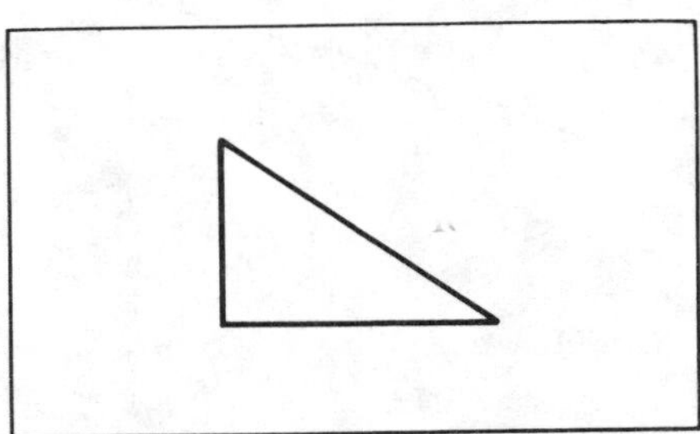

FIGURE 7.2 Output of the programs GRAPH2A and GRAPH2.

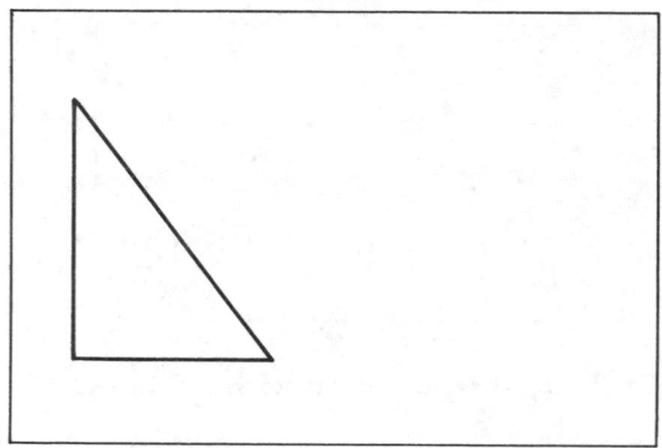

FIGURE 7.3 Output of the program GRAPH3.

The program SQRP1 follows.

```
REM  Square root plotter

SET WINDOW -1, 4, -1, 3

FOR x = 0 to 4 step 1/8          ! Loop through line segments
    PLOT LINES: x, sqr(x);
NEXT x

END
```

The `PLOT LINES` statement specifies that the y-coordinate is `sqr(x)`. It ends in a semicolon; consecutive points will thus be connected by line segments. We have chosen an ample coordinate system, allowing a margin around the graph. (See Figure 7.4.)

However, our result is unsatisfactory. We will have to make several improvements in our program. First, we make the drawing smoother by choosing a smaller step size. The choice is a trade-off—the smaller the step the more accurate the graph but the longer it takes to draw it. Second, we draw axes. The two `PLOT LINES` statements near the start of the program plot the x-axis and y-axis, respectively. Finally, we label the graph by means of a

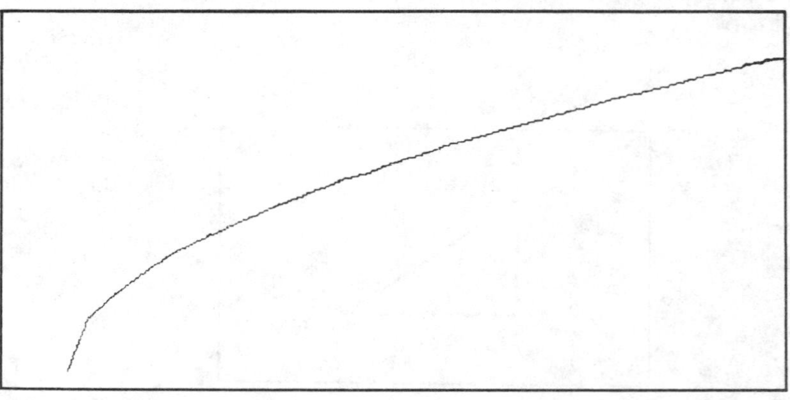

FIGURE 7.4 Simple graph of the square root function.

PLOT TEXT statement. The at portion specifies where the lower left corner of the label shall be placed.

The program SQRP2 follows.

```
REM  Square root plotter
REM  With axes and label

SET WINDOW -1, 4, -1, 3
PLOT LINES: -1,0; 4,0          ! Axes
PLOT LINES: 0,-1; 0,3

FOR x = 0 to 4 step .05        ! Loop through line segments
    PLOT LINES: x, sqr(x);
NEXT x
PLOT TEXT, at 1,2.5: "Square root"

END
```

The output is shown in Figure 7.5.

7.4 WINDOWS

As a more interesting example we shall draw a spiral. A well-known spiral is specified by the equations

```
LET x  =  t * cos(t)
LET y  =  t * sin(t)
```

where t starts at 0 and runs through some appropriate range. As t increases the curve *spirals out*. The program itself is quite similar to SQRP1.

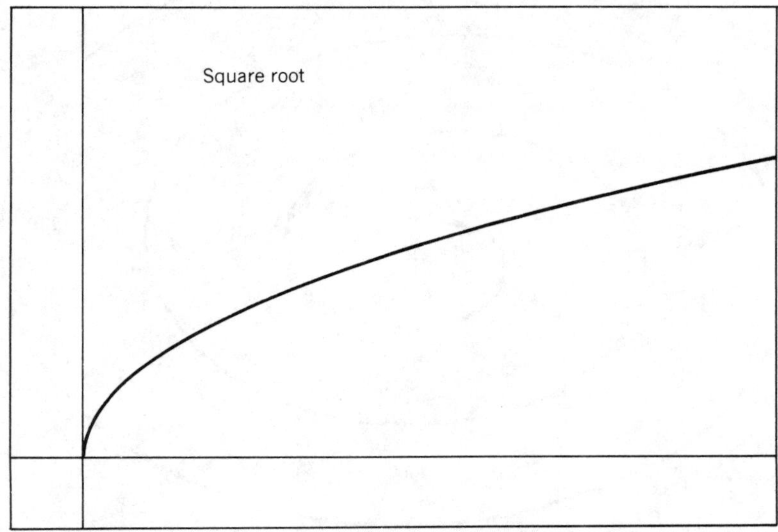

FIGURE 7.5 Fancier graph of the square root function.

The program SPIRAL1 follows.

```
REM  Draw spiral

SET WINDOW -20, 20, -20, 20

FOR t = 0 to 20 step 1/4
    PLOT LINES: t*cos(t), t*sin(t);
NEXT t

END
```

The resulting picture is shown in Figure 7.6. It is not as attractive as we might like, as it was drawn on a screen that is wider than it is tall. We would prefer to draw it on a square area of the screen. To do this we open a *window*.

The statement

```
OPEN #1: screen .25, .75, .1, .9
```

provides us with a window consisting of a portion of the screen. We call this window #1, to distinguish it from other windows we might open. The screen coordinates specified are relative to the physical screen, with both horizontal and vertical coordinates ranging from 0 to 1. Thus we have specified the middle half horizontally, and have left a slight margin on both the bottom and the top.

Whether the area is actually square shaped depends less on the computer than on the display device. Some experimentation with the `OPEN` statement may be necessary to get the exact dimensions you desire.

The program `SPIRAL2` draws the same spiral in a roughly square window. It also *frames* the picture by drawing the sides of the square. The result is shown in Figure 7.7.

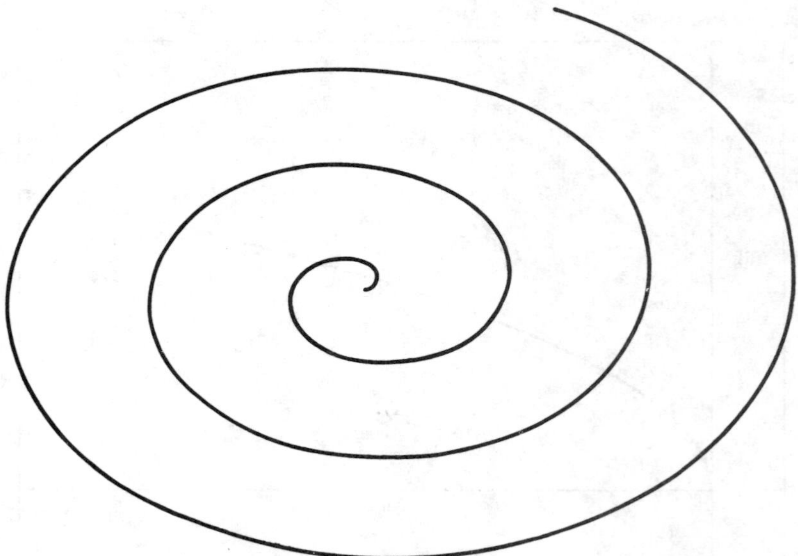

FIGURE 7.6 Simple spiral.

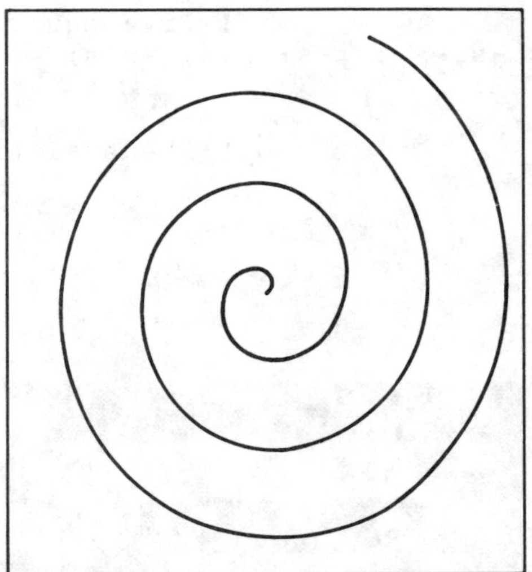

FIGURE 7.7 Fancier spiral in a square window.

The program SPIRAL2 follows.

```
REM  Draw spiral in a window

OPEN #1: screen .25, .75, .1, .9   ! Open window
SET WINDOW -20, 20, -20, 20        ! Coordinates
PLOT LINES: -20,-20; 20,-20; 20,20; -20,20; -20,-20 !Frame

FOR t = 0 to 20 step 1/4
    PLOT LINES: t*cos(t), t*sin(t);
NEXT t

END
```

We now turn to `SQUARES1`, which draws *nested squares* within the same square window. We let both coordinates range from -5 to 5, and draw squares whose sides go from `-s` to `s`. We do this in a loop, so that `s=1` produces a small square, while `s=5` fills the window.

To make the picture more interesting, we will fill in alternate regions. The `FLOOD` statement starts at a specified point and fills in, or shades, the smallest closed area containing the point. Our program points, in turn, to a position in the largest square, in the middle square, and in the smallest square, and shades them. If we draw in black on white (as with the Apple Macintosh), the shading will be in black. If we display white on black (as with the IBM PC), we shade in white. And, if we are drawing in color, the program will shade in the current color (see the next section). The result is shown in Figure 7.8.

The program SQUARES1 follows.

```
REM  Nested squares

OPEN #1: screen .25, .75, .1, .9   ! Open window
SET WINDOW -5, 5, -5, 5            ! Coordinates
```

```
FOR s = 1 to 5                        ! Five squares
    PLOT LINES: -s,-s; s,-s; s,s; -s,s; -s,-s
NEXT s

FLOOD 0,4.5                           ! Shade alternate squares
FLOOD 0,2.5
FLOOD 0,0.5

END
```

FIGURE 7.8 Nested squares, alternately shaded.

7.5 COLOR PICTURES

If color displays are available, it is very simple in BASIC to produce color output. **SET COLOR** specifies the color in which the drawing is to be carried out. When we wish to change color, we simply issue another **SET COLOR** statement. And, **SET BACKGROUND COLOR** will set the color on the screen before we draw on it. (See the notes on color in the Summary.)

These statements are used to produce a color picture of the nested squares. For our program we pick a blue background, draw the squares in red, and switch to yellow before the **FLOOD** statements, so that alternate squares are colored yellow. The picture is shown in Figure 7.9.

The program SQUARES2 follows.

```
REM  Nested squares, in color

OPEN #1: screen .25, .75, .1, .9  ! Open window
SET WINDOW -5, 5, -5, 5           ! Coordinates
SET BACKGROUND COLOR "blue"
```

```
SET COLOR "red"
FOR s = 1 to 5                        ! Five squares
    PLOT LINES: -s,-s; s,-s; s,s; -s,s; -s,-s
NEXT s

SET COLOR "yellow"
FLOOD 0,4.5                           ! Shade alternate squares
FLOOD 0,2.5
FLOOD 0,0.5

END
```

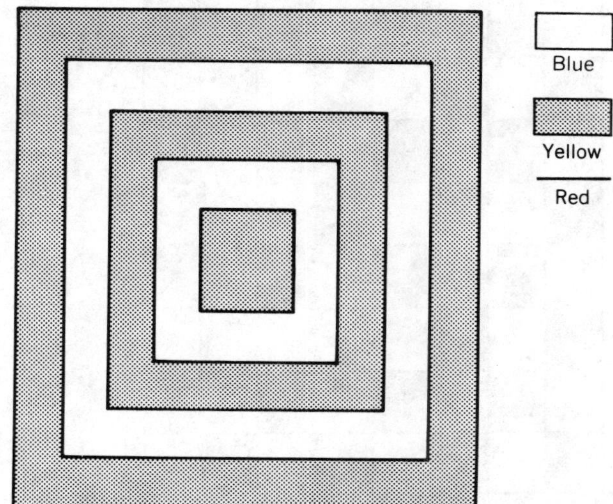

FIGURE 7.9 Nested squares in color.

Next we produce a checkerboard. The program should be self-explanatory if you keep the following two observations in mind: The `IF` statement inside the nested `FOR` loops has a even-odd test in it that picks out alternate squares. (The use of `mod` will be explained later.) And, because the background is black, it suffices to color alternate squares in red to obtain a red/black board. (See Figure 7.10.)

The program BOARD follows.

```
REM  Checker board

OPEN #1: screen .25, .75, .1, .9   ! Open window
SET WINDOW 0, 8, 0, 8              ! Coordinates

SET BACKGROUND COLOR "black"
SET COLOR "yellow"
FOR s = 0 to 8
    PLOT LINES: 0,s; 8,s           ! Horizontal
    PLOT LINES: s,0; s,8           ! Vertical
NEXT s
```

```
SET COLOR "red"
FOR x = 0 to 7
    FOR y = 0 to 7
        IF mod(x+y,2)=0 then           ! Alternate ones
           FLOOD x+.5,y+.5
        END IF
    NEXT y
NEXT x

END
```

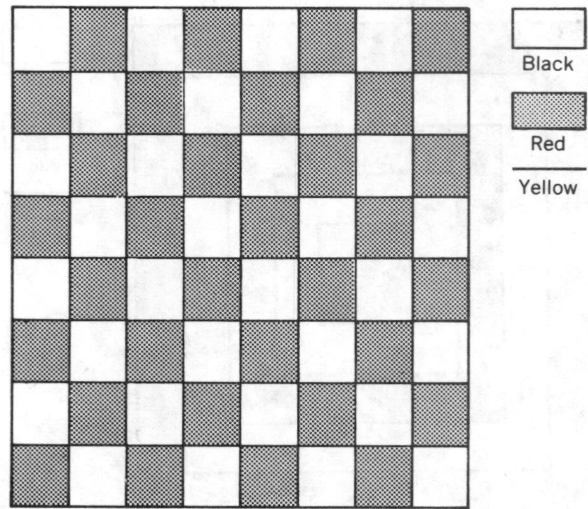

FIGURE 7.10 Checkerboard in color.

7.6 MULTIPLE WINDOWS

It is often convenient to have several windows open at once. The program **WINDOWS** opens three windows of different size and shape. We draw a spiral in the first, nested squares in the second, and place text in the third.

It is important to note that the choice of the screen coordinates for a window are independent of the code that produces a picture within the window. Thus, if we do not like the shape of the spiral, we can simply change the **OPEN #1** statement without having to change the code for drawing the spiral.

The program WINDOWS follows.

```
REM  Multiple windows

OPEN #1: screen 0, .25, .5, .9     ! Three windows
SET WINDOW -20, 20, -20, 20
OPEN #2: screen .4, .9, .1, .9
SET WINDOW -6, 6, -6, 6
OPEN #3: screen 0, .3, 0, .3
SET WINDOW 0, 2, 0, 2
```

```
FOR w = 1 to 3                     ! Loop through windows
    WINDOW #w                      ! Select window
    ASK WINDOW x1, x2, y1, y2      ! Get coordinates
    PLOT LINES: x1,y1; x2,y1; x2, y2; x1,y2; x1,y1 ! Frame
NEXT w

WINDOW #1                          ! Spiral
FOR t = 0 to 20 step 1/4
    PLOT LINES: t*cos(t), t*sin(t);
NEXT t

WINDOW #2                          ! Squares
FOR s = 1 to 5                     ! Five squares
    PLOT LINES: -s,-s; s,-s; s,s; -s,s; -s,-s
NEXT s
FLOOD 0,4.5                        ! Shade alternate squares
FLOOD 0,2.5
FLOOD 0,0.5

WINDOW #3                          ! Text
PLOT TEXT, at .5,1: "No. 3"

END
```

Notice that we can specify a different coordinate system for each window. The **OPEN** statement specifies the portion of the screen to be used for the window, while **SET WINDOW** specifies the coordinate system within the window.

We switch from window to window by using a **WINDOW** statement. We can loop through all the windows, using a variable, **w**, for the number of the window. This loop, which draws frames around the three windows, should

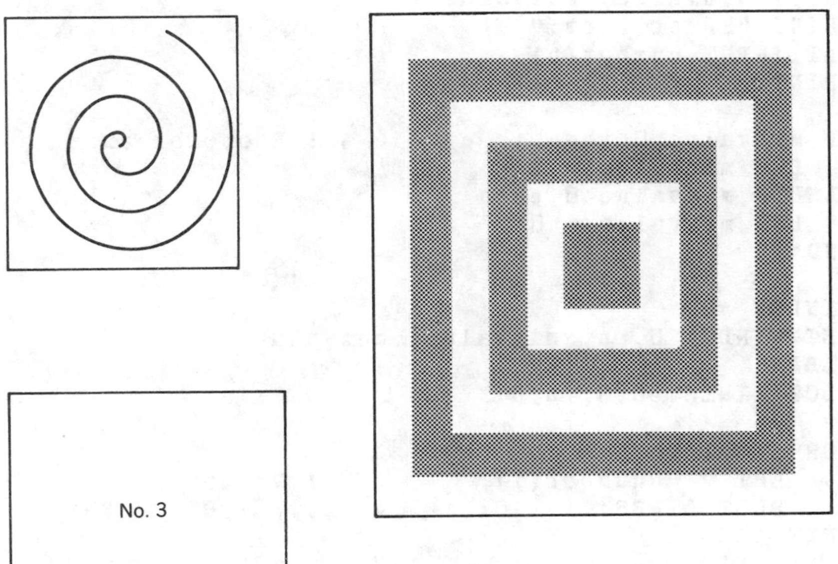

FIGURE 7.11 Multiple windows.

be studied carefully. The **ASK WINDOW** statement gives us the user coordinates of the current window, which are then used to draw the frame.

The rest of the program is simple. We pick a window and draw a picture or print text within it. The result is shown in Figure 7.11.

We will close with a practical application, a program to draw bar graphs. We start by opening two windows. The small window on the bottom is used to get data from the user, while the larger window on top will contain the graph.

Next we ask the user for the data for the bars. First we ask how many numbers there will be. Next we ask for the range of values, which we use for our y-coordinates. (See Exercise 9.) And finally, we obtain the actual values.

Before issuing a **SET WINDOW** statement we must make a small adjustment. If the values are all positive (or all negative) we cannot use the range specified by the user for our y-axis. Suppose the values range from 100 to 300. Unless y-values start with 0, the bottom of the bars will not show. The **IF** structure makes a correction, if necessary. The x-axis is scaled from 0 to **n**. The first bar will be in the interval 0 to 1, the second in 1 to 2, and so on.

The program BARS follows.

```
REM  Bar chart

OPEN #1: screen 0, 1, 0, .25          ! For text
OPEN #2: screen .2, .8, .3, 1         ! For chart

DIM number(20)

DO
   WINDOW #1
   PRINT "How many";
   INPUT n
   IF n=0 then EXIT DO                ! Exit convention
   PRINT "Min, max";
   INPUT minvalue, maxvalue
   PRINT "Enter them:"
   MAT INPUT number(n)
   PRINT

   IF minvalue>0 then                 ! Room for axis
      LET minvalue = 0
   ELSEIF maxvalue<0 then
      LET maxvalue = 0
   END IF

   WINDOW #2
   SET WINDOW 0, n, minvalue, maxvalue
   CLEAR
   PLOT LINES: 0,0; n,0               ! Axis

   FOR i = 1 to n
      LET v = number(i)               ! Value
      PLOT LINES: i-1,0; i-1,v; i,v; i,0   ! Bar
   NEXT i
LOOP

END
```

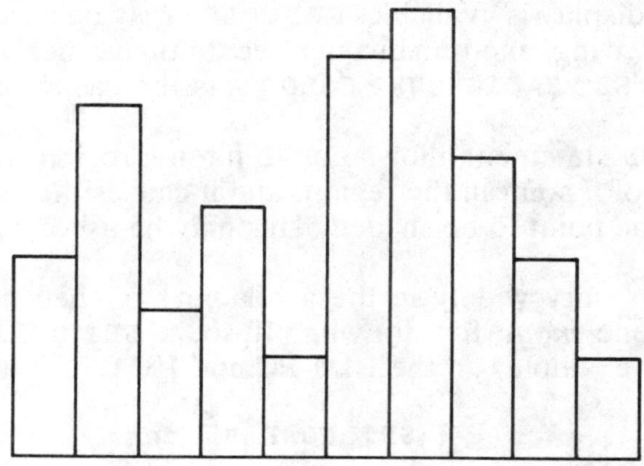

Enter them:
? 4, 7, 3, 5, 2, 8, 9, 6, 4, 2

How many?

FIGURE 7.12 A simple bar chart.

Next we `CLEAR` window #2 to erase any previous bar graph, plot the x-axis and, within a loop, draw the three sides of each bar. A sample bar chart is shown in Figure 7.12.

7.7 SUMMARY

The user introduces a coordinate system for the display device by a `SET WINDOW` statement of the form

```
SET WINDOW xlow, xhigh, ylow, yhigh
```

Within this coordinate system points and lines are plotted by `PLOT POINTS:` and `PLOT LINES:` statements. Each requires the x and y coordinates of a point. In the latter, a semicolon indicates that the point is to be connected to the next one. (True BASIC allows `PLOT` as an abbreviation for either `PLOT POINTS:` or `PLOT LINES:`; check your reference manual for details.) A label may be printed by

```
PLOT TEXT, at x,y: "....."
```

Instead of using the whole screen, the user may open one or more windows with a statement of the form

```
OPEN #3: screen xlow, xhigh, ylow, yhigh
```

where the entire screen has range 0 to 1 in both directions. Each window may have its own coordinate system. `CLEAR` erases the current window. A `WINDOW` statement allows the user to switch windows. `ASK WINDOW` supplies the coordinate system for the current window.

If a color display is available, **SET COLOR** may be used to choose the color for future drawing, and remains in effect until another **SET COLOR** statement is executed. **SET BACKGROUND COLOR** sets the background color of the display screen.

The **FLOOD** statement allows one to fill in a region. Its arguments are the coordinates of a point in the region, and it causes the smallest closed region containing the point to be shaded. This may be used in either black/white or with colors.

Computers vary widely in the availability of their colors and may have more than one *mode* for drawing. If so, a **SET MODE** statement may be needed. For example, on the IBM PC and IBM PC-compatible computers

```
SET MODE "hires"
```

will produce accurate drawings in white-on-black.

```
SET MODE "graphics"
```

will result in cruder drawings, but makes several colors available. If no color is available, **SET COLOR** may produce shadings of grey. Consult the BASIC User Manual for the capabilities of your particular computer.

EXERCISES

1. Draw a rectangle whose lower left corner has coordinates (.5,.5) and whose upper right corner has coordinates (2,2). Also draw the diagonals of the rectangle.
2. From the program of Exercise 1 remove the **SET WINDOW** statement. Explain the resulting picture.
3. On a piece of paper draw a *screen* with horizontal and vertical sides running from 0 to 1. Try to sketch the three windows opened in **WINDOWS** on your paper. Compare the results with Figure 7.11.
4. Run **BARS** to produce several bar graphs. Watch what happens in the lower window. (This is known as *scrolling*.)
5. Open a square window. Draw a square and then draw two lines to cut it into four smaller squares. Flood two of the small squares. (If the square isn't square, adjust the **OPEN** statement.)
6. Write a program to draw a circle. A circle is produced by the equations

   ```
   LET x = cos(t)
   LET y = sin(t)
   ```

   where `t` goes from 0 to 2π. (In BASIC, 2π is denoted `2*pi` and is equal to about 6.2832.) Try to produce a true circle by adjusting the **OPEN #1: screen** statement.
7. In Exercise 6 change the circle to ellipses of various shapes by changing the **SET WINDOW** statement.
8. Modify Exercise 1 to label the picture. Use **PLOT TEXT**.
9. Modify the program **BARS** so that you need not ask the user for **minvalue** and **maxvalue**. Your program should compute these.

The remaining exercises require the use of color.

10. In `SQUARES2` use three different colors for flooding.

11. Modify Exercise 5 to produce an attractive color picture.

12. Modify `BARS` so that bars above the axis are flooded in yellow, while those below the axis are flooded in red.

13. Write a program to produce a color picture of your own choice.

CHAPTER 8

FILES AND TABLES

8.1 INTRODUCTION

Besides the working memory (sometimes, and incorrectly, called *core storage*) of a computer, there is usually an external memory. For personal computers *floppy disks* or a *hard disk* serve as external memory. Information on such devices are stored in *files*. For example, when a program is saved, it is saved in a file. Files in the external memory are also used to store blocks of data.

Small amounts of data can be supplied to a program in **DATA** statements. But if there are a large number of data items, or data has to be shared among several programs, the data should be removed from the program and put into a separate file. In this chapter we examine *display-format* files, and inputting from and printing to them.

We will also show how a file may be listed by means of a BASIC program. The file may be either a data file or a saved program.

A *table* is like a list, except that it has two subscripts instead of one. The first subscript indicates the *row* of the table, the second the *column*. Lists are sometimes called *vectors*, whereas tables are sometimes called *matrices*. Both are called *arrays*.

8.2 DATA FILES

There are several types of files in BASIC. We will use only *display-format* files. These can be typed in from the keyboard and can be listed. For example, a saved program is a display-format file. Such files may also be used to store data.

Let us consider the example of a professor who keeps the names and grades of her students in a file. At the end of the term she uses a simple program to compute and print the average grades. The file GRADES contains the data needed by the program.

The data file GRADES follows.

```
6
Baker, 87, 65, 79, 82
Fisher, 66, 51, 45, 70
Gardner, 77, 75, 79, 82
Hunter, 91, 89, 95, 100
Smith, 75, 75, 69, 77
Taylor, 88, 82, 85, 83
```

The first line contains the number of students. Subsequent lines have the name of a student, followed by four grades. They are separated by commas, just as if they were typed in answer to an INPUT request. Indeed, one obtains information from such a file by means of an INPUT statement, which picks up the next line in the file.

One must first obtain access to the file by means of an OPEN statement. Because several files may be opened by the program, a file number must be assigned. This is similar to opening a window, except that in place of the keyword screen one uses the keyword name for a file. This is followed by the filename.

The program AVERAGE follows.

```
REM  Averages grades from a file

OPEN #1: name "GRADES"              ! File of grades

INPUT #1: n                         ! Number of students
FOR i = 1 to n
    INPUT #1: name$, a, b, c, d     ! Name, four grades
    LET average = (a+b+c+d)/4
    PRINT name$, average
NEXT i

END
```

Because we used OPEN #1:, we use INPUT #1: to obtain a line of data. First we input the number of students. This n is then used in the FOR loop. We then input five items for each student, compute the average, and print the name and the average.

```
run

Baker          78.25
Fisher         58
Gardner        78.25
Hunter         93.75
Smith          74
Taylor         84.5
```

Although we showed a very small class in this example, the program works without change for a class of any size.

In the `OPEN` statement we used a string constant, `"GRADES"`, for the name of the file. Alternatively, we may use a string variable. This allows us to ask the user what file to open, and to use that name in the `OPEN` statement. This will be illustrated by our next program, which lists a file.

We illustrate two other features in the program `LISTER`. The previous program required the professor to have a first line that indicated the number of students (the number of lines of data). We can avoid this by using a `DO` loop in place of `FOR` loop, starting it with

```
DO while more #1
```

which is practically self-explanatory. The condition `more #1` is true as long as there is more information in the file. Once we reach the end of the file, `more #1` will be false, and hence we exit the `DO` loop.

If the file we list contains commas, then `INPUT` will not give us the whole line. And, if there are blank lines, then `INPUT` will object. Both problems are avoided by using a `LINE INPUT` statement, which inputs an entire line (even if that line is empty).

The first run lists the datafile `GRADES`. In the second run it is asked to list the file `LISTER`. In other words, it lists itself!

```
run

Filename? GRADES

6
Baker, 87, 65, 79, 82
Fisher, 66, 51, 45, 70
Gardner, 77, 75, 79, 82
Hunter, 91, 89, 95, 100
Smith, 75, 75, 69, 77
Taylor, 88, 82, 85, 83

run

Filename? LISTER

REM  Lists a file

PRINT "Filename";           ! Filename from user
INPUT file$
OPEN #1: name file$
PRINT

DO while more #1            ! Go through file
   LINE INPUT #1: line$
   PRINT line$
LOOP

END
```

8.3 TABLES

Whenever data fall naturally into a row and column arrangement, we automatically think of a table. In the following example, each of several salespersons (the rows of the table) sells a certain number of each item (the columns of the table). If we add the numbers in any particular column, we get the total number of items sold by all the salespersons. If we multiply each number in a row by a price, and add the resulting products, we get the total sales by each salesperson.

The program SALES follows.

```
REM  Calculates total sales for several salespersons,
REM  and total sales by item

! Uses a list for the prices and a table for the number
! of each item sold by each salesperson

DIM price(10)                                  ! Price list
DIM sales(10, 10)                              ! Table of amounts sold

! Read price list, sales table
READ items
MAT READ price(items)
READ persons
MAT READ sales(persons, items)

DATA  5
DATA  1.20, 2.15, 0.65, 4.30, 2.00
DATA  3
DATA  5,  3,  0,  2,  2
DATA  7,  1, 12,  1,  5
DATA  3,  3,  6,  6,  8

! Sales by salesperson
PRINT "Salesperson", "Number sold", "Gross($)"
FOR i = 1 to persons
    LET count = 0
    LET gross = 0
    FOR j = 1 to items
        LET count = count + sales(i,j)
        LET gross = gross + price(j) * sales(i,j)
    NEXT j
    PRINT i, count, gross
NEXT i
PRINT

! Sales by items sold
PRINT "Item", "Count", "Gross($)"
FOR j = 1 to items
    LET count = 0
    FOR i = 1 to persons
        LET count = count + sales(i,j)
    NEXT i
    PRINT j, count, count * price(j)
NEXT j
PRINT

END
```

The **MAT READ** statement works the same for tables as for lists. It fills the table, by rows, from data in the **DATA** statements. For example,

```
MAT READ sales(persons, items)
```

reads a table in which the number of rows is specified by `persons` and the number of columns by `items`. We show a run, and you are encouraged to check some of the results.

```
run

Salesperson   Number sold   Gross($)
 1             12            25.05
 2             26            32.65
 3             26            55.75

Item          Count         Gross($)
 1             15            18
 2             7             15.05
 3             18            11.7
 4             9             38.7
 5             15            30
```

8.4 MORE ON FILES

We will convert the program **SALES** to allow the sales data to be kept in a separate file. There are four steps to this conversion:

1. Remove the data from the program.
2. Add an **OPEN** statement to provide the name of the data file.
3. Replace the **MAT READ** statement by a **MAT INPUT #1:** statement.
4. Place the data in a separate file.

The data can be organized as they were in **DATA** statements except for one slight modification. The **MAT INPUT** statement assumes that its data is on a single line in the file. If the data are spread over several lines, then commas must be added at the end of every line except the last. This is shown in the file **SALEDATA**.

The data file SALEDATA follows.

```
3
5,  3,  0,  2,  2,
7,  1, 12,  1,  5,
3,  3,  6,  6,  8
```

Notice the trailing commas on the ends of the second and third lines of the file.

We now present the first part of the modified program. The remainder of the program is unchanged.

A portion of the program SALES2 follows.

```
REM  Calculates total sales for several salespersons
REM  and total sales by item

! Uses a list for the prices and a table for the number
! of each item sold by each salesperson.
! The table is input from a file.

DIM price(10)                          ! Price list
DIM sales(10, 10)                      ! Table of amounts sold

! Read price list
READ items
MAT READ price(items)

DATA  5
DATA  1.20, 2.15, 0.65, 4.30, 2.00

! Sales from file
PRINT "Data file";
INPUT file$
OPEN #1: name file$
INPUT #1: persons
MAT INPUT #1: sales(persons,items)


run

Data file? saledata
Salesperson   Number sold   Gross($)
 1             12            25.05
 2             26            32.65
 3             26            55.75

Item          Count         Gross($)
 1             15            18
 2             7             15.05
 3             18            11.7
 4             9             38.7
 5             15            30
```

Let us now consider how we can put information into a file. The program POWERS in Chapter 4 printed a small table of powers of numbers. Suppose we wish to refer to that table frequently without having to recalculate it each time. We can accomplish this by printing the table to a file, instead of to the screen. POWERS3 does the job.

The program POWERS3 follows.

```
REM  Powers, printed to file

OPEN #1: name "TABLE"                  ! Output file
ERASE #1                               ! Clear it
SET #1: zonewidth 10
```

```
PRINT #1: "Number", "Square", "Cube", "Fourth power"

FOR x = 1 to 3 step 1/4                 ! Outer loop
    FOR p = 1 to 4                      ! Inner loop
        PRINT #1:x^p,
    NEXT p
    PRINT #1:                           ! New line
NEXT x

END
```

The changes are minimal. We added an **OPEN #1:** statement. We follow this by

```
ERASE #1
```

in case the file contained some previous (now not needed) information. Additionally, we change **PRINT** to **PRINT #1:**, and **SET** to **SET #1:**.

We will not show the sample run because there is nothing to see. Instead, we present the file that this program has just created.

The output file TABLE follows.

```
Number    Square    Cube      Fourth power
 1         1         1         1
 1.25      1.5625    1.95312   2.44141
 1.5       2.25      3.375     5.0625
 1.75      3.0625    5.35937   9.37891
 2         4         8         16
 2.25      5.0625    11.3906   25.6289
 2.5       6.25      15.625    39.0625
 2.75      7.5625    20.7969   57.1914
 3         9         27        81
```

Printing to a file is similar to inputting from a file. Both require an **OPEN** statement. Both also require a **PRINT** or **INPUT** statement, but with the file number attached. However, there are differences. In printing to a file, we either want to be sure the file is empty to begin with, or we want to add new material to what is already there. In the first case, which we just illustrated, we make sure the file is empty with an **ERASE** statement.

If we had wished, instead, to add new material to the end of the file, we would have had to use a statement like

```
SET #1: pointer end
```

to prevent attempting to overprint what was already there. Attempting that action happens to be an error that will stop the program.

8.5 SUMMARY

The simplest form of file is the *display-format* file. It consists solely of characters that can be typed from a keyboard, and can be created in a way similar to creating a BASIC program—by using the screen editor and the keyboard. Such files can be displayed on the screen.

Programs wishing to use files must (1) first *open* the files, and (2) use special file input - output instructions. To open a file, use a statement such as

```
OPEN #3: name "filename"
```

Thereafter, the program will use #3 to refer to that file.

What constitutes a legal filename varies from computer to computer. We used names of not more than eight characters, consisting of letters and digits. Most computers allow such names.

For display-format files, the special file input and output instructions are similar to ordinary INPUT and PRINT instructions, except that a phrase like #3: follows the INPUT or PRINT keyword. The following two examples are typical.

```
INPUT #3: x, y, z
PRINT #2: "The answer is", 2*x + 3
```

To input an entire line, including commas, or to allow empty lines, one uses

```
LINE INPUT #3: line$
```

Before printing to a file, one must exercise either

```
ERASE #3                ! Empty out file
```

or

```
SET #3: pointer end    ! Point to end of file
```

One can input an entire file by using a DO loop starting with

```
DO while more #3
```

EXERCISES

1. Modify **AVERAGE** to (a) ask the user for the name of the datafile, and (b) not require that the number of students be in the file.
2. Modify **LISTER** to produce a double-spaced listing.
3. Modify **SALES2** to allow it to read in the price list, as well as the sales data.
4. In **SALES** we multiply by price(j) twice. The first multiplication occurs inside a loop, the second after the loop. Why?
5. Run the program **POWERS3** twice. Does **TABLE** have two tables in it? Why? Modify the program to add the new material to the end of the file, and repeat the experiment.
6. Write a program that constructs a table mtable containing the multiplication table up to 10×10. Use **MAT PRINT** to print it. (You will need a **SET** zonewidth statement.)
7. Write a program that reads numbers from **DATA** statements into a 4-by-5 table and then computes and prints the row sums.

8. Modify the previous program to obtain its data from a file. Create a suitable data file with numbers of your choice.
9. Write a program that will input an entire computer program from a file and print all the **LET** statements. (Hint: Remember that the statement may be indented. Use the function **ltrim$**.)
10. Modify the previous program to print all **REM**, **SUB**, and **DEF** statements. For a long program this produces a useful *table of contents*.

CHAPTER 9

FUNCTIONS

9.1 INTRODUCTION

BASIC provides a number of functions to make programming simpler. Some of them are mathematical, such as the square root `sqr` or logarithm to the base 10 `log10`. Others provide special services, such as the next random number `rnd` or the ratio of the circumference to the diameter of a circle `pi` (which is equal to the constant π). Still others help us deal with strings, like the uppercase function `ucase$` and the blank-trimming function `trim$`. This chapter describes some of the commonly used functions and gives examples of their use.

The user can define additional functions that can be used just as if they were part of the language. Some consist of a single formula; they could be defined in one-line `DEF` statements. More complicated functions might require a multiple-line `DEF` structure; this structure becomes, in effect, a short program that defines the function.

Function definitions commonly appear early in a program, before they are used. If this is not the case, a `DECLARE DEF` statement is needed.

9.2 BUILT-IN NUMERIC FUNCTIONS

We have already seen the square root function `sqr`. It and some other common mathematical functions are defined in the following list:

`sqr(x)`	Square root of x, x >= 0
`sin(x)`	Sine of x
`cos(x)`	Cosine of x
`tan(x)`	Tangent of x
`log(x)`	Natural logarithm of x
`log10(x)`	Common logarithm of x
`exp(x)`	Natural exponential of x (e^x)

The functions `sin(x)` and `cos(x)` can take either radian measure arguments (2*π for a complete circle) or degree measure arguments (360 degrees for a complete circle). The easiest way to accomplish this is to use the **OPTION ANGLE** statement, as in the following two simple programs.

The program TRIG1 follows.

```
REM  Trig functions using degrees

OPTION ANGLE DEGREES                        ! Work in degrees

FOR a = 0 to 90 step 15                     ! Up to 90 degrees
    PRINT a, cos(a), sin(a)
NEXT a

END


run

 0              1              0
 15             .965926        .258819
 30             .866025        .5
 45             .707107        .707107
 60             .5             .866025
 75             .258819        .965926
 90             0              1.
```

The program TRIG2 follows.

```
REM  Trig functions using radians

OPTION ANGLE RADIANS                        ! May be omitted

FOR a = 0 to pi/2 step pi/12                ! pi/2 = 90 degrees
    PRINT a, cos(a), sin(a)
NEXT a

END


run

 0              1              0
 .261799        .965926        .258819
 .523599        .866025        .5
 .785398        .707107        .707107
 1.0472         .5             .866025
 1.309          .258819        .965926
 1.5708         0              1.
```

Although the numerical values of the angles differ in the two systems, the values of `sin` and `cos` are the same. In `TRIG2` we may omit the `OPTION ANGLE` statement because, if none is supplied, radians are used.

Several other useful numeric functions in BASIC are as follows:

`abs(x)`	Absolute value of x
`int(x)`	Integer part of x
`sgn(x)`	Sign of x if $x > 0$, `sgn(x)` = 1 if $x = 0$, `sgn(x)` = 0 if $x < 0$, `sgn(x)` = -1
`max(x,y)`	Maximum of x and y
`min(x,y)`	Minimum of x and y
`mod(x,y)`	The remainder of x when divided by y

Some of these functions need further explanation. The absolute value of -1.345 is 1.345. The integer part of 1.345 is 1; the integer part of -1.345 is -2 (not -1). The sign of 1.345 is 1; the sign of -1.345 is -1. The maximum of -4 and +2 is +2; the maximum of -7.65 and -3.45 is -3.45. `Mod(10,3) = 1`, the remainder of 10 when divided by 3. We have already seen a use of `mod`, for if `n` is an integer, `mod(n,2) = 0` if and only if `n` is even. This was used in `BOARD`.

9.3 BUILT-IN STRING FUNCTIONS

In addition to numeric functions, BASIC provides several functions to deal with strings. Some of these were illustrated in Chapter 6, and others will be discussed in more detail in Part II. Some string functions convert strings into strings, such as the following:

`ucase$(s$)`	Turns all lowercase letters in s$ to uppercase
`lcase$(s$)`	Turns all uppercase letters in s$ to lowercase
`ltrim$(s$)`	Removes all leading spaces in s$
`rtrim$(s$)`	Removes all trailing spaces in s$
`trim$(s$)`	Removes all leading and trailing spaces in s$

Note that the arguments are string variables and that the names of the functions end in a `$`. The following functions assign a number to a string.

`len(s$)`	Gives the length of the string s$ (number of characters)
`ord(s$)`	Gives the ASCII character number of the one-character string s$
`val(s$)`	If s$ is a string of characters that represents a legal number, converts to that number

---

BASIC provides still other numeric functions; consult your Reference Manual for details.

The following functions, on the other hand, create a string from a number:

`chr$(n)`	Generates the character whose ASCII character number is n
`str$(x)`	Converts the value x into a string of characters, similar to what the **PRINT** statement produces, but with no leading or trailing spaces.

Note that if a function returns a string, its name ends in a dollar sign, while if it returns a number, the dollar sign is absent.

The following program illustrates the `ord` and `chr$` functions. The two functions allow us to get the ASCII number of a character, and to convert a number into the corresponding ASCII character.

The program ASCII follows.

```
REM  Illustrates the ord and chr$ functions

FOR c = 65 to 90                      ! ASCII of capital letters
    PRINT chr$(c);                    ! Convert to letter
NEXT c
PRINT

LET name$ = "John Smith"
FOR i = 1 to len(name$)               ! Each character
    PRINT ord(name${]i:i[});          ! Convert to ASCII code
NEXT i
PRINT

END


run

ABCDEFGHIJKLMNOPQRSTUVWXYZ
 74  111  104  110  32  83  109  105  116  104
```

This program uses the `chr$` function to show that ASCII characters numbered 65 through 90 stand for the uppercase letters. The `ord` function is used to show the ASCII numbers of the letters in "John Smith". The lowercase letters (a through z) are numbered 97 through 122.

9.4 SINGLE-LINE DEFINED FUNCTIONS

We are often interested in converting from one set of units to another. For instance, the Fahrenheit temperature scale is commonly used in the United

---

The ASCII code associates a standard number from 0 to 127 with each of the frequently used characters, such as the letters, the digits, and the common mathematical symbols. Most computers have additional characters associated with numbers higher than 127, but these are not standard. See Appendix 1 for a table of ASCII codes.

States, while the Celsius temperature scale enjoys favor in Europe and in science. Although there is no function in BASIC to carry out the conversion, it is easy to add one with a **DEF** statement, as follows:

```
DEF fahr(c) = 9/5*c + 32
```

The program CELSIUS4 illustrates the use of the **DEF** statement.

The program CELSIUS4 follows.

```
REM  Converts from Celsius to Fahrenheit degrees

DEF fahr(c) = 9/5*c + 32           ! Conversion function

FOR example = 1 to 3
    PRINT "Celsius";
    INPUT degrees
    PRINT "Converts to "; fahr(degrees); "degrees Fahrenheit."
    PRINT
NEXT example

END


run

Celsius? 37
Converts to  98.6 degrees Fahrenheit.

Celsius? 100
Converts to  212 degrees Fahrenheit.

Celsius? -40
Converts to -40 degrees Fahrenheit.
```

BASIC provides a function to compute the square root, sqr. However, BASIC does not happen to provide a function to compute the cube root. (Nor does it provide a function to compute any other root, for that matter.) But that doesn't stop us. To get our cube root function, we simply use the **DEF** statement, as follows:

```
DEF cubrt(x) = x^(1/3)
```

In fact, any time BASIC does not include a function that one might wish to use, one can use the **DEF** statement to define it. And, because we are defining our function, we are free to choose its name.

The program **DEGREE** in Chapter 1 converts from Celsius to Fahrenheit, but does so directly without using a function.

9.5 MULTIPLE-LINE DEFINED FUNCTIONS

Sometimes new functions can be defined with simple formulas that fit onto a single line, as just described. But often new functions need several, perhaps many, lines for their definition. For example, suppose we did not have the `sgn` function available and wished to create one. We could define it as follows (we use a different name for it, `sign`):

```
DEF sign(x)
    IF x<0 then
       LET sign = -1
    ELSEIF x=0 then
       LET sign = 0
    ELSE
       LET sign = +1
    END IF
END DEF
```

The structure starts with a **DEF** statement that includes the name of the function and its argument (or arguments) in parentheses. It must end with an **END DEF** statement. At one or more places in the definition a value must be assigned to the function. In this example, see the three **LET sign** = statements.

As another example, consider the problem of finding the greatest common divisor of two positive whole numbers. The standard method is the celebrated *Euclid's Algorithm*. The idea is to divide the first number by the second, and keep the remainder. Then, divide the second number by the remainder to get a new remainder, and keep on doing so until the remainder is zero. The final divisor (which is the previous remainder) is then the greatest common divisor. This algorithm takes on the following form as a multiple-line defined function.

```
DEF gcd(x,y)
    DO
       LET r = mod(x,y)
       IF r = 0 then EXIT DO
       LET x = y
       LET y = r
    LOOP
    LET gcd = y
END DEF
```

A complete program, together with example runs, is shown.

The program EUCLID follows.

```
REM  Euclid's Algorithm

DEF gcd(x,y)                           ! g.c.d. of two numbers
    DO
       LET r = mod(x,y)                ! Remainder
       IF r = 0 then EXIT DO           ! Done
       LET x = y                       ! Next division
       LET y = r
```

```
    LOOP
    LET gcd = y                     ! Assign value to function
END DEF

FOR example = 1 to 3
    PRINT "Two numbers";
    INPUT x, y
    PRINT "The gcd of"; x; "and"; y; "is"; gcd(x,y)
    PRINT
NEXT example

END


run

Two numbers? 100, 64
The gcd of 100 and 64 is 4

Two numbers? 1001, 77
The gcd of 1001 and 77 is 77

Two numbers? 201, 103
The gcd of 201 and 103 is 1
```

We may also define string functions for ourselves. In the following, the function `double` double-spaces a string, in the sense that it inserts a space after every character.

The program DOUBLE follows.

```
REM  Defined string function

DEF double$(s$)                     ! Double space function
    LET t$ = ""                     ! Start with empty string
    FOR c = 1 to len(s$)            ! For each character
        LET c$ = s${]c:c[}
        LET t$ = t$ & c$ & " "      ! Add character and space
    NEXT c
    LET double$ = t$                ! Value of function
END DEF

FOR example = 1 to 3
    PRINT "A string";
    INPUT x$
    PRINT double$(x$)
    PRINT
NEXT example

END
```

```
run

A string? Jones
J o n e s

A string? A very nice day.
A   v e r y   n i c e   d a y .

A string? !>#$%^&*
! > # $ % ^ & *
```

9.6 DECLARE DEF

In the preceding examples, the function definition, whether single-line or multiple-line, appears near the beginning of the program (earlier than the first use of the function). However, we sometimes prefer to have function definitions appear later in the program. In that case, we must include a **DECLARE DEF** statement earlier in the program. A modified version of **EUCLID** illustrates this idea.

The program EUCLID2 follows.

```
REM  Euclid's Algorithm

DECLARE DEF gcd                      ! Must declare

FOR example = 1 to 3
    PRINT "Two numbers";
    INPUT x, y
    PRINT "The gcd of"; x; "and"; y; "is"; gcd(x,y)
    PRINT
NEXT example

DEF gcd(x,y)                         ! g.c.d. of two numbers
    DO
       LET r = mod(x,y)              ! Remainder
       IF r = 0 then EXIT DO         ! Done
       LET x = y                     ! Next division
       LET y = r
    LOOP
    LET gcd = y                      ! Assign value to function
END DEF

END
```

The only difference between this and **EUCLID** is that here the function definition appears toward the end of the program, and the function is used (in the **PRINT** statement) earlier in the program.

9.7 SUMMARY

BASIC includes a variety of built-in numeric and string functions. Only a few are illustrated in this text. The Reference Manual should be consulted for further details.

New functions can be defined using the single-line `DEF` statement or the multiple-line `DEF` structure, and may have any number of arguments, including none. They may be numeric-valued or string-valued, and their arguments may be numbers or strings. The names of functions that take on string values end in a `$`.

New functions are often defined in the program before they are used. If they are not defined before they are used, then a `DECLARE DEF` statement is needed.

For trigonometric functions angles may be measured either in degrees or radians, although the *default* is radians. To use degrees, an `OPTION ANGLE DEGREES` statement is required.

EXERCISES

1. Define a function `max3(x,y,z)` that yields the largest of its three arguments.
2. Write a program to find the shortest word in a list of words. (Hint: Use the string function `len`, which gives the number of characters in its argument.)
3. Print a table of `log(exp(x))` for a range of x-values, say, for x = 1 to 10 in steps of .25. What conclusion do you draw from the result?
4. Define a function to convert from Fahrenheit to Celsius degrees.
5. Modify `EUCLID` to compute the greatest common divisor of three numbers.
6. Define a function `lcm(x,y)` that finds the least common multiple of the two numbers. (Hint: The product of `gcd(x,y)` and `lcm(x,y)` is `x*y`.)
7. Define a function `roots` that, given the coefficients `a`, `b`, and `c` of a quadratic equation, will yield the number of real roots.
8. Define a function `root(x,n)` that computes the nth root of `x`.
9. Define a function `length$`, which takes a string as its argument, and whose value is ''short'' if the string has no more than three characters, ''long'' if more than seven characters, and ''medium'' otherwise.
10. The function `double` leaves too much space between words. Modify the definition so that it does not insert a space after a character that is a space.
11. Define a function `listsum(x(),n)` whose value is the sum of the first `n` numbers in the list `x`. (The first argument in the definition must be `x()`; the parentheses indicate that `x` is a list variable.)

CHAPTER 10

SUBROUTINES

10.1 INTRODUCTION

We urge you to read this Introduction twice—once before starting the chapter and once after finishing it.

One of the fundamental concepts in programming is the *subroutine*. Subroutines serve many purposes, the most important of which is allowing one to write very large programs by dividing them into smaller, more manageable pieces.

Subroutines may be located inside the main body of a program, in which case they serve to help organize the program. Or, they may be outside the program, and give the program capabilities that it would otherwise have to provide for itself. In the latter case, subroutines may be collected together into *libraries*. Such libraries of subroutines may be shared by many programs and hence are key building blocks for large programs.

Subroutines may have parameters, or they may lack them. Except in extremely rare circumstances, external subroutines need parameters, for that is the only way in which they can communicate with the rest of the program. Internal subroutines may also have parameters. But, unlike external subroutines, internal subroutines can also communicate with the main program containing them through the variables of program, which are also available to the subroutine.

Defined functions are like subroutines in that they, too, can be made external to the program and be collected into libraries.

10.2 INTERNAL SUBROUTINES

Perhaps the commonest use of subroutines is to simplify a program. The following program requires the user to supply three numbers, all of which must be positive. It is good programming practice to check that the user actually supplied positive numbers. The purpose of this elementary program is to compute a sales price, including tax.

The program SUB0 follows.

```
REM  Needs three positive numbers
REM  Poorly programmed

PRINT "Number of items";                ! Ask for number
DO                                      ! Get and check
   INPUT n
   IF n<=0 then PRINT "Must be positive."
LOOP until n>0

PRINT "Price per item";
DO
   INPUT p
   IF p<=0 then PRINT "Must be positive."
LOOP until p>0

PRINT "Percent tax";
DO
   INPUT t
   IF t<=0 then PRINT "Must be positive."
LOOP until t>0

LET sale = n*p                          ! Cost without tax
LET tax = sale * (t/100)                ! Tax on sale
LET total = sale + tax                  ! Total cost
PRINT "You owe $"; total

END


run

Number of items? 15
Price per item? 0
Must be positive.
? .32
Percent tax? -5
Must be positive.
? 5
You owe $ 5.04
```

A major portion of the program is taken up with checking whether the supplied numbers are positive. Each test requires a `DO` loop because the user may supply a bad number several times. Additionally, the code within the loops are almost identical. So we introduce a *subroutine*, named `positive`, to shorten and simplify the program. It will ask for a number `x` and, if it is not positive, it will print an error message and ask again.

The program SUB1 follows.

```
REM  Needs three positive numbers
REM  Uses a subroutine

PRINT "Number of items";          ! Ask for number
CALL positive                     ! Use subroutine
LET n = x

PRINT "Price per item";
CALL positive
LET p = x

PRINT "Percent tax";
CALL positive
LET t = x

LET sale = n*p                    ! Cost without tax
LET tax = sale * (t/100)          ! Tax on sale
LET total = sale + tax            ! Total cost
PRINT "You owe $"; total

SUB positive                      ! Get positive number
    DO                            ! Get and check
       INPUT x
       IF x<=0 then PRINT "Must be positive."
    LOOP until x>0
END SUB

END
```

The subroutine starts with a `SUB` statement that contains the name of the subroutine, and ends with `END SUB`. The program uses the subroutine by means of a `CALL` statement, which contains the name of the subroutine called. The effect of `CALL` is to execute the code within the subroutine, just as if it appeared in place of the `CALL` statement. Thus, we have three `CALL` statements, but the repetitious code occurs only once, within the subroutine. We will show an improved version later in the chapter.

The output of `SUB1` is the same as of `SUB0`, and is therefore not shown.

Recall the program `SALES`, first introduced in Chapter 8. It could be divided into three major pieces: reading in the data, computing results by salesperson, and computing results by item. We can quickly scan the entire program and learn its functions, for the program is small enough. But let us use subroutines and reorganize the program as follows, to get `SALES3`.

The program SALES3 follows.

```
REM  Calculates total sales for several salespersons,
REM   and total sales by item.

! Uses a list for the prices and a table for the number
! of each item sold by each salesperson.
! Organized into subroutines

DIM price(10)                     ! Price list
DIM sales(10, 10)                 ! Table of amounts sold
```

```
CALL readdata                    ! Skeleton of program
CALL personresults
CALL itemresults

SUB readdata                     ! Read price list, sales table
    READ items
    MAT READ price(items)
    READ persons
    MAT READ sales(persons, items)
END SUB

DATA  5
DATA  1.20, 2.15, 0.65, 4.30, 2.00
DATA  3
DATA  5,  3,  0,  2,  2
DATA  7,  1, 12,  1,  5
DATA  3,  3,  6,  6,  8


SUB personresults                ! Sales by salesperson
    PRINT "Salesperson", "Number sold", "Gross($)"
    FOR i = 1 to persons
        LET count = 0
        LET gross = 0
        FOR j = 1 to items
            LET count = count + sales(i,j)
            LET gross = gross + price(j) * sales(i,j)
        NEXT j
        PRINT i, count, gross
    NEXT i
    PRINT
END SUB

SUB itemresults                  ! Sales by items sold
    PRINT "Item", "Count", "Gross($)"
    FOR j = 1 to items
        LET count = 0
        FOR i = 1 to persons
            LET count = count + sales(i,j)
        NEXT i
        PRINT j, count, count * price(j)
    NEXT j
    PRINT
END SUB

END
```

From the three-line *skeleton* at the top level, we can quickly see what the program does and how it is organized. If we want to examine the details, we can look at the subroutines.

There are several points to be made. First, in the skeleton, there are three **CALL** statements. Each one of these *calls* or *invokes* a major task. One can think of this first part as akin to a top executive in a company who issues major orders but doesn't worry about the details of carrying them out. The subroutines play the role of subordinates in the company.

Another point is that it is not possible to "fall into" a subroutine in BASIC inadvertantly; the only way to invoke it is to use a **CALL** statement. Thus, there need not be a **STOP** statement after the third **CALL** statement.

If the programmer wishes to reorder the second and third tasks, only two CALL statements need to be switched; there is no need to reorder the actual code of the subroutines. In other words, the order in which the code of each subroutine appears is immaterial.

The reader may notice that the revised program, with subroutines, is longer than the original program. This results from the addition of CALL, SUB, and END SUB statements, and the extra blank lines. In large programs these extra instructions are well worth it, and are often the difference between being able to write the program and not be able to write it. It also makes modifying the program much easier.

10.3 EXTERNAL SUBROUTINES

We now come to one of the most important ideas in programming—that of sharing or reusing code. In BASIC, this is accomplished through libraries of external subroutines and defined functions.

Suppose a programmer in the office across the hall needs to write a program, one of whose features is the accumulation of gross sales by salesperson. He has heard of a program that you wrote that contains a subroutine (personresults) to carry out this task. He asks to use your subroutine. Because you both work for the same organization, it is acceptable to share code in this way. One way he could do this would be to copy the subroutine and include it in his program. However, for internal subroutines this is messy and wasteful. And, it can be dangerous. For instance, the routine personresults uses the variables i and j, and it is quite likely that his program uses the same variables for other purposes. Calling your subroutine will change the values of i and j and very likely mess up the rest of his program.

He could, alternatively, read your subroutine carefully and eliminate any conflicting variables. But this too is a waste. He really would just like to send your subroutine the numbers items and persons and the arrays price and sales, and have your subroutine produce the desired results. He should not have to examine your code or worry about what variable names you used. It is precisely for these purposes that BASIC has *external subroutines*.

An external subroutine has *parameters*, a list of variables that indicate the quantities the main program sends to it and any quantities the subroutine is to send back. Otherwise, the variables of the subroutine are a private matter. BASIC considers an i or j in an external subroutine to be different from an i or j in the main program.

To allow subroutines to be safely and conveniently shared, we remove them from the program and put them into *libraries*. Then any program can make use of these routines by indicating that it wishes to use the library.

To illustrate, we will create a small library consisting of personresults and itemresults.

The library SALESLIB follows.

```
REM  SALESLIB

!    External subroutines for computing sales.
!
!    personresults    computes and prints results by salesperson
!    itemresults      computes and prints results by items sold
```

```
EXTERNAL

SUB personresults (items, persons, price(), sales(,))

    PRINT "Salesperson", "Number sold", "Gross($)"
    FOR i = 1 to persons
        LET count = 0
        LET gross = 0
        FOR j = 1 to items
            LET count = count + sales(i,j)
            LET gross = gross + price(j) * sales(i,j)
        NEXT j
        PRINT i, count, gross
    NEXT i
    PRINT

END SUB

SUB itemresults (items, persons, price(), sales(,))

    PRINT "Item", "Count", "Gross($)"
    FOR j = 1 to items
        LET count = 0
        FOR i = 1 to persons
            LET count = count + sales(i,j)
        NEXT i
        PRINT j, count, count * price(j)
    NEXT j
    PRINT

END SUB
```

BASIC has the rule that the keyword `EXTERNAL` must appear at the beginning of any such library file, before the first `SUB` statement. It is a good idea to include comments that give the names and purposes of all the subroutines in a particular library, so a person can see at a glance what subroutines are in the library file without having to read the entire file. We can now simplify `SALES3` to get `SALES4`.

The program SALES4 follows.

```
REM  Calculates total sales for several salespersons,
REM  and total sales by item.

REM  Uses a list for the prices and a table for the number
REM  of each item sold by each salesperson.
REM  Uses library of subroutines.

LIBRARY "SALESLIB"

DIM price(10), sales(10, 10)

CALL readdata                         ! Skeleton
CALL personresults (items, persons, price, sales)
CALL itemresults (items, persons, price, sales)
```

```
SUB readdata
    READ items
    MAT READ price(items)
    READ persons
    MAT READ sales(persons, items)
END SUB

DATA  5
DATA  1.20, 2.15, 0.65, 4.30, 2.00
DATA  3
DATA  5,  3,  0,  2,  2
DATA  7,  1, 12,  1,  5
DATA  3,  3,  6,  6,  8

END
```

The **LIBRARY** statement indicates to BASIC that some of the subroutines will be found in the file **SALESLIB**.

In the **SUB** statement of the external subroutines, the parameter `price` is followed by "()" to indicate that it is a `list`, whereas `sales` is followed by "(,)" to show that it is a `table`. (These are sometimes called *bowlegs*.) But they are not needed in the **CALL** statements because the main routine knows from the **DIM** statement that they are lists or tables.

There is one more feature of external subroutines that we wish to illustrate. It is not necessary to use the same names for parameters in the main program as those that occur in the subroutines. For example, the following very simple program uses an external subroutine to add two numbers. You should observe that the names of the parameters are different in the two **CALL** statements and different from those in the subroutine `add`. In this trivial example we did not bother to create a library, but added the subroutine to our program. And, because it occurs after **END**, it is external. The variables `num1` and `num2` are used as *input parameters*, i.e. they provide information for the subroutine. The variable `sum` is used as an *output parameter*; it supplies the result back to the main routine.

The program SUBADD follows.

```
REM   Illustrates parameter naming in subroutines

PRINT "Two numbers";
INPUT x, y
CALL add (x, y, z)
PRINT "The sum is"; z
PRINT

PRINT "Two more";
INPUT a, b
CALL add (a, b, c)
PRINT "The new sum is"; c

END

SUB add (num1, num2, sum)          ! Adds two numbers

   LET sum = num1 + num2

END SUB
```

We show a run resulting in the expected results.

```
run

Two numbers: 17, 23
The sum is 40

Two more: 9, 8
The new sum is 17
```

This idea—collecting external subroutines together into libraries so that they can be shared—is one of the most important ideas of programming. To use one of these subroutines, all one must know is (1) the name of the library containing it, (2) the name of the subroutine, and (3) the calling sequence (the number, type, and purpose of the parameters in the `CALL` statement, but not their names).

There is an additional major advantage of libraries of external procedures. Compiling a large number of routines (i.e. translating them from BASIC into machine language) can take several minutes. Libraries can be saved in compiled form, thus speeding up the execution of the main program.

We should mention that internal subroutines may also contain parameters. In such a case they may use both the parameters and the other variables of the main program. As an example we include an improved version of `SUB1`.

The program SUB2 follows.

```
REM  Needs three positive numbers
REM  Uses a subroutine with parameters

CALL positive ("Number of items", n)    ! Use subroutine
CALL positive ("Price per item", p)
CALL positive ("Percent tax", t)

LET sale = n*p                          ! Cost without tax
LET tax = sale * (t/100)                ! Tax on sale
LET total = sale + tax                  ! Total cost
PRINT "You owe $"; total

SUB positive (prompt$, x)               ! Get positive number
    DO                                  ! Get and check
       PRINT prompt$;
       INPUT x
       IF x<=0 then PRINT "Must be positive."
    LOOP until x>0
END SUB

END
```

All the work to obtain and check a positive number is now contained within the subroutine `positive`. Including `prompt$` provides the advantage that, in case of an error, the prompt is repeated (see the run). And, having the variable as a parameter eliminates the need for statements such as the `LET n = x` in `SUB1`.

```
run

Number of items? 15
Price per item? 0
Must be positive.
Price per item? .32
Percent tax? -5
Must be positive.
Percent tax? 5
You owe $ 5.04
```

10.4 EXTERNAL FUNCTIONS

Defined functions can be internal to programs, or can be external and appear in libraries. External defined functions always need to be named in a `DECLARE DEF` statement. As with internal subroutines, internal defined functions can use variables in the program that contains them. Unlike subroutines, defined functions provide their results through their *name*, by using it in an expression like any other function. For example, in Chapter 9 we defined a function `fahr`. We use it by writing statements such as

```
LET y = fahr(100)
```

or

```
PRINT fahr(-20)
```

There is one other major difference between subroutines and defined functions. Parameters in subroutines work *both ways*. That is, a given parameter may be an input parameter, an output parameter, or both. However, with defined functions, parameters can be only input parameters. In other words, subroutines can change the values of parameters sent to them but functions cannot change the values of parameters.

To show why it is important for functions not to change the value of a parameter, consider the following loop:

```
FOR x = 0 to 100 step 10
    PRINT x, fahr(x)
NEXT x
```

If `fahr` could change the value of `x`, our loop would not work as intended.

10.5 SUMMARY

Subroutines and defined functions can be internal to another program, in which case they can operate on and change the values of variables in that program.

Subroutines and defined functions can also receive information through parameters. For subroutines, the information can be both *input* and *output*. For defined functions, the parameters can provide only *input* information, and cannot be permanently changed. For defined functions, the result is provided by using the name of the function in an expression.

Subroutines and defined functions may be made external to a program and collected into libraries. An external function requires a **DECLARE DEF** declaration.

All variables not appearing in the calling sequence of external subroutines and defined functions are *private* to each subroutine or defined function.

Subroutines and defined functions can be internal to the main program or to external subroutines or functions. In this case, they can communicate with the procedure that contains them both through their parameters and through the other variables of the program.

EXERCISES

1. In **SMALL5** make the routine that finds the smallest number and its position an internal subroutine. (See Section 5.2.)
2. Modify the previous program by moving the routine to a library. (What are the necessary parameters?)
3. Expand the library of Exercise 2 by including the corresponding string routine from **ALPHA** (Section 6.4). Modify **ALPHA** to use this library.
4. Add a third routine to **SALESLIB** that opens a file and reads data from it (as in **SALES2**). Write a version of **SALES2** that uses this library.
5. Create a library containing two functions—one that converts from Fahrenheit to Celsius, and another that converts from Celsius to Fahrenheit. Write a short program that uses the library.
6. Modify **QUAD2** (Section 3.3) to make the equation-solving routine a subroutine. The skeleton of the new program should be a loop that repeatedly asks the user for coefficients and then calls the subroutine.
7. We often need to ask the user a question to which the answer is "yes" or "no". Write an external subroutine that receives a question from the main routine, asks it, and checks to make sure that the response is valid. (It should accept "yes" or "no" in any combination of uppercase and lowercase letters.) Write a short program that uses this subroutine repeatedly and bases some decision on the answers.
8. External subroutines normally require parameters. Think of an example of an external subroutine that has no parameters.
9. Prepare two subroutines that do graphics. The first should draw a rectangle, and the parameters should be the coordinates of the lower left corner and the lengths of the sides. The second should draw a rectangle and flood it. The second subroutine should call the first one. The main program should issue a series of calls, producing an attractive pattern.
10. (Requires availability of color.) Modify the subroutines of Exercise 9 by adding string parameters to specify a color for drawing (and one for flooding in the second routine).

CHAPTER 11

HOW TO PROGRAM

11.1 INTRODUCTION

By the time you have reached this point, you should agree that writing small programs is pretty easy stuff. True, there were some details that had to be learned, as well as new concepts. But, the basic mechanics were simple.

Writing large programs is quite another matter. If writing a 10-line program takes 10 minutes, that comes to one line of BASIC per minute. Does that mean that a 1000-line program will take 1000 minutes (about 17 hours, or about a half of a working week)? Decidedly not—it will take much longer. Writing long programs is inherently more complex than writing short programs.

There are several reasons why long programs are more difficult to write. One is that short programs are often used just once, and then discarded. Long programs, on the other hand, are often designed for use by others. Consequently, they have to be written more carefully, to anticipate all forms of misuse. They must also be provided with elaborate documentation and manuals.

Another reason, many believe, is the limitation of a human being's short-term memory. Most persons can understand or grasp a short 10-line program in a few seconds. And they can keep it in mind while they contemplate changes. With large programs, the programmer must have all useful information written down so it can be referred to when attempting to understand or change the program.

Still another reason is the limit of what can appear on a single screen or page. Short programs that in their entirety occupy but one page, or one screenful, are easier to understand than longer programs, which require page-turning or screen-scrolling.

Whatever the reasons, writing large programs is not easy. Even professional programmers have trouble. One hears about rockets crashing because of programming errors. And one hears that large programs may have hundreds, or even thousands, of errors many months after they were allegedly completed.

It is almost impossible to write a program that has no errors. If for no other reason, we often do not know exactly what the program is supposed to do, to the last detail, until after we have built it. But there is much we can do to bring us closer to that error-free goal. The first step is to understand the stages in developing a large program. These stages are often referred to as the *software development life cycle*. Our version is

1. Specification
2. Program Design
3. Code Design
4. Construction and Testing

If, despite all our efforts with these four stages, errors still exist in our program, then we will have to consider techniques to isolate errors. This process is often called *debugging*, and is usually considered to be part of step 4. However, we will discuss debugging in a separate section.

Software developers usually add a fifth stage,

5. Maintenance

Maintenance involves repairing errors that surface after the software is completed and delivered to the customer. It also includes changes and additions requested by the customer or user. In the software industry, it is generally accepted that as much time and effort (i.e., money) is spent on the maintenance stage as on the first four stages taken together. (Despite its importance, we will not discuss maintenance any further in this chapter, but will concentrate on the first four stages of our version of the software development life cycle.)

Read this chapter once through for ideas. Later, when you are becoming involved with writing medium to large-sized programs, reread it. Many of the ideas will make more sense once you have had some experience with larger programs.

11.2 SPECIFICATION

We will not dwell on *specification*. But, it is important to know what the program is supposed to do *before* starting to build it. This is especially true if the program is being built for someone else.

Matters to be determined during this stage include the user interface, algorithms, data structures, generality, and robustness. We will now discuss each of these matters.

The User Interface

What should the user have to do to interact with the program? Should there be commands to be typed in? Should one use menus? How much freedom should be allowed the user, with respect to, say, spelling errors? What should the output displays look like?

It is at this stage that you should decide how best to *prompt* the user for proper input, and how best to label the output. This is not always as easy as it sounds. For example, suppose that we want the user to enter the number of coins to flip. We offer three candidates for the input prompt message.

```
Enter n:
Number of coins?
Please type the number of coins that you want to flip?
```

The first is too short, and assumes that the user knows what `n` is. The third is too verbose, fills up too much of the screen, and ends with a "?" even though it is not a question. The middle one is about right and has the proper punctuation.

For many large programs, specifying what the user should see for input and output is the hard part; writing the program is often much easier.

Algorithms

If the program requires extensive computation, what methods should be used? For example, if a list of names needs sorting, which sorting algorithm should be used. *Algorithm* is merely the name given to a computational method that (a) might require input, (b) always produces some output, (c) completes its work in a finite amount of time, and (d) does what it is supposed to do.

Data Structures

How should the data of a problem be organized? Should one use lists or tables? Should the data itself be sorted, or should use be made of an indexed sort (see Chapter 14)? Which, if any, data should be stored in files? One should spend as much time answering questions like these as questions of what algorithms to use. For, the efficiency of a well-written sorting algorithm will be lost if the data are stored clumsily.

Generality

Should the program be a special purpose program limited for use in a small number of situations? Or should the program be general purpose, of use in a wider variety of circumstances? There are arguments to be made for each choice. A special purpose program is almost always easier to use. Fewer commands have to be given, and fewer choices have to be made, to get it to do its job. More general programs, besides being much longer, require the user to make more choices and issue more commands to get it to work. And, the user may have to study a much larger manual before using the program.

On the other hand, a general purpose program will do more things for the user. And perhaps, only one general purpose program might be needed for a series of tasks, whereas several special purpose programs would be needed.

Many well-designed programs are general purpose and easy to use at the same time. They provide *default values* for most of the common cases. This relieves the user from having to answer a long series of questions just to run a short problem. For example, a word processing program might assume that the page size is 8.5 by 11 inches. An expert who needs a different size page will not object to the long series of questions needed to change the size.

Robustness

Robustness is the degree to which a program responds "gracefully" to being fed bad data or bad commands. For example, does it give the user a second chance if the user misspells the file name?

These are but a few of the kinds of questions that must be asked during the specification or planning stages of building a large program.

11.3 PROGRAM DESIGN

Program design is often the most difficult part of building a large program. For the most part, it involves deciding how a large program should be divided into subroutines. A design is often represented by a *structure chart*, which is simply a chart that shows which subroutines call which other subroutines.

For example, the structure chart for the `SALES4` example from Chapter 10 appears in Figure 11.1. This chart shows that the top-level subroutine, which is actually the main program, calls three other subroutines. That's all there is, as the three other subroutines do not call other subroutines.

Structure charts show the names of the data that are used and produced by each subroutine. If the data are *passed* to and from the subroutine as parameters, their names appear next to small arrows close to the line connecting the subroutines. If the data are not passed, we use arrows that originate and terminate inside the rectangles that represent the subroutines. In the program `SALES4`, the data for the subroutines `personresults` and `itemresults` are parameters, while the data provided by the subroutine `readdata` are not parameters. The structure chart shows this distinction.

It is important to choose names for subroutines that reflect their purpose. Perhaps a better name for the middle of the three lower-level subroutines might be "COMPUTEANDPRINTPERSONRESULTS", as that would indicate its dual purpose (computing, and then printing). But it is also important that the names be short.

Given a particular design (i.e,. a particular structure chart), there are two important questions that need to be raised. First, how does one evaluate the design? And second, how does one develop a design in the first place? Although there are design methodologies whose purpose is to come up with a design, we will not describe them here. Suffice to say, they require a careful and thorough understanding of the underlying problem, and take some time to explain and understand.

Instead, we will concentrate on a few ideas that can be used to evaluate a

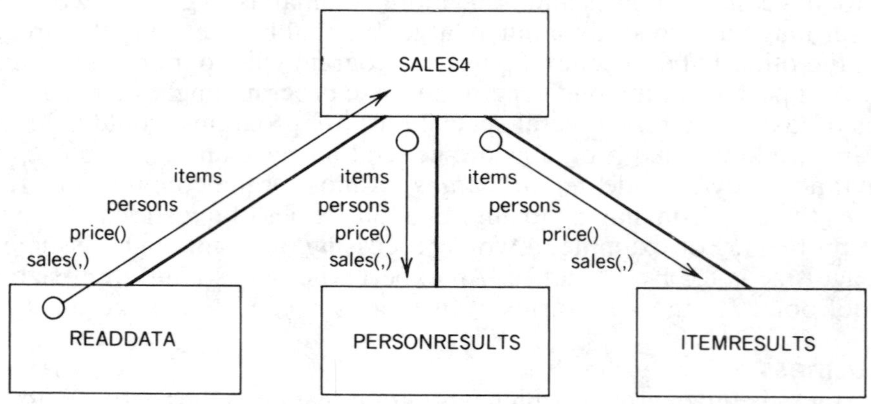

FIGURE 11.1 Structure chart for `SALES4`.

design, once one has been made. These ideas are *heuristic* because following them usually, but not necessarily, leads to a good design.

Keep Subroutines Short

We recommend that subroutines be shorter than one page, or one screenful, in length. If that is not possible, then so be it. But it is much harder to understand a subroutine if you must constantly shift pages or screens back and forth.

One exception to this principle occurs when a subroutine consists of, say, an `IF` structure with a large number of `ELSEIF` parts. Here, the cure (having several short subroutines) is worse than the illness (having one long subroutine.)

Keep Subroutines Single-Purpose

A subroutine that does one single task is almost always easier to write and test than a subroutine that does several tasks. A single task may, however, be quite complicated. For example, a subroutine that solves a linear programming problem is necessarily quite complicated, and may indeed call other subroutines. But it still has as *its* purpose, a single task.

Software engineers use the term *cohesion* to describe the degree to which subroutines can range from being single-purpose (*functional* cohesion) to being a disjointed collection of unrelated tasks (*coincidental* cohesion). Being able to rate subroutines in this fashion is obviously desirable, but further details are beyond the scope of this text.

Keep Calling Sequences Short

If a subroutine needs four data elements to do its work, then the calling sequence must contain four parameters. For example, the subroutine `personresults` needs four parameters (the number of persons, the number of items, the price list, and the sales table). Four is not too many, but if a calling sequence contains ten or more parameters, perhaps it is time to reconsider the design.

Communicate Data Through Calling Sequences

As much as it is possible, one should supply the data needed by subroutines through their calling sequences. The reason is that it is then clearer what data are needed by the subroutine and therefore less likely that errors will occur.

This goal seems like the antithesis of our third goal. If we communicate the data through calling sequences, then the calling sequences will be longer. In Chapter 10 we recommended the use of internal subroutines without parameters to subdivide a large program into smaller pieces. This is still a good idea. But if all the data needed by a subroutine is provided through its calling sequence, then the subroutine can be made external. And, we have already learned that external subroutines are much less likely to contribute to errors than internal subroutines that share data. Furthermore, an internal subroutine that has no parameters per se, but that uses ten or fifteen chunks of data, is likely to be quite complicated.

Software engineers use the term *coupling* to measure the degree to which two subroutines are interrelated. Subroutines are *loosely coupled* if they share only a few data elements, and then only as parameters in their calling sequences. Subroutines that have long calling sequences or share data with other subroutines outside the calling sequences are said to be *tightly coupled*. Loose coupling is generally better inasmuch as changes made to one subroutine are then less likely to require changes to other subroutines. As with cohesion, coupling is an important matter in rating a particular design, but a more detailed discussion is beyond the scope of this text.

Limit Use of Flags

Flags are signals that one subroutine sends to another. The first subroutine decides something or other. It then sets a flag so that a different subroutine can know what the first subroutine decided. In BASIC flags are usually variables that are set to either 0 or 1. For example, setting the variable `error` to 0 may mean that no errors have occurred, whereas setting `error` to 1 may mean that one or more errors have occurred.

Programs that contain many flags are extremely difficult to write and to test. And it is very difficult to make sure they are free from error.

Sometimes it is hard to avoid the use of flags. Examples are subroutines that test for errors. If these subroutines occur at a lower level, they must communicate their results (*errors* versus *no errors*) back to the higher level through a flag. (An example occurs in the program **CALENDAR** in Chapter 12.) Another occurs when a lower-level subroutine is assigned the job of reading information from a file. When the end of the file is reached, this subroutine must use a flag (or its equivalent) to inform the higher-level routines. (An example occurs in the program **UPDATE** in Chapter 13, where the end-of-file signal is the special code "zzzzz".)

Make Design Hierachical

The structure chart of a large program should usually look like an upside down tree. That is, there is one box at the top (the main program) that calls several subroutines at the second level. The second-level subroutines often call more subroutines at the third level, and so on.

A good design idea is to have the high-level subroutines deal in high-level concepts, like the top executives in a company. The often messy details should be left to the lower-level subroutines. In this way it is more likely that you will be able to separate "the forest from the trees", to separate the general concepts from the specific details.

11.4 CODE DESIGN

Once we settle on the general design, if only temporarily, we can begin thinking about coding each subroutine. There are several issues to keep in mind.

1. Choice of construct or instruction
2. Choice of variable names
3. Use of variables
4. Flow of code
5. Comments and documentation
6. Indentation and blank spaces

We discuss each of these in turn.

Choice of Construct or Instruction

How does one decide which BASIC statements to use? To be more specific, should one use a **FOR** loop or a **DO** loop? Our advice is to use the more general

DO loop unless (a) one knows in advance how many times the loop is to be executed, or (b) one needs to use a *loop-variable* that takes on successive values. Then use a FOR loop.

Another example is the choice between an IF - THEN - ELSEIF - ELSE construct and a SELECT - CASE construct, which is discussed in Part II. In general, any SELECT - CASE construct can be easily converted into an equivalent IF - THEN - ELSEIF - ELSE construct, although the reverse is not true. If both are possible, we recommend the SELECT - CASE structure if the choices being made are of equal importance, but the IF - THEN - ELSEIF - ELSE structure if several choices are more important and will be placed ahead of the others.

Choice of Variable Names

Choosing good variable names is important, and can make the code more readable. For example, in SALES4 we used the variable persons to represent the number of salespersons. This is an acceptable choice. But we can err either by making them too short or too long. Let us consider some alternatives.

number_of_persons	a bit too long
n	too short; doesn't convey meaning
numberofpersons	too long; hard to read
person	short, but gives the wrong idea
persons	short, but clearer
numpersons	about right
num_persons	about right

Different programmers will make different decisions about selecting variable names. (In fact, the authors have slightly different preferences.) But the principles to keep in mind are: (a) they should accurately reflect their purpose, and (b) they should not be too long.

Use of Variables

Variables should be explicitly initialized. For example, a program fragment to add the numbers from 1 to 5 might be written

```
LET sum = 0
FOR i = 1 to 5
    LET sum = sum + i
NEXT i
```

Why is LET sum = 0 necessary, you might ask, since BASIC sets all numeric variables to zero anyhow? The answer is this: If you expand your program and include this fragment in some larger loop, the variable sum would be zero the first time but not the subsequent times.

Variables in any program should have a single purpose. It is not efficient to use some variable, like temp, for several purposes to save storage if it leads to an obscure *bug* that takes several hours to find. You should be especially careful in choosing variable names for internal subroutines (see Section 10.2). A common culprit is to use the variable i for all FOR loops. Better to use i1 and i2. Better still, choose a more meaningful name for the FOR variable, such as row, if that's what the FOR variable represents.

Finally, avoid numerical constants such as 5. Instead, choose a variable name that describes that number, and initialize that variable with a **LET** or **READ** statement. To see why this practice is important, imagine that you have written a program to play a card game in which each player gets five cards, but that you have not established that number as a variable.

That number would appear throughout the program. Sometimes the number 4, being one less than 5, will also appear. Suppose you now change the program to deal six-card hands. You must change all 5s to 6s, and some 4s to 5s. It gets tricky if there are other 4s or 5s in the program that have nothing to do with the number of cards in a hand.

Flow of Code

When we read an essay, our understanding is increased if related ideas are near one another. Nothing is more jarring than a sudden shift in thought for no apparent reason. The same goes for programming. In the previous example that added the numbers from 1 to 5, suppose we had initialized the variable **sum** much earlier in the program. A reader seeing that initialization might wonder what the purpose was. Keep things together that should go together.

You should make single statements *flow* naturally, and therefore be more readable. For example, suppose that cost is equal to price minus discount. Two ways to write this are

```
LET cost = price - discount
LET cost = -discount + price
```

The first is obviously more readable. Where there is a choice, BASIC statements should flow naturally as they are read.

Comments and Documentation

A subroutine is the basic building block of a program. Consequently, each subroutine should be accompanied by information that describes in general terms the purpose of the subroutine and any of its special or unusual features. In addition, the main program should be headed by a series of comments or **REM** statements that identify and introduce the program, like the title page and preface of a book. We recommend including the name of the program, its author, the original date and the dates of modifications, and any other information that would help the reader. (Up to now, we have not followed our own advice—the programs in Part I are short and are explained fully in the text, often on the same page. From here on, we will include these headers.)

It is a matter of style whether you use **REM** statements or lines beginning with exclamation points; the two are equivalent. We have chosen to use **REM** statements for the program header, and the exclamation points for all other comments.

If variable names are carefully chosen, the BASIC code will be quite readable and need no further explanation. But sometimes one must use a cryptic construction whose purpose is not obvious at first glance. Those constructions should be accompanied by explanatory comments.

Surprisingly, it is possible to include too many comments. For example, in

```
LET sum = sum + amount          ! Accumulate sum
```

the comment is superfluous and can be removed. It is perfectly obvious from the LET statement itself what is going on. Indeed, the variable names were chosen to make the purpose quite clear.

Comments should be written in good and correct English. They should be succinct rather than verbose. Whether or not they are constructed like English sentences, which start with a capital letter and end with a period, is a matter of personal style. It is just important that the style be consistent. Comments should be edited or rewritten if they are unclear or are too long.

Indentation and Blank Spaces

When properly used, indentation can show the extent of structures. For example, compare the following:

```
FOR i = 1 to n
IF name$ = list$(i) then
LET position = i
EXIT FOR
END IF
NEXT i

     FOR i = 1 to n
IF name$ = list$(i) then
  LET position = i
      EXIT FOR
   END IF
NEXT i

FOR i = 1 to n
    IF name$ = list$(i) then
       LET position = i
       EXIT FOR
    END IF
NEXT i
```

The first example reflects a common coding style. The second shows that improperly used indentation can confuse rather than clarify. The third shows indentation that helps reveal the extent of the two structures—the IF structure nested within the FOR loop.

Blanks and lowercase letters also help due to the fact that most people are accustomed to reading English sentences in lowercase with spaces between the words. For example, compare the following equivalent instructions:

```
LET SUM=SUM+AMOUNT
LET SUM = SUM + AMOUNT
LET sum=sum+amount
LET sum = sum + amount
```

Which of the four is easiest to read? You decide. It is not necessary to capitalize the keywords of BASIC, although we have chosen that style for this text. The reader may prefer to keep all in lowercase, as in

```
let sum = sum + amount
```

or to blend uppercase and lowercase, as in

```
Let sum = sum + amount
```

The point is to make the code as readable as possible.

In the previous examples, we saw the use of blank space, as well as the use of lowercase, to improve readability. Sometimes blank space can be left out to improve readability. Compare

```
LET total = x * y + z
LET total = x * y+z
LET total = x*y + z
```

All three have exactly the same effect because BASIC ignores spaces in arithmetic expressions. But the second example is hard to read as it may suggest that the addition is done first, as would be the case with

```
LET total = x * (y+z)
```

but it is not. Because one is accustomed in ordinary algebra to seeing $xy + z$, where the two variables to be multiplied are simply juxtaposed, the third example of the three is more readable.

Finally, blank lines should be used to separate major portions of programs, just as blank lines are used to separate paragraphs in printed English.

11.5 CONSTRUCTION AND TESTING

One way to write a large program is to type in all the code, and then press the RUN key and hope. Of course, the program will probably not work correctly; there will almost certainly be errors in it. So then begins the extensive and challenging job of locating the errors, or *debugging*, as the process is called.

An alternative is to code and test each subroutine in turn. This is called *incremental construction and testing*. Although the subroutine will contain an error or two, it will be much easier to locate the errors in a small subroutine than in a large program.

There are two general approaches to incremental construction and testing—*top down* and *bottom up*. In top-down construction and testing one builds the top-level routine first, and tests it. How can one do this when the lower-level routines called by the top-level routine haven't yet been built?

The answer is that you can replace subroutines that are not yet written by dummy subroutines called *stubs*. You must include the name of the subroutine and its calling sequence (its parameters), but its inner workings can be "faked". That is, you might use a **LET** statement that always gives the same value, or a **PRINT** statement to print crucial parameters.

As the construction proceeds, you replace each of the stubs with a real subroutine, and test the new subroutine immediately. If necessary, you can create additional stubs. This process continues until the program is finished.

In bottom-up construction and testing, the lower-level routines are written and tested first. Because the entire program has yet to be written, one needs small programs that can call the lower-level subroutines for the purpose of testing. These small programs are called *drivers*.

In practice, neither pure top-down nor pure bottom-up is the ideal, but rather some combination of the two. The main point is to construct a subroutine and then test it, and not to construct all the subroutines and then test all of them in one fell swoop.

Finally, in testing a subroutine, one should make sure that all alternatives are tested. For instance, suppose the subroutine contains the following:

```
IF a < b then
   LET x = x + 1
ELSE
   LET x = x + 2
END IF
IF c < d then
   LET x = x + 3
ELSE
   LET x = x + 4
END IF
```

There are four ways in which the tests can go (a < b can be true or false, c < d can be true or false). To be thorough, one should test at least four cases:

1. a < b and c < d
2. a < b and c >= d
3. a >= b and c < d
4. a >= b and c >= d

Another important idea is *boundary testing*. For example, if a subroutine is supposed to print "Correct" if the parameter n is a whole number from 1 through 10, and is supposed to print "Incorrect" for a whole number less than 1 or greater than 10, one should make sure it works properly for n = 0, 1, 10, and 11. If there were a mistake in using "<" where "<=" should have been used, it will be quickly discovered.

Finally, supply erroneous or extreme data to see how *robust* your program is, that is, how well is behaves under adverse circumstances. We can think of this testing phase as a "shakedown cruise," where the main purpose is to find all flaws and weaknesses. Passing all tests does not mean the program is perfect, but it certainly increases one's confidence about using the program.

11.6 DEBUGGING

If, despite our best efforts, the program still contains errors, we must *debug* it. If the program is well-designed, and the subroutines individually tested, any newly discovered errors can often be quickly diagnosed. We will not be concerned with those. Rather, we will discuss here what to do if and when an error appears whose cause is mysterious.

One of the best strategies, and the one you should try first, is to read your code carefully and thoroughly. Examine each line, asking yourself if it does what it is supposed to do. If you are working in a group, have someone else read your code and criticize it. Another person is often able to recognize a flaw that may lurk behind your blind spot. If you have a printer, make a clean listing. Reading a listing of the code is much easier than reading it on the computer screen.

If code reading doesn't reveal the problem, you can attempt to isolate the part of the program that generates the error. This can be done by inserting breakpoints or `PRINT` statements into the middle of the program. When the program stops at such a breakpoint, various values can be printed out in the hopes that some clue will appear. Although this strategy is sometimes necessary as a last resort, it should be avoided for several reasons. First, it is extremely time consuming, especially with a large program. Second, if you have no idea what caused the error, you will really be probing in the dark and may also have no idea which variables to examine when the program stops.

A much better approach is to formulate a hypothesis as to what caused the error. Then, carefully read the code of the suspected subroutine or subroutines. If this code reading does not illuminate the error, then insert breakpoints or `PRINT` statements into the suspicious subroutine or subroutines. This approach is quite different from the "shot in the dark" approach of trying to deal with the entire program without a working hypothesis.

Sometimes errors are caused through misuse of the structures and instructions of the language. Go back to the reference manual and be sure you understand the precise way the features work. It is a good idea to avoid using features with which you are not thoroughly familiar and comfortable.

Our final advice: Working at the keyboard of a computer is a classic example of the adage "more isn't always better." In fact, if you have worked at the computer for a long time, or if you are tired, additional debugging work may not only be nonproductive, it may even leave your program in a worse condition, with more errors than before. The chance of accidentally destroying your entire program increases the longer you sit "staring at the screen."

The best advice is to plan your debugging sessions at the keyboard to last no more than one-half to one hour. We even go so far as to prescribe how to manage your sessions at the computer to make the most efficient use of your own time. This advice assumes that you have a printer available.

1. Start with a fresh and up-to-date listing.
2. Read the listing and write down changes to be made.
3. Make the changes at the computer, as well as any other obvious changes.
4. If an hour goes by, or if you are not getting anywhere, get a fresh listing, leave the computer, go to a quiet place, and read the code. You might even consider taking a lunch or coffee break. *Then* go back to step 1.

The important advice is to get a fresh listing and to *leave* the computer. Thinking is needed, not typing. We close this chapter with a timeless reminder from computer pioneer Richard W. Hamming that

TYPING IS NO SUBSTITUTE FOR THINKING

11.7 SUMMARY

Developing a large program is usually divided into several stages: specification, program design, code design, construction and testing, and maintenance. (We did not consider maintenance here.)

Specification involves determining such matters as the user interface, the algorithms to be used, the amount of generality to include, and the amount of robustness to include.

Program design is often represented with a *structure chart*, which is a diagram showing which subroutines call which other subroutines. Important heuristics to consider are keep the subroutines short, keep the subroutines single-purpose, keep the calling sequences as short as possible, communicate between subroutines through the calling sequences, limit the use of flags, and try to place the messy details in lower-level subroutines.

Code design involves choosing the right structure or instruction, choosing good variable names, constructing expressions that can be easily read, including comments and documentation, and using indentation and blank space to reveal the structure of the code.

Construction and testing can be done in several ways, but should be done incrementally if possible. That is, as each subroutine is coded, it should be tested. This can be done top-down or bottom-up. Top-down construction requires the use of *stubs*, which are dummy subroutines. Bottom-up construction requires the use of *driver* programs to test the subroutines.

If errors persist, debugging will be required. It is not a good idea to try to find an error in a large program without a theory. It is better to formulate a hypothesis about the cause of the error. This hypothesis will then suggest which subroutines to examine. A careful reading of the code will often reveal the error. Only when all else fails should one resort to inserting **PRINT** statements or using breakpoints.

PART TWO

TEXT APPLICATIONS

CHAPTER 12

TEXT PROCESSING

12.1 INTRODUCTION

Strings were introduced in Chapter 6 and several string operations and functions were considered in Chapters 6 and 9. The reader should review that material before starting the current chapter.

In this chapter we expand the use of these operations and introduce one new function and one new operation that can be performed on strings. The new string function is `pos`, which is used for finding the location of one string in another string. The new operation is assigning *into* the string with a `LET` statement. The string variable on the left uses a substring expression to specify which of its characters are to be changed.

We also introduce the **`WHEN USE`** structure that can be used to intercept a *fatal error* that might otherwise cause the program to stop at an inconvenient time.

Many of these string functions and operations are used to develop a library of string manipulating subroutines. Some of these subroutines are then used in a perpetual calendar program.

12.2 BASIC OPERATIONS ON STRINGS

We saw in Chapter 6 that we can carry out certain operations on strings of characters. One important operation is joining two strings together to form one long string; this operation is called *concatenation* and is denoted by the ampersand symbol `&`. As an example, if `a$ = "abc"` and `b$ = "xyz"`, then after `LET c$ = b$ & a$`, we have `c$ = "xyzabc"`.

Another important operation is extracting a piece of a string. This operation is called the *substring* operation, and is provided through notation that specifies the character numbers of the first and last characters to be retained. As an example, suppose that `a$ = "Dartmouth"`; then `a$[3:5] = "rtm"`, i.e., the third through the fifth characters of the original string.

These operations are illustrated in the program `STROPS`, which also introduces the new string function `pos`.

```
REM  STROPS
REM
REM  Demonstrates string operations
REM  and functions

READ a$, b$
DATA Dartmouth, College

PRINT "Concatenation"
PRINT a$, b$
PRINT a$ & b$

PRINT
PRINT "Substringing and the len function"
PRINT a$[5:9]
PRINT len(a$), len("College")

PRINT
PRINT "The pos function"
PRINT pos(a$, "t"), pos(a$, "t", 5)
PRINT pos(a$, "t", 9), pos(b$, "ll")

END

run

Concatenation
Dartmouth      College
DartmouthCollege

Substringing and the len function
mouth
 9              7

The pos function
 4              8
 0              3
```

The `pos` function locates where in a string one can find some specified substring. That is, `pos(a$,b$)` gives the character position in `a$` of the first character of the first occurrence of `b$`.

The `pos` function is more easily understood with examples. In the run of `STROPS`, the `pos` function is used four times. In the first, we ask for the first occurrence of the single character string "t" in the string `a$`. And, because `a$` = "Dartmouth", the first "t" occurs in the fourth character position.

In the second example we want to find the next occurrence of "t". Due to the fact that a repeated use of the first example will merely repeat the first answer, we ask instead that `pos` find the first occurrence of "t" in `a$` that occurs in position 5 or later. For this use, the `pos` function has three arguments; the third argument tells pos where to start the search. This search finds this second occurrence in character position 8.

In the third example, we ask pos to find yet another occurrence of "t". This time there is none, and the value returned by pos is 0. Finally, we ask pos to search for a string containing several characters. It gives us the character position of the first character of the match, which is 3.

As another application, the program **NAME** uses several of the string operations and functions to reverse peoples' names, that is, to separate the last name from the first name and the middle initial.

```
REM  NAME
REM
REM  Prints last name first

FOR i = 1 to 3
    READ fullname$
    LET length = len(fullname$)
    LET space1 = pos(fullname$, " ")
    LET space = pos(fullname$, " ", space1 + 1)
    IF space = 0 then LET space = space1
    LET lastname$ = fullname$[space + 1: length]
    LET rest$ = fullname$[1: space - 1]
    PRINT lastname$ & ", " & rest$
NEXT i

DATA  John G. Kemeny
DATA  Thomas E. Kurtz
DATA  Laurie Snell

END

run

Kemeny, John G.
Kurtz, Thomas E.
Snell, Laurie
```

The program **NAME** depends on the fact that the last name follows the space that follows the middle initial, or, if there is no middle initial, follows the space that follows the first name. First, let us assume that there is a middle initial. The pos function locates the first space. Then it locates the space after the middle initial. The last name consists of the original string starting after the second space. The rest of the name (first name and middle initial) is obtained similarly.

Now assume that the name contains no middle initial. The search by pos for the second space fails, so that the variable space is equal to 0. The **IF** statement then adjusts the variable space to point to the first (and only) space.

One limitation of the program **NAMES** is that it will not handle more complicated names like "John Brown III" or "John Brown, Jr" (see Exercise 3).

For our final example of simple string operations, we illustrate assigning *into* a string. Suppose we wish to have the string "XXX" replace characters 2 through 4 in a string variable a$. We will use a **LET** statement with the variable a$ followed by the substring expression [2:4], followed by the equal sign of the **LET** statement. The string constant **"XXX"** will be on the right of the equal sign. Thus,

```
LET a$[2:4] = "XXX"
```

will replace characters 2 through 4 of a$ with the characters "XXX".

Without being able to assign into a string, one might have to use something like

```
LET a$ = a$[1:1] & "XXX" & a$[5:len(a$)]
```

which is precisely equivalent. In place of `len(a$)` one may use any equal or larger number. Thus, if one knows that the string cannot have more than 100 characters, then `a$[5:100]` will return the entire string from the fifth character. Or, one can use the special variable `maxnum`, the largest number that BASIC can handle, as in

```
LET a$ = a$[1:1] & "XXX" & a$[5:maxnum]
```

The program **STRLET** illustrates assigning into a string.

```
REM  STRLET
REM
REM  Illustrates assignment into a string

LET a$, b$, c$, d$ = "abcdefgh"
PRINT a$
LET a$[2:4] = "XXX"
PRINT a$
LET b$[2:3] = "XXX"
PRINT b$
LET c$[2:2] = "XXX"
PRINT c$
LET d$[2:1] = "XXX"
PRINT d$

LET pres$ = "Dwight Eisenhower"
PRINT pres$
LET pres$[8:7] = "D. "
PRINT pres$

END

run

abcdefgh
aXXXefgh
aXXXdefgh
aXXXcdefgh
aXXXbcdefgh
Dwight Eisenhower
Dwight D. Eisenhower
```

The first **LET** statement illustrates assigning one value to several variables all at once. The second **LET** statement replaces the second through fourth characters of **a$**, which consist of the three characters "bcd", with another string of three characters "XXX". The third **LET** statement replaces two characters of **b$** with the three characters. The fourth **LET** statement replaces but one character of **c$** with three characters. And the fifth **LET** statement replaces *no* characters of **d$** with the three characters. That is, it inserts the three characters into **d$**. Note that if the substring expression on the left of the "=" denotes a *null string* (a string having no characters, that is, of zero length), then the string value is inserted *just in front of* the *from* character.

12.3 EXCEPTION HANDLING

As long as the user is careful to provide correct data for a correct program, the program will run smoothly. But if not, conditions might arise that BASIC just cannot handle; these are called *fatal exceptions* or *fatal errors*. When these occur, BASIC has no alternative but to stop.

For example, the following simple program calculates square roots of nonnegative numbers.

```
REM  WHEN1
REM
REM  Illustrates fatal errors

DO
   INPUT x
   PRINT x, sqr(x)
LOOP
END
```

All is well as long as the user supplies non-negative numbers. What happens when the user supplies a negative number? Because BASIC cannot take the square root of a negative number, all it can do is to print an error message and stop.

```
run

? 64
 64                  8
? 24
 24                  4.89898
? -32
SQR of negative number.
```

The smart programmer knows this and takes the precaution to check **x** first.

```
REM  WHEN2
REM
REM  Illustrates protecting against fatal errors
```

```
DO
   INPUT x
   IF x >= 0 then
      PRINT x, sqr(x)
   ELSE
      PRINT "Can't take square root of a negative number."
   END IF
LOOP
END
```

When the user provides a negative number, the program now prints the programmer's error message and continues, rather than printing BASIC's error message and stopping. (The sample run is not shown.)

It is always a good idea for the programmer to forestall fatal errors by prechecking whenever possible. However, not all potentially fatal errors are easy to check for. For these cases, BASIC provides a new structure—the `WHEN USE` structure, as follows:

```
WHEN EXCEPTION IN
     (If anything occurs here that would stop the program,)
USE
     (... this section of code is executed instead.)
END WHEN
```

Of course, if no fatal error occurs between `WHEN EXCEPTION IN` and `USE`, the code between `USE` and `END WHEN` is ignored.

In Chapter 9 we mentioned the two functions `val` and `str$`. `str$` converts a number into a string, the same string that would be produced by a `PRINT` statement but without leading or trailing spaces. The `val` function converts a string into a number, provided that the string represents a number according to the rules of the `INPUT` or `DATA` statements. The program `WHEN3` illustrates these two functions.

```
REM  WHEN3
REM
REM  Illustrates val and str$ functions

DO
   INPUT x$
   LET x = val(x$)
   LET y$ = str$(x)
   PRINT x$, x, y$
LOOP
END


run

? 123e-4
123e-4            .0123             .0123
? -123e-4
-123e-4          -.0123            -.0123
? e-4
VAL string isn't a proper number.
```

The sample run shows what happens when the user provides a string that the `val` function cannot handle; a fatal error occurs, BASIC provides an error message, and the program stops.

Unfortunately, the smart programmer cannot precheck the value of **x$** without asking the `val` function to convert it. It is just too complicated. This is where the **WHEN USE** structure comes in handy.

```
REM  WHEN4
REM
REM  Illustrates protecting the val function

DO
   INPUT x$
   WHEN EXCEPTION IN
        LET x = val(x$)
        LET y$ = str$(x)
        PRINT x$, x, y$
   USE
        PRINT "Improper val string "; x$
   END WHEN
LOOP
END
```

```
run

? 123e-4
123e-4             .0123             .0123
? e-4
Improper val string e-4
? -123e-4
-123e-4           -.0123            -.0123
?
```

It must be noted that *any* fatal error that occurs between **WHEN EXCEPTION IN** and **USE** will cause the code between **USE** and **END WHEN** to be executed. It is therefore wise to *protect* only what is necessary. In the program **WHEN4** a fatal error is not possible in the second and third lines following **WHEN EXCEPTION IN**. Consequently, it is safe to assume that any error must be caused by an improper argument to the `val` function.

The **WHEN USE** structure is also useful with files, and will be discussed further in Chapter 13.

12.4 A TEXT PROCESSING UTILITY

We now present a series of examples that will culminate in a set of subroutines that are useful for both interactive input and general text processing. The interactive input problem is this: How can we allow the user to enter several commands all at one time, or enter the commands one at a time? A novice may choose the latter method, while the experienced user may prefer the former.

We start by asking how the user can enter, for instance, three items at once? If we insist that the user separates the items with commas and always enters three items, the solution is easy. The user simply uses an `INPUT` statement with three variables, as in

```
INPUT x, y, z
```

If, on the other hand, we wish to avoid using commas, but want to use spaces instead to separate the items, then we cannot conveniently use the `INPUT` statement. Furthermore, the `INPUT` statement does not allow the user the choice as to how many items to enter.

In general, what we must do is input the *entire* line, exactly as typed by the user, and then examine it character by character to find where the spaces are.

Looking at the problem another way, the `INPUT` statement relies on commas to separate items in the user's response. This convention is adequate for entering numbers, or even lists of names. But what if we want to enter a line of English text and have the computer separate the words? Clearly, the `INPUT` statement cannot be used because the line may or may not contain commas. In that case, we want to input the entire line, without regard to commas.

The `LINE INPUT` statement inputs an entire line of text, exactly as typed, including commas and other punctuation, and leading or trailing blank spaces. It assigns the entire line to a string variable.

A program that uses `LINE INPUT` and prints individual words follows, and assumes that there is a subroutine that can *extract* the leading word from a line of text. (This process is sometimes called *parsing*.) Such a subroutine would be used as follows:

```
CALL nextword (word$, line$)
```

The string variable `line$` provides the line of text to the subroutine, which then returns the first word in the variable `word$`. It also returns the rest of the line in `line$`.

As examples of how `nextword` works, we show typical values of `line$` before the call to `nextword`, and the resulting values of `word$` and `line$`.

Before CALL	**After CALL**	
`line$`	`word$`	`line$`
`"Smith Jones Brown"`	`"Smith"`	`"Jones Brown"`
`"Jones Brown"`	`"Jones"`	`"Brown"`
`"Brown"`	`"Brown"`	`""` (empty string)
`"  RED white "`	`"RED"`	`" white "`
`" white "`	`"white"`	`""`
`"John Smith"`	`"John"`	`"Smith"`
`"Smith, John"`	`"Smith,"`	`"John"`

We therefore see that the subroutine `nextword` delivers the first word of the string, which has been completely *stripped* of leading and trailing spaces. The value of the variable `line$` may afterwards contain both leading and trailing spaces, but these are dealt with later. Notice in the last example that the comma is part of `word$` because it follows "Smith" without an intervening space.

We now show how simple this subroutine is.

```
SUB nextword (word$, line$)

! Extracts first word from line$, returns it in word$.
! The first word is the string of characters from the
! start of line$, after leading blanks have been
! removed, up to the first following blank or up to
! the end of the line if there are no remaining blanks.

    LET line$ = ltrim$(line$)
    LET first = 1
    LET last = pos(line$, " ")    ! Ending blank
    IF last = 0 then LET last = len(line$) + 1
    LET word$ = line$[first: last-1]
    LET line$ = line$[last+1: len(line$)]

END SUB
```

The subroutine first removes leading spaces from `line$` by using the BASIC `ltrim$` function. Next, the subroutine searches for the first blank space, which indicates the end of the word. If none is present, we want to take the rest of the line. We do this by pretending that the first blank space occurs *after* the end of the line. Whichever is the case, we next extract the desired word and shorten the line accordingly. If `line$` is empty (contains no characters) or contains nothing but blanks, then `word$` will contain the null string and have length zero.

A simple text parsing program that uses the subroutine `nextword` is `PARSE0`, which follows. (The library `Textlib` contains an improved version of the subroutine `nextword`, and is discussed later.)

```
REM  PARSE0
REM
REM  Parses words

LIBRARY "Textlib"

PRINT "Line to be parsed";
LINE INPUT line$
DO
   CALL nextword (word$, line$)
   IF len(word$) = 0 then EXIT DO
   PRINT word$
LOOP

END

run

Line to be parsed? Now is the time
Now
is
the
time
```

When all the words in **line$** have been extracted, **word$** will have length zero. The **EXIT DO** statement will then cause the **DO** loop to be exited and the program to end.

The preceding program responds to but a single line of input. If we want to respond to a continuous supply of lines, we must include another loop in the program. The following program, **PARSE1**, continues until it has extracted 10 words, regardless of the number of lines of input needed.

```
REM  PARSE1
REM
REM  Parses words

LIBRARY "Textlib"

FOR i = 1 to 10
    DO
       CALL nextword (word$, line$)
       IF len(word$) > 0 then EXIT DO
       PRINT "New line, please";
       LINE INPUT line$
    LOOP

    REM  Here is where word$ is processed
    PRINT word$
NEXT i

END

run

New line, please? Now is the time
Now
is
the
time
New line, please? The     quick brown   fox.
The
quick
brown
fox.
New line, please? nine ten eleven
nine
ten
```

Under normal conditions, the **DO** loop will be entered, a word extracted, and the loop exited. If there are no more words in **line$**, the loop is not exited. Rather, the program asks the user for more input. If a troublesome user then enters a line consisting entirely of blanks, the program continues to ask for more input.

Although this example is a reasonable program to process words, there is a better way to structure it. In **PARSE1** we had to be concerned with inserting lines of text (**LINE INPUT**) whenever one was needed. But what if the subroutine that gives us the next word takes over that responsibility? The resulting program might then look something like this:

```
REM  PARSE2
REM
REM  Shows use of Input subroutine
```

```
LIBRARY "Textlib"

FOR i = 1 to 10
    CALL input ("New line, please", word$, line$)

    REM  Here is where word$ is processed
    PRINT word$
NEXT i

END
```

Notice how much shorter and cleaner `PARSE2` is than `PARSE1`. However, the subroutine `input` is now responsible for obtaining a new line of text from the user, and must be told what to tell the user in such cases. We therefore supply the prompt message as an argument of the subroutine.

```
run

New line, please? Now is the time for all good men
Now
is
the
time
for
all
good
men
New line, please? John Smith
John
Smith
```

In the subroutine `nextword` a word is defined as a string of characters that ends with the first blank (or the end of the line), after stripping the leading blanks. However, a user may occasionally wish to treat a phrase containing blanks as a *single word*, and we would like to offer this choice. The convention we will propose is that a string of characters containing blanks but enclosed in quotes (") will be treated as a single word. (In this discussion, the word "quote" and the symbol " refer to the keyboard symbol. They do not refer to the open-quote and close-quote used to surround quoted material in typeset text.)

Recall the earlier example of "John Smith". The subroutine `nextword` yielded the two words "John" and "Smith". If the user wanted to keep the full name intact, he or she would enter the following: `"John Smith"`.

We can easily modify the subroutine `nextword` to be sensitive to such quoted strings. (This version of `nextword` appears in the library `TEXTLIB`.)

```
SUB nextword (word$, line$)

! Extracts first word from line$, returns it in word$.
! The first word is the string of characters from the
! start of line$, after leading blanks have been
! removed, up to the first following blank, or up to
! the end of the line if there are no remaining blanks.
```

```
    ! If line$ starts with a quote, the first word is the
    ! string of characters between the first and second
    ! quotes, not including the quotes.  If there is no
    ! second quote, the rest of line$ is included.

    LET line$ = ltrim$(line$)
    LET first = 1
    IF line$[1:1] = """" then  ! Check for quoted string
       LET first = 2
       LET last = pos(line$, """", first)   ! Ending quote
    ELSE
       LET last = pos(line$, " ") ! Ending blank
    END IF
    IF last = 0 then LET last = len(line$) + 1
    LET word$ = line$[first: last-1]
    LET line$ = line$[last+1: len(line$)]

END SUB
```

The subroutine first determines whether it is supposed to be looking for the ending blank space or an ending quote. From then on, the treatment is identical, except that the word will start with character number 2 in the case of a quoted string, because character number 1 is a quote mark!

The symbol `""""` (four quotes) appearing in the subroutine `nextword` is a notation for, believe it or not, a *single* quote, (`"`). Because the quote mark serves to surround a string constant, BASIC uses two quotes (`""`) to represent a quote mark *inside* a quoted string. For example, suppose we wanted the following sentence to appear in a `PRINT` statement in a program:

```
"Ouch," he said.
```

It would not be sufficient to surround the entire sentence with quotes, for we would then have:

```
""Ouch," he said."
```

which would be interpreted as a null string (`""`), followed by the meaningless characters (`Ouch,`), followed by the quoted string (`" he said."`). The solution in BASIC is to double up each quote that appears inside the quoted string. Thus, we have

```
"""Ouch,"" he said."
```

There are now six quotes, whose interpretations are:

1. The opening quote of the quoted string constant.

2.-3. The first quote character in the quotation.

4.-5. The second quote character in the quotation.

6. The closing quote of the quoted string constant.

With that background, it is easy to see that, to represent a single quote (`"`) as a string constant in a program, we must first double it and then surround it with quotes (`""""`)!

We will now exhibit the subroutine `input` that, along with the subroutine `nextword`, constitute the library **TEXTLIB**.

```
SUB input (message$, word$, line$)

    ! Parses word from front of line$.  Returns word in word$,
    ! the rest of the line in line$.  If word$ is empty,
    ! requests input from user, using message$ as the prompt.

    DO                       ! Be sure we have a non empty line
       CALL nextword (word$, line$)
       IF len(word$) > 0 then EXIT DO   ! All is okay
       PRINT message$;     ! Get a new line
       LINE INPUT line$
    LOOP

END SUB
```

As noted previously, the **DO** loop keeps asking for input until the user enters a nonblank line. Entering a blank line is a remote possibility, but one that the subroutine should be sensitive to.

The subroutine `nextword` does the actual word extraction for the subroutine `input`. It allows a phrase that contains blanks to be treated as a *word*, as long as the phrase is enclosed in quotes. The reader should work through both the quoted string case, and the ordinary case to verify that the subroutine operates as claimed.

12.5 A PERPETUAL CALENDAR

Determining the day of the week on which a particular date falls is an interesting problem. We observe that January 1, in the year 1 AD would have been a Monday in our (Gregorian) calendar. So we merely count the number of days starting with January 1, 1, and ending at the date of interest. To convert this number to the day of the week, we simply divide by seven and examine the remainder. If the remainder is 0, that day was a Sunday; if the remainder is 1, it was a Monday, and so on.

Computing the number of days starting with January 1, 1, is surprisingly easy; after all, we know that most years have 365 days, and we know the number of days in each month. Of course, we have to take into account that leap years have 366 instead of 365 days, and that leap Februarys have 29 instead of 28 days.

The Gregorian Calendar requires any year that is a multiple of four to be a leap year, except that multiples of 100 are *not* leap years. Furthermore, it dictates that multiples of 400 *are* leap years. Testing in BASIC that a year **y** is a leap year can be as simple as

```
IF mod(y,4) = 0 and mod(y,100) <> 0 or mod(y,400) = 0 then
```

The subroutine `nextword` does not accept quoted strings that contain quote marks.

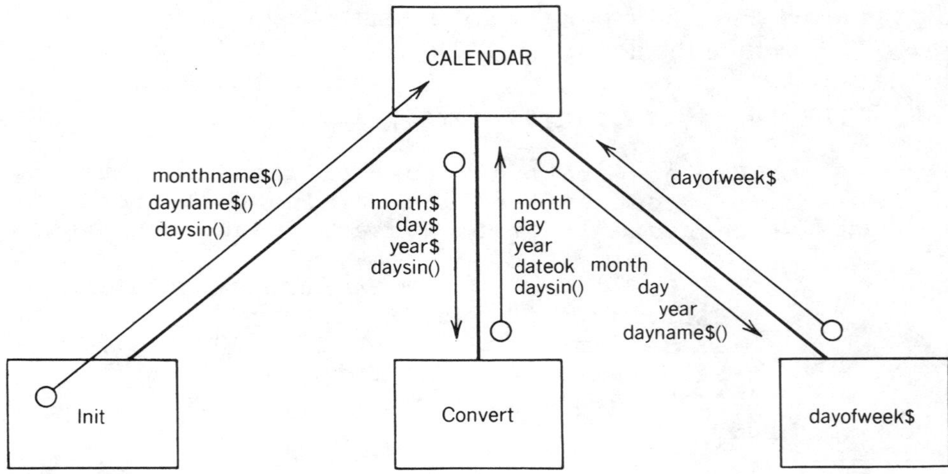

FIGURE 12.1
Structure chart for `CALENDAR`.

It is just as easy to compute the number of days in the years before the specified year `y`:

```
LET days = (y-1)*365+int((y-1)/4)-int((y-1)/100)+int((y-1)/400)
```

The program **`CALENDAR`**, shown later, carries out these relatively trivial calculations. But as with other programs designed to be used by many people, most of the program is devoted to coaching the user for input and then checking the inputted data for validity. Actually computing the day of the week (the defined function `dayofweek$`) is done in but six lines.

The program repeatedly asks the user for dates. Each date consists of three pieces of string data. Each piece must be converted to a number, and then checked for validity, i.e., the month number must be from 1 to 12, and the day number must be from 1 to 28, 29, 30, or 31, depending on the month. Because different checking rules are required for each of the three pieces of data, we need to apply them in sequence. If the data pass all checks, the program can then calculate the day of the week. If the data fail a particular check, then all later checks are meaningless and must be bypassed. This checking process is very lengthy, so we *package* it as a subroutine, which incidentally also converts the string data to numeric form.

The subroutine `Convert` makes separate checks for the month, year, and day of the month, in that order. The day number is checked after the year number, due to the fact that February has different numbers of days depending on leap years. If any of these checks fails, the subroutine is exited immediately (after an error message) by the **`EXIT SUB`** statement. The valid data indicator (`dateok` in the subroutine) was first set to 0 so that an error exit would result in a bad status. If all checks pass, this indicator is set to 1 (the signal for good data).

Two features of the month-checking code need further explanation. First, we use the `lcase$` function for both the official month names and the month name supplied by the user. In this way the month-checking code is not sensitive to case (lower or upper). Second, if the month name entered is one of the valid twelve month names, the **EXIT FOR** statement will cause an exit from the **FOR** loop with a correct value for the variable **month**. If the month name entered is invalid, the **FOR** loop is exited normally, with the value of the variable **month** being 13, the first value *not* used in the loop. The **IF THEN** structure following the **FOR** loop will then print the error message and exit from the subroutine.

We now examine the top level of the program. It first initializes three lists—the names of the months, the number of days in each month, and the names of the days of the week.

The main **DO** loop first asks the user for the input data. This is done using the subroutine **Input**, which is found in the library **Textlib**. Notice that the prompt message is supplied to **Input** as the first argument. Because three pieces of data are needed, the subroutine is called three times. If a prompt message is needed the second or third time, it must be a different message, because the user has already entered some data. This feature allows the user to enter the three components of the data—the month, the day, and the year—on a single line or on separate lines.

After receiving the data, the program calls on the subroutine **Convert** to convert and determine the validity of the data. If the data passes all the tests, the program then uses the defined function **dayofweek$** to compute the answer, which is then printed.

The subroutine **Convert** is long, as it carries out several tasks: it converts each piece of the date to numeric form, and then checks it for validity. Such multipurpose subroutines are sometimes hard to understand. But, checking for errors is also complicated, especially in this example where the checking must be done sequentially. (The reader is invited to attempt dividing the subroutine **Convert** into three smaller subroutines, and then decide if the result is easier to understand.)

```
REM  CALENDAR
REM
REM  An eternal Gregorian calendar

DECLARE DEF Dayofweek$

LIBRARY "Textlib"

DIM monthname$(1 to 12), daysin(1 to 12), dayname$(0 to 6)

CALL Init
DO                              ! Main loop
   LET line$ = ""               ! Start with empty line$
   CALL Input ("Month, day, year", month$, line$)
   CALL Input ("Day, year", day$, line$)
   CALL Input ("Year", year$, line$)

   !  Convert date to numeric, and check for errors
   CALL Convert (month$, month, day$, day, year$, year, dateok)

   IF dateok=1 then
      PRINT "     That day is a "; Dayofweek$(month, day, year)
      PRINT
   END IF
LOOP
```

```
SUB Init

    MAT READ monthname$, daysin, dayname$
    DATA January, February, March, April, May, June
    DATA July, August, September, October, November, December
    DATA 31, 28, 31, 30, 31, 30, 31, 31, 30, 31, 30, 31
    DATA Sunday, Monday, Tuesday, Wednesday
    DATA Thursday, Friday, Saturday


END SUB

DEF Dayofweek$(m, d, y)

    ! Compute total number of days starting January 1, 1 AD

    LET days = 365*(y-1)+int((y-1)/4)-int((y-1)/100)+int((y-1)/400)
    FOR i = 1 to m - 1
       LET days = days + daysin(i)
    NEXT i
    LET days = days + d
    LET dayofweek$ = dayname$(mod(days, 7))


END DEF

SUB Convert (month$, month, day$, day, Year$, year, dateok)

    ! Convert date and check for errors

    LET dateok = 0                  ! Assume date is bad


    !  Convert and check month
    FOR month = 1 to 12
       IF lcase$(monthname$(month)) = lcase$(month$) then EXIT FOR
    NEXT month
    IF month > 12 then
       PRINT "No such month."
       EXIT SUB                     ! Error found; exit with dateok = 0
    END IF


    !  Convert and check year
    LET year = val(year$)           ! Convert to a number
    IF year <> int(year) or year <= 0 then
       PRINT "Year must be an integer and AD."
       EXIT SUB                     ! Error found; exit with dateok = 0
    END IF


    !  Adjust for leap year
    LET daysin(2) = 28              ! Check for leap year
    IF mod(year,4)=0 and mod(year,100)<>0 or mod(year,400)=0 then
       LET daysin(2) = 29
    END IF
```

```
    !  Convert and check day
    LET day = val(day$)           ! Convert to a number
    IF day <> int(day) or day < 1 or day > daysin(month) then
       PRINT "Day must be an integer between 1 and";
       PRINT daysin(month)
       EXIT SUB                   ! Error found; exit with dateok = 0
    END IF

    LET dateok = 1                ! Passed all tests
END SUB

END

run

Month, day, year? May 31 1926
     That day is a Monday

Month, day, year? January
Day, year? 1 1900
     That day is a Monday

Month, day, year? december 31
Year? 1999
     That day is a Friday

Month, day, year? February 29 1972
     That day is a Tuesday

Month, day, year? February 29 1973
Day must be an integer between 1 and 28
Month, day, year? nov 11 1980
No such month.
Month, day, year? MAY     3     1979
     That day is a Thursday
```

12.6 SUMMARY

BASIC provides the string function `pos`. It works as follows:

`pos(s$,t$,n)` The character number in the string `s`, of the first character of a *match* of `t$` in `s$`, starting the search in the string `s$` at character `n`.

When the substring notation appears on the left of the equal sign in a `LET` statement, the string on the right is *assigned* into the position designated by the substring notation. Thus, if `a$ = "abcdefghi"`, and

```
LET a$[2:5] = "yup",     a$ = "ayupfghi"
```

then characters 2 through 5 (''bcde'') will be replaced by ''yup''. Notice that the length of `a$` is changed.

If a null substring expression appears on the left in a `LET` statement, the string on the right is *inserted* in front of the first position. Thus, if `a$` is again `"abcdefghi"`, and

```
LET a$[2:1] = "wow",        a$ = "awowbcdefghi"
```

then ''wow'' will be inserted in front of character 2, which is a ''b''.

The **INPUT** statement is intended to be used to input a list of items, where the items are separated by commas. Thus, the **INPUT** statement is sensitive to commas. If commas are present in strings being inputted, then such strings need to be enclosed in quote marks. The **INPUT** statement also strips leading and trailing spaces.

The **LINE INPUT** statement is intended to allow inputting of an entire line of text, without regard to leading and trailing spaces, and commas that might be embedded in the text.

The **WHEN USE** structure is used to ''protect'' a section of code that could, under certain circumstances, cause the program to stop. It is used as follows:

```
WHEN EXCEPTION IN
     (If anything occurs here that would stop the program,)
USE
     (... this section of code is executed instead.)
END WHEN
```

EXERCISES

1. Write a program to accept as data names in the form last-name first-name, and then to print them in normal order. That is, data should be of the form ''Kemeny John G.'' and the output of the form ''John G. Kemeny''. There should be no commas in the data or the output.
2. Rewrite **NAME** to allow for the possibility of multiple middle initials (not just two or three).
3. Further modify **NAME** to allow for the possibility of suffices like ''Jr'' or ''III''.
4. The subroutine `input` never returns a zero-length word. (a) Prove this by examining the code. (b) Show that, if the subroutine `nextword` is called with the variable `line$` consisting of nothing but blanks, the subroutine correctly returns a null string in `word$`.
5. Make the following three improvements in **CALENDAR**.
   a. If the user types ''stop'', the program should stop.
   b. Allow (but do not require) three-letter abbreviations for the months.
   c. Protect the two uses of the `val` function with **WHEN USE** structures. (Why does `val` need protecting?) Allow the user to reenter the correct data.
6. Redesign **CALENDAR** so that the subroutine `Convert` will call `Dayofweek$` if the date is valid, and then return the day of the week to the main program. What are the advantages and disadvantages of this revised design? Think of other ways to organize the program and consider their advantages and disadvantages.

7. Turn `CALENDAR` into a subroutine, and test the conjecture that the 13th of a month is more likely to be Friday than any other day of the week. Try a 400-year cycle. (Due to B. H. Brown.)
8. Write a subroutine `FileInput`, similar to `Input`, that obtains words from a file rather than from the user. You should assume that the main program has opened the file.
9. Write a subroutine that asks the user for the name of a file and then opens it. If there is no such file, the subroutine should ask for another name. (Hint: Use a `WHEN USE` structure.)

CHAPTER 13

FILE APPLICATIONS

13.1 INTRODUCTION

We introduced files in Chapter 8 and learned that the **OPEN** statement associates a file with the program and provides a convenient "nickname" (the *file number*) to refer to the file. We also learned that the program obtains data from the file with an **INPUT #** statement.

Additionally, we discovered that data is put into a file with a **PRINT #** statement. For *display-format* files (which we use in this text), printing must be done to an *empty* file (see the **ERASE #** statement) or to the end of the file if it already has data in it (see the **SET POINTER** statement).

Files can be created, if they do not yet exist, with the *create* option in the **OPEN** statement. Another useful statement is the **CLOSE** statement, which *closes* a file. It is the opposite of the **OPEN** statement.

We will discuss several applications of files in this chapter. The first is a set of two simple programs for keeping scores of, for instance, a basketball team. The second is a text filling program; it takes unfilled text from one file and places filled text into a second file. (In word processing, *filling* is the process of making the lines of a paragraph roughly the same length.) Finally, we present a classic application in simple form—a *master file update* program.

13.2 A SIMPLE SCOREKEEPING APPLICATION

Suppose we wish to use the computer to help keep track of the scoring averages of, say, a basketball team. We shall keep the current data in a file. And, we shall use two separate programs for manipulating this data. The first program will retrieve the data and print the current averages of the players. The second program will add the individual scores from the the most recent game to the data, to *update* the data. (Sometimes these two activities are combined into one program, but for simplicity, we choose to use two separate programs.)

We need to keep both the players names and their scores for all the games played to date. How should we organize this data? We could, for instance, keep the players names in one file and the scores in another. We choose instead to keep all the data in one file. (Exercise 3 calls for using two files.) We also choose to use display-format files, so that we can examine them on the screen. Finally, we choose to use one line per number. (For a large file, this can waste space, but our files are small because teams rarely contain more than twelve players and seasons are rarely longer than thirty games. This comes to but 360 numbers.)

We first show the data file SCORES as it might look after two games have been played. (We assume only five players do the scoring.)

The data file SCORES in midseason.

```
Brown
Green
Jones
Smith
White
zzzzz
 9
 14
 15
 22
 8
 7
 17
 7
 9
 19
```

Notice that the players' names appear at the beginning of the file, one per line. The "zzzzz" is *not* the name of a sleepy player, but is a special signal to indicate that the last name has been reached. Such a special value is called a *sentinel.*

A sentinel is one of three possible ways to tell the program that a certain point in a file has been reached. (This point could be the end of the file.) Alternatively, we could tell the program in advance how many names there were (that number might occur in the first line of the file), or we could keep the names and the scores in separate files (since BASIC can easily detect the end of a file, as we shall see). Using a sentinel here makes it possible for the two programs to operate (a) with but a single file, and (b) without including the number of players as an entry in the file.

Notice also that there is only one score on each line. This is reflected in the **INPUT #** statements in the program, each of which contains one variable.

The program that computes the averages is the more complicated of the two. It must first input the names, then all the scores. Only then can it compute and print the averages. Because the scores are kept *by game* but the averages must be computed *by player*, the program must keep running totals for each player. This is done with a list `scores`. Its dimension is set high enough to work for most teams.

```
REM   AVERAGE2

REM   Computes average scores for players
REM   from data in a file.

DIM names$(15)                       ! Names of the players
DIM scores(15)                       ! Scores of the players

INPUT prompt "Data file: ": datafile$
OPEN #1: name datafile$

LET num_players = 0
DO
   LINE INPUT #1: name$
   IF name$ = "zzzzz" then EXIT DO
   LET num_players = num_players + 1
   LET names$(num_players) = name$
LOOP

LET num_games = 0
DO while more #1
   LET num_games = num_games + 1
   FOR i = 1 to num_players
       INPUT #1: points
       LET scores(i) = scores(i) + points
   NEXT i
LOOP

PRINT "Name", "Average"
PRINT
FOR player = 1 to num_players
    LET average = scores(player)/num_games
    PRINT names$(player), average
NEXT player

END
```

The first **INPUT** statement in the program uses the *prompt option*. The string constant following the word `prompt` is printed on the screen in place of the usual question mark. Without the `prompt option`, prompted input would require two statements, a **PRINT** statement and an **INPUT** statement. A more general string expression can also follow the word `prompt`.

We can understand the role of the sentinel value "zzzzz" when we examine the first **DO** loop. It inputs players' names until the special name "zzzzz" is encountered. At that point, the loop is exited with the proper value for the variable `num_players`. Thus, this first loop serves the dual purpose of establishing the names of the players in the program and counting their number.

The next loop retrieves the players' scores for the several games. Because the number of games is not known to the program, we use a **DO** loop. As long as there are more data in the file (i.e., there are more games), the **DO** loop should continue. The **DO** loop therefore uses the condition `more #1`, which is *true* if there are more data (i.e., more games) in the file, and is *false* otherwise. When the file runs out of data, (i.e., when `more #1` is *false*), then there are no more games.

Once within the **DO** loop, we use a **FOR** loop to input each player's scores and enter them into the list `scores`. The **FOR** loop is chosen because the number of players *is* known at this point. The **FOR** loop assumes that if the score for the first player is present, then the scores for all the players will be present.

The final **FOR** loop prints the players' names and their averages, and is self-explanatory.

So much for computing and printing the averages. What does the manager do after each game when new data must be recorded? The companion program **AVUPDATE** operates on the same data file, and adds new data to its end.

Before explaining how **AVUPDATE** works, we need to introduce the concept of a *file pointer*. The file pointer is used inside BASIC to "point to" or keep track of the next item in the file to be used. For example, each time an item (string or number) is inputted from a file, the file pointer is adjusted to point to the *next* item to be inputted.

For display-format files in BASIC a program can start inputting only from the beginning of the file, and can print only to the end of the file. In **AVUPDATE** we need to input the first part of the file and then add (print) data to the end of the file. Thus, we need to move the file pointer from somewhere in the middle of the file to the end of the file. This is done with a **SET** statement, as follows:

```
SET #1: pointer END
```

We now examine the program **AVUPDATE**. It starts by inputting names from the file, and responding to the sentinel value "zzzzz" just as **AVERAGE2** does.

After it uses a **SET** statement to position the *file pointer* at the end of the file, the program merely transcribes (to the end of the file) the scores entered by the manager. Notice that the manager is *prompted* with the name of each player, and so does not have to remember the order of the players' names.

```
REM   AVUPDATE

REM   Adds data to the data file used by the
REM   program AVERAGE2

DIM names$(10)                      ! Names of the players

INPUT prompt "Data file: ": datafile$
OPEN #1: name datafile$

LET num_players = 0
DO
   LINE INPUT #1: name$
   IF name$ = "zzzzz" then EXIT DO
   LET num_players = num_players + 1
   LET names$(num_players) = name$
LOOP

SET #1: pointer END
```

```
PRINT "Enter new points for each player."
FOR i = 1 to num_players
    PRINT names$(i);
    INPUT points
    PRINT #1: points
NEXT i

END
```

Any database system, of which this is a very simple example, needs some way to get it started. This program needs the players' names in a file. At the beginning of the season, the manager must create a file containing only the names and the sentinel, as follows:

The SCORES file before the season starts.

```
Brown
Green
Jones
Smith
White
zzzzz
```

This can probably be done most easily with the screen editor.

For the sample run, we shall show a run of the program **AVERAGE2** after two games have been played (see the first version of the file **SCORES**). We will then show a run of the program **AVUPDATE**, followed by another run of the program **AVERAGE2**. Finally, we show the file **SCORES** as it exists after the third game has been played.

```
run

Data file: scores
Name              Average

Brown              8
Green              15.5
Jones              11
Smith              15.5
White              13.5

run

Data file: scores
Enter new points for each player.
Brown? 13
Green? 19
Jones? 8
Smith? 17
White? 12
```

```
run

Data file: scores
Name             Average

Brown             9.66667
Green             16.6667
Jones             10
Smith             16
White             13
```

The SCORES file after updating.

```
Brown
Green
Jones
Smith
White
zzzzz
 9
 14
 15
 22
 8
 7
 17
 7
 9
 19
 13
 19
 8
 17
 12
```

13.3 A WORD PROCESSING UTILITY

Word processing consists of a complex set of tasks including creating the text, formatting it, and finally printing the text or sending it as *electronic mail* to a recipient. Creating or modifying the text is often done with a *word processor* that has a *screen editor*. Most word processors come equipped with a host of special features to aid in the task; we will not consider these. Nor will we consider the problem of printing the document or sending it over a network.

The one function of word processors that we will consider is that of formatting. Formatting can be sophisticated and deal effectively with such difficult issues as positioning footnotes and handling *widows* and *orphans*. (*Widows* are single lines of text that appear at the bottom of a page. *Orphans* are single lines of text that appear at the top of a page.) Formatting also includes

---

We will not discuss *justification*, the process of causing the left margin and the right margin to "line up". For typed text, justification involves placing extra spaces between some of the words of a line to make the rightmost word end at the right margin. It is the authors' opinion that typed text is more attractive when unjustified than when justified. However, see Exercise 4.

filling the text, that is, making sure there is approximately the same amount of text on each line. We shall examine *filling* in this section.

To keep things simple, the filling program will use two files—an input file that contains the text to be filled, and an output file that will receive the filled text.

The fundamental strategy of text filling is deceptively simple: If the new word can fit onto the line, add it; otherwise, print that line to the output file and start a new line. To this simple requirement we add several others:

1. Any line beginning with a space is either an indented line or signifies the start of a paragraph; therefore, do not add any part of it to the previous line.
2. There should be two spaces following a period, except when specified otherwise by item 3, which follows.
3. More than one space between words should be taken as intentional, and such extra spaces should be retained.
4. A blank line (a line consisting of zero or more blanks and no other characters) should appear as a blank line in the output text as well.

These seemingly simple features make the filling algorithm complicated. The reason is that what needs to be done with the output file is dictated by what has yet to be examined from the input file. For example, if a line is half filled but not yet printed to the output file, and a new line starting with a blank is received from the input file, then the half-filled line must be printed to the output file.

Let us now examine the program `FILLTEXT`. After opening the two files it needs, the main part of the program consists of a `DO` loop that obtains lines from the input file and determines what is to be done with each one. If the line is a blank line, it is sent directly to the output file. The test for a blank line is to use the function `trim$` to remove the leading and trailing blanks, and then check to see if it has zero length.

If there is a partially filled line waiting, it must be sent to the output file before putting out the blank line. This action—putting out a partially filled line—appears throughout the program.

An incoming line that is not entirely blank but that starts with a blank requires putting out a partially filled line before starting the new line. The filling operation is then carried out by the subroutine `fill`, as it also is for a line that starts with a nonblank character.

Finally, after all the lines from the input file have been processed, any remaining partially filled output line must be printed to the output file.

```
REM   FILLTEXT

REM   Fills lines in the text from a file and
REM   puts filled text into a second file

LET width = 65                       ! Line width
CALL Getfiles

LET prevline$ = ""                   ! Previous line, starts empty
DO while more #1
   LINE INPUT #1: line$
   IF len(trim$(line$)) = 0 then ! Signal to put out empty line
```

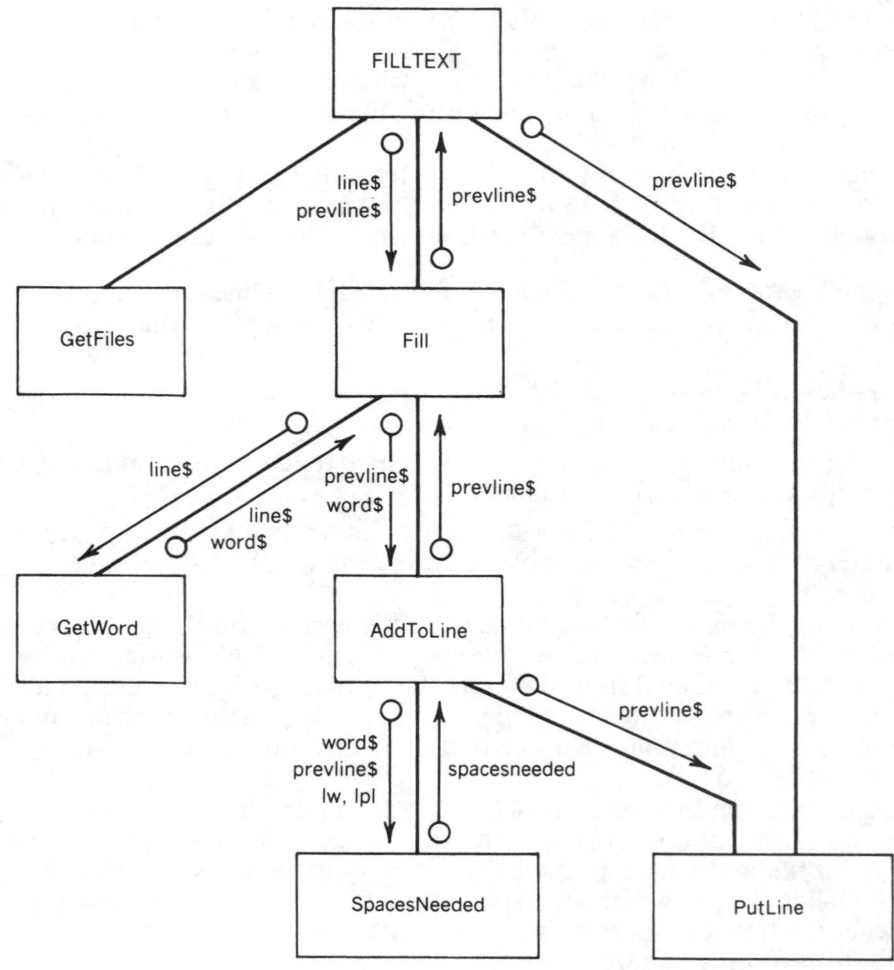

FIGURE 13.1
Structure chart for FILLTEXT.

```
      CALL Putline (prevline$)
      LET line$, prevline$ = ""
      CALL Putline (" ")        ! Put out a blank line
   ELSE
      IF line$[1:1] = " " then ! New paragraph means a new line
         CALL Putline (prevline$)
         LET prevline$ = ""
      END IF
      CALL Fill (line$, prevline$)
   END IF
LOOP
CALL Putline (prevline$)
PRINT "Done."
```

```
SUB Getfiles

    INPUT prompt "File containing text to fill: ": infile$
    OPEN #1: name infile$, access input
    INPUT prompt "Output file to contain filled text: ": outfile$
    OPEN #2: name outfile$, access outin, create newold
    ERASE #2

END SUB


SUB Fill (line$, prevline$)

    DO while len(trim$(line$)) > 0
       CALL Getword (word$, line$)
       CALL AddToLine (prevline$, word$)
    LOOP

END SUB


SUB Getword (word$, line$)

    LET lenl = len(line$)
    FOR i = 1 to lenl             ! Include leading blanks
       IF line$[i:i] <> " " then EXIT FOR
    NEXT i
    LET p = pos(line$, " ", i) ! Look for trailing blank
    IF p = 0 then LET p = lenl + 1
    LET word$ = line$[1:p-1]
    LET line$ = line$[p:lenl]

END SUB


SUB AddToLine (prevline$, word$)

    LET lpl = len(prevline$)
    LET lw = len(word$)
    IF lpl = 0 then               ! newline is empty
       LET prevline$ = word$
    ELSE

       CALL SpacesNeeded (numspaces)

       !  Add to "prevline$" or start a new line
       IF lpl + numspaces + lw <= width then ! If room, add it
          LET prevline$ = prevline$ & repeat$(" ", numspaces) & word$
       ELSE
          CALL Putline (prevline$) ! If no room, put out line
          LET prevline$ = ltrim$(word$) ! ... and start new one
       END IF
    END IF

END SUB
```

```
SUB SpacesNeeded (numspaces)

    IF prevline$[lpl:lpl] = " " or word$[1:1] = " " then
       LET numspaces = 0
    ELSE IF prevline$[lpl:lpl] = "." then
       LET numspaces = 2
    ELSE
       LET numspaces = 1
    END IF

END SUB


SUB Putline (prevline$)

    ! Print the line only if it is not null

    IF len(prevline$) > 0 then PRINT #2: prevline$

END SUB

END
```

The subroutine `Getfiles` is largely self-explanatory. Notice that the input file is *opened* with `access input` and the output file is *opened* with `access outin`. These access options may be omitted in both cases, as the *default* is `access outin`, which allows both input and output. In addition, the output file is opened with a `create newold` option. It allows the file to be opened whether it existed previously or not. If the file exists, it is simply opened; if it doesn't exist, it is first *created* and then opened.

The subroutine `Fill` *parses* or ''peels off'' the words from the input line (see Section 12.3), and feeds them one-by-one to the subroutine `AddToLine`.

The subroutine `Getword` provides a word from the front of the input line, including any *leading* spaces. Because we wish to retain leading spaces, we cannot use the subroutine `nextword` from the library `TEXTLIB`.

The subroutine `AddToLine` first determines the correct number of spaces in front of the new word, by calling the subroutine `SpacesNeeded`. If there is room at the end of the output line, it adds these spaces and the new word to it; if not, it puts out the filled line and starts a new line with the new word.

There are three rules for determining the correct number of spaces.

1. If there are leading blanks on the word, retain them.
2. Use two blanks after a period that occurs at the end of a line.
3. Otherwise, use one blank to separate words.

In each case, the subroutine first calculates the length of the line as if the new word and its leading spaces were to be added. If the line is too long, it first puts out the now-filled output line, and then starts a new line. If not too long, it *concatenates* the new word onto the end of the output line with the appropriate number of intervening blanks.

The file TEXT1 before filling follows.

```
     Now is the time for
all good men to come
to the aid of their party.
The quick brown fox...

     This indented block should
     not be changed.  Each line
     goes to the output file as is.

     Retaining extra spaces is useful for special emphasis.
For example,  LET x = 5  is clearer than LET x = 5 is.

run

File containing text to fill: text1
Output file to contain filled text: text2
Done.
```

The file TEXT1 after filling follows.

```
     Now is the time for all good men to come to the aid of their
party.  The quick brown fox...

     This indented block should
     not be changed.  Each line
     goes to the output file as is.

     Retaining extra spaces is useful for special emphasis.  For
example,  LET x = 5  is clearer than LET x = 5 is.
```

13.4 A MASTER FILE UPDATE PROGRAM

We shall now consider an important computing application, that of updating information in a large file. The file may, for example, contain information on credit card customers. The file consists of *records*, and each record corresponds to an account. Each day certain records need to be *updated* with the transactions of that day, such as paying a credit card bill or incurring a new charge.

The file that contains the current information on each customer is called the *master file*. The file that contains the day's transactions is called the *transaction file*. For simplicity, we identify each customer by last name only, and retain only the current outstanding balance in the master file. (Positive balances represent money owed to the bank.)

The master file MFILE follows.

```
Brown, 150
Green, 200
Jones, 25.50
Mason, 35
Price, 42
Smith, 230
White, 100
```

Each line in the file is a *record* and each record has two *fields*, the "name" and the "balance".

Looking at a typical transaction file. we notice that each of its lines is also a record containing two fields, the name and the transaction amount. (Positive transactions are new charges to be added to the balance. Negative transactions are payments that, when *added* to the balance, will reduce it.)

The transaction file TFILE follows.

```
Adams, 25
Jones, -12.50
Lewis, 19
Smith, 47.50
```

We adopt the following rules:

1. If a name in the transaction file matches a name in the master file, then the transaction amount will be added to the balance.
2. If a name in the transaction file does *not* match any name in the master file, then the transaction record will be inserted into the master file as a new master record.

With these rules, it is easy to verify that the revised master file, produced by the program `UPDATE`, is correct as shown following the run.

```
run

Master file? mfile
Transaction file? tfile
New master file? nmfile
Update completed.
Ready
```

The modified master file NMFILE follows.

```
Adams,   25
Brown,   150
Green,   200
Jones,   13
Lewis,   19
Mason,   35
Price,   42
Smith,   277.5
White,   100
```

Before we discuss the program that actually produced the new master file, notice that we are using display-format files. These correspond to magnetic tape or cassette tape files in that no program can write new information into the *middle* of them. (Remember that attempting to `PRINT` into the middle of a file will cause the program to stop.) Therefore, the only way we can make changes in such a file is to *copy* it, making the needed changes as the records "pass by". For this strategy to work, it is essential that both the master file and the transaction file be in order (sorted alphabetically by name).

The results of *merging* the transaction file into the master file will go into a

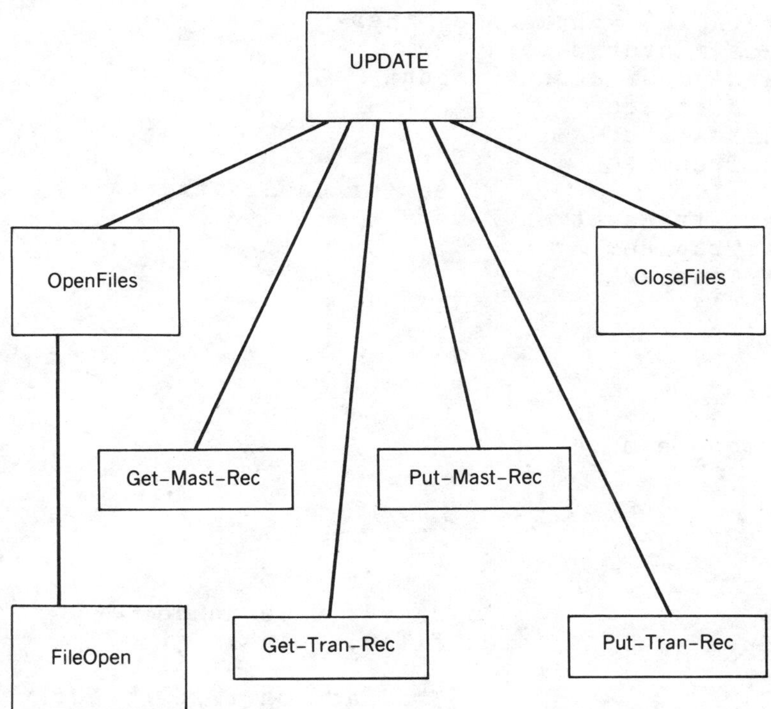

FIGURE 13.2
Structure chart for UPDATE.

new master file, which is initially empty. Let us now examine the program **UPDATE**.

```
REM   UPDATE
REM
REM   A simple sequential master file update program
REM
REM   Master file records are in the form
REM        Name, balance
REM   Transaction file records have the same form.
REM
REM   If a transaction file name matches a master file name,
REM        add the transaction amount to the balance.
REM
REM   If there is no corresponding name in the master file,
REM        insert the transaction record in the master file.

CALL OpenFiles

CALL Get_Mast_Rec
CALL Get_Tran_Rec

DO while mastername$ < "zzzzz" or tranname$ < "zzzzz"
   IF mastername$ < tranname$ then
      !   Keep searching
      CALL Put_Mast_Rec
      CALL Get_Mast_Rec
```

```
   ELSEIF mastername$ = tranname$ then
      !   Update master record
      LET balance = balance + amount
      CALL Put_Mast_Rec
      CALL Get_Mast_Rec
      CALL Get_Tran_Rec
   ELSE                           ! mastername$ > tranname$
      !   Insert transaction record
      CALL Put_Tran_Rec
      CALL Get_Tran_Rec
   END IF
LOOP

CALL CloseFiles

PRINT "Update completed."

STOP

SUB OpenFiles

    LET mf = 1                    ! Master file number
    CALL FileOpen (#mf, "Master file", "old")

    LET tf = 2                    ! Transaction file number
    CALL FileOpen (#tf, "Transaction file", "old")

    LET nmf = 3                   ! New master file number
    CALL FileOpen (#nmf, "New master file", "newold")
    ERASE #nmf

END SUB


SUB FileOpen (#1, prompt$, create$)

    DO
       WHEN exception in
            PRINT prompt$;
            INPUT filename$
            OPEN #1: name filename$, create create$
            EXIT DO
       USE
            PRINT "That file not available; try again."
       END WHEN
    LOOP

END SUB

SUB Get_Mast_Rec

    IF more #mf then
       INPUT #mf: mastername$, balance
    ELSE
       LET mastername$ = "zzzzz"
    END IF

END SUB
```

```
SUB Get_Tran_Rec

    IF more #tf then
       INPUT #tf: tranname$, amount
    ELSE
       LET tranname$ = "zzzzz"
    END IF

END SUB

SUB Put_Mast_Rec

    PRINT #nmf: mastername$; ", "; balance

END SUB

SUB Put_Tran_Rec

    PRINT #nmf: tranname$; ", "; amount

END SUB

SUB CloseFiles

    CLOSE #mf
    CLOSE #tf
    CLOSE #nmf

END SUB

END
```

We will describe only the main part of the program and parts of the subroutines `OpenFiles` and `Get_Mast_Rec` at length.

Sometimes it is easier to understand a program by assuming that it has already gotten underway. Consequently, we'll worry about the initialization and closedown later. Here, we assume that we have both a master record and a transaction record in front of us. That is, the variables `mastername$`, `balance`, `tranname$`, and `amount` have values obtained from the corresponding files.

We now compare the two names. Three possibilities arise. If the `mastername$` occurs earlier in the alphabet than `tranname$`, then we must cycle through the master file. This is done by first writing out the current master file record, and then reading in a new master file record. (According to the principles of top-down structure, these two tasks are assigned to a subroutine, which appears later.)

Before going any further, notice that we act on a particular record from a file by first reading it in, then by updating it, and finally by writing it out.

Continuing, if `mastername$` and `tranname$` agree, we then recompute the balance in the master record. Because we have now "used up" both the master record and the transaction record, we must obtain a new one from each file.

Finally, if `mastername$` occurs later alphabetically than `tranname$`, it means that there is no matching name for this transaction, and it should be *inserted* into the master file. Thus, we arrange to write out the transaction record, and then obtain a new one. In this case, the master record stays around because there might be a later transaction record destined to update it.

We illustrate these three cases by examining our current example in detail. Assume that "Adams" and "Brown" have already been processed, and that the program is now examining the master record for "Green" and the transaction record for "Jones". The arrowheads "—>" indicate the position of each file's pointer.

```
          m-record: Green, 200
          t-record: Jones, -12.50

    mfile             tfile               nmfile
    -----             -----               ------
    Brown, 150        Adams, 25           Adams, 25
    Green, 200        Jones, -12.50       Brown, 150
-->               -->                 -->
    Jones, 25.50      Lewis, 19
    Mason, 35         Smith, 47.50
    Price, 42
    Smith, 230
    White, 100
```

At this point, the program has obtained, and is now examining, a record from the master file "Green, 200" and a record from the transaction file "Jones, -12.50". "Green" comes before "Jones"; therefore, the program simply writes the "Green" record to the new master file and reads a new record from the master file. These actions produce the following situation:

```
          m-record: Jones,  25.50
          t-record: Jones, -12.50

    mfile             tfile               nmfile
    -----             -----               ------
    Brown, 150        Adams, 25           Adams, 25
    Green, 200        Jones, -12.50       Brown, 150
    Jones, 25.50  -->                     Green, 200
-->                   Lewis, 19       -->
    Mason, 35         Smith, 47.50
    Price, 42
    Smith, 230
    White, 100
```

This time, the program examines a master record for "Jones" and a transaction record for "Jones". Because these names are the same, the program adds the transaction amount to the balance and then writes the revised master record to the new master file. (The negative amount, -12.50, represents a payment by Jones to the bank.) The program has "used up" both records, so now it must read both a new master record and a new transaction record. The situation is now as follows:

```
        m-record: Mason, 35
        t-record: Lewis, 19

    mfile              tfile              nmfile
    -----              -----              ------
    Brown, 150         Adams, 25          Adams, 25
    Green, 200         Jones, -12.50      Brown, 150
    Jones, 25.50       Lewis, 19          Green, 200
    Mason, 35    -->                      Jones, 13
-->                    Smith, 47.50  -->
    Price, 42
    Smith, 230
    White, 100
```

This time, "Lewis" comes before "Mason", and "Lewis, 19" is from the transaction file. Therefore, the program merely writes the transaction record to the new master file and reads a new transaction record. This produces the following situation:

```
        m-record: Mason, 35
        t-record: Smith, 47.50

    mfile              tfile              nmfile
    -----              -----              ------
    Brown, 150         Adams, 25          Adams, 25
    Green, 200         Jones, -12.50      Brown, 150
    Jones, 25.50       Lewis, 19          Green, 200
    Mason, 35          Smith, 47.50       Jones, 13
-->                -->                    Lewis, 19
    Price, 42                         -->
    Smith, 230
    White, 100
```

We have covered the cases where records of both types are examined. Three other cases can arise. First, the transaction file may become empty (there is no transaction record to process). Second, the master file may become empty (there is no master record to process). Third, both files might become empty concurrently.

If the transaction file is empty, we should cycle through the rest of the master file, writing out records and reading in new records until the copying operation is complete. Thus, we want to carry out the part of the main loop commented with "Keep searching" until the master file becomes empty. This will be done automatically if `mastername$` < `tranname$`. We therefore arrange that, whenever the transaction file becomes empty, `tranname$` is set to some name that is guaranteed to occur later in the alphabet than any real name. Here we choose "zzzzz" as this signal. We follow the same strategy if the master file should run out first; because `mastername$` is now "zzzzz", the part of the main loop commented with "Insert transaction record" is carried out until the transaction file becomes empty.

When both files become empty, then both `mastername$` and `tranname$` will be "zzzzz". In this case, the condition for continuing the `DO` loop is no longer met, and the loop is exited.

Using a *high value* (here, "zzzzz") to signal that the end of the file has been reached is standard practice for programs of this type.

The subroutine `OpenFiles` illustrates that the *create* option can be specified with a string variable or expression as well as by a keyword. That is, we can use any of the following (assume `c$ = "old"`):

```
..., create old
..., create "old"
..., create c$
```

The `create old` option, in any of the three forms above, guarantees that the attempt to *open* the file will be successful if and only if the file already exists. This is also the default; that is, including the `create old` option or omitting it will have the same effect.

There are two other create options, `create new` and `create newold`. `Create new` will ensure that an attempt to open the file will be successful if and only if the file does *not* exist; BASIC will, of course, create a new file. `Create newold` will succeed in all cases. If the file already exists, BASIC will merely open it. If the file does not exist, BASIC will create and open it.

The subroutine `Get_Mast_Rec` and `Get_Tran_Rec` use `more #` to detect the end of the file. If there is more data in the file, then the program simply reads the record. If not, the program reads nothing, but sets the variable `mastername$` to the artificially high value, "zzzzz", to signal the rest of the program that the end of the file has been reached.

The other subroutines are self-explanatory.

13.5 SUMMARY

The `OPEN` statement finds the file, if it is available, and associates with it a numerical file number. The following is typical:

```
OPEN #3: name "datafile"
```

With display-format files, which are the only kind discussed in this chapter, `INPUT #` statements are used to obtain data from the file and `PRINT #` statements are used to place data into the file.

Erasing the contents of a file can be done with the `ERASE` statement. If we wish to add to the data already present in the file, we must position the file pointer to the end of the file with a `SET` statement. The following are typical:

```
ERASE #3
SET #2: pointer end
```

If a file with a certain name does not yet exist, it can be created by an `OPEN` statement with a *create* option. Another useful statement is the `CLOSE` statement, which *closes* a file and which is the opposite of the `OPEN` statement. Closing a file is necessary in BASIC only when it will be re-opened later in the same program. The following are typical:

```
OPEN #2: name "temp", create new
CLOSE #3
```

There are four ways for a program to detect the end of a file.

1. The program knows in advance how many data elements are in the file. (See, for example, `SALES2` in Section 8.4.)

2. The program can detect a sentinel value as the last element of the file. (See **AVERAGE2** and **AVUPDATE** in this chapter.)
3. The program can use the `more #` condition in a **DO** loop or **IF THEN** structure or statement. The `end #` is similar but has the opposite truth value. (See **AVERAGE2** in this chapter.)
4. The program can use a **WHEN USE** structure, as for example

```
WHEN EXCEPTION IN
     INPUT #1: mastername$
USE
     LET mastername$ = "zzzzz"
END WHEN
```

EXERCISES

1. Write a program to produce a listing of a specified range of lines in the program. (For example, list the 4th through the 17th lines.)
2. Write a program that copies one file into a second file, and deletes a specified range of lines from the first, for example, the 4th through the 17th. Don't forget to *erase* the second file ahead of time.
3. Redesign **AVERAGE2** and **AVUPDATE** to use two files, one for names and one for scores, and therefore eliminate the need for the sentinel "zzzzz".
4. The program **FILLTEXT** *fills* lines, that is, makes sure that each line contains the most words that it can. The program does not *justify* the filled lines. Justification involves inserting additional spaces between the words so that the first word is at the left margin and the last word is at the right margin. Modify **FILLTEXT** to justify the filled lines. (Remember, partially filled lines, such as the last line of a paragraph, should not be justified.)
5. Modify **UPDATE** to allow several transaction records to update the same master record. (Hint: Two statements have to be removed. Which two?)
6. (Continuation) Assume that there are two or more transaction records with the same name but there is no corresponding master record. If the modification called for in Exercise 5 is carried out, then each transaction record will be inserted into the new master file. Introduce code to prevent such occurrences.
7. Make the subroutine **FILEOPEN** in **UPDATE** external and place it in a library **FILELIB**. (There are three ways in which the **OPEN** statement in that subroutine can fail: first, the file might not exist; second, we might not be able to obtain the desired accesses; and third, the file might already be open. We can avoid the third failure by first closing the file. Therefore, also add a **CLOSE** statement to the subroutine **FILEOPEN**.) Modify **UPDATE** to make use of this subroutine.
8. Modify **UPDATE** to check for the following errors in the transaction file:
   a. Names out of order.
   b. A new balance is negative.

   If the program detects an error, it should report it and continue.

CHAPTER 14

SEARCHING AND SORTING

14.1 INTRODUCTION

This chapter discusses two tasks that are essential to many computer applications: *searching*, as in searching a list of names to find a particular name, and *sorting*, or putting a list of names or numbers into order. The searching and sorting routines discussed here are all packaged as subroutines. The numeric versions are included in the library file `SORTNLIB`, and the string versions are in the library file `SORTSLIB`.

We will first explore how to search a list for a particular name or number. *Linear searching* is simple, but slow for long lists. *Binary searching* is much faster, especially for long lists, but requires that the list be in order.

We begin our study of sorting by analyzing the simple *selection sort*. We shall show that the selection sort is unbearably slow for long lists.

We will also study an efficient sorting algorithm. The one we have chosen is both efficient for long lists and adaptable for sorting very long files. It is called the *sort merge*.

We will then present a modification of the sort merge algorithm that is useful for large data bases in that the sorting can take place without ever moving or exchanging the actual data.

Finally, we will present a simple application of sorting, an *indexing* program. The simplest examples of indexing appear as the last section in many books, where selected words are associated with particular pages in the book. We shall use as our example the indexing of the keywords in a computer program.

14.2 SIMPLE SEARCHING

A common problem in computing is to locate a certain name in a list of names. Suppose the list of names is in `list$(1)` through `list$(n)`, and `key$` contains the name being searched for. One possible approach is as follows:

```
LET place = -1
FOR i = 1 to n
    IF list$(i) = key$ then
       LET place = i
       EXIT FOR
    END IF
NEXT i
```

The `FOR` loop examines each entry of the list in turn. As soon as a match is found, the variable `place` is set to that value, and the loop exited. If the name is not in the list, the variable `place` will still have the value -1 when the loop is finished.

If the desired name is in the list exactly once, the variable `place` will contain its position in the list. If the desired name is in the list more than once, then our program fragment will find the first occurrence. Suppose we wish to find the last, not the first, occurrence. All we have to do is to remove the `EXIT FOR` statement. Then, each time a match is found, the variable `place` will be set to this new position. At the end of the loop, the variable `place` will obviously refer to the last match in the list.

The subroutine `linsrchs`, which follows, is patterned on the code fragment shown earlier, but allows the search to start at an entry other than entry 1 in the list. (Because the *not found* signal is -1, the starting entry should be no less than 0.)

```
SUB linsrchs (list$(), start, finish, key$, place)

    ! Linear search.  Searches linearly for key$ in
    ! list$(start), ..., list$(finish).  If found, place
    ! is the subscript; if not found, place = -1.

    LET place = -1
    FOR i = start to finish
        IF list$(i) = key$ then
           LET place = i
           EXIT FOR
        END IF
    NEXT i

END SUB
```

The subroutine `linsrchs` searches a string list, and can be found in `SORTSLIB`. `SORTNLIB` contains a similar subroutine, `linsrchn`, for searching numerical lists.

This search method is called *linear* because the list containing the names is examined one entry at a time, starting with the first. If the desired name happens to be first, then we are lucky; we found it as quickly as we possibly could have. If the desired name happens to be the last, then we are unlucky; we will have examined each and every entry in the list. The same is true for failure to find the name in the list. On the average, we will have to examine a number of entries somewhere between the least (1) and the most (n), or about n/2. The time needed for the search is determined roughly by the number of entries examined, and is therefore proportional to n/2, which is a *linear* function of n. If n is small, no problem. But if n is large, say one million, then each search carried out by this method will have to examine 500,000 entries on the average.

14.3 EFFICIENT SEARCHING

The generally poor efficiency of linear searching can be significantly improved if the list of names (or numbers) happens to be in order. We can then use the *binary search*, which starts by looking at the middle element in the list. If that matches the key, then it is done. If not, and this is the important idea, the binary search chooses either the lower half or the upper half of the list for another try. Because the list is in order, this choice is easily made by comparing the middle element with the key. We then repeat the process of examining the middle element, but this time for a list that is about half as long.

```
SUB binsrchs (list$(), start, finish, key$, place)

    ! Binary search.  Assumes list$() is sorted.
    ! Searches for key$ in list$(start), ..., list$(finish).
    ! If found, place is the subscript; if not found,
    ! place = -1.

    LET first = start
    LET last = finish
    LET place = -1
    DO until last < first or place >= 0
       LET mid = int((first + last)/2)
       LET mid$ = list$(mid)
       IF mid$ = key$ then
          LET place = mid             ! Found it!
       ELSEIF mid$ > key$ then
          LET last = mid - 1          ! Work with lower half
       ELSE                           ! Here, mid$ < key$
          LET first = mid + 1         ! Work with upper half
       END IF
    LOOP

END SUB
```

The subroutine `binsrchs` computes the *middle* position by taking the integer part of the average of the first and last positions. (It is not necessary that the middle be exact for the binary search to work properly.) The middle element is compared with the key. If a match is found, the variable `place` is set to the correct entry number. Otherwise, if the middle element is larger than the key (`mid$` > `key$`), then the desired element, if it exists, will be found in the lower half of the list, i.e., the half whose subscripts are < `mid`. We therefore adjust the variable `last` to point to the upper end of the *lower* half of the list (the variable `first` already points to the first element in the lower half). On the other hand, if the middle element is smaller than the key (the `else` case), then we look further in the *upper* half of the list. In this case, we adjust the variable `first` to point to the first element in the upper half

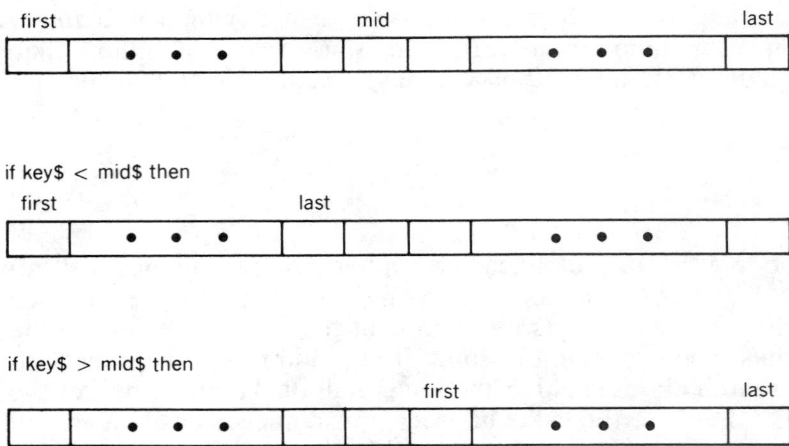

FIGURE 14.1
One stage of the binary search cuts the size of the list roughly in half.

(again, the variable `last` already points to the last element in the upper half). This action is illustrated in Figure 14.1.

Eventually, we either find the desired element (`place` points to it, or to one of them, if there are more than one), or we don't. In the latter case, `place = -1`, as in `linsrchs`. In this subroutine, failure to find the desired element is detected when `last` is actually less than `first`.

It is beyond the scope of this text to fully analyze the performance of searching methods. But a simple argument will show that the binary search is much, much faster than the linear search. For one million elements, we have already seen that the linear search requires about 500,000 *probes* on the average. (A probe is the examination of a single element in the list.) For the binary search, we consider the worst case, that of finding the desired element at the latest possible time. This situation would arise roughly as follows. We start with 1,000,000 elements and check the middle one. Assume it doesn't match. We then check the middle element of the appropriate half, which contains roughly 500,000 elements. We have now examined but two elements, but we know that the desired element must be one of only 250,000 elements. We summarize this process in table form.

After This Many Probes	This Number of Elements Remain
1	500,000
2	250,000
3	125,000
...	......
10	976
11	488
...	...
17	7
18	3
19	1
20	Found it!

Thus, the worst case for the binary search of a list containing one million items is 25,000 (= 500,000/20) times faster than the average case for the linear search. Of course, the binary search requires that the list be presorted, but that price is worth paying if more than just a few searches are to be made.

The maximum number of *probes* required by the binary search can be approximated by the logarithm-to-the-base-2 of the total number of elements in the list. For 1,000,000 elements, this comes to

```
log2(1000000) = 19.9316
```

which is pretty close to 20.

The library `SORTNLIB` contains a similar binary search subroutine for searching numeric lists.

14.4 SORTING

Sorting a list of names or numbers sounds like a complicated task. Indeed, there are many different sorting methods, and a complete analysis of how fast they work can be quite complex. We will limit our study to two sorting routines. The one presented in this section, the *selection sort*, is chosen because it is easy to understand. Later, in Section 14.5, we present the *sort-merge* routine, which is quite fast.

```
SUB selsortn (list(), first, last)

    ! Sorts a numeric list from list(first) to list(last)
    ! using a selection sort

    FOR i = first to last - 1
        ! Find minimum in list(), starting at position i.
        LET p = i                     ! Trial position for minimum
        LET newmin = list(p)          ! Trial minimum
        FOR j = i+1 to last
            IF list(j) < newmin then
               LET p = j              ! New position
               LET newmin = list(p)       ! and new minimum
            END IF
        NEXT j
        ! Move newmin to list(i), move others down
        FOR j = p to i+1 step -1
            LET list(j) = list(j-1)
        NEXT j
        LET list(i) = newmin
    NEXT i

END SUB
```

We can demonstrate that this subroutine works with a simple example, which sorts a list of random integers. The random numbers are generated by the `rnd` function, which will be discussed in Chapter 17.

```
REM   TESTSORT

LIBRARY "Sortnlib"

DIM x(10)
```

```
FOR i = 1 to 10
    LET x(i) = int(100*rnd)
NEXT i

PRINT "Unsorted."
MAT PRINT x

CALL selsortn (x, 1, 10)

PRINT "Sorted."
MAT PRINT x

END

run

Unsorted.
 54            7             68            33            95
 82            54            8             39            58

Sorted.
 7             8             33            39            54
 54            58            68            82            95
```

The library `SORTSLIB` contains a similar selection sort routine that sorts a string list.

14.5 MEASURING EFFICIENCY

The most important fact about any sorting routine is how long it takes to sort a list of a certain size. Naturally, the precise answer depends on many factors, such as whether the list is already in order or not, or how well the programming has been done. For these and other reasons, we generally are content to classify sorting routines according to some formula based on n that will tell us about how long it will take to sort a list of n elements, roughly speaking.

These ideas can be made quite precise, but here we will be content to perform timing experiments. We will conclude that the selection sort is an *n-squared* sort; that is, it will take four times as long to sort a list twice as long, because 2-squared is 4.

To carry out these experiments, all we need is a simple program like the one that follows. In it, `time` is a no-argument function in BASIC that gives the current time in seconds. (If your computer does not have an internal clock, then this method of timing will not work.)

```
REM   TIMER
REM
REM   Measures running time for numerical sorting
REM   subroutines using lists of random numbers
REM   of any desired length n
```

```
LIBRARY "Sortnlib"

DIM x(1000)

DO
   PRINT "Length of list";
   INPUT n

   IF n = 0 then EXIT DO

   FOR i = 1 to n
       LET x(i) = rnd
   NEXT i

   LET start = time
   CALL selsortn (x, 1, n)
   LET finish = time
   PRINT "Time to sort"; finish - start
   PRINT
LOOP

END

run

Length of list? 50
Time to sort 2.2

Length of list? 100
Time to sort 7.86

Length of list? 200
Time to sort 31.81

Length of list? 400
Time to sort 127.76

Length of list? 0
```

Comparing the results for n = 50, 100, 200, and 400, we can easily see that if the length of the list is doubled, the time is increased roughly fourfold, which is consistent with our assertion that the selection sort is an n-squared method. In fact, we can easily see that the time needed for a random list of length n is, roughly,

$$\text{time} \approx .000786 * n^2$$

We can now estimate how long it would take to sort a long list of, say, 100,000 entries. Because 100,000 is 1000 times as large as 100, the sorting time will increase a million-fold (= 1000^2) from 7.86 to 7,860,000 seconds, or about 91 days!

14.6 SORT MERGE

We next present a sorting method called the *sort-merge*. It is a two-stage process—a sorting stage is followed by several merging stages. Although longer and more complicated than the selection sort (which it uses in the first stage), the payoff is that it is much, much faster for large lists. In fact, in terms of speed, sort-merge bears the same relation to selection sorting that binary searching bears to linear searching.

The sort-merge starts with a sorting stage. However, instead of sorting the entire list at one time, it sorts it in pieces. For instance, it might divide a list of 100,000 entries into 5000 pieces containing 20 entries each. Each of the pieces is then sorted using, for example, the selection sort. We can estimate the total time to be spent on this stage by multiplying our previous experimental estimate by the number of pieces.

Time for each piece = .38 seconds
Time for all pieces = 5000 × .38 = 1900 seconds

As we can plainly see, 1900 seconds is a good deal less than 7,860,000 seconds, the time needed by a selection sort alone.

The second stage comprises merging the pieces pairwise to produce larger pieces, and continuing until there is only one piece left. The merging process is more easily understood with a simple example. We will use pieces containing only three entries each. To start, a pointer `p1` points to the first element of the first piece, and `p2` points to the first element of the second piece. There is an auxiliary list and a pointer, `ptemp`, that points to the previously entered element (`ptemp = 0` at the start).

```
        list                     temp
                        ptemp
p1      100
        500
        700
p2      200
        400
        800
```

We compare the entries pointed to by `p1` and `p2`, and choose the smaller (here, "100"). We then move this value to the next available space in the auxiliary list `temp`, which we find by incrementing `ptemp`. We then increment either `p1` (if the entry moved came from the first piece) or `p2` (if the entry moved came from the second piece). In the example, "100" came from the first piece, so `p1` is incremented. The picture now looks like this:

```
        list                     temp

        100             ptemp    100
p1      500
        700
p2      200
        400
        800
```

Next, we compare the entries pointed to by `p1` and `p2`; the values are "500" and "200", respectively. Because "200" is the smaller, we move this value to the next available spot in the list `temp`. We then increment `p2` because "200" came from the second piece. The picture now looks like this:

```
              list                temp

              100                 100
      p1      500       ptemp     200
              700
              200
      p2      400
              800
```

We continue in this fashion until all entries from both pieces have been moved. Of course, when we run out of entries in either piece, we simply move all the remaining entries from the other piece. And, in case of ties, we move the entry from the first piece. After all entries have been moved, the picture looks like this:

```
              list                temp

              100                 100
              500                 200
              700                 400
      p1      200                 500
              400                 700
              800       ptemp     800
      p2
```

Notice that `p1` points to the entry just *after* the last entry of piece one, and `p2` points to the entry just *after* the last entry of piece two. This condition signals the end of this part of the routine.

As a final step, we transfer the entries back from the auxiliary list `temp` to the original list `list`.

Each pair of pieces in the original list is similarly merged. The list now contains sorted pieces twice as long (six instead of three), but there are only about half as many of them!

The entire process is repeated, and the sorted piece size doubled, until there is only one sorted piece, which is our goal.

The subroutine `mergen` merges numerical lists. The first `DO` loop is in charge as long as there are elements remaining in both pieces. The subroutine `move` does the actual transfer of data and adjusting of pointers. Following the main `DO` loop are two *run out* `DO` loops, whose purpose is to move whatever remaining elements there are into one of the two pieces. Finally, the data are transferred back from the temporary list `temp` to the original list `list`.

```
SUB mergen (list(), first1, last1, last2)

    ! Merge list(first1), ..., list(last1)
    ! and list(last1+1), ..., list(last2)
    ! into list(first1), ..., list(last2)

    DIM temp(1000)            ! Need temporary work space
    LET p1 = first1           ! Pointer first segment
    LET p2 = last1 + 1        ! Pointer second segment
    LET ptemp = 0             ! Pointer in temp()
```

```
      DO while p1 <= last1 and p2 <= last2
         IF list(p1) <= list(p2) then     ! Move smaller one
            CALL move(p1)
         ELSE
            CALL move(p2)
         END IF
      LOOP
      DO while p1 <= last1
         CALL move(p1)              ! Run out first piece
      LOOP
      DO while p2 <= last2
         CALL move(p2)              ! Run out second piece
      LOOP

      LET i = first1                ! Copy temp() back into list()
      FOR j = 1 to ptemp
          LET list(i) = temp(j)
          LET i = i+1
      NEXT j

      SUB move(ptr)                 ! list(ptr) to next temp slot
          LET ptemp = ptemp + 1
          LET temp(ptemp) = list(ptr)
          LET ptr = ptr + 1
      END SUB

   END SUB
```

The subroutine `srtmergn` is the supervisor routine for sorting a numeric list by the sort-merge process. It calls on the subroutine `selsortn` to sort the pieces (here the piece size is 20). It then repeatedly calls the subroutine `mergen` (shown in the preceding display) that merges two pieces into one piece that is twice as long. The calling sequence

```
CALL mergen (list, i, j, k)
```

specifies that, in the `list()`, the first piece goes from entry `i` through entry `j`, and the second piece goes from entry `j+1` through entry `k`.

```
SUB srtmergn (list(), first, last)

    ! Sort-merge for numeric list, list(first), ..., list(last).
    ! First sort pieces using selection sort.
    ! Then merge these pieces, iterating until
    ! only one piece left.

    LET piecesize = 20              ! Size to sort
    FOR i = first to last step piecesize
        LET j = min(i + piecesize - 1, last)
        CALL selsortn (list, i, j)      ! Sort piece
    NEXT i
```

```
    DO while piecesize < last - first + 1    ! Need to merge
       FOR i = first to last step 2*piecesize
           LET j = min(i + piecesize - 1, last)
           LET k = min(j + piecesize, last)
           IF j < last then CALL mergen (list, i, j, k)
       NEXT i
       LET piecesize = 2*piecesize
    LOOP

END SUB
```

It remains for us to perform timing experiments for the sort-merge. We use the program **TIMER**, shown earlier, but change the call to the sort routine to

```
CALL srtmergn (x, 1, n)
```

These are the results:

```
run

Length of list? 50
Time to sort 1.37

Length of list? 100
Time to sort 3.07

Length of list? 200
Time to sort 7.25

Length of list? 400
Time to sort 16.31

Length of list? 0
Ready
```

The times are less than those for the selection sort, and clearly do not quadruple as the length of the list is doubled. In fact, the time is roughly proportional to **n*log(n)**. That is,

$$\text{time} \approx .00680 * n * \log(n)$$

This formula works pretty well for $n = 50$, 100, 200, and 400. Using it, we estimate that sorting a list containing 100,000 entries by the sort-merge method would take about 7830 seconds, which is about 2.2 hours, a good deal less than what the selection sort would require. In fact, the improvement ratio is enormous, being about 1000:1 (7,860,000/7830).

Finally, we show graphically the timing results for the selection and the sort-merge sorts.

The library **SORTSLIB** contains similar routines for carrying out a sort-merge on a list of strings.

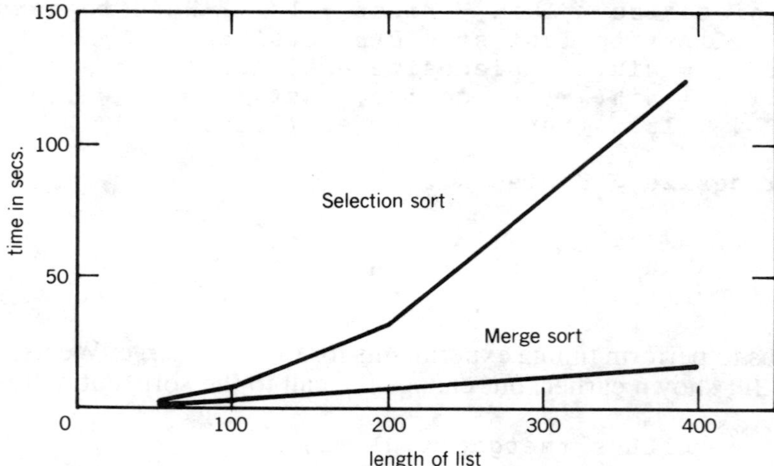

FIGURE 14.2
Timing comparisons for the selection and merge sorts.

14.7 AN INDEXED SORT

In the sorting routines examined so far, the actual data in the list being sorted are rearranged. In many applications, this rearrangement can be inefficient. For example, suppose we wish to sort a list of names and addresses into zip code order. Each time we discover an address that is *out of order*, we would want to exchange it with some other address. This means exchanging the name, the street address, the town, the zip code, and any other information that might be part of the address. This would be true if the names were in a string list `names$()`, the addresses in a string list `addresses$()`, and so on.

This problem can be avoided entirely by *never* moving the data. Instead, we introduce a companion numeric list called an *index list*. The entries in this numeric list will *point* to the actual data. At the start, the index list will simply contain the numbers 1 through n, where n is the number of entries in the data list. Then, in whatever sorting method we use, whenever we would otherwise move data entries, we move the index list entries instead!

The idea of an indexed sort can be grasped through a simple example. Suppose that we have a data list containing the names of the days of the week, and that we wish to put that list into alphabetical order. The following figure shows the state of the index list and the data list both before and after the sorting.

	Before
Index List	**Data List**
x(1) = 1	list$(1) = "Sunday"
x(2) = 2	list$(2) = "Monday"
x(3) = 3	list$(3) = "Tuesday"
x(4) = 4	list$(4) = "Wednesday"
x(5) = 5	list$(5) = "Thursday"
x(6) = 6	list$(6) = "Friday"
x(7) = 7	list$(7) = "Saturday"

Index List	After Data List
x(1) = 6	list$(1) = "Sunday"
x(2) = 2	list$(2) = "Monday"
x(3) = 7	list$(3) = "Tuesday"
x(4) = 1	list$(4) = "Wednesday"
x(5) = 5	list$(5) = "Thursday"
x(6) = 3	list$(6) = "Friday"
x(7) = 4	list$(7) = "Saturday"

Thus word number 6, "Friday", is first in alphabetic order, word number 2, "Monday", is next, and so on. Notice that the data list is unchanged; only the index list has been modified.

An indexed sort can be made from any sorting method. The modifications are almost trivial. Basically, one must establish the index list, for instance **x()**. Then, instead of examining entries such as **list$(i)**, one examines **list$(x(i))**. However, one never rearranges the entries in **list$()**, only those in **x()**.

```
SUB indsrmgs (list$(), first, last, x())

    ! Sorts a string list list$(), indexed by x(),
    ! from list$(x(first)) to list$(x(last)),
    ! using an indexed sort-merge routine.
    ! It first sorts pieces using an indexed selection
    ! sort.  It then merges these pieces, iterating
    ! until there is only one piece left.

    LET piecesize = 20          ! Size to sort
    FOR i = first to last step piecesize
        LET j = min(i + piecesize - 1, last)
        CALL indsorts (list$, i, j, x)  ! Sort piece
    NEXT i

    DO while piecesize < last - first + 1 ! Need to merge
       FOR i = first to last step 2*piecesize
           LET j = min(i + piecesize - 1, last)
           LET k = min(j + piecesize, last)
           IF j < last then CALL indmrgs (list$, i, j, k, x)
       NEXT i
       LET piecesize = 2*piecesize
    LOOP

END SUB

SUB indsorts (list$(), first, last, x())

    ! Sorts a string list indexed by x(),
    ! from list$(x(first)) to list$(x(last)),
    ! using a stable indexed selection sort.

    FOR i = first to last - 1
        ! Find minimum in list$(x()), starting at position i.
        LET p = i                   ! Trial position for minimum
        LET newmin$ = list$(x(p)) ! Trial minimum
```

```
          FOR j = i+1 to last
              IF list$(x(j)) < newmin$ then
                 LET p = j         ! New position
                 LET newmin$ = list$(x(p)) ! and new minimum
              END IF
          NEXT j
          ! Move x(p) to x(i), move others down
          LET temp = x(p)
          FOR j = p to i+1 step -1
              LET x(j) = x(j-1)
          NEXT j
          LET x(i) = temp
      NEXT i

END SUB

SUB indmrgs (list$(), first1, last1, last2, x())

    ! Merges list$(x(first1)), ..., list$(x(last1))
    ! and list$(x(last1+1)), ..., list$(x(last2))
    ! into list$(x(first1)), ..., list$(x(last2))

    DIM xtemp(1000)              ! Need temporary work space
    LET p1 = first1              ! Pointer first segment
    LET p2 = last1 + 1           ! Pointer second segment
    LET ptemp = 0                ! Pointer in temp()

    DO while p1 <= last1 and p2 <= last2
       IF list$(x(p1)) <= list$(x(p2)) then
          CALL move(p1)          ! Move smallest from piece one
       ELSE
          CALL move(p2)          ! Move smallest from piece two
       END IF
    LOOP
    DO while p1 <= last1
       CALL move(p1)             ! Run out first piece
    LOOP
    DO while p2 <= last2
       CALL move(p2)             ! Run out second piece
    LOOP

    LET i = first1               ! Copy xtemp() back into x()
    FOR j = 1 to ptemp
        LET x(i) = xtemp(j)
        LET i = i+1
    NEXT j

    SUB move(ptr)                ! x(ptr) to next xtemp slot
        LET ptemp = ptemp + 1
        LET xtemp(ptemp) = x(ptr)
        LET ptr = ptr + 1
    END SUB

END SUB
```

The problem alluded to in the first paragraph of this section (in which companion string lists of data would have to be moved when one part, such as the name list, were sorted) can be circumvented if all the information were in a single string list. Each string might contain, for example, the name in positions 1 through 30, the address in positions 31 through 50, and so on. The sorting would then be done by comparing, not the entire string with another string, but a *substring* in each string. To sort by address, for example, compare

```
list$(p1)[31:50]
```

with

```
list$(p2)[31:50]
```

See Exercise 7.

14.8 AN INDEXING PROGRAM

We are all familiar with the index that appears at the end of most books. It consists of certain keywords, ordered alphabetically, along with the numbers of the pages on which they occur. In literary studies, all words, not just certain words, are included. And in addition to page numbers, the numbers of the lines in which the word appears may be given. An index, then, consists of a list of words, along with enough information to allow locating each word in the original text.

To construct an *index*, the words are gathered in the order they appear in the text, starting from page 1. But an *index* requires that they appear alphabetically. This necessitates a gigantic sort, which is a natural application for a computer. Indeed, computers have revolutionized the preparation of literary *indices* and *concordances* (similar to indices), an extremely time-consuming task when done manually.

We will illustrate the idea of indexing with a simple program that has a simple task, one that could just as easily have been done by hand. But the same principles apply to large indexing programs working on immense tasks.

The program `INDEX` examines a BASIC program that has line numbers, and constructs an index showing on which lines a given *word* appears. It operates by examining each line of the sample program, and extracting each *word* that appears on the line. It inserts that word, along with the corresponding line number, into parallel lists. This continues until the text file is exhausted, the signal for which is `alldone=1`. The subroutine `GetWord` takes care of the details of obtaining a word and its line number, along with handling the end of the file. After all words have been input, the word list is sorted using an indexed sort merge `Indsrmgs`. The index list `x()` must, of course, first be established.

Finally, the sorted list is printed. The printing is done so that each word appears only once and is followed by the line numbers of the lines in which it appears, arranged in a neat format. We use the `tab` function, in the next-to-last PRINT statement, to achieve this format. If column = 1, the printing cursor is moved to position 16, just as if there were a preset *tab* at that point. When column = 2, we move to position 22, and so on.

The subroutine GetWord looks suspiciously like the subroutine input, which was discussed and used in Section 12.3. However, there are several minor differences. First, the line number num$ is carried along as essential information. Second, there is no prompt message, because the next line comes from a file instead of from the user. Third, the subroutine nextwd1 differs from the subroutine nextword found in TEXTLIB in that nextwd1 uses a variety of special characters to denote the end of a word, whereas nextword uses only a space.

The subroutine GetLine is similar to the subroutine Get_Mast_Rec in the program UPDATE (see Section 13.5), except that when the file is exhausted, GetLine sets the signal flag alldone to 1. In addition, GetLine extracts the line number from in front of the line.

We again point out that we do not use the library TEXTLIB because the subroutines GetWord and nextword are slightly different in purpose. Here, GetWord discards all words having length 2 or less. Furthermore, Nextword uses any of the special characters to end a *word*, not just a blank space.

```
REM   INDEX
REM
REM   Constructs and prints an index
REM   of all words of at least three letters,
REM   truncating all trailing punctuation

LIBRARY "Sortslib"

DIM wordlist$(1000)                    ! Words
DIM linelist$(1000)                    ! Line numbers
DIM x(1000)                            ! Index list
DIM specchar$(20)                      ! Special character
list

CALL Setup

! Main routine

LET numwords = 0                       ! Wordlist subscript
DO
   CALL GetWord (word$, lineno$, alldone)
   IF alldone=1 then EXIT DO
   LET numwords = numwords + 1
   LET wordlist$(numwords) = word$
   LET linelist$(numwords) = lineno$
LOOP

FOR i = 1 to numwords                  ! Establish index list
    LET x(i) = i
NEXT i

CALL Indsrmgs (wordlist$, 1, numwords, x)
```

```
CALL PrintIndex

SUB Setup

    ! Set up special character list, and
    ! open the text file

    READ numspec                    ! Number of special characters
    MAT READ specchar$(numspec)
    DATA 15
    DATA " ", "(", ")", "+", "-", ",", ";", ".", "$", """"
    DATA "*", "[ ", " ]", ":", "/"

    LET infile = 1                  ! Number of input file
    DO
       WHEN exception in
            PRINT "File name";
            INPUT filename$
            OPEN #infile: name filename$
            EXIT DO                 ! If all is okay
       USE
            PRINT "File not available; try again."
       END WHEN
    LOOP

END SUB

SUB GetWord (word$, num$, done)

    ! Returns a word, containing at least three characters,
    ! and its line number.  If no more words, done = 1.

    LET done = 0
    DO
       IF len(line$) = 0 then CALL GetLine (line$, num$, done)

       IF done = 1 then EXIT DO

       LET line$ = ltrim$(line$)
       IF len(line$) > 0 then
          CALL Nextwd1 (word$, line$)
          IF len(word$) >= 3 then EXIT DO
       END IF
    LOOP
    LET word$ = lcase$(word$)

END SUB

SUB GetLine (line$, lineno$, alldone)

    ! Gets a new line from the file.
    ! Returns the line number, which is assumed to exist,
    ! and also the rest of the line.
    ! When the file is empty, alldone = 1.
```

```
        DO while len(line$) = 0 and alldone = 0
           IF more #infile then
              LINE INPUT #infile: line$
              CALL Nextwd1 (lineno$, line$)     ! Get line number
           ELSE
              LET alldone = 1
           END IF
        LOOP

    END SUB

    SUB Nextwd1 (word$, line$)

        ! Nextwd1 "parses" the first word in line$, which is the
        ! string up to but not including the earliest occurring
        ! special character, and puts it into word$.

        LET p1 = len(line$) + 1         ! First position after line
        FOR k = 1 to numspec
            LET p2 = pos(line$, specchar$(k))
            IF p2 > 0 then LET p1 = min(p1, p2)
        NEXT k
        LET word$ = line$[1:p1 - 1]
        LET line$ = line$[p1+1:len(line$)]

    END SUB

    SUB PrintIndex

        ! Prints the word list in the order determined by the
        ! index list x().  After each word, the corresponding
        ! line numbers are listed across the page.

        LET prevword$ = ""              ! To get started
        FOR i = 1 to numwords
            LET word$ = wordlist$(x(i))
            IF word$ <> prevword$ then
               PRINT                    ! If new word, start new line
               PRINT word$;             ! Print the word
               LET prevword$ = word$
               LET column = 0
            END IF
            LET column = column + 1     ! Move over one column
            IF column > 6 then
               PRINT                    ! If too far, reset to column 1
               LET column = 1
            END IF
            PRINT tab(10+6*column); linelist$(x(i));
        NEXT i
        PRINT

    END SUB

    END
```

The following run shows an index of the program **TIMERLN**, which is the program **TIMER** (see Section 14.5) with line numbers added. Included are all words of three characters or more. As it turns out, most of these words are either English words, or BASIC variables or keywords. The index also includes *words* that don't look like English words, such as large numbers (e.g., "1000").

```
100 REM   TIMER
110
120 LIBRARY "Sortnlib"
130
140 DIM x(1000)
150
160 DO
170     PRINT "Length of list";
180     INPUT n
190
200     IF n = 0 then EXIT DO
210
220     FOR i = 1 to n
230         LET x(i) = rnd
240     NEXT i
250
260     LET start = time
270     CALL selsortn (x, 1, n)
280     LET finish = time
290     PRINT "Time to sort"; finish - start
300     PRINT
310 LOOP
320
330 END

run

File name? timerln

1000            140
call            270
dim             140
end             330
exit            200
finish          280    290
for             220
input           180
length          170
let             230    260    280
library         120
list            170
loop            310
next            240
print           170    290    300
rem             100
rnd             230
selsortn        270
sort            290
sortnlib        120
start           260    290
then            200
time            260    280    290
timer           100
```

To produce an index of English text, one might want to modify `nextwdl` by changing the list of special characters and using a different method of determining the line number. (See Exercise 5.)

14.9 SUMMARY

We examined two searching algorithms. The simpler is called a *linear* search because the time needed for the search is roughly proportional to the length of the list. The more efficient method, the *binary* search, requires time roughly proportional to *log(n)*. For small lists, it matters little. But when *n* is large, the binary search is faster by a factor of *n/log(n)*, which can be quite large.

Similarly, sorting algorithms can be classified according to the time needed. The *selection sort* requires a time proportional to *n-squared*. The *merge sort* was shown by experiment to require a time proportional to $n \times log(n)$. When *n* is small, it matters little. But when *n* is large, the ratio $n^2/(n \times log(n)) = n/log(n)$ can be quite large.

Finally, we can avoid any movement of the data in the list to be sorted by using an *index*. Only the *pointers* in the index list are ever changed.

EXERCISES

1. Confirm the termination condition for the binary search (`last < first`) with simple examples. (Assume that the item is not in the list. Then consider lists of length one, and follow the values of `first` and `last` for all possibilities. Do the same for lists of length two. Because longer lists always lead eventually to lists of length one or two, this would constitute a proof.)
2. Carry out timing experiments, similar to those shown in the text for sorting, to compare linear and binary searching.
3. The selection sort can be speeded up slightly by simply interchanging `list(i)` and `list(p)` instead of moving the intervening elements downwards. (a) Make this change to `selsortn` and run the timing tests for both the original and modified versions. (b) The faster selection sort is *not* stable; that is, tied values do not necessarily retain their original order. Construct a simple numeric example to demonstrate this lack of stability. (Note: A stable sort is necessary for the database application in the next chapter, where we may wish to sort two or more times but do not want the later sorts to rearrange the earlier sorts.)
4. Carry out experiments to determine the optimum *piecesize* for the sorting phase of the sort-merge routine. To keep things simple, use numeric lists. You may want to add a parameter to the calling sequences of `srtmergn` and `mergen` to allow you to change the initial piece size easily.
5. Modify the program `INDEX` to work with general text files that have no line numbers. You will have to keep track of the line number in the program by means of a counter. Each time a new line is obtained, increment the counter by one. (Optional) Change the list and the variables that handle the line numbers to be of *numeric*, rather than *string*, type.

6. Set up a library `INDEXLIB` to do an index sort on strings. It should contain the following routines:

a. A protected file open subroutine.

b. The routine `indsorts`.

c. A routine that reads a file, one line at a time, into a string list.

d. A routine to initialize an index of n elements.

e. A routine to print a string list of n elements in the order given by an index.

Then, write a program that asks the user for a file, sorts it, and prints it. Use *all* the above routines. Your program should be very short! Generate a test file to sort by generating 25 random sequences of strings having length 30. A random lowercase letter can be generated by

```
LET a$ = chr$(int(26*rnd) + 97)
```

`26*rnd` generates a *random* number in the range (0,25). Adding 97 puts the number in the range (97,122), exactly the numbers of the lowercase letters in the ASCII scheme.

7. Modify `indsorts` to sort only on the substring from character number 12 through character number 20. Test the program on the random test file of Exercise 6.

8. Modify the routine `indsrmgs` and its two companion routines `indsorts` and `indmrgs` to make all comparisons on the substring in positions `c1` through `c2`, which must also be added to the parameter lists.

CHAPTER 15

A DATABASE SYSTEM

15.1 INTRODUCTION

In this chapter we will present a database system that is capable of handling large databases. Our main programming objective is to illustrate the organization and segmentation of a large program, and we will stress the use of previously written libraries of subroutines. We will also illustrate a user interface that can accommodate both the novice and the expert user.

BASIC's **SELECT CASE** structure is also introduced.

15.2 ORGANIZATION OF THE DATA

Consider a large database, such as information on the faculty of a college or all the art objects in a museum. We say that the *database* consists of a set of *entities* and their associated *attributes*. For a college faculty the entities are the members of the faculty, and their attributes are *name*, *rank*, *department*, *date of birth*, and so forth. For the museum example the entities are the objects of art, and the attributes might include *type* (e.g. painting), *country of origin*, *location*, and *purchase price*.

When each entity has one attribute value for each attribute category, the database is said to be *rectangular*. Sometimes, the term *flat file* is used. With a faculty database, for example, each faculty member (i.e., each entity) has one *lastname*, one *rank*, and so forth.

Database information is stored in an *external* memory device. For a microcomputer, this will be a floppy disk or a hard disk. There is a fundamental choice as to whether the data is stored by entities (in *records*) or by attributes. Because there are usually many attributes, but only a few are needed for a given run, we elect to store by attributes, making it easy to bring only the portion of the information needed into main memory. Thus, our basic storage unit is a file that contains all the values of a given attribute; for example, the location of each art object or the rank of a faculty member.

To be able to find the data files we need a database *directory*, which will also contain other needed information. It is stored in a file whose name is the name of the database. Thus the directory is easy to find, and it tells us where to find all other information.

For our system, the first line of a directory is a one-line title, which is useful in reassuring the user that the right information is being retrieved. Then the directory contains one line for each attribute, each line containing four pieces of information:

1. The name of the attribute.
2. Its type ("str" for string or "num" for numeric attributes).
3. Its width (field width for printing).
4. The name of the file containing the data for that attribute.

We will illustrate the system with a small database containing information about a class of 16 students. We show the directory (`CLASS`) and the eight files containing the data on eight attributes:

The directory file CLASS and the eight data files.

```
Data on a small class
lastname,  str, 12, DATA1
firstname, str, 10, DATA2
class,     num,  5, DATA3
hw,        num,  2, DATA4
ex1,       num,  3, DATA5
ex2,       num,  3, DATA6
final,     num,  5, DATA7
sex,       str,  3, DATA8

DATA1          DATA2          DATA3
Adams          John            84
Baker          Mary            86
Cook           William         85
Einstein       Albert          85
Gross          Samuel          87
Harvey         Ann             84
King           Susan           87
Longhorn       Barbara         86
Martin         Lu              86
Norton         John            85
Osborne        Paul            85
Price          Jean            85
Rice           Peter           86
Smith          John            87
Smith          Mary            84
Taylor         Robert          84
```

```
DATA4 DATA5   DATA6   DATA7  DATA8
  35    39      40      75      M
  42    45      55      83      F
  37    31      47      89      M
  50    50      60     100      M
  46    29      28      55      M
  32    37      51      67      F
  41    37      33      78      F
  39    32      25      43      F
  47    45      56      92      F
  29    29      38      87      M
  38    21      47      69      M
  40    44      55      75      F
  38    36      31      91      M
  45    48      44      83      M
  31    29      47      79      F
  41    50      51      62      M
```

We see, for example, that the attribute *lastname* is a string attribute, that we allow 12 characters to print it, and that it is in the file **DATA1**. And, *final* (final exam grade) is numeric, we allow five characters (needed to be able to print the header "final"), and it is stored in **DATA7**.

15.3 ORGANIZATION OF THE PROGRAM

Our database system is called **FIND**. After naming the libraries of subroutines (discussed in Section 15.11), **FIND** dimensions a series of arrays to hold the database information. The assumptions reflected in the **DIM** statements are that there may be up to 200 entities, up to 30 attributes, but no more than 10 of the attributes can be used at one time. The first four arrays contain the directory information on all the attributes of the database. Thus, we need to read the directory only once.

The data retrieved will be stored in an array `data$`, with one column for each attribute retrieved. The rows correspond to entities. To be able to store all data in one two-dimensional array, we must retrieve all the data as strings. (For some uses we must later convert data that represents numbers to numeric form.) The array `col` keeps track of the column of `data$` in which an attribute is stored.

The remaining arrays are for the internal use of **FIND**. One array, **index**, deserves special mention. Any good database system allows the user to select entities having a special property (e.g. faculty members in a given department) and to sort on any attribute. We establish the list **index** for use by an index sorting routine (see Chapter 14.) We use the same list to make selections.

```
REM  FIND

REM  A Database System

LIBRARY "DBLIB.trc", "TEXTLIB.trc", "STATLIB.trc", "SORTSLIB.trc"
DECLARE DEF compare            ! In DBLIB
```

```
!  Directory information

DIM att$(30)                ! Attribute names
DIM type$(30)               ! "str" or "num"
DIM wide(30)                ! Width in characters
DIM file$(30)               ! Files containing attribute data
```

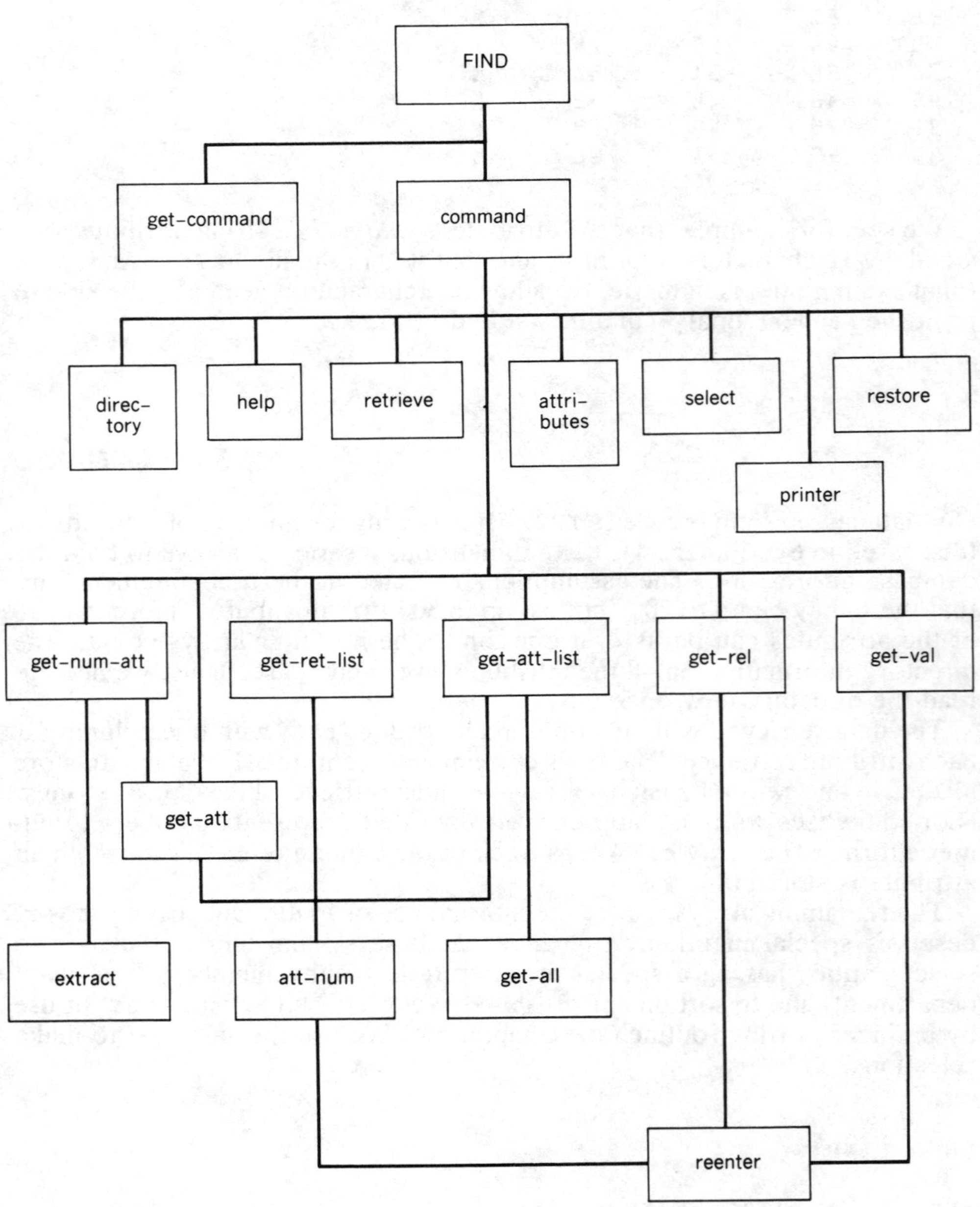

FIGURE 15.1
Structure chart for FIND.

```
!  Working storage

DIM data$(200,10)        ! Retrieved data
DIM index(200)           ! Index for sorting and selection
DIM col(30)              ! Column of data$(,) having attr.
                         ! col = 0 if not retrieved
DIM field(10)            ! Printing fields (starting column)
DIM attlist(10)          ! List of attributes asked for
DIM temp(200)            ! For numerical data

DIM rel$(7)              ! List of relations
MAT READ rel$
DATA =, <, >, <=, >=, <>, :
```

The structure chart of the program `FIND`, shown in Figure 15.1, includes most of the internal routines. It excludes several low-level utility routines, such as the subroutine `error`, which are used by many of the other routines.

15.4 THE MAIN ROUTINE

The program `FIND` is *command driven*. That is, it waits until the user types a command and then executes it. Then it is ready for another command. To protect the user, it also checks for a variety of errors.

We want the program to accommodate users from novices to experts. The novice should be allowed to type only one item at a time and be prompted as to what is required next. But the experienced user would become annoyed waiting for the prompts. We therefore allow such users to type an entire command line. In Chapter 12 we constructed a subroutine `input` that accomodates both kinds of users, and we use `input` here. But we will go one step further and allow typing several commands at once. This is the task of the routine `get_command`.

FIND (continued).

```
LET comline$ = "base"                 ! Force base command
CLEAR

DO                                    ! Main routine

   ! Comline$ is entire input, may contain multiple commands.
   ! Line$ contains a single command, possibly with arguments.

   CALL get_command (comline$, line$)  ! Handle multiple commands
   CALL nextword (com$, line$)         ! Current command

   WHEN EXCEPTION IN                   ! For error recovery
        CALL command (com$[1:3])       ! Carry out command
```

```
   USE                              ! Error comes here
        PRINT extext$               ! Error message
        IF extype=100 then          ! Illegal directory
           LET comline$ = "base" ! Must try again
        ELSE
           LET comline$ = ""        ! The rest now useless
        END IF
   END WHEN

LOOP

SUB get_command (comline$, line$)  ! Get command line


    IF comline$="" then            ! Need new input
       PRINT
       LINE INPUT prompt "Command? ": comline$ ! New command line
    END IF

    LET p = pos(comline$, " # ") ! Check for multiple command
    IF p=0 then LET p = len(comline$) + 1
    LET line$ = comline$[1:p-1] ! First command
    LET line$ = lcase$(line$)     ! Everything in lowercase
    LET comline$ = ltrim$(comline$[p+3:len(comline$)]) ! Save rest

END SUB
```

Multiple commands are separated by a number sign (#), which must have spaces around it. The subroutine `get_command` checks whether a previously typed command still needs to be executed. If not, it asks for a new command line, which then goes into `comline$`. It then splits off one command into `line$` and keeps the rest (if any) in `comline$`. Thus, `line$` contains only a single command, possibly with arguments.

The variable `comline$` is initialized to "base", forcing the user to open a database. The main loop calls `get_command` and then looks at the first word of `line$`, which is the command. Next it calls the routine `command` to execute the command, and then loops.

Two features of this loop should be noted. First, only the first three letters of the command are passed on, to allow either typing the full command or just an abbreviation of three or more letters. Thus, in place of the command "attributes", the user may type "attrib" or "att".

Second, the execution of commands is protected by a **WHEN USE** structure (see Section 12.3). If any error occurs while a command is being carried out, the program returns to the main loop. In addition, situations can arise in many subroutines that we wish to treat as a serious error and return control to the main loop. When that happens, the subroutine merely calls the routine `error`, which causes an exception that bounces control back to the main loop. When the **WHEN USE** structure detects an exception, it prints an error message (which is contained in the string `extype$`), and discards `comline$` so that the user may start afresh. However, if the error occurs when the program is opening a database (exception type 100), then the user is forced to try again.

This use of the **WHEN USE** structure allows the top level of the program to handle all errors and provides a simple method for *aborting* commands.

15.5 THE COMMAND ROUTINE

When the subroutine `command` is called in the main loop, it is passed a lowercase, three-letter abbreviation of the command. To choose which of the many possible commands to carry out, we introduce the **SELECT CASE** structure, an alternative to a long **IF THEN** structure with many **ELSEIF** lines. In the **SELECT CASE** statement we specify the variable on whose value the selection is to be made; in our routine this is `c$`. Each **CASE** statement specifies one or more possible values of this variable. The program will execute only one case; if none fits, the computer executes the **CASE ELSE** case. This powerful structure makes this routine easy to read.

FIND (continued).

```
SUB command (c$)                          ! Carry out command

    SELECT CASE c$
    CASE "bas"                            ! New database
         CALL input ("Name of database",f$,line$)
         CALL directory
         PRINT title$

    CASE "att"                            ! List of attributes
         CALL attributes

    CASE "ret"                            ! Retrieve
         CALL get_ret_list (attlist, al_max)
         FOR i = 1 to al_max
             CALL retrieve (attlist(i))
         NEXT i
         CALL restore

    CASE "sel"                            ! Select
         CALL get_att (anum, cnum)
         CALL get_rel (r)
         CALL get_val (type$(anum), v$)
         CALL select (cnum, r, v$, type$(anum))

    CASE "sor"                            ! Sort
         CALL get_att (anum, cnum)
         ! Use "<", relation 2
         CALL indsort (data$, cnum, index, i_max, type$(anum), 2)

    CASE "rso"                            ! Reverse sort
         CALL get_att (anum, cnum)
         ! Use ">", relation 3
         CALL indsort (data$, cnum, index, i_max, type$(anum), 3)

    CASE "pri"                            ! Print
         CALL get_att_list (attlist, al_max)
         CALL printer (attlist, al_max)
```

```
        CASE "sta"                          ! Statistics
             CALL get_num_att (temp)
             CALL statprint (temp)

        CASE "res"                          ! Restore index
             CALL restore

        CASE "hel"                          ! Help
             CALL help

        CASE "exi", "sto"                   ! Exit or stop
             STOP

        CASE ELSE                           ! Unknown
             PRINT "Illegal command: "; com$
             CALL error ("Type 'help'.")

        END SELECT
        IF line$<>"" then CALL error ("Extra material in command")

   END SUB
```

For the typical case we ask the user for some additional information and then call the appropriate subroutine to carry out the command. Every request by the program for information uses the subroutine `input`, so that if the user has already supplied all the necessary information, no more prompts are issued.

If the user types "exit" or "stop", the run is terminated. If an illegal command is typed, the program suggests that user type "help", which results in simple instructions. This is much kinder than printing a lengthy message every time there is an illegal command. Additionally, an experienced user who mistyped one word will be annoyed by an unnecessary lengthy message.

We shall now consider the various commands.

15.6 RETRIEVING DATA

The first command is always "base". It calls `directory`, which attempts to read the directory. This reading is protected by a **WHEN USE** structure, in case the user furnishes an illegal name or the name of a file that is not a directory. In case of failure, `error` is called.

The command "retrieve" reads from the data files those attributes specified by the user. It asks for a list of attributes to retrieve, reads the files one at a time, and places the values into columns of `data$`. From the first attribute it finds out how many entities there are and checks that all subsequently retrieved attributes have the same number of entities.

The "attribute" command furnishes a list of attributes in the database. If any have been retrieved, a list of them is also printed.

"Restore" sets up the index list `index` to refer to all the entities in their original order. (See Chapter 14.)

FIND (continued).

```
!  Command routines

SUB directory                         ! Get directory

    CLOSE #1
    WHEN exception in                 ! Check directory
         OPEN #1: name f$
         LINE INPUT #1: title$
         LET a = 0                    ! Attribute number
         DO while more #1
            LET a = a+1
            INPUT #1: att$(a), type$(a), wide(a), file$(a)
         LOOP
    USE
         CALL error ("Not a legal directory.")
    END WHEN

    LET a_max = a                     ! Total number of attributes
    MAT col = zer(10)                 ! Nothing retrieved yet
    LET c_max = 0                     ! Columns of data$ used
    LET i_max = 0                     ! Entries in index
    LET ents = 0                      ! Total entities

END SUB

SUB help                              ! List of commands

    PRINT
    PRINT "The commands are:"
    PRINT
    PRINT "Base, Attributes, Retrieve, Select, Restore"
    PRINT "Sort, Rsort, Print, Stats, Exit"
    PRINT
    PRINT "Commands may be abbreviated to 3 letters."
    PRINT "Items on command line are separated by spaces."
    PRINT "Multiple commands are separated by ' # ' ."
    PRINT "Attributes must be retrieved before they are used."
    PRINT

END SUB

SUB attributes                        ! Print list of attributes

    PRINT
    PRINT "List of attributes:"
    FOR a = 1 to a_max
       PRINT att$(a); "   ";
    NEXT a
    PRINT
    IF c_max = 0 then EXIT SUB ! None retrieved

    PRINT
    PRINT "Retrieved:"
    FOR a = 1 to a_max
```

```
      PRINT
      PRINT "Retrieved:"
      FOR a = 1 to a_max
          IF col(a)>0 then PRINT att$(a); "    ";
      NEXT a
      PRINT
      PRINT

END SUB

SUB retrieve (anum)              ! Bring in data on attribute a

      LET cnum = c_max + 1        ! Column to use
      CALL read (file$(anum), data$, cnum, n)
      IF ents = 0 then LET ents = n         ! Take ents from first

      IF n = ents then            ! Right number
         LET c_max = cnum
         LET col(anum) = cnum
      ELSE
         CALL error ("Wrong number of entities: " & att$(anum))
      END IF

END SUB

SUB restore                       ! Reinitialize index

      FOR i = 1 to ents
          LET index(i) = i
      NEXT i
      LET i_max = ents
      PRINT ents; "entities"

END SUB
```

15.7 MANIPULATING DATA

The next set of routines carries out the actual data manipulations. The user may sort on any attribute, either in increasing order (''sort'') or decreasing order (''rsort''). Each calls the same subroutine but uses a different relation for comparison. The user may also select a subset of the entities, using the seven available relations. Six of these are the usual relations in BASIC. Thus, one may select entities for which ''dept = Math'' or ''salary >= 30000''. The seventh relation checks for the occurrence of a substring. For example, ''firstname : ann'' will find all people whose first name is Ann, Anne, Anna, Hannah, etc.

The key to sorting and selection is that we do not change the large amount of information in the array `data$`; we manipulate only the index. For selection, we examine each value of the designated attribute to see whether it satisfies the specified condition. Only those entities that meet the condition are retained in `index`. Because all uses of `data$` are through `index`, we look only at selected entities, in the order of the most recent sort.

After selecting and sorting, the user would normally print the result. `Printer` asks for a list of attributes ("all" means that all attributes should be printed). It then prints the attributes for the selected entities in the order specified by the user. (The previous sorts determine the order of the entities.)

FIND (continued).

```
SUB printer (attlist(), al_max) ! Print selected entities

    LET where = 1                  ! Set up field widths
    FOR a = 1 to al_max
        LET anum = attlist(a)
        LET field(a) = where
        LET where = where + wide(anum) + 2 ! Tab position
    NEXT a

    PRINT                          ! Print header
    FOR a = 1 to al_max
        LET anum = attlist(a)
        PRINT tab(field(a)); att$(anum);
    NEXT a
    PRINT

    PRINT                          ! Print values
    FOR i = 1 to i_max
        FOR a = 1 to al_max
            LET anum = attlist(a)
            PRINT tab(field(a)); data$(index(i),col(anum));
        NEXT a
        PRINT
    NEXT i
    PRINT

END SUB

SUB select (cnum, r, v$, t$)   ! Select entities

    LET j = 0                      ! Insertion pointer
    FOR i = 1 to i_max
        LET s$ = lcase$(data$(index(i),cnum))
        IF compare(s$,v$,t$,r) = 1 then ! Relation holds
           LET j = j+1
           LET index(j) = index(i)
        END IF
    NEXT i
    IF j=0 then CALL error ("None selected")
    PRINT j; "selected"
    LET i_max = j

END SUB
```

The program uses the library `STATLIB` to provide statistics on a numerical attribute. A call to `get_num_att` converts the values of the attribute to numbers and places into the list `temp`. Then the `statprint` routine in `STATLIB` is called.

It is important to remember that when we print or compute statistics, the commands apply only to the selected entities. Thus, if one has made a selection and wants the next command to apply to the entire data base, a "restore" command is needed.

15.8 UTILITY ROUTINES

The next portion of FIND contains the utility routines. They have a similar design so we shall explain only one of them. The routine get_rel asks the user for a relation (for "select"). After the relation is inputted, it is checked to see whether it is one of the seven legal relations. If it is, rel becomes the number of the relation. If not, the routine reenter is called. This allows the user to try again, or to cancel the command. The routine loops until the user either specifies a legal relation or cancels.

It is important to allow the "cancel" option in each such routine because the user is allowed to type multiple inputs on a line and may have gotten out of step with the program. If cancellation is requested, error is called. The result is an appropriate message and a return to the main routine.

Inputs are always requested by calling the input routine developed in Chapter 12, so that the user has the option either of being prompted for each input or of anticipating the program by typing several items on a line.

FIND (continued).

```
!  Utility routines

SUB get_att (anum, cnum)           ! Ask for an attribute

    CALL input ("Attribute", a$, line$)
    CALL att_num (a$, anum, cnum)
    IF cnum=0 then CALL error ("Have not retrieved: " & att$(anum))

END SUB

SUB get_rel (rel)                  ! Ask for a relation

    CALL input ("Relation", r$, line$)
    DO
       CALL linsrchs (rel$, 1, 7, r$, rel)
       IF rel<0 then
          PRINT "Do not recognize: "; r$
          CALL reenter ("relation", r$)
       END IF
    LOOP until rel>0

END SUB

SUB get_val (t$, v$)             ! Ask for type t$ comparison value
```

```
    CALL input ("Value", v$, line$)
    IF t$="num" then                    ! Must be number
       DO
          CALL convert (v$, v, isnum)
          IF not isnum=1 then
             PRINT "Must be a number."
             CALL reenter ("value", v$)
          END IF
       LOOP until isnum=1
    END IF

END SUB

SUB get_num_att (temp())               ! Numeric attribute, values to temp

    CALL get_att (anum, cnum)
    IF type$(anum) <> "num" then
       CALL error ("Not a numeric attribute: " & att$(anum))
    END IF
    CALL extract (cnum, temp)

END SUB
```

Next there are two routines that obtain lists of attributes and place the attribute numbers in `attlist`. They differ in that `get_att_list`, which is used by `printer`, must check that all the attributes have been previously retrieved. It must also allow the command ''print all'', which calls the routine `get_all`.

FIND (continued).

```
SUB get_ret_list (attlist(), n)    ! Get attributes to retrieve

    CALL input ("Attributes to retrieve", a$, line$)

    LET n = 0
    DO
       CALL att_num (a$, anum, cnum)
       LET n = n + 1
       LET attlist(n) = anum
       CALL nextword (a$, line$)
       LET a$ = lcase$(a$)
    LOOP until a$=""

END SUB

SUB get_att_list (attlist(), n)    ! Get list of retrieved attributes

    CALL input ("List of attributes", a$, line$)

    IF a$ = "all" then
       CALL get_all (attlist,n)
```

```
        ELSE
           LET n = 0
           DO
              CALL att_num (a$, anum, cnum)
              IF cnum=0 then
                 CALL error ("Have not retrieved " & att$(anum))
              END IF
              LET n = n + 1
              LET attlist(n) = anum
              CALL nextword (a$, line$)
              LET a$ = lcase$(a$)
           LOOP until a$=""
        END IF

END SUB

SUB get_all (attlist(), n)        ! All retrieved attributes

    LET n = 0
    FOR a = 1 to a_max            ! Look at all attributes
        IF col(a) > 0 then        ! Has been retrieved
           LET n = n + 1
           LET attlist(n) = a
        END IF
    NEXT a

END SUB
```

15.9 LOW-LEVEL ROUTINES

Four short routines are at the bottom of the pyramid. The routine `att_num` is used every time the user supplies the name of an attribute. It searches the list of attribute names to see whether such an attribute exists, and calls `reenter` if it does not. The parameter `anum` returns the number of the attribute, while `cnum` returns the column of `data$` in which that attribute's values are stored. In particular, if the attribute has not yet been retrieved, then `cnum = 0`.

`Extract` is used to convert the values of a numeric attribute to numbers, and to place them in the array `temp`. `Reenter` is called whenever an illegal item is typed. The user may try again or cancel.

Finally there is the routine `error`, which causes an exception, and sends the program back to the main routine. It generates the error message specified by the calling routine. It sets the error number to 100 or 200, for the sole purpose of recognizing an error in opening a database.

FIND (continued)

```
SUB att_num (a$, anum, cnum)

    ! Is a$ the name of an attribute?
    ! If so, anum is its number, cnum its column.
    ! Else ask to reenter.
```

```
    DO
       CALL linsrchs (att$, 1, ubound(att$), a$, anum)
       IF anum < 0 then
          PRINT "Do not recognize: "; a$
          CALL reenter ("attribute", a$)
       END IF
    LOOP until anum > 0          ! Found
    LET cnum = col(anum)

END SUB

SUB extract (cnum, temp())       ! Column cnum of data$ into temp

    MAT temp = zer(i_max)        ! Correct dimension
    FOR i = 1 to i_max           ! Selected entities only
        LET temp(i) = val(data$(index(i),cnum))
    NEXT i

END SUB

SUB reenter (what$, x$)              ! Try again

    PRINT "Reenter "; what$; " or cancel";
    INPUT x$
    LET x$ = lcase$(x$)
    IF x$ = "cancel" then CALL error ("Cancelled")

END SUB

SUB error (err$)                 ! Print message, return to Command

    ! 100 is the special number for an illegal directory
    IF pos(err$,"directory")>0 then LET e = 100 else LET e = 200
    CAUSE EXCEPTION e, err$

END SUB

END
```

15.10 SAMPLE SESSIONS

We illustrate the use of **FIND** by showing two runs. The first might be a typical run by a user not familiar with **FIND**. The second is a run by a user familiar with both **FIND** and the database **CLASS**.

```
run

Name of database? class
Data on a small class

Command? show
Illegal command: show
Type 'help'.
```

```
Command? help

The commands are:

Base, Attributes, Retrieve, Select, Restore
Sort, Rsort, Print, Stats, Exit

Commands may be abbreviated to 3 letters.
Items on command line are separated by spaces.
Multiple commands are separated by ' # ' .
Attributes must be retrieved before they are used.


Command? attributes

List of attributes:
lastname  firstname  class  hw  ex1  ex2  final  sex

Command? retrieve
Attributes to retrieve? lastname sex final
 16 entities

Command? select
Attribute? sex
Relation? +
Do not recognize: +
Reenter relation or cancel? =
Value? F
 7 selected

Command? rsort
Attribute? final

Command? print
List of attributes? lastname final

lastname      final

Martin        92
Baker         83
Smith         79
King          78
Price         75
Harvey        67
Longhorn      43


Command? Stop


run

Name of database? class
Data on a small class

Command? ret lastname sex final # sel sex = F # rso final # pri lastname final
 16 entities
 7 selected
```

```
lastname         final

Martin           92
Baker            83
Smith            79
King             78
Price            75
Harvey           67
Longhorn         43


Command? res # stat final # stat ex1
 16 entities

Range: 43 to 100
Median: 78.5
Mean: 76.8
Variance: 206.7
Std. dev.: 14.4

Have not retrieved: ex1

Command? ret ex1 # sor name # pri all
 16 entities
Do not recognize: name
Reenter attribute or cancel? lastname

lastname       ex1   final   sex

Adams          39    75      M
Baker          45    83      F
Cook           31    89      M
Einstein       50    100     M
Gross          29    55      M
Harvey         37    67      F
King           37    78      F
Longhorn       32    43      F
Martin         45    92      F
Norton         29    87      M
Osborne        21    69      M
Price          44    75      F
Rice           36    91      M
Smith          48    83      M
Smith          29    79      F
Taylor         50    62      M


Command? exit
```

15.11 THE LIBRARIES

FIND depends on subroutines from four libraries: **DBLIB**, **TEXTLIB**, **SORTSLIB**, and **STATLIB** (**STATLIB** depends on a routine from **SORTNLIB**). In this section we will discuss **DBLIB** at length.

The library **DBLIB** contains four routines. The subroutine `convert` changes a string to a number. It uses `val`, but is protected by a **WHEN USE** structure (see Section 12.3). Thus we can safely test whether `num$` represents a number.

The routine `read` reads a datafile into the specified column of `data$`. It also reports the number of entries found.

The subroutine `indsort` carries out an index sort. It sorts a column of `data$` in either increasing or decreasing order. However, instead of shuffling the entries of `data$` (which would require changing all the columns) only `index` is changed. It is similar to the routines developed in Chapter 14, but it handles both string and numeric data.

Finally, the defined function `compare` is used for all comparisons. It compares two strings, of specified type, according to the stated relation. If the relation is ":", substring containment, the comparison is made through the `pos` function. However, for ordinary relations, such as "<", a different routine is needed for string and numeric attributes. Unless numeric attributes are changed to numbers, incorrect comparisons occur. For example, in `DATA7`, the string "100" would be the *smallest* if a string comparison were made; as a number, it is the largest entry.

```
EXTERNAL

!  DBLIB
!
!     Convert         Converts a string to a number
!     Reads           Reads an attribute data file
!     Indsort         Special index sort
!     Compare         Special compare function

SUB Convert (num$, num, ok)

    ! Converts num$ to num using "val"
    ! If not a number, ok = 0

    LET ok = 1
    WHEN exception in
         LET num = val(num$)
    USE
         LET ok = 0
    END WHEN

END SUB

SUB Read (file$, data$(,), c, howmany)

    ! Read data from file$ into col c of data$(,)
    ! howmany = number of items read

    OPEN #1: name file$
    LET i = 0

    DO while more #1
       LET i = i+1
       LINE INPUT #1: data$(i,c)
    LOOP
    LET howmany = i                       ! Number of items found
    CLOSE #1

END SUB
```

```
SUB Indsort (data$(,), c, ind(), n, t$, rel)

    ! Index sort column c of data$
    ! Using index ind() with n elements
    ! t$ = "str" or "num",  rel  as in compare
    ! rel specifies one of seven relations

    DECLARE FUNCTION compare

    FOR k = 1 to n-1             ! Selection sort with index
        LET p = k
        LET small$ = lcase$(data$(ind(p),c))
        FOR i = k+1 to n
            LET d$ = lcase$(data$(ind(i),c))
            IF compare(d$, small$, t$, rel) = 1 then
               LET p = i
               LET small$ = d$
            END IF
        NEXT i
        LET temp = ind(p)
        LET ind(p) = ind(k)
        LET ind(k) = temp
    NEXT k

END SUB

DEF Compare(s$, t$, type$, rel)

    ! Compare s$ and t$
    ! type$ = "str" or "num"
    ! rel = relation number
    ! If type$ = "num", assumes that s$ and t$ are numbers
    ! compare = 1 if relation holds; else 0

    LET compare = 0
    IF rel = 7 then               ! Containment; do as string
       IF pos(s$,t$) > 0 then LET compare = 1
    ELSEIF type$ = "str" then ! String comparison
       SELECT CASE rel
       CASE 1
            IF s$ = t$ then LET compare = 1
       CASE 2
            IF s$ < t$ then LET compare = 1
       CASE 3
            IF s$ > t$ then LET compare = 1
       CASE 4
            IF s$ <= t$ then LET compare = 1
       CASE 5
            IF s$ >= t$ then LET compare = 1
       CASE 6
            IF s$ <> t$ then LET compare = 1
       END SELECT
    ELSE                          ! Numeric comparison
       LET s = val(s$)
       LET t = val(t$)
```

```
        SELECT CASE rel
        CASE 1
             IF s = t then LET compare = 1
        CASE 2
             IF s < t then LET compare = 1
        CASE 3
             IF s > t then LET compare = 1
        CASE 4
             IF s <= t then LET compare = 1
        CASE 5
             IF s >= t then LET compare = 1
        CASE 6
             IF s <> t then LET compare = 1
        END SELECT
     END IF

END DEF
```

The library **TEXTLIB** contains **input** and **nextword**, and was discussed in Chapter 12. **SORTSLIB** and **SORTNLIB** were discussed in Chapter 14. **STATLIB**, which we will not discuss, contains routines for computing and printing statistical quantities.

EXERCISES

1. Add a command "sum" to **FIND**. It should create a new numeric attribute that equals the sum of two existing attributes.
2. Expand the "sum" command (see Exercise 1) to form a linear combination of several previous numeric attributes.
3. Add an "explain" command to **FIND** that furnishes a brief explanation of a command specified by the user.
4. Add a "hist" command to **FIND** to plot a histogram of a numerical attribute.
5. Set up your own database on the topic of your choice. Create a directory and files for the attributes. Use **FIND** on your database.

PROJECTS

1. Write a program package that allows a user to create a new database.
2. Write a program package that allows the user to make the following changes in a database:
   a. Change the value of an attribute for a given entity.
   b. Delete an entire attribute.
   c. Add an attribute and write the values into a previously saved file.

   Notes: For projects a and c, the computer must prompt the user as to which entity's values are being input. The user should be allowed to specify this attribute (e.g., for `CLASS` the natural prompt would be "lastname").

If the directory is changed, it must be written out before the end of the session.

If an attribute is changed or added, its values must also be written out.

PART THREE

MATHEMATICAL APPLICATIONS

CHAPTER 16

ELEMENTARY MATHEMATICS

16.1 INTRODUCTION

We have chosen four topics from elementary mathematics to illustrate a variety of programming techniques. Each is entirely independent of the others, and any of the applications may be taken up after Part I has been mastered.

First, we will consider solving triangles, and provide a simple program for finding the missing side(s) of a triangle. It illustrates the usefulness of defined functions to help organize a program. Additionally, it makes use of the `SELECT CASE` structure.

Next, we will consider finding roots of an equation. Our program will provide numerical solution of equations that cannot be solved without a computer. The program employs the bisection method to close in on a root rapidly.

In our third application we will find prime numbers and factor integers into prime factors. A small library will be built that may be used for a variety of number theory applications.

The fourth topic is the use of matrix methods. BASIC has very powerful instructions for matrix manipulation. These will be applied first to the solution of simultaneous equations and then to the famous Leontief input - output model of the economy.

16.2 TRIGONOMETRY

Many problems in elementary mathematics lend themselves to simple computer solutions. An almost perfect example is the *solution of triangles*.

The program `TRIG` solves the three classical cases in which, from three pieces of information about a triangle, we must find an unknown side (or two sides). The standard names for these cases are as follows:

SAS given two sides and the included angle
ASA given two angles and the included side
SSA given two sides and a non-included angle

The labeling of sides and angles is shown in Figure 16.1.

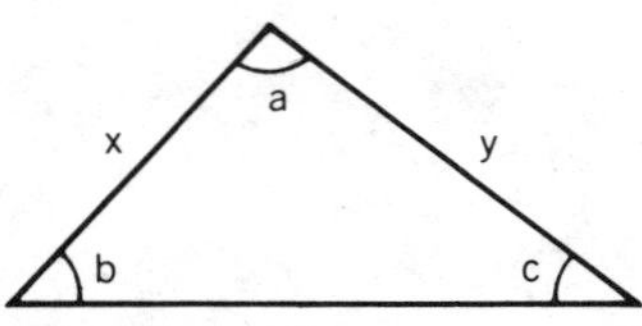

FIGURE 16.1
Labeling of the sides and angles of a triangle.

At the high school level, trigonometry is usually done in degrees. Although BASIC normally works in radians, the declaration

```
OPTION ANGLE degrees
```

changes all the trigonometric functions to ones that use degrees. Next the program introduces three functions that help us organize the program.

The Law of Sines states (see Figure 16.1):

$$z/\sin(a) = x/\sin(c)$$

or

$$z = \sin(a) * x/\sin(c)$$

Thus, we can compute a side from the angle opposite the side (a) and another side together with the angle opposite it (x and c). This is the essence of the defined function `lawsin`.

The Law of Cosines allows us to calculate a side from knowledge of the other two sides and the angle opposite the unknown side. This is incorporated into `lawcos`.

We will also need an *arcsin* function, which is not part of the language. But it can be defined in terms of `atn` (the arctangent). This leads to the defined function `asin`.

The main part of the program is a `DO` loop structure, which allows the user to try many cases. The program prompts the user for a case and `SELECT CASE` chooses the appropriate routine. Note that `ucase$` is applied to the input so that the selection will work whether the user typed the input in uppercase, lowercase, or some mixture of the two. (`SELECT CASE` is a more sophisticated version of the `IF` structure. See the discussion in Section 15.5.) One of the cases is "STOP". It allows the user to signal the end of the session. Each of the other cases requires the user to input three numbers. The subroutine `input3` allows us to organize our prompts and inputs very simply. Let us now consider the three cases.

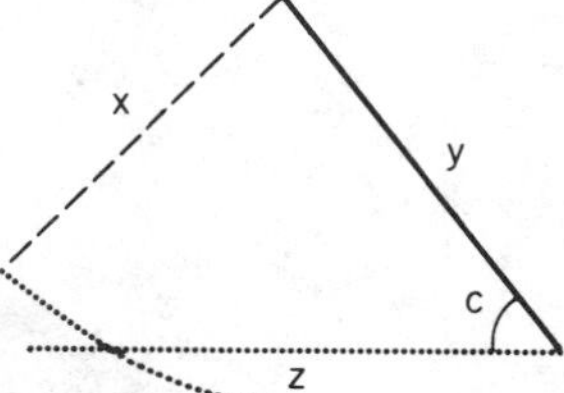

FIGURE 16.2
The ambiguous SSA triangle.

The case "SAS" asks for the sides **x** and **y**, and the included angle **a**. This is a straightforward application of the Law of Cosines.

The case "ASA" requires us to find the third angle **c**, the angle opposite **x**. We find this by knowing that the sum of the angles is 180 degrees. Then each of the missing sides is found from the Law of Sines.

The most interesting case is "SSA", in which there may be one solution, two solutions, or none. Given **x**, **y**, and **c**, Figure 16.2 illustrates the solution. We mark the side **y** (fixing two corners) and know the direction of the side **z**. Then from the top corner we draw a circle of radius **x**. If this does not cut the side **z**, there is no solution. If it is tangent to the line we have a unique solution. And, if there are two intersections we may have two solutions, but one might be on "the wrong side"—which will occur if **x** is longer than **y**.

We first find **sinb**, the sine of the angle opposite **y**. Because it is crucial whether this is equal to or greater or less than 1, we round it to eight places to guard against round-off errors. (The function **round** is a built-in function that rounds a number to a specified number of places.) If **sinb** > **1**, which is impossible, **x** was too short to reach the third side. If **sinb** = **1** then we have tangency and a unique right triangle solution. In the most interesting case we find the angle **b** using **asin** and angle **a** from the fact that the sum is 180 degrees. However, we must test both **b** and **180-b** because they have the same sine. And in each case we must test whether the angle **a** turned out to be positive.

```
REM  TRIG
REM
REM  Find missing side(s) of triangle
REM  Handles three cases

OPTION ANGLE degrees

!  Functions to find side by law of sines, cosines

DEF lawsin(oppang,x,oppx) = sin(oppang) * x/sin(oppx)
DEF lawcos(x,y,oppang) = sqr(x^2 + y^2 - 2*x*y*cos(oppang))
DEF asin(a) = atn(a/sqr(1-a^2))    ! Arcsin

DO
   PRINT "Case";
   INPUT c$

   SELECT CASE ucase$(c$)

   CASE "SAS"
        CALL input3 ("Side ", x, "Angle", a, "Side ", y)
        PRINT "Third side = "; lawcos(x,y,a)
```

```
CASE "ASA"
     CALL input3 ("Angle", a, "Side ", x, "Angle", b)
     LET c = 180 - a - b
     PRINT "Second side = "; lawsin(b,x,c)
     PRINT "Third side  = "; lawsin(a,x,c)

CASE "SSA"
     CALL input3 ("Side ", x, "Side ", y, "Angle", c)
     LET sinb = round(y * sin(c)/x, 8)
     IF sinb>1 then
        PRINT "Not possible"
     ELSEIF sinb=1 then         ! Unique
        LET a = 90 - c
        PRINT "Third side  = "; lawsin(a,x,c)
     ELSE                       ! Ambiguous
        LET b = asin(sinb)      ! First case
        LET a = 180 - b - c
        IF a>0 then
           PRINT "Third side  = "; lawsin(a,x,c)
        ELSE
           PRINT "Not possible"
        END IF
        LET b = 180 - b         ! Second case
        LET a = 180 - b - c
        IF a>0 then
           PRINT "Or"
           PRINT "Third side  = "; lawsin(a,x,c)
        END IF
     END IF

CASE "STOP"
     STOP

CASE ELSE
     PRINT "Please choose from:"
     PRINT "SAS  ASA  SSA  STOP"

END SELECT

   PRINT
LOOP

SUB input3 (p1$, x1, p2$, x2, p3$, x3)      ! Get three quantities

    PRINT p1$;                       ! Prompt
    INPUT x1                         ! Get quantity
    PRINT p2$;
    INPUT x2
    PRINT p3$;
    INPUT x3

END SUB

END
```

Several cases are illustrated in the run. The first is a simple case of SAS. The second is a 30 - 60 - 90 triangle. Next we show our error handling (CASE

ELSE) if a case is mistyped. Finally we illustrate examples of SSA with no, one, and two solutions.

```
run

Case? sas
Side ? 10
Angle? 40
Side ? 12
Third side =   7.7556

Case? asa
Angle? 30
Side ? 10
Angle? 60
Second side =   8.66025
Third side  =   5.

Case? aas
Please choose from:
SAS   ASA   SSA   STOP

Case? ssa
Side ? 3
Side ? 4
Angle? 90
Not possible

Case? ssa
Side ? 10
Side ? 8
Angle? 40
Third side   =   14.7049

Case? ssa
Side ? 8
Side ? 10
Angle? 40
Third side   =   12.423
Or
Third side   =   2.89784

Case? stop
```

16.3 ROOTS OF AN EQUATION

In this section we will develop a general-purpose routine for finding real roots of the equation

$$f(x) = 0$$

where f(x) is any continuous function definable in BASIC. This type of problem occurs in many applications of mathematics. Even the special case where f(x) is a polynomial is far from trivial; when the degree is greater than 4, there is no general formula for the roots.

We start from the simple fact that if a continuous function is negative at one end of an interval and positive at the other, it must have a root (be equal to 0) somewhere in between. The program **ZERO** assumes that f(a) and f(b) have opposite signs, and finds a zero in between.

```
REM  ZERO
REM
REM  Solve f(x) = 0
REM  Finds one root in [a,b]
REM  Assumes f(a) and f(b) have different signs

DEF f(x) = x^5 + 2*x^3 - 1

READ a, b                                   ! From, to
DATA 0, 1
LET err = 1e-7                              ! Error tolerance

LET s = sgn(f(a))                           ! Sign on left
DO
   LET x = (a+b)/2                          ! Midpoint
   IF sgn(f(x)) = s then                    ! New left end
      LET a = x
   ELSE                                     ! New right end
      LET b = x
   END IF
LOOP while abs(b-a) > err

PRINT "One root at "; x

END
```

We picked a fifth degree polynomial, which is introduced in a **DEF** statement. We selected (0,1) as our interval. Because f(0) = -1 and f(1) = +2, there must be a root in the interval. We also specify the permissible error `err`. By picking `1e-7`, we should have six-decimal accuracy in the root.

The main routine is very simple. The function `sgn` assigns +1 to a positive number, -1 to a negative number, and 0 to 0. Hence, it is very convenient for testing the sign of a value of the function f. We start by letting `s` be the sign of the value at `a`. Then we loop, always cutting the interval containing the root in half, until we have an interval whose length is within the specified error. In each iteration we compute f for the midpoint x. If this has the same sign as f(a), then we narrow the interval to (x,b); otherwise, we choose (a,x). Finally we print `x`, which must be within `err` of the root.

```
run

One root at  .733157
```

The run shows that the polynomial has a root at about .733.

The program **ZERO2** tries to find all real roots within a specified interval (a,b). It incorporates the main portion of **ZERO** as the subroutine `oneroot`. It divides (a,b) into 100 subintervals and checks for a change of sign. If it finds one, it calls `oneroot`.

Three other features deserve comment. A root may occur at `x1`, the beginning of the subinterval. We check for this to avoid having to call `oneroot`.

For the final step (100) we want to check the beginning point (which is `b`), but not the rest of the interval, which lies to the right of `b`. This explains the `ELSEIF` clause. And, `found` counts the number of roots found.

```
REM  ZERO2
REM
REM  Solve f(x) = 0
REM  Finds all roots in (a,b)

DEF f(x) = sin(x) - log10(x)

READ a, b                               ! From, to
DATA 1, 10
LET err = 1e-7                          ! Error tolerance
LET found = 0                           ! Number of roots

LET h = (b-a)/100                       ! Step size
FOR step = 0 to 100
    LET x1 = a + step*h                 ! Next point to try
    IF f(x1) = 0 then                   ! Root at point
       PRINT "One root at "; x1
       LET found = found + 1
    ELSEIF step < 100 then
       LET x2 = x1 + h                  ! End of interval
       IF f(x1)*f(x2)<0 then            ! Change of sign
          CALL oneroot (x1, x2)
          LET found = found + 1
       END IF
    END IF
NEXT step
PRINT found; "roots found"

SUB oneroot (a, b)                      ! Find root in (a,b)

    LET s = sgn(f(a))                   ! Sign on left
    DO
       LET x = (a+b)/2                  ! Midpoint
       IF sgn(f(x)) = s then            ! New left end
          LET a = x
       ELSE                             ! New right end
          LET b = x
       END IF
    LOOP while abs(b-a) > err

    PRINT "One root at "; x

END SUB

END


run

One root at  2.69626
One root at  7.32835
One root at  8.26383
 3 roots found
```

The function in our program is the difference between `sin(x)` and `log10(x)`. The latter is the logarithm to the base 10, or the *common logarithm*. The difference will be zero where the two curves cross. It is easy to see that any such crossing must be on the interval (1,10). And, we find three such crossings. The reader is encouraged to plot the two curves (using BASIC) on the same graph to observe the crossings.

16.4 PRIME NUMBERS

The study of prime numbers has fascinated both professional and amateur mathematicians for centuries. Part of the interest stems from the fact that much can be achieved through totally elementary methods. We will discuss two famous algorithms, one for finding primes and another for finding the prime factors of a given number.

The first algorithm is the ancient *sieve* for finding primes. By definition, 1 is not a prime and larger positive integers are prime if not divisible by a smaller one (except for 1). Thus, to find the primes to 100 we write down the numbers from 2 to 100. The first number, 2, must be a prime. Its multiples are not prime, so we cross them out. The next number not crossed out, 3, is a prime. We cross out its multiples. The next, 5, is again prime. And so on.

The short program **PRIMES** carries out this process. Instead of writing out the numbers, we have a list `slot` and `slot(n)` represents the number `n`. BASIC initializes any list of numbers to zeroes, and we cross numbers out by setting `slot(n) = -1`. (Any number other than zero would do.) For each `n`, the program **PRIMES** checks whether it has been crossed out. If not, it prints it and calls **sieve** to cross out its multiples.

We have incorporated one well-known shortcut. If `x` has a factor `n` then `x/n` is also a factor. Additionally, one of these must be no greater than `sqr(x)`, the square-root of `x`. For example, 77 = 7*11. There is no point in trying 11, which is greater than sqr(77), because we already know that 7 divides 77. Hence, once `n*n` is greater than `upper`, there is no point in calling **sieve**.

The run shows the prime numbers up to 100.

```
REM  PRIMES
REM
REM  Prime numbers by the sieve method

DIM slot(1000)                  ! For crossing out
LET upper = 100                 !     up to 100
FOR n = 2 to upper
    IF slot(n) = 0 then         ! Prime
       PRINT n;
       IF n*n <= upper then CALL sieve
    END IF
NEXT n

SUB sieve                       ! Does actual crossing out
```

```
        FOR i = 2*n to upper step n
            LET slot(i) = -1          ! Cross out
        NEXT i

    END SUB

    END

    run

 2   3   5   7   11   13   17   19   23   29   31   37   41   43   47   53
 59  61  67  71  73   79   83   89   97
```

Next we will build a small library of subroutines that are useful for working with primes. The first routine in NUMLIB is a prime sieve.

NUMLIB (first part).

```
SUB primes (pr(), k)               ! Primes to 1000, how many

    DIM slot(1000)                 ! For crossing out
    LET upper = 1000               ! Up to 1000
    LET k = 0                      ! Subscript for pr()
    FOR n = 2 to upper
        IF slot(n) = 0 then        ! Prime
           LET k = k+1             ! Put on list
           LET pr(k) = n
           IF n*n <= upper then CALL sieve
        END IF
    NEXT n

    SUB sieve                      ! Does actual crossing out

        FOR i = 2*n to upper step n
            LET slot(i) = -1       ! Cross out
        NEXT i

    END SUB

END SUB
```

This routine is almost identical to PRIMES. It finds the prime numbers up to 1000. But instead of printing them, which is usually not what we want, it puts them in a list pr for further use. And, k ends up equal to the number of primes found.

Such libraries may be saved separately, and in compiled form. This is a convenience for any programmer wishing to use the library. The following very short program, PRIMES2, illustrates the use of the library. The program calls the subroutine to find the primes to 1000 and, just to show that it has done so, prints the number of primes found and the largest one.

```
REM  PRIMES2
REM
REM  Prime sieve, save in list

LIBRARY "NUMLIB.trc"                     ! Compiled library
DIM pr(200)                              ! List of primes

CALL primes (pr, npr)
PRINT npr; "primes to 1000"
PRINT pr(npr); "is the largest"

END

run

 168 primes to 1000
 997 is the largest
```

The second routine in `NUMLIB`, `factor`, finds the prime factors of a number `n` and prints them. The routine is speeded up by using a list of primes up to 1000.

The key subroutine is `try`, which determines whether `p` divides `n`. The `mod` function has the property that `mod(n,p)` is zero only when `p` divides `n`. If it does, the factor is printed, `n` is divided by `p`, and we loop to see whether `p` still divides the quotient. Thus, the subroutine removes all factors of `p` from `n`.

The main portion of `factor` first tries the primes on our list, then switches to consecutive odd numbers as possible divisors. When `p` passes the `sqr(n)`, there is no point in proceeding further. We either have reduced `n` to 1, or the quotient is now prime (because it is not divisible by a smaller number).

NUMLIB (continued).

```
SUB factor (n, pr(), k)                  ! Prints factors of n

    LET i = 1                            ! Try primes first
    DO
       IF i<=k then
          LET p = pr(i)                  ! Prime
          LET i = i+1
       ELSE
          LET p = p+2                    ! Next odd number
       END IF
       CALL try                          ! Is it a factor?
    LOOP while n>p*p
    IF n>1 then PRINT n else PRINT           ! Last factor, if any
```

```
    SUB try

        DO while mod(n,p)=0          ! Found factor
           PRINT p;
           LET n = n/p
        LOOP

    END SUB

END SUB
```

The program FACTOR shows how we may use this routine. It first calls primes to construct the prime list pr and then allows the user to type in integers and have them factored. To make it somewhat more interesting, we time the factoring routine for each n. The function time gives time in seconds. Hence, calling it before and after the factoring gives us the elapsed time in seconds.

```
REM  FACTOR
REM
REM  Factors an integer into its primes

LIBRARY "NUMLIB.trc"
DIM pr(200)                          ! List of primes
CALL primes (pr, npr)

DO
   PRINT "Number to factor";
   INPUT n                           ! Number to factor
   IF n=0 then EXIT DO               ! Signal to stop
   LET t1 = time                     ! Time it
   CALL factor (n, pr, npr)          ! Print factors
   PRINT time-t1; "secs."            ! Show time to factor
   PRINT
LOOP

END

run

Number to factor? 1024
 2  2  2  2  2  2  2  2  2  2
 .33 secs.

Number to factor? 101
 101
 .16 secs.

Number to factor? 123456789
 3  3  3607  3803
 9.11 secs.

Number to factor? 12345677654321
 11  73  101  137  239  4649
 .55 secs.

Number to factor? 0
```

The times shown are for an IBM PC. All are less than a second, except for the third example where the program had to factor 3607 * 3803. These times also include not only the factoring but also printing the factors. The speed of the factoring of the 16-digit number seems remarkable. However, once the factor 239 is found, n = 4649, which is less than 239 * 239, and hence the routine knows that it is prime.

16.5 MAT INSTRUCTIONS

This section assumes familiarity with the mathematical use of *vectors* and *matrices*. It is designed to show that BASIC has a set of powerful commands for manipulating them. Each of these commands starts with **MAT** to show that the statement refers to vectors and/or matrices.

The program **EQU** shows that it is trivial to write a program for the solution of n equations in n unknowns, for the case where the solution is unique. If one collects the coefficients of the equations into an n-by-n matrix **A**, the right sides in a vector **b**, and the unknowns in a vector **x**, the equations may be written as

$$Ax = b$$

If A has an inverse, $A^{-1}b$, then the unique solution is

$$x = A^{-1}b$$

```
REM  EQU
REM
REM  Linear equation solver

DIM  A(10,10), Ainv(10,10), b(10), x(10)

READ n                              ! Number of equations, unknowns
MAT READ A(n,n)                     ! Coefficients of left side
MAT READ b(n)                       ! Right side

MAT Ainv = inv(A)                   ! Invert A if possible
MAT x = Ainv * b                    ! Then easy solution

PRINT "Solution:"                   ! Answers
MAT PRINT x

DATA 3                              ! Three equations
DATA 1, 2, 4                        ! Left side
DATA 5, 4, 4
DATA 0, 1, -2
DATA -2, 6, 2                       ! Right side

END
```

The program reads **n**, the number of equations, then reads **A** and **b** with single **MAT** statements and computes the answer by two more **MAT** statements. The first is a single command to invert the matrix **A** (and call its inverse **Ainv**). The second carries out the matrix multiplication necessary to find **x**. We then print a label and use **MAT PRINT** to print the answer vector, **x**.

Let us review the need for the **DIM** statement. It serves a double purpose: It declares **A** and **Ainv** as matrices (two-dimensional arrays), and **b** and **x** as vectors (one-dimensional arrays). It also tells BASIC how much room to save for them. For example, **A** is allowed to have up to 10 rows and 10 columns. The actual dimensions of **A** and **b** are determined by the **MAT READ** statements; **A** is n x n, while **b** has n components. Because **Ainv** and **x** are computed, BASIC automatically makes them the correct size.

Two runs of **EQU** follow.

```
run

Solution:
 2.              0               -1

DATA 3, 0, -4                   ! Change last row of A

run

Can't invert singular matrix.
```

The first run shows the simple solution of the equations. For the second run we changed the last row of the matrix and obtained an error message indicating that **A** does not have an inverse. In such a case there may be no solution or there may be infinitely many, and a more sophisticated program is needed.

Our second example is the *Open Leontief model* from the field of economics. In this model the economy of a country is divided into industrial groups. Knowing the interrelations among the industries, the model predicts what the total production of each industry will be for given levels of consumer demand.

Although the computer program **LEONTIEF** can handle a large realistic model, our data will be for a highly oversimplified example and does not attempt to represent an actual country. We will use the following six industrial groups:

A: Automobile
M: Manufacturing, other
S: Steel
C: Coal/Oil
T: Transportation
P: Power

The key tool is a matrix Q of *technological coefficients*:

$$Q = \begin{matrix} \mathrm{A} \\ \mathrm{M} \\ \mathrm{S} \\ \mathrm{C} \\ \mathrm{T} \\ \mathrm{P} \end{matrix} \begin{pmatrix} .1 & .2 & .3 & 0 & .1 & .15 \\ .1 & .2 & .2 & 0 & .15 & .2 \\ .08 & .2 & .3 & .2 & .1 & .1 \\ .1 & .4 & .1 & 0 & .2 & .05 \\ .4 & .1 & .1 & .1 & 0 & .2 \\ .1 & .1 & .2 & .5 & .05 & 0 \end{pmatrix}$$

A row of the matrix corresponds to one industry and indicates how much the industry must purchase from each industry for a unit of production. For example, Q(3,4) = .2, which means that for each $1000 the steel industry produces, it orders $200 worth of the output of the coal/oil industry.

The consumers put a demand on the industries, represented by the demand row vector d expressed in convenient units, say, billions of dollars. In our example

$$d = (20, 50, 5, 15, 30, 25)$$

Thus, consumers order 20 billion dollars worth of goods from the automobile industry, 50 billion of other manufactured goods, etc.

The most interesting question is what the total output of each industry will be. This output must meet not only the consumer demand, but also the orders from other industries resulting from this demand. If we let the row vector

$$p = (p_1 , p_2 , p_3 , p_4 , p_5 , p_6)$$

stand for the (unknown) total production, then we must have

$$p = d + pQ$$

or

$$p(I\text{-}Q) = d$$

If the matrix `I-Q` has an inverse (call it `N`), then the solution is

$$p = dN$$

Under simple assumptions, which are normally met in real life, the inverse `N` exists and is a non-negative matrix. For a large model we have to invert a sizable matrix. But once this inverse is found, the preceding formula tells us how to find the production `p` for any demand `d`.

Another interesting quantity is obtained by letting `c` be a column vector of all ones, and letting

$$t = Nc$$

Then the total production for the entire country, or its *gnp* is

$$gnp = pc = dt$$

Thus, a given component of `t` tells us how much a unit addition to the orders for an industry will add to the *gnp*.

The program `LEONTIEF` calculates these quantities. It illustrates a number of additional `MAT` instructions. First of all, we can set up matrices of special form. The function `idn` sets up an identity matrix, and `con` sets up a matrix (or vector, in our case) of all ones. There also exists a function `zer` that sets up an all-zero matrix. Additionally, we use the function `dot`, which computes the *dot product* of two vectors. The rest of the program uses `MAT` instructions, which were previously explained. You should note how short and simple a program solves this famous problem.

```
REM  LEONTIEF
REM
REM  Demonstrates the Open Leontief model

DIM Q(10,10), I(10,10), X(10,10), N(10,10)  ! Matrices
DIM d(10), p(10), c(10), t(10)     ! Vectors

READ m                             ! Number of industries
MAT READ Q(m,m)                    ! Input matrix
MAT READ d(m)                      ! Consumer demand

MAT I = idn(m)
MAT X = I - Q                      ! Solution
MAT N = inv(X)
MAT p = d * N                      ! Production
MAT c = con(m)
MAT t = N * c                      ! GNP per unit order
LET order = dot(d,c)               ! Consumer order total
LET gnp = dot(d,t)                 ! GNP

PRINT "Total production:"          ! Print answers
MAT PRINT p
PRINT "GNP per unit order:"
MAT PRINT t
PRINT "Consumer orders ="; order
PRINT "GNP ="; gnp

DATA 6                             ! 6 industry example

DATA .1 , .2, .3,  0, .1 , .15     ! Q matrix
DATA .1 , .2, .2,  0, .15, .2
DATA .08, .2, .3, .2, .1 , .1
DATA .1 , .4, .1,  0, .2 , .05
DATA .4 , .1, .1, .1,  0 , .2
DATA .1 , .1, .2, .5, .05,  0

DATA 20, 50, 5, 15, 30, 25

END
```

The run shows the total production resulting. For example, the automobile industry will produce about 210 billion dollars. It also shows the t-vector, indicating that each unit order to an industry will generate total production ranging from 9.6 to 10.8 units. In total we see that 145 billion dollars ordered by consumers resulted in about 1.4 trillion dollars worth of goods produced.

```
run

Total production:
 210.361        335.331        303.612        193.636
 180.412        199.746

GNP per unit order:
 9.67537        9.60072        10.8453        9.38888
 9.91097        10.2867

Consumer orders = 145
GNP = 1423.1
```

EXERCISES

1. Write a program to handle the case SSS in trigonometry. Given three sides, it should print the three angles. (Hint: Any side must be less than the sum of the other two sides.)
2. Find all the x-values for which sin(x) = cos(3x) between 0 and 10. If you have graphics available, plot the two functions to observe the crossing points.
3. Write a program for the following game. Each of two players types in a seven-digit number. The one having the largest prime factor wins.
4. Speed up `factor` as follows: After it has used up the primes, skip multiples of 3 among the odd numbers. Alternately increase p by 2 or 4. (Be careful how you get started.)
5. The subroutine `factor` prints a factor as many times as it occurs. Modify it to print the prime factors in one column and their *multiplicity* in the next.
6. Write a program to find all proper divisors of an integer n. That is, find all numbers, including 1, that are less than n and divide n.
7. Modify the previous program to compute the sum of the proper divisors of a number. A number is called *perfect* if it is equal to the sum of its proper divisors. Find the perfect numbers up to 30.
8. Use `EQU` to find three numbers such that their sum is 12, the difference of the first two is 1, and the sum of the first two minus the third is 6.
9. Make up a Leontief model of a 10-industry system. Explore its behavior as the consumer demand `d` varies.
10. In Exercise 9, suppose that the government wishes to place a billion dollar order to stimulate the *gnp*. Which industry should get the order?

PROJECT

Create a library for elementary number theory. Some possible routines are:

1. Find the greatest common divisor of two numbers. (See Chapter 9.)
2. Find the least common multiple of two numbers.
3. Find how many divisors a number has.
4. Compute the sum of the divisors of a number.
5. Find how many numbers less than n are relatively prime to n, i.e. have no factor in common with n.

Write a program that uses a compiled version of the library and illustrates the various routines.

CHAPTER 17

SIMULATION

17.1 INTRODUCTION

An important use of computers is the imitation of processes of real life. This is known as *simulation*. These processes often depend, or appear to depend, on chance events. Imitation of these chance events is thus an important part of simulation models. In BASIC, the imitation of chance events, no matter how complicated, is carried out by the simple function `rnd`.

In this chapter we start with simple processes to illustrate the `rnd` function—flipping coins and rolling dice. We then describe how to simulate dealing cards, as for the games of poker and bridge. Again, we will use the simple `rnd` function.

Next we describe a simulation model for exploring the behavior of the spread of a gene mutation. We follow with an example of the Monte Carlo method to estimate the area of an irregularly-shaped region.

We close the chapter with two more complex simulations. The first is a baseball team's batting for nine innings—one half of a baseball game. The second is a resource allocation model that simulates the use of disk storage on a computer system.

17.2 RANDOM NUMBERS

The basis of most simulations is the generation of so-called *random numbers*. In BASIC this is accomplished by the function `rnd`. Every time it is used, its value is a randomly picked point on the unit interval. That is, if we

```
LET a = rnd
```

then a will be set equal to a number between 0 and 1, not inclusive, and this is done at random. The simple program RANDOM picks 20 such random numbers, and prints them to three decimal places.

```
REM  RANDOM
REM
REM  Print 20 random numbers

FOR i = 1 to 20
    LET x = rnd
    PRINT round(x,3),
NEXT i

END


run

 .549          .078          .688          .335          .952
 .824          .541          .085          .391          .582
 .751          .514          .032          .421          .495
 .588          .101          .825          .484          .779
```

We see that the values are fairly evenly distributed. Indeed, if we pick many random numbers, about 50 percent will be less than .5, about 10 percent will lie between .2 and .3, etc. In general, we may simulate a probability of p by using the statement

```
IF rnd < p then
```

We illustrate this with coin tossing.

```
REM  COIN
REM
REM  Simulate tossing a coin

FOR i = 1 to 10
    IF rnd < .5 then
       PRINT "heads",
    ELSE
       PRINT "tails",
    END IF
NEXT i

END


run

heads          heads          tails          heads          tails
tails          heads          tails          tails          tails
```

Another important use of rnd is to pick integers at random. Suppose that we wished to simulate the roll of a die. We may first try

```
LET a = 6*rnd
```

Then, a will be a point picked at random from the interval (0,6). We add 1 to the result, so that the point is picked from (1,7). It has probabilty 1/6 of being in (1,2), 1/6 in (2,3), and so forth. If we take the integer part of the answer, we get the numbers 1, 2, 3, 4, 5, 6 with equal probabilities. Thus,

```
INT(6*rnd + 1)
```

simulates the roll of a die. (Here it is important that `rnd` never equals 1, so that 7 is not a possible result.)

We use this to simulate the well-known dice game *shooting craps*. A pair of dice is rolled. If the sum of the dice is 7 or 11 we win. If the sum is 2, 3, or 12, we lose. Any other sum becomes our *point*, and we must try to roll a sum equal to our point before we roll a sum of 7. These rules are fairly complicated, but they are designed to make the chances of winning just slightly less than 0.5.

The program `DICE` simulates 10 games. It uses the function `roll` to simulate one die, so that `roll + roll` gives us the sum of two dice. (Note that each call to `roll` generates a new `rnd`.) The `SELECT CASE` structure (see Chapter 15) is ideal for handling the three cases on the first roll. And, a `DO` loop is ideal for the the subroutine `make_point`, because the number of rolls depends on what happens. The statement

```
LOOP until dice=point or dice=7
```

expresses the condition for termination very simply.

This program shows that a well-structured program may be easier to understand than a verbal description of a problem.

```
REM  DICE
REM
REM  Simulate shooting craps

DEF roll = int(6*rnd+1)              ! Roll of a die
RANDOMIZE

FOR game = 1 to 10                   ! 10 games
    LET dice = roll + roll           ! Sum of two dice
    PRINT dice;
    SELECT CASE dice
    CASE 2, 3, 12
         PRINT "You lose on first roll."
    CASE 7, 11
         PRINT "You win on first roll."
    CASE ELSE
         LET point = dice            ! Becomes your "point"
         CALL make_point
    END SELECT
NEXT game

SUB make_point                       ! Try making point

    DO
       LET dice = roll + roll
       PRINT dice;
    LOOP until dice=point or dice=7
```

```
    IF dice=point then
       PRINT "You win by making point."
    ELSE
       PRINT "You lose."
    END IF

END SUB

END
```

The 10 runs illustrate various cases. We win four and lose six.

```
run

 11 You win on first roll.
 3 You lose on first roll.
 4  4 You win by making point.
 6  3  9  3  7 You lose.
 3 You lose on first roll.
 6  8  3  5  5  10  7 You lose.
 8  10  8 You win by making point.
 2 You lose on first roll.
 7 You win on first roll.
 10  7 You lose.
```

We need to explain the statement **RANDOMIZE**. If the programs **RANDOM** or **COIN** are rerun, they will produce exactly the same result. And, although `rnd` picks points in a random manner, it generates the same sequence of random numbers each time. This is important for the debugging of simulation models. Suppose that we get a test run that shows that in a very rare case our program performs incorrectly. We may never be able to duplicate that case! But by getting the same random numbers, we can fix the bug and retry the run. So, once a program is debugged, we will want to add **RANDOMIZE** near its beginning to assure that we get different random numbers on each run.

17.3 DEALING CARDS

We will now construct a library that is useful for simulating card games. We number our cards from 0 to 51, with 0 representing the 2 of clubs, and 51 the ace of spades. This is a simple numeric representation that can easily be decoded.

The routine `decode`, given the card number `c`, computes `s` the number of the suit (from 0 to 3) and the value `v` (from 0 to 12). This is accomplished in two statements, using `int` and `mod`. We employ the string lists `s$()` and `v$()` to print actual symbols, and these are set up in the initializing routine `initial`. We use lowercase letters to designate the suits.

The convenience of this approach is that for most of the simulation we may use the code number `c`, and yet we can print intelligible output through the routine `printcard`.

The coding scheme is illustrated in Table 17.1. It is based on the relation

$$c = 13*s + v$$

The most interesting parts of the library are the routines `newdeck` and `deal`. There are well-known routines for shuffling a deck, but they tend to be

TABLE 17.1
Coding Scheme for the Library CARDLIB

	s = 0	s = 1	s = 2	s = 3
v = 0	0 = c2	13 = d2	26 = h2	39 = s2
v = 1	1 = c3	14 = d3	27 = h3	40 = s3
v = 2	2 = c4	15 = d4	28 = h4	41 = s4
v = 3	3 = c5	16 = d5	29 = h5	42 = s5
v = 4	4 = c6	17 = d6	30 = h6	43 = s6
v = 5	5 = c7	18 = d7	31 = h7	44 = s7
v = 6	6 = c8	19 = d8	32 = h8	45 = s8
v = 7	7 = c9	20 = d9	33 = h9	46 = s9
v = 8	8 = c10	21 = d10	34 = h10	47 = s10
v = 9	9 = cJ	22 = dJ	35 = hJ	48 = sJ
v = 10	10 = cQ	23 = dQ	36 = hQ	49 = sQ
v = 11	11 = cK	24 = dK	37 = hK	50 = sK
v = 12	12 = cA	25 = dA	38 = hA	51 = sA

complex. Instead, we will use a much simpler idea. We start with a sorted deck and pick cards at random! In `newdeck` we set up the cards in their natural order in the list `deck()` and note that the number of remaining cards, `nc`, is 52. When we `deal`, we pick a card at random from the deck. We remove that card by replacing it with the last card in the deck and reducing `nc` by one.

```
EXTERNAL

!  CARDLIB
!  Library for card games
!
!      initial          Initializes names of suits and values
!      newdeck          Sets up a new deck
!      deal             Deals one card
!      printcard        Prints a card
!      decode           Decodes suit and value from card number

SUB initial (s$(), v$())                ! Initialize

    RANDOMIZE

    MAT READ s$                         ! Suits
    DATA c, d, h, s

    MAT READ v$                         ! Values
    DATA 2, 3, 4, 5, 6, 7, 8, 9
    DATA 10, J, Q, K, A

END SUB

SUB newdeck (deck(), nc)                ! Fresh deck of cards

    LET nc = 52                         ! Number of cards left
    FOR i = 0 to 51                     ! Set up in order
        LET deck(i) = i
    NEXT i

END SUB
```

```
SUB deal (deck(), nc, c)             ! Deal a card

    LET i = int(nc*rnd)              ! Pick random card
    LET c = deck(i)                  ! Card number
    LET nc = nc - 1                  ! One less card
    LET deck(i) = deck(nc)           ! Remove from deck

END SUB

SUB printcard (c, s$(), v$())        ! Print card number c

    CALL decode(c, s, v)
    PRINT s$(s); v$(v); " ";

END SUB

SUB decode (c, s, v)                 ! Suit and value

    LET s = int(c/13)                ! Suit number
    LET v = mod(c,13)                ! Value

END SUB
```

As a simple application, we write a program to deal a hand of 13 cards. The program `DEAL1` is self explanatory.

```
REM   DEAL1
REM
REM   Deal a bridge hand

LIBRARY "CARDLIB.trc"

DIM s$(0 to 3), v$(0 to 12)          ! Suit, value symbols
DIM deck(0 to 51)

CALL initial (s$, v$)
CALL newdeck (deck, nc)
FOR card = 1 to 13                   ! Deal, print 13 cards
    CALL deal (deck, nc, c)
    CALL printcard (c, s$, v$)
NEXT card

END

run

d8 c5 h3 d4 c6 d5 s2 c9 s10 dJ d9 h5 s8
```

For a more interesting example, we deal four hands and print them in the same order as an experienced bridge player might arrange them.

```
REM  DEAL2
REM
REM  Deal four bridge hands

LIBRARY "CARDLIB.trc", "SORTNLIB.trc"
```

```
DIM s$(0 to 3), v$(0 to 12)        ! Suit, value symbols
DIM deck(0 to 51)
DIM hand(13)

CALL initial (s$, v$)
CALL newdeck (deck, nc)
FOR n = 1 to 4                     ! Four hands
    FOR card = 1 to 13             ! Deal 13 cards
        CALL deal (deck, nc, hand(card))
    NEXT card

    CALL selsortn (hand, 1, 13)    ! Sort hand
    FOR card = 1 to 13             ! Print it
        CALL printcard (hand(card), s$, v$)
    NEXT card
    PRINT
    PRINT
NEXT n

END

run

c4 c5 c6 c8 d2 d10 dQ dK h7 hJ hQ s5 s10

c2 c3 c9 cJ cQ d4 d9 dA h2 h9 hA s7 sK

c7 c10 d3 d5 d6 d7 d8 dJ h3 h4 h5 s2 s6

cK cA h6 h8 h10 hK s3 s4 s8 s9 sJ sQ sA
```

If the players with the second and fourth hands are partners, they should be successful in a bid of *7 spades*.

Another important use of simulation is the estimation of probabilities. We illustrate this by estimating how likely it is that a poker hand contains a pair.

In **POKER** we only need to explain the two new subroutines. **Dealhand** deals a five-card hand. It deciphers the code number **c** and stores the value of the card in a list **hand()**. We are not interested in suits in this program. Two sevens form a pair no matter what their suits are. The other routine, **checkpair**, compares the values in **hand()** two-at-a-time. If any two are the same, the flag **yes** is set to 1. If none is found, it ends up being 0. The main routine simply counts the number of hands having a pair and prints the fraction at the end.

```
REM  POKER
REM
REM  Probability of a pair in a poker hand

LIBRARY "CARDLIB.trc"

DIM s$(0 to 3), v$(0 to 12)        ! Suit, value symbols
DIM deck(0 to 51)
DIM hand(5)                        ! Five-card hand

LET nhands = 100                   ! Hands to simulate
LET count = 0                      ! Number with a pair
```

```
CALL initial (s$, v$)
FOR try = 1 to nhands                   ! Simulate "nhands" hands
    CALL newdeck (deck, nc)             ! Fresh deck for each hand
    CALL dealhand
    CALL checkpair (yes)
    IF yes=1 then LET count = count + 1      ! Had a pair
NEXT try
PRINT "In"; nhands; "hands a fraction"; count/nhands; "had a pair"

SUB dealhand

    FOR card = 1 to 5                   ! Deal five cards
        CALL deal (deck, nc, c)
        CALL decode (c, s, v)
        LET hand(card) = v              ! Only care about value
    NEXT card

END SUB


SUB checkpair (yes)                     ! yes = 1 if a pair present

    LET yes = 0                         ! Until we find one
    FOR i = 1 to 4                      ! Cards to compare
        LET card1 = hand(i)
        FOR j = i+1 to 5                ! Compare to
            LET card2 = hand(j)
            IF card1=card2 then         ! Found one
               LET yes = 1
               EXIT SUB                 ! No need to go on
            END IF
        NEXT j
    NEXT i

END SUB

END


run

In 100 hands a fraction .51 had a pair

run

In 100 hands a fraction .53 had a pair

run

In 100 hands a fraction .47 had a pair

run

In 100 hands a fraction .54 had a pair

run

In 100 hands a fraction .51 had a pair
```

The five runs show that it is plausible that the probability of having a pair is near to 0.5. That is true. We might also guess that it is slightly higher than 0.5. The actual probability is .493. This illustrates what simulation is good at and what its weakness is; that is, we can get a quick estimate of a probability that we may not know how to compute, but we would have to run a very large number of cases to obtain an accurate answer.

In this example we would need to simulate about 10,000 hands to settle with any confidence that the probability is less than 0.5. We include such a run. However, it takes a long time on a personal computer.

```
run

In 10000 hands a fraction .4962 had a pair
```

17.4 SPREAD OF A MUTATION

Let us suppose that a mutation occurs in one gene in a human being. We wish to simulate the spread of the mutant gene among the descendants of that person.

By the laws of genetics, there is probability 1/2 that the chromosome containing the mutant gene will be passed on to a given child. We will assume that the mutation is rare, so that the spouse of a descendant does not have it. Thus, if a given child does not inherit the mutation, his or her descendants will be mutation free.

The program **GENES** assumes that each person has exactly two children, and it follows the spread of the mutation through 15 generations. The variable n is the number of individuals in a given generation having the mutation. Initially, n is equal to 1. The loop determines at random (with probability 1/2) which of the 2*n children inherit the mutation. If $n = 0$ in any generation, there is no point in continuing the simulation, so we use an **EXIT FOR** to get out of the loop. We will print the value of n for each generation.

```
REM  GENES
REM
REM  Spread of a mutation

RANDOMIZE
LET children = 2                         ! Children per family

LET n = 1                                ! Original mutation
FOR gener = 1 to 15                      ! Simulate 15 generations
    LET sum = 0                          ! Offspring with mutation
    FOR i = 1 to n*children
        IF rnd<.5 then LET sum = sum + 1
    NEXT i
    LET n = sum                          ! For next generation
    PRINT n;
    IF n=0 then EXIT FOR                 ! Disappeared
NEXT gener
PRINT

END
```

The runs suggest that there is high probability for the mutation to die out–often very fast. In only one run is the mutation still present after 15 generations.

```
run

 1  1  1  1  1  1  0

run

 1  1  1  1  2  2  1  0

run

 0

run

 2  4  3  5  6  10  13  13  13  15  15  12  9  7  6

run

 2  1  0
```

Next we change the number of children per family to three. We note that now there is a high probability of survival for the mutation and there are usually many mutants in the fifteenth generation.

```
run

 3  5  9  14  18  27  37  52  75  112  169  259  383  564
 838

run

 2  3  4  7  14  13  20  34  51  69  97  151  211  311
 449

run

 1  1  2  2  2  4  4  4  5  10  17  25  36  54  68

run

 0

run

 3  4  5  9  13  19  31  45  62  94  141  207  308  482
 745
```

17.5 MONTE CARLO METHOD

An interesting application of random numbers is the estimation of the area of an irregularly shaped region. Suppose that we have a map that represents a known area. On it is a country whose area we do not know. Imagine throwing darts at random, but uniformly distributed, at the map. The fraction of the darts that land within the country is an estimate of the fraction of the total area that is within the country. This is known as the *Monte Carlo Method* of estimation.

For example, suppose that we have a map representing 10 square miles, and a park of irregular shape. We pick points at random on the map and count the number that fall within the park. If they constitute, say, 73 percent of the total number, then the park has an approximate area of 7.3 square miles.

We now need an example in which it is easy to determine whether a given point falls within an area, so that we can judge the accuracy of the method. We choose a unit circle, with the circumscribed square as our *map*. Because each side has length 2 (from -1 to 1), the area is 4. The fraction of *hits* times 4 will be an estimate for the area of the circle—i.e., an estimate for the number π.

The program `CIRCLE` carries this out in a simple manner. It picks 1000 random points, whose (x,y) coordinates are within the square. We count how many are within the circle (i.e., have a distance from the origin of no more than 1). Then we print 4 times the fraction of *hits*. We again see how easy it is to obtain rough answers by simulation, but that the answers are not very accurate.

```
REM  CIRCLE
REM
REM  Estimate pi
REM  Monte Carlo simulation

RANDOMIZE
LET n = 1000                           ! Number of tries
LET hits = 0                           ! Inside circle

FOR try = 1 to n
    LET x = 2*rnd - 1                  ! From -1 to 1
    LET y = 2*rnd - 1
    IF x^2 + y^2 <= 1 then             ! Hit
       LET hits = hits + 1
    END IF
NEXT try

PRINT 4*hits/n

END

run

 3.16

run

 3.108

run

 3.116
```

The program `CIRCLE2` illustrates the method visually. (See Chapters 7 and 21 for an explanation of graphics commands.) It draws both the square and the circle, and it draws a point for each *dart*. Hits are plotted in red, misses in green. Figure 17.1 is a black-and-white representation of the result.

```
REM  CIRCLE2
REM
REM  Estimate pi
REM  Monte Carlo simulation with graphics

OPEN #1: screen 0, .2, .1, .9      ! For printed result
OPEN #2: screen .25, .75, .1, .9   ! Target square
SET WINDOW -1,1,-1,1
SET COLOR "yellow"
BOX LINES  -1,1,-1,1
BOX CIRCLE -1,1,-1,1

RANDOMIZE
LET n = 1000                       ! Number of tries
LET hits = 0                       ! Inside circle

FOR try = 1 to n
    LET x = 2*rnd - 1
    LET y = 2*rnd - 1
    IF x^2 + y^2 <= 1 then         ! Hit
       LET hits = hits + 1
       SET COLOR "red"
       PLOT x,y
    ELSE
       SET COLOR "green"
       PLOT x,y
    END IF
NEXT try

WINDOW #1
PRINT 4*hits/n

END
```

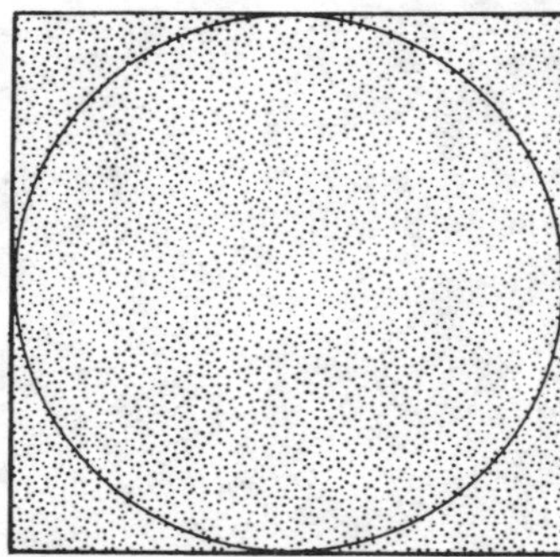

FIGURE 17.1
Estimating π by the Monte Carlo Method.

TABLE 17.2
Batting Averages of the 1963 Los Angeles Dodgers

Order	Player	Batting Average	Slugging Average
1.	Wills, Maury (ss)	.302	.349
2.	Gilliam, Junior (2b)	.282	.383
3.	Davis, Willie (of)	.242	.365
4.	Davis, Tommie (of)	.326	.457
5.	Howard, Frank (1b)	.273	.518
6.	Fairly, Ron (of)	.271	.388
7.	McMullen, Ken (3b)	.236	.339
8.	Roseboro, John (c)	.236	.351
9.	Pitcher (average)	.117	.152

17.6 A BASEBALL SIMULATION

In a more light-hearted vein, one of the authors (Kemeny) was interested in the effect that batting order would have on the runs produced by a baseball team. It is widely believed by fans and managers alike that batting order is crucial. That is, the players most likely to *walk* or *hit singles* should bat first or second, the best sluggers should bat fourth or fifth, and so on. This is a complicated question and involves such issues as the way a pitcher pitches to a batter when there are runners on base.

We choose to address a simpler situation. We assume that all pitchers and batters perform the same regardless of the number of outs, the number of men on base, and so on. In other words, we assume that the probability of a particular batter getting a hit is the same regardless of the situation. We can then explore the effects of batting orders on the number of runs produced.

We shall start with a simulation of one side of a nine-inning game. Each of the nine batters has certain probabilities of making an out, receiving a walk, getting a single, and so on. We will then use the `rnd` function to determine, according to these probabilities, the outcome. For realism, we chose as our team the 1963 world champion Los Angeles Dodgers. Their batting and slugging averages are shown in Table 17.2.

To further simplify the simulation, we consider only five possible outcomes of an *at bat*: out, walk, single, double, and home run. Triples are lumped with doubles, as they are rare and usually have the same effect on producing runs as doubles. We also ignore stolen bases, sacrifice bunts, and flies, etc. Finally, we assume that all singles will advance a runner from first to third, and that all doubles will score a runner from first base.

To determine the end result of a particular batter's outcome, we must devise a code to keep track of base runners. Because there are three bases, and a base can be occupied or empty, we use a *three bit* binary number. A "1" will mean that the base is occupied, and a "0" will mean that it is empty. It is not necessary to understand binary numbers to understand this coding scheme. The reader may think of this merely as using code numbers 0 - 7 for the eight outcomes, as shown in Table 17.3.

Under these assumptions, Kemeny's original simulations showed that the batting order had a neglible effect on the outcome. See Kemeny, Snell, Thompson, *Introduction to Finite Mathematics*, Third Edition, Prentice-Hall, Englewood Cliffs, NJ, 1974, pp. 308-311.

TABLE 17.3
Codes for Representing Runners on Base

Code	Binary Representation: Third base	Second base	First base	Meaning
0	0	0	0	Bases empty
1	0	0	1	Runner on first
2	0	1	0	Runner on second
3	0	1	1	Runners on first and second
4	1	0	0	Runner on third
5	1	0	1	Runners on first and third
6	1	1	0	Runners on second and third
7	1	1	1	Bases loaded

We next form a table `P(batter,result)` that gives the probability of each of the five results, based on their percentages for 1963. (Actually, we need give the probabilities for only four results on the grounds that if none of the four occurs, then the fifth must occur.)

The result of a batter's effort will be a new configuration of base runners, and the number of runs scored. We thus start with a result and a configuration of base runners, and end with a number of runs and a new configuration of base runners. We can represent this effect with a *state transition table*.

```
State(result,code) = 10*(number of runs) + (new code)
```

For example,

```
State(1,1) = 5 = 05
```

because a single (result = 1) with a runner on first (code = 1) yields 0 runs and runners on first and third (code = 5). And,

```
State(4,6) = 30
```

because a home run, with runners on second and third, produces three runs and leaves the bases empty. This computation is contained in the subroutine `action`.

```
REM   DODGER
REM
REM   This program simulates one side of a nine inning
REM   baseball game. It is based on a program originally
REM   written by John G. Kemeny to celebrate the 1963
REM   World Series victory of the Los Angeles Dodgers.

DIM P(9,0 to 3)            ! Batting probabilities
DIM State(4,0 to 7)        ! The state table gives runs and
                           !    new state from result, state
DIM result$(0 to 4)        ! Batting result in English
DIM LOB(0 to 7)            ! Number left on base from state

CALL initialize            ! Main program
CALL new_game
FOR i = 1 to 9
    CALL play_inning
```

```
NEXT i
CALL game_results                      ! End of main program

SUB new_game                           ! Initialize for game

    LET score = 0                      ! Totals runs
    LET batter = 0                     ! Current batter
    LET tot_hits = 0                   ! Total hits
    LET left_on = 0                    ! Total left on base

END SUB

SUB play_inning                        ! Simulate an inning

    CALL new_inning
    DO
       CALL next_batter
       CALL outcome                    ! Simulate result
    LOOP until outs = 3
    CALL inning_results

END SUB

SUB new_inning                         ! Initialize for inning

    PRINT "Inning"; i                  ! Inning number
    LET inning_runs = 0                ! Runs in the inning
    LET outs = 0                       ! Outs
    LET code = 0                       ! Bases empty

END SUB

SUB next_batter

    LET batter = batter + 1
    IF batter > 9 then LET batter = 1

END SUB

SUB outcome

    LET x = rnd                        ! For probability
    FOR result = 0 to 3
        LET x = x - P(batter,result) ! Keep subtracting
        IF x < 0 then EXIT FOR  ! Until it turns
negative
    NEXT result
    PRINT result$(result); "   ";     ! Print outcome
    CALL action                        ! Do bookkeeping

END SUB

SUB action

    IF result > 0 then          ! Not an out
       IF result <> 2 then LET tot_hits = tot_hits + 1 ! Not a walk
       LET x = State(result,code)
```

```
            LET runs = int(x/10)    ! Runs produced
            LET code = mod(x,10)    ! New code
            LET inning_runs = inning_runs + runs
        ELSE
            LET outs = outs + 1
        END IF

END SUB

SUB inning_results

    LET left_on = left_on + LOB(code) ! Runners left on base
    PRINT
    PRINT inning_runs; "runs"
    PRINT
    LET score = score + inning_runs ! Total runs

END SUB

SUB game_results

    PRINT
    PRINT "Game Totals:";
    PRINT
    PRINT score; "runs"
    PRINT tot_hits; "hits"
    PRINT left_on; "Runners left on base"

END SUB

SUB initialize

    ! Batting averages; based on those of the 1963 Dodgers

    MAT READ P
    DATA  .644, .240, .077, .039
    DATA  .644, .190, .103, .053
    DATA  .720, .167, .046, .050
    DATA  .641, .244, .050, .038
    DATA  .673, .153, .073, .038
    DATA  .651, .182, .106, .038
    DATA  .704, .162, .079, .036
    DATA  .709, .162, .071, .040
    DATA  .836, .090, .053, .016

    ! The state table

    MAT READ State
    DATA  1, 5, 11, 15, 11, 15, 21, 25
    DATA  1, 3, 3, 7, 5, 7, 7, 17
    DATA  2, 12, 12, 22, 12, 22, 22, 32
    DATA  10, 20, 20, 30, 20, 30, 30, 40

    MAT READ result$
    DATA  Out, Single, Walk, Double, Home Run
```

```
    ! The left-on-base function

    MAT READ LOB
    DATA  0, 1, 1, 2, 1, 2, 2, 3

    RANDOMIZE

END SUB

END
```

The program is carefully structured into a main program and short subroutines (see Figure 17.2). After `initialize`, which sets up the arrays, the main routine calls `new_game`, nine times calls `play_inning`, and then calls `game_results`. This is a simple and clear *skeleton* for the program. It makes modifications easy. (See Exercise 10.)

The routine `play_inning` is structured similarly. It calls `new_inning`, then it loops through `new_batter` and `outcome` until there are three outs. Then, it calls `inning_results`.

We need to explain the subroutine `outcome`. Based on the value of the `rnd` function, a particular result from 0 to 4 is selected. This is done by subtracting probabilities from the `rnd` value until it turns negative. The `FOR` loop checks results 0 through 3. If any of these is selected, the loop is exited with the variable `result` set to the selected value. If the `FOR` loop ends *normally*, then the value of the loop variable `result` will be equal to 4, the first value not used within the loop.

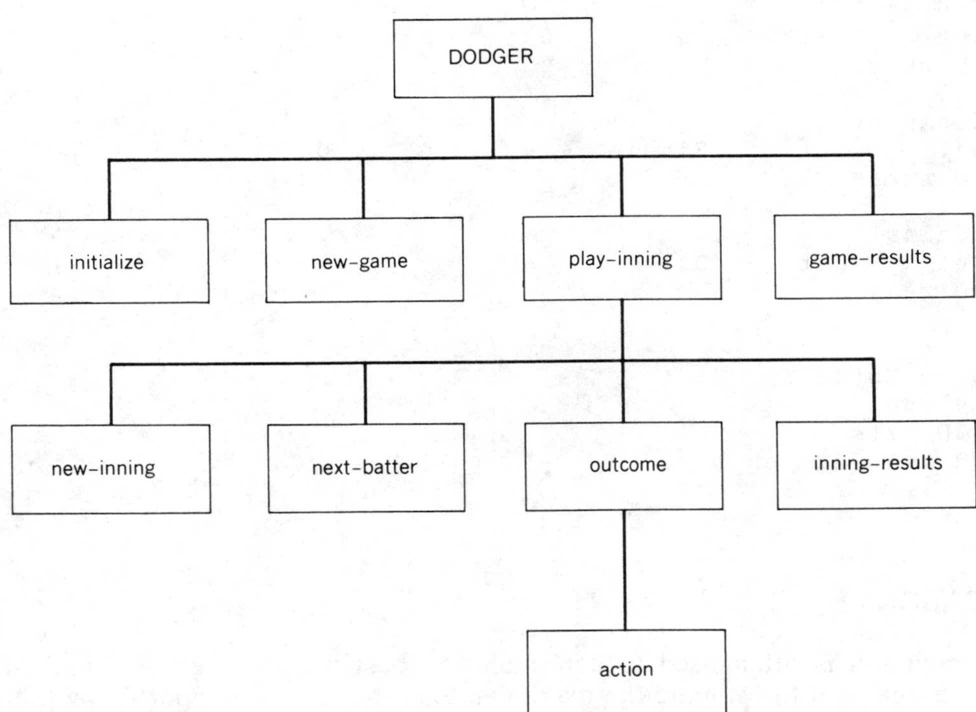

FIGURE 17.2
Structure Chart for DODGER.

Then `outcome` calls `action` to figure out the consequences and keep score.

A typical Dodger game is shown.

```
run

Inning 1
Out       Out       Out
 0 runs

Inning 2
Single      Home run      Out       Out       Out
 2 runs

Inning 3
Out       Single      Walk      Out       Out
 0 runs

Inning 4
Single      Walk      Out       Out       Out
 0 runs

Inning 5
Single      Out       Out       Out
 0 runs

Inning 6
Double      Single      Double      Out       Out       Out
 2 runs

Inning 7
Out       Walk      Out       Out
 0 runs

Inning 8
Out       Out       Single      Single      Out
 0 runs

Inning 9
Out       Out       Out
 0 runs


Game Totals:
 4 runs
 10 hits
 9 men left on base
```

17.7 RESOURCE ALLOCATION

Simulation is often used to determine the best way to use some limited resource, and to estimate the maximum load that can be supported by that resource. Common examples are the number of check-out counters needed at a supermarket, or the number of trunk telephone lines needed for a given city.

We have chosen the problem of allocating space on a computer disk. This may be the (external) disk memory of a large computer a hard disk on a personal computer, or a file server on a local area network.

We assume that a number of people use the same computer, that they save files, that they delete files no longer needed, and that the system operates six days per week. We shall simulate one year, plotting the number of saved files at the end of each week.

The outcome depends, of course, on what we assume about the way files are created and deleted (i.e., unsaved). We assume that only a limited number of new files can be created each day. We will take this number to be from 0 to 10, and assume that all of these numbers are equally likely. We use a variable `maxnew` for the upper bound (10), to make it easy to change the number.

We assume that for each saved file there is a fixed small probability `unspr` that the file will be deleted on a given day. We will use 2 percent in our model. (See Exercise 11 for an exploration of how the outcome depends on `maxnew` and `unspr`.)

MEMORY asks for the original number of files, and then simulates 52 weeks. For each day it decides at random whether any given file gets deleted. Then it picks a random integer, between 0 and `maxnew` inclusive, as the number of files added. It plots the total number saved at the end of each week.

```
REM  MEMORY
REM
REM  Simulate saved files on a disk

LET unspr = .02                      ! Prob. unsave old file
LET maxnew = 10                      ! 0 to maxnew new files

LIBRARY "PLOTLIB.trc"

CALL data_setup (52, 500, 100)       ! Get ready for graph
PRINT "Initial no. of files";
INPUT files                          ! Initial number of files

RANDOMIZE
PLOT 0,files;
FOR t = 1 to 52*6                    ! One year
    FOR i = 1 to files               ! Unsave old
        IF rnd<unspr then LET files = files - 1
    NEXT i
    LET newn = int((maxnew+1)*rnd)       ! Add new files
    LET files = files + newn
    IF mod(t,6)=0 then PLOT t/6,files;       ! Plot weekly
NEXT t

END
```

The program uses **PLOTLIB** to set up the window and to draw and label axes. This library will be discussed in Chapter 21.

In our first run we begin with 100 files. We note that initially the number of files climbs steadily. Then it settles down to a range in the mid-200s and

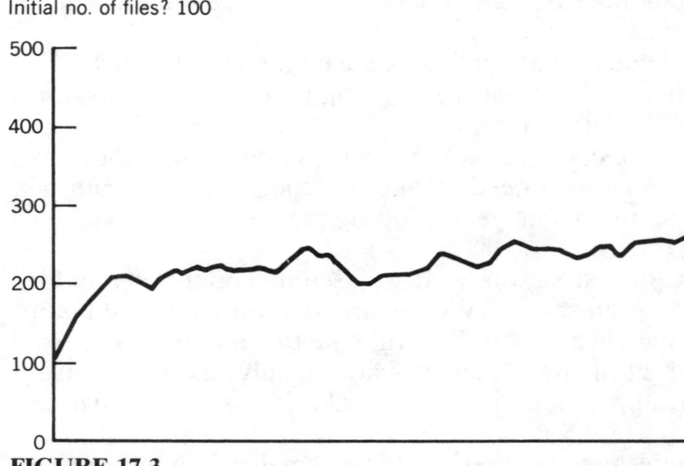

FIGURE 17.3
Number of Saved Files Starting from 100.

oscillates. When we start with 400 files, we experience a steady decrease, then it settles down to what appears to be the same range. Indeed, it can be shown that the initial number of files has no effect on the long-range behavior. (See Figures 17.3 and 17.4.)

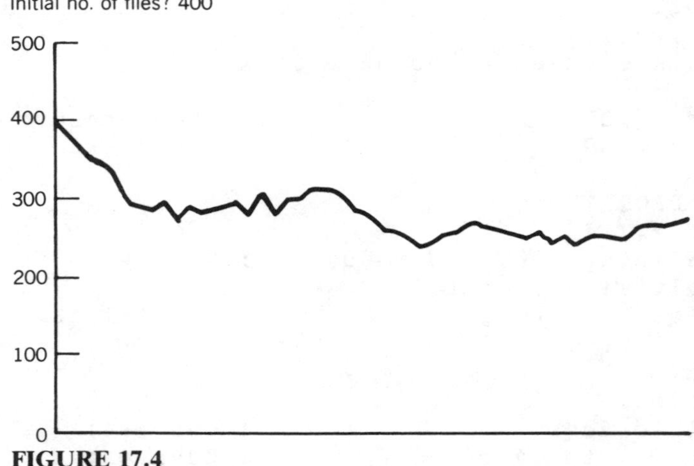

FIGURE 17.4
Number of Saved Files Starting from 400.

It would appear that if we have room for 300 files and start with less than that number, then a user will hardly ever get a "disk full" message.

EXERCISES

1. Random integers from a consecutive set of integers may be formed by the command

```
LET x = int(a*rnd + b)
```

where `b` is the smallest integer in the set and `a` is the number of different integers. Write appropriate commands for choosing a random integer from each of the following two sequences.
a. 0, 1, 2, ..., 10
b. 13, 14, 15, ..., 25

2. Modify **DICE** to serve as a gambling game. Each time we win it credits us with one dollar, and when we lose it debits one dollar. Your program should play 100 games, and print only the final net gain or loss.

3. In **CARDLIB** the cards are numbered from 0 to 51. Make the necessary changes so that cards are numbered from 1 to 52. Which is simpler?

4. Modify **CARDLIB** so that `printcard` will print a more easily readable name for a card, e.g. "King of Hearts".

5. Modify **DEAL2** so that for each hand it prints the high card point count (A = 4, K = 3, Q = 2, J =1).

6. Write a program to deal a poker hand (five cards) and check for
a. a flush (all of the same suit)
b. a straight (a run like 5-6-7-8-9, ignoring the suit)

7. Modify **GENES** to allow the presence of a mutation to influence whether the chromosome is passed on to child. Simulate the following situations:
a. Each person has two children. The probability of inheriting the mutant gene is .6.
b. Each person has three children. The probability of inheriting the mutant gene is .3.

8. The formula for the volume of a sphere is $c * \pi * r^3$. Pretend that we do not know the value of c and modify **CIRCLE** to estimate this constant.

9. Modify **CIRCLE2** so that instead of inscribing a circle, it inscribes the square whose corners are the middles of the four sides of the outside square. It should produce a visual image of the Monte Carlo method and an estimate of the area of the inscribed square. (Hint: Test on `abs(x) + abs(y)`.)

10. Modify **DODGER** to simulate 10 games. It should *not* print the inning results, only the game results.

11. Explore varying `maxnew` and `unspr` in **MEMORY**, noting the effect on the long-term behavior. Try the following cases:
a. `maxnew` = 20
b. `unspr` = .04
c. `maxnew` = 20 and `unspr` = .04

Take a guess on how these two parameters influence the *typical* number of files in the long run.

12. If `files` gives the current number of saved files in the program **MEMORY**, and we know `unspr`, what is the average number of files deleted on a given day? From `maxnew` calculate the average number of new files. What must `files` equal so that the average number deleted is equal to the number created (equilibrium)? Compare your result with the guess you took in Exercise 11.

PROJECTS

1. Build a simulation model for the game of tennis. Assume that the better player has probability $p > 0.5$ of winning each point.

a. Simulate one game. A player wins by scoring four points, but the player must be ahead by two points to win.
b. Simulate a set, without a *tie-breaker*. The winner must win six games and be ahead by two games.
c. Simulate a match, in which the first player to win three sets wins the match.

Try your model for $p = .6$ (a much better player) and $p = .51$ (a slightly better player). Estimate for each the probability of winning a match.

2. Simulate a drunkard's walk. A drunkard's home is on corner number 0 on Main Street, and the jail is on corner number `n` on Main Street. He starts at corner number `k` (between 0 and `n`) and walks to a neighboring corner. He is just as likely to walk to `k-1` as to `k+1`. This *random walk* continues until he reaches home or lands in jail.

Estimate the probability of his getting home safely for various starting positions. How does the answer depend on `n` and `k`?

3. Write a program to simulate playing a hand of *draw poker*. A five-card hand is dealt. The computer may discard up to three cards and have new cards dealt in their place. The program should announce what kind of a hand it has after the draw.

4. Write a program to do Monte Carlo estimation of the area under $y = f(x)$ for a function f, which takes on only non-negative values. Provide a suitable graphic output.

CHAPTER 18

COMPUTER MODELS

18.1 INTRODUCTION

A *computer model* is a program that acts out a real-life situation. It attempts to imitate as much of a real situation as possible, so that one may study its behavior under varying circumstances. In this chapter we explore three different computer models that do not involve random processes. (Computer models that involve random processes were studied in Chapter 17.) The situations they imitate nonetheless are difficult to understand. Consequently, the computer model provides insight through trial and error, a luxury we would certainly not have with the real-life situation.

The first model is the classic Lotka-Volterra model of a simple ecological system in which there are two species—a predator species (foxes) and a prey species (rabbits). The predators are assumed to live off the prey, whereas the prey are assumed to have an unlimited food source (grass).

The second model attempts to project the future population of the United States. The model employs a standard device for population modeling—the *cohort*. Each age group is treated distinctively in terms of death rate and contribution to the birth rate.

The third model shows how the computer can be useful to study a complex situation that defies mathematical analysis. The model is of a small college, which has a faculty size, a student body size, a tuition rate, and so on. One of the main points is that a computer model can not only explore overall behavior, but can also pinpoint sensitivities—those areas where a relatively small change in one of the factors can cause a major change in the results.

In the runs of the models we illustrate ways of displaying a large number of results in graphic or tabular form.

18.2 A MODEL FROM ECOLOGY

This topic illustrates an important application of the ecological and environmental sciences, that of the interaction between species as they struggle for survival.

We will consider the interaction of two species, such as foxes and rabbits, where the first species feeds on the second. The model was developed by A. J. Lotka, but we follow the treatment of *Mathematical Models in the Social Sciences*, Chapter III (The MIT Press, Cambridge, 1972.) The model assumes that if `r` is the number of rabbits and `f` is the number of foxes, the sizes of two populations change according to the laws, which are differential equations:

$$\frac{dr}{dt} = A*r - B*r*f \qquad \frac{df}{dt} = C*r*f - D*f$$

for suitable constants A, B, C, and D. In our model we use the parameter values:

$$A = .5 \quad B = .01 \quad C = .001 \quad D = .4$$

We may describe the two equations roughly as follows. If there were no foxes, the rabbits would increase at a fixed rate (`A*r` term), while if there were no rabbits the foxes would die out at a rate (`D*f` term). The `r*f` terms indicate that interaction between the species helps the fox population grow, but depletes the rabbit population.

We will use a very simple method to obtain a numerical solution for the equations. The method assumes that the new value of the population (foxes or rabbits) is given by the old value plus the rate of change times the time interval. This method is reasonably accurate if the time interval is small (we use .1).

The program **FOXRAB** carries out this calculation. First it defines two functions (`dr` and `df`), representing the two differential equations. Then it

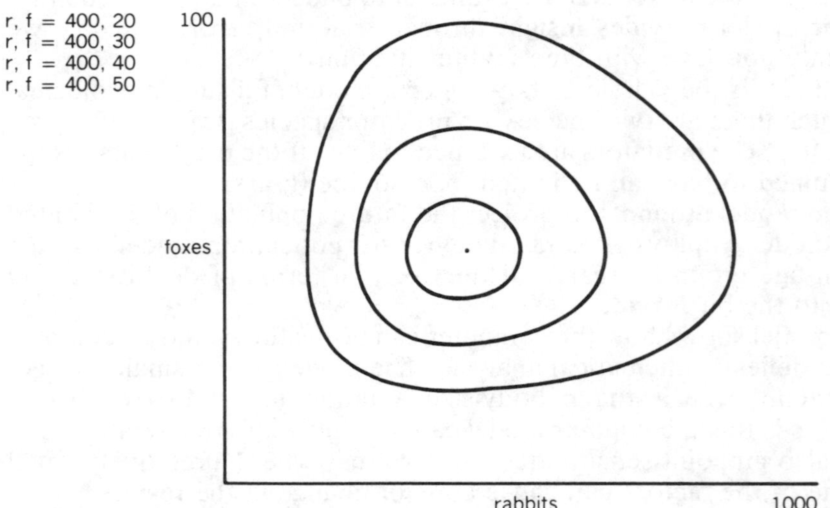

FIGURE 18.1
The predator - prey model: Graphical output.

sets up the parameters `A`, `B`, `C`, `D`, `tmax`, and `dt`. Next it sets up window coordinates, allowing a good-sized margin on the left for communication with the user. Finally, it carries out the calculations, plotting as it goes.

We run four cases to allow comparison of results for varying initial conditions. For each case we allow the user to specify the initial conditions (number of rabbits and foxes to start with). The result is shown in Figure 18.1. The values `r` = 400 and `f` = 50 represent an equilibrium. For the other initial conditions we find cyclic behavior, with the populations cycling around the equilibrium values.

```
REM  FOXRAB
REM
REM  Simple predator/prey model
REM  Uses Lotka-Volterra equations

DEF dr(r,f) = A*r - B*r*f               ! Rate of change of rabbits
DEF df(r,f) = C*r*f - D*f               ! Rate of change of foxes

LET A = .5                              ! Parameters
LET B = .01
LET C = .001
LET D = .4
LET rmax = 1000
LET fmax = 100
LET tmax = 20                           ! Length of simulation
LET dt = .1                             ! Step size

CALL setup                              ! Axes, labels
FOR n = 1 to 4                          ! Show 4 cases
    INPUT prompt "r, f = ": r, f
    FOR t = 0 to tmax step dt
        PLOT r,f;
        LET r = r + dr(r,f)*dt          ! Compute next cycle
        LET f = f + df(r,f)*dt
    NEXT t
    PLOT
NEXT n

SUB setup

    SET mode "hires"                    ! For IBM-pc
    SET WINDOW  -rmax/2,rmax,-fmax/4,fmax
    PLOT LINES: 0,fmax; 0,0; rmax,0       ! Axes
    PLOT TEXT, at -.1*rmax, .5*fmax: "foxes"
    PLOT TEXT, at -.1*rmax, .9*fmax: str$(fmax)
    PLOT TEXT, at .5*rmax, -.1*fmax: "rabbits"
    PLOT TEXT, at .9*rmax, -.1*fmax: str$(rmax)

END SUB

END
```

Starting at the bottom, both populations increase until the number of foxes grow to a critical value. Then rabbits decline in number. Eventually there are too few rabbits and the number of foxes starts to decline. This allows rabbits to increase again. We return to the starting position, and the pattern repeats. Such cycles in predator - prey populations have indeed been observed in nature.

18.3 A POPULATION MODEL

It is often important to attempt to predict population growth. For example, school and college planners would like to know how many persons of school or college age there will be in 5 or 10 years; social security planners would like to know how many persons aged 70 and above there will be in 20 or 50 years. These questions are easy to answer using census data of the population by age. However, other questions are more difficult to answer. For example, suppose health care is improved substantially, how would such a change affect the number of persons aged 70 and above? Or how would the school-age population be affected by a certain change in the birth rate? These questions, and many like them, can be answered through the use of a population, or *demographic*, model of the United States.

The key idea in such models is to keep track of certain groups in the population, called *cohorts*, as time goes on. The model we present in this section divides the total population into cohorts according to age. As one year goes by, the cohort size will diminish according to the mortality rate; mortality rates are known for the population as a whole as well as for major subdivisions (such as sex and race) of the population. In addition, new individuals enter the population at age 0, subject to birth rates that vary according to the age of the mother.

The population of the United States is actually affected by other major factors such as immigration and emigration, which, for simplicity, we will not consider. Neither will we take into account that slightly different mortality rates apply to the different races and sexes or to different parts of the country. (See Project 5.)

The program `POPULUS` assumes that the population of the United States is divided into cohorts with ages 0 through 100. As the cohort at a particular age becomes one year older, its size is reduced by the mortality rate for that age. In addition, a new cohort at age 0 comes from births. Multiplying the birth rate for a given age of women by the number of women at that age and summing these products gives the number of births. (`POPULUS` assumes that exactly half of the individuals at a given age are women.) `POPULUS` projects the population for several years into the future. In addition, it allows the user to change the birth rate and the mortality rate (due to improved health care) at a specified time.

We want to produce the results in a nice tabular form, reporting every ten years. To achieve this, we save the results (in the table `out$`) until we are ready to print a table.

Following the precepts of top - down design, the main part of the program is very short. It calls the initalization routine and then loops through the specified years, saving the output every `cycle` of years. It asks for the changes in the birth and mortality rates in `change_year`. Its structure chart is shown in Figure 18.2.

The subroutine `initial` establishes the length of the simulation and the change point. It also reads the age groups into the output table `out$`. It then opens the file `popdata`, which contains the census information and inputs

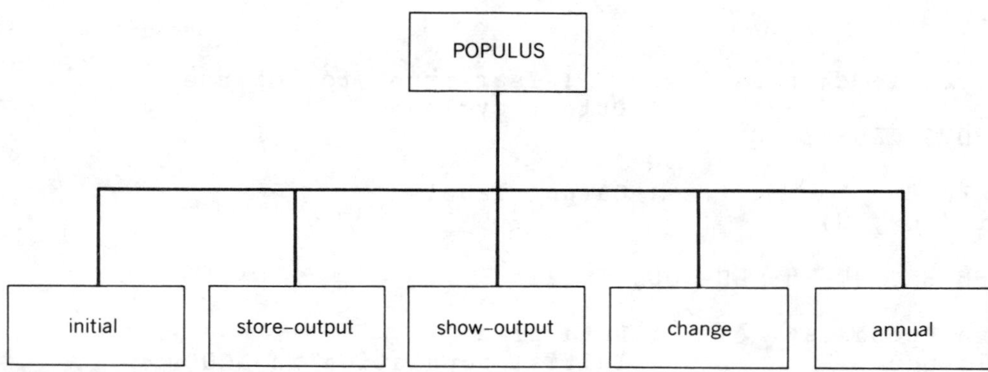

FIGURE 18.2.
Structure chart for the program POPULUS.

the values of pop(), br(), and dr(). Because the Statistical Abstract gives the birth and mortality rates per 1000 individuals, we multiply by .001 to adjust.

```
REM   POPULUS
REM
REM   Population growth model
REM
REM   This program follows each age group in a population
REM   as it ages, applying birth and mortality rates.
REM   It allows a change in birth and health care rates
REM   after a specified number of years.
REM
REM   Population, birth rate, and mortality rate
REM   are taken from Tables 28, 77, and 96 of
REM        U. S. Bureau of the Census
REM        Statistical Abstract of the United States: 1977
REM        98th Edition, Washington, D. C., 1977.
REM   Mortality rates above age 65 have been extrapolated.

DIM pop(0 to 100)                ! Population by age
DIM br(0 to 100)                 ! Birth rate by mother's age
DIM dr(0 to 100)                 ! Death rate by age
DIM hist(0 to 5)                 ! Used for summary printing
DIM out$(5, 0 to 6)              ! Formatted output

CALL initial

FOR year = year0 to year1
    IF mod(year-year0, cycle) = 0 then CALL store_output
    IF year = change_year then
       CALL show_output          ! Part 1 results
       CALL change               ! Change rates
    END IF
    CALL annual                  ! Population for next year
NEXT year
CALL show_output                 ! Part 2 results
```

```
SUB initial

    READ year0, year1, change_year     ! Year from, to, change
    READ cycle                         ! Output cycle
    DATA 1975, 2075, 2025, 10

    FOR row = 1 to 5                   ! Output labels
        READ out$(row, 0)
    NEXT row
    DATA 0-19, 20-39, 40-59, 60-100, Total

    OPEN #1: name "popdata"            ! Data file
    MAT INPUT #1: pop                  ! Initial population in 1000s
    LINE INPUT #1: x$                  ! Blank line
    MAT INPUT #1: br                   ! Birth rate per 1000 women
    LINE INPUT #1: x$                  ! Blank line
    MAT INPUT #1: dr                   ! Mortality rate per 1000 persons
    CLOSE #1

    MAT br = (.001)*br                 ! Birth rate per woman
    MAT dr = (.001)*dr                 ! Mortality rate per person

    LET birthrate = 0
    FOR age = 0 to 100
        LET birthrate = birthrate + br(age)
    NEXT age

    PRINT "Starting birth rate is"; birthrate

END SUB

SUB annual

    FOR age = 99 to 0 step -1          !   Age pop. by one year
        LET pop(age+1) =  pop(age)*(1 - dr(age))
    NEXT age

    LET pop(0) = 0                     !   Calculate new births
    FOR age = 1 to 100
        LET women = pop(age)/2         !   Assume half are women
        LET pop(0) = pop(0) + br(age)*women
    NEXT age

END SUB

SUB change

    PRINT "Change in birth rate, death rate";
    INPUT deltabr, deltahc

    FOR age = 0 to 100
        LET br(age) = br(age)*(1 + deltabr)
    NEXT age
    LET birthrate = birthrate*(1 + deltabr)
    PRINT "New birth rate is"; birthrate
```

```
    LET dr(0) = dr(0)*(1 - deltahc)     ! Infants
    FOR age = 51 to 100                ! Older age groups
        LET dr(age) = dr(age)*(1 - deltahc)
    NEXT age

    LET year0 = year                   ! New base year
    CALL store_output                  ! Begin new output

END SUB

DEF form$(x) = using$("###.#", x/1000)        ! Millions, formatted

SUB store_output                       ! Population: age group, total

    MAT hist = zer
    LET popul = 0
    FOR age = 0 to 100
        LET decade2 = int(age/20)
        LET hist(decade2) = hist(decade2) + pop(age)
        LET popul = popul + pop(age)
    NEXT age

    LET col = (year - year0)/cycle + 1        ! Column of output
    LET out$(1, col) = form$(hist(0))
    LET out$(2, col) = form$(hist(1))
    LET out$(3, col) = form$(hist(2))
    LET out$(4, col) = form$(hist(3) + hist(4) + hist(5))
    LET out$(5, col) = form$(popul)

END SUB

SUB show_output                        ! Print contents of out$

    SET zonewidth 9                    ! Narrow columns
    PRINT
    PRINT "Ages",                      ! Header
    FOR i = 0 to 5
        PRINT year0 + i*cycle,
    NEXT i
    PRINT
    PRINT repeat$("-", 60)             ! Underline
    MAT PRINT out$                     ! Body of output

END SUB

END
```

The population for each age is given in the Statistical Abstract for 5 or 10-year age groups. Here we make the somewhat unrealistic assumption that these numbers should be apportioned equally to each age in the age group. The birth rate is likewise given in the Statistical Abstract for age groups; we assume that the same rates apply to all women in the age group. Finally, the mortality rates in the Statistical Abstract are given for each year of age up to age 65, and for ages 70, 75, and 80. The values for ages above 65 were obtained by interpolating in and extrapolating from these values.

The resulting data file **POPDATA** is shown. The numbers for each array are typed in convenient length lines, with all items except the last one followed by a comma. The data arrays are separated by blank lines, which are handled in `initial` by using **LINE INPUT** statements.

```
3067.8, 3067.8, 3067.8, 3067.8, 3067.8, 3661.7,
3661.7, 3661.7, 3661.7, 3661.7, 3661.7, 3661.7, 3661.7, 3661.7,
4224.0, 4224.0, 4224.0, 4224.0, 4155.5, 4155.5, 4155.5, 4155.5,
3766.7, 3766.7, 3766.7, 3189.1, 3189.1, 3189.1, 3189.1, 3189.1,
3189.1, 3189.1, 3189.1, 3189.1, 3189.1, 2301.2, 2301.2, 2301.2,
2301.2, 2301.2, 2301.2, 2301.2, 2301.2, 2301.2, 2301.2, 2363.6,
2363.6, 2363.6, 2363.6, 2363.6, 2363.6, 2363.6, 2363.6, 2363.6,
2363.6, 2006.4, 2006.4, 2006.4, 2006.4, 2006.4, 2006.4, 2006.4,
2006.4, 2006.4, 2006.4, 1720.0, 1720.0, 1720.0, 1720.0, 1720.0,
1720.0, 1720.0, 1720.0, 1720.0, 1720.0, 430.0, 430.0, 430.0,
430.0, 430.0, 430.0, 430.0, 430.0, 430.0, 430.0, 107.5,
107.5, 107.5, 107.5, 107.5, 107.5, 107.5, 107.5, 107.5, 107.5,
59.7, 59.7, 59.7, 59.7, 59.7, 59.7

0, 0, 0, 0, 0, 0, 0, 0, 0, 0, 1.3, 1.3, 1.3, 1.3, 1.3,
56.3, 56.3, 56.3, 56.3, 56.3, 114.7, 114.7, 114.7, 114.7, 114.7,
110.3, 110.3, 110.3, 110.3, 110.3, 53.1, 53.1, 53.1, 53.1, 53.1,
19.4, 19.4, 19.4, 19.4, 19.4, 4.6, 4.6, 4.6, 4.6, 4.6,
.3, .3, .3, .3, .3, 0, 0, 0, 0, 0, 0, 0, 0, 0, 0, 0,
0, 0, 0, 0, 0, 0, 0, 0, 0, 0, 0, 0, 0, 0, 0, 0, 0, 0, 0, 0,
0, 0, 0, 0, 0, 0, 0, 0, 0, 0, 0, 0, 0, 0, 0, 0, 0, 0, 0, 0

16.06, .95, .75, .60, .50, .44,
.39, .36, .32, .28, .25, .25, .30, .42, .57, .75,
.91, 1.05, 1.16, 1.23, 1.30, 1.37, 1.41, 1.42, 1.41, 1.38,
1.36, 1.35, 1.36, 1.38, 1.40, 1.44, 1.49, 1.57, 1.66, 1.78,
1.91, 2.07, 2.25, 2.45, 2.68, 2.94, 3.22, 3.53, 3.88, 4.25,
4.66, 5.09, 5.55, 6.04, 6.57, 7.15, 7.78, 8.47, 9.23, 10.02,
10.87, 11.84, 12.95, 14.19, 15.56,
16.99, 18.35, 19.59, 20.77, 21.95,
23.45, 25.35, 27.61, 30.23, 33.21,
36.41, 39.83, 43.47, 47.33, 51.44,
55.85, 60.59, 65.66, 71.06, 76.69,
82.86, 89.47, 96.52, 104.01, 111.94,
120.42, 129.45, 139.03, 149.16, 159.84,
171.18, 183.18, 195.84, 209.16, 223.14,
237.89, 253.41, 269.70, 286.76, 1000.00
```

The subroutine `annual` merely moves the number of persons of a given age to the next age, applying the mortality rate as it goes. Notice that the loop must go backwards, using a step size of -1. The subroutine then calculates the number of new individuals by applying the birth rate to the number of women at each age. (We assume that women constitute one-half the population at each age.) Although the population size, `pop(age)`, is given in thousands, it is not necessary to multiply by 1000 before applying the birth and death rates, for we would immediately divide by 1000 to return to the original units.

The subroutine `change` allows the user to alter the birth rate by a multiplicative factor, with the factor applying to all the birth rates. The adjustment in death rate is similarly taken to be a multiplicative factor that reduces the mortality rate. In this case, the reduction is assumed to apply only to infants and persons aged 50 and older, the groups most affected by the quality of health care.

The subroutine `store_output` first calculates population by decile groups and then stores a nicely formatted summary in a column of `out$`. The function `form$` creates a formatted output; the formatting string "###.#" will round to one decimal place, and put three digits before the decimal point and one after it. Our output will thus line up nicely. (See Appendix III for details or `PRINT using`.)

The routine `show_output` prints the table. It labels all columns, then underlines the header. The function `repeat$` is used to duplicate a dash 60 times for the underlining. Then `MAT PRINT` is used to print the formatted table. This routine is called twice, once before calling `change` and once at the end. Thus pre-change and post-change results are shown separately.

```
run

Starting birth rate is 1.8

Ages        1975      1985      1995      2005      2015      2025
------------------------------------------------------------------
0-19        73.5      66.7      64.9      60.7      57.1      54.6
20-39       63.0      74.5      71.9      65.3      63.5      59.4
40-59       45.2      48.6      59.3      69.9      67.2      61.1
60-100      33.0      38.5      40.4      43.5      51.7      60.0
Total      214.6     228.3     236.5     239.4     239.6     235.1

Change in birth rate, death rate? .2, .1
New birth rate is 2.16

Ages        2025      2035      2045      2055      2065      2075
------------------------------------------------------------------
0-19        54.6      56.3      58.7      58.3      59.8      60.8
20-39       59.4      55.9      53.4      55.1      57.5      57.0
40-59       61.1      59.6      55.6      52.5      50.0      51.8
60-100      60.0      61.4      59.6      56.9      53.5      50.9
Total      235.1     233.3     227.4     222.8     220.8     220.5
```

The sample run shows how we might project the population of the United States into the future. Notice that the birth rate for the population, 1.8, is lower than the ZPG (zero population growth) rate. Nonetheless, the population continues to grow until the year 2015, when it reaches almost 240 million. Although the younger age groups are declining due to the low birthrate, we can see a "population bulge" move through the age groups, with an increase in the older groups offsetting the decline of the younger ones. (For a discussion of ZPG see Project 4(a).)

In the year 2025, we introduce a 20 percent increase in the birth rate and assume improved health care. The birth rate then becomes almost equal to the ZPG rate, and the population, although decreasing for awhile, appears to

---

To fit the output table on the screen, we recommend inserting `SET MODE "hires"` into the program for the IBM PC, and selecting "small font" on the Macintosh.

level off at around 220 million. Without these changes there would be a steady decline of the population.

18.4 MODEL OF A SMALL COLLEGE

The use of mathematical models is common to all the sciences. The ability to formulate physical laws in mathematical terms has enabled physicists to use the full power of mathematics to analyze the physical world. Although some mathematical models have proved equally useful in the social sciences, it is common for the mathematics to be so complex as to be beyond our means of analysis. In such situations, computer models can be useful.

In a computer model the scientist formulates a number of quantitative relations as a computer program. The purpose of the program is to "act out nature". If the model is reasonably accurate, the scientist may be able to predict the effects of changes in the environment and of different policies imposed by man.

There is no sharp boundary between mathematical models and computer models. In general, however, social science models are both more complicated and less certain. Precise mathematical solutions for them are less likely. We may therefore be forced to bypass the mathematical analysis stage and to go directly to the computer model.

As an illustration, we will construct two models of enrollments at a small college. We will imagine that only the student/faculty ratio and the tuition influence enrollment. Before we examine the actual models, we should warn the reader that any agreement between these models and the real world is purely coincidental. Our purpose is not to simulate reality but to show that even simple models such as these can exhibit non-intuitive behavior, which often is a characteristic of real life.

We will first consider `COLLEGE`, a simple model consisting of mathematical equations that can actually be solved by a combination of algebra and calculus. But, when we introduce even slightly more realistic assumptions (in `COLLEGE2`), the behavior of the model will be dramatically different. In the latter case, a study of the model without computers is nearly hopeless.

The key variables in both models are

pool = applicant pool
faculty = size of the faculty
students = size of the student body
ratio = student/faculty ratio
tuition = tuition

One difficulty in modeling social behavior is that of quantifying intangibles. For example, how attractive is the institution to students in the applicant pool? We will model an attractiveness factor, depending on `ratio` and `tuition`, that determines the fraction of the pool that actually comes to the college.

In addition, our model depends on five parameters. Of these, `cost`, `fixed`, and `endow` are known quantities determining the expense of running the institution; `tuitmin` and `ratiomin` are intangibles used to compute the attractiveness factor.

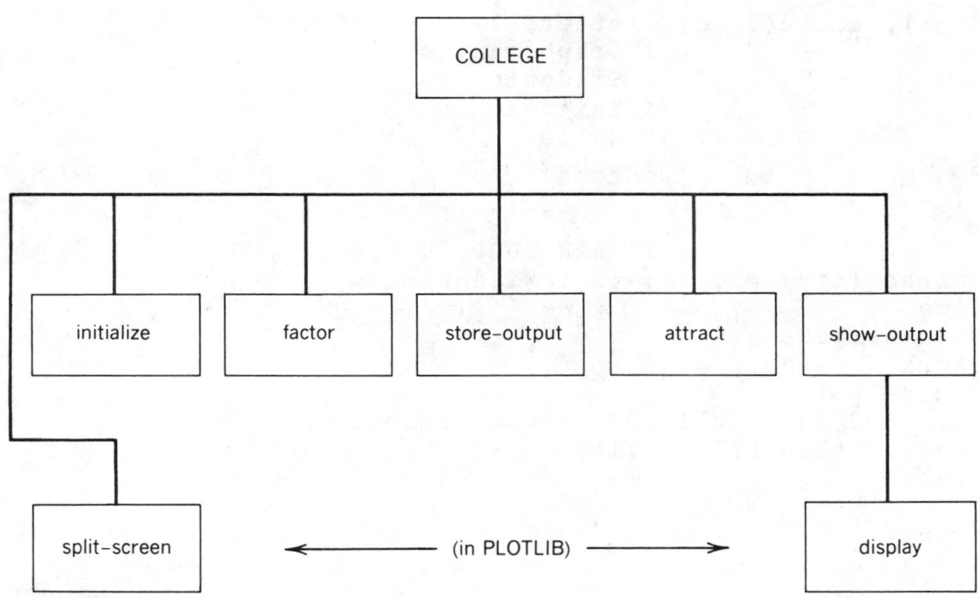

FIGURE 18.3
Structure chart for the program COLLEGE.

The model starts in equilibrium. If no change is made in the faculty of 100, the student body remains at 2000, with a ratio of 20 (poor) and the tuition at a very low $4000. The trustees are considering a five-year build-up of the faculty to improve the quality of the institution, and COLLEGE is designed to help in this decision. It asks for the new (target) faculty size and increases the faculty in five equal steps to this size. It shows what happens to the institution in the next 15 years.

The skeleton of COLLEGE is a FOR loop, allowing four examples. Results of all four will be shown graphically on the same screen, thus allowing comparisons. Its structure chart is shown in Figure 18.3. The graphics routines are in PLOTLIB, which will be explained in Chapter 21.

```
REM  COLLEGE
REM
REM  Model of a small college

LIBRARY "PLOTLIB.trc"                ! For graphics output
SET MODE "hires"

! Parameters

LET cost = 40000                     ! Cost per faculty
LET fixed = 7.8e6                    ! Fixed costs
LET endow = 3.8e6                    ! Endowment income
LET tuitmin = 4000                   ! Minimum tuition
LET ratiomin = 10                    ! Minimum ratio
LET maxyear = 15                     ! Length of simulation
LET nyears = 5                       ! Years of faculty increase
```

```
DIM data(0 to 40, 3), range(3, 2), letter$(3)
MAT READ range                          ! Graph ranges
DATA 500, 3000                          ! Students
DATA 3200, 8000                         ! Tuition
DATA 10, 22                             ! Ratio
MAT READ letter$                        ! Labels
DATA S, T, R

FOR try = 1 to 4                        ! MAIN LOOP, 4 cases
    CALL split_screen (try, #1, #2)        ! Windows
    CALL initialize
    FOR year = 0 to maxyear
        CALL factors
        CALL store_output
        IF students<500 then EXIT FOR   ! Out of business
        IF year<nyears then LET faculty = faculty + delta
        CALL attract
    NEXT year
    CALL show_output
NEXT try

SUB initialize

    LET pool = 1000                     ! Applicant pool
    LET faculty = 100                   ! Faculty size
    LET students = 2000                 ! Student body size

    WINDOW #2
    PRINT "Faculty";
    INPUT newfaculty                    ! New faculty size
    LET delta = (newfaculty-faculty)/nyears       ! Over five years

END SUB

SUB factors                             ! Key variables

    LET ratio = students/faculty
    LET tuition = (faculty*cost + fixed - endow)/students

END SUB

SUB attract                             ! Students next year

    LET a1 = max(ratio/ratiomin, 1)
    LET a2 = max(tuition/tuitmin, 1)
    LET frosh = pool/(a1 * a2^1.5)
    LET frosh = pool/(a1 * a2^1.5)
    LET students = 4 * frosh            ! Oversimplified

END SUB

SUB store_output                        ! Save for graphics

    LET data(year,1) = students
    LET data(year,2) = tuition
    LET data(year,3) = ratio

END SUB
```

```
SUB show_output

    WINDOW #1
    LET lastyear = min(year, maxyear)
    CALL display (#1, data, range, maxyear, lastyear, letter$)

    WINDOW #2
    PRINT "Students ="; round(students,0)
    PRINT "Tuition  ="; round(tuition,0)
    PRINT "Ratio    ="; round(ratio,2)

END SUB

END
```

The first call is to `split_screen`, which sets up four graphics windows, one at a time. Next, `initialize` initializes our variables and asks for the new faculty size. Then follows the main loop that runs through the annual cycle. At the end, we call `show_output`, which displays both graphic and numeric output.

In the main loop, `factors` computes the variables `ratio` and `tuition`. Tuition is determined by taking the net expense of the college and dividing by the number of students. Next `store_output` is called. This routine stores the results in the array `data` for later graphic output. If `students` drops below 500 we use an `EXIT FOR` to exit the loop, because this case is hopeless. If we are in the build-up period, the faculty is increased. Finally we call `attract` to determine the number of students.

The heart of the model is `attract`. It assumes that the number of freshmen is the `pool` divided by the factor

$$a1 * a2^{1.5}$$

where

$$a1 = \max(ratio/ratiomin, 1)$$
$$a2 = \max(tuition/tuitmin, 1)$$

The smaller this factor is, the more attractive the college is to students. Let us examine `a1` first. The larger the ratio, the larger `a1`, hence the smaller the number of freshmen. Twice the ratio will produce half the freshmen. The use of `max` insures that `a1` cannot be less than 1 (can't attract more students then there are in the pool). It also has the effect that a ratio lower than `ratiomin` does not help the college. Similar remarks apply to `a2`. But this variable is raised to the power 1.5. Consequently, doubling the tuition would reduce the number of students not by a factor of 2, but by a factor of about 2.8. We have thus built into the model the assumption that students are more sensitive to tuition changes than to changes in the student/faculty ratio. The usefulness of the model depends in large measure on how well this attractiveness factor reflects reality.

We then compute the total number of students as 4 times the number of freshmen. This is quite unrealistic; a smaller incoming group of students does

---

To fit the output table on the screen, we recommend inserting `SET MODE "hires"` into the program for the IBM PC, and selecting "small font" on the Macintosh.

not normally reduce the number of upperclassmen. This will be corrected in the second version of the model. If `students` drops below 500, the college goes out of existence, and we stop the output.

It may appear that another unrealistic feature is built into the model; we did not take inflation into account. However, we may view the model as working with *constant dollars*. Attractiveness depends on the ratio of `tuition` and `tuitmin`. If both increase by the same inflationary factor, the ratio does not change.

Four runs are shown in Figure 18.4. The first shows that the college is in equilibrium, with a ratio of 20 and tuition at the minimum level of $4000. The next runs explore the effect of increasing the faculty. (Because the tuition is at the minimum level, it is clear that there is no advantage in decreasing the faculty.) We see that increases to 160 or 200 faculty members do increase the attractiveness of the college and hence the size of the student body. But 240 is past the optimum. The ratio drops below 10 and, hence, no longer helps, while tuition keeps climbing. The result is a disaster.

We also see that, in all reasonable cases, after a few transitional years the college settles down to a new equilibrium. It can be shown mathematically that, under the given assumptions, a faculty of 200 is optimal (leads to the largest student body) for our college.

We now change the initial values for the faculty to 200 and students to 2370. This is a new, better, equilibrium. We have a much higher quality institution that is somewhat more costly and has a larger student body. But what if changed conditions disturb this equilibrium?

Let us suppose that the fixed costs of the college rise from $7.8 million to $8.3 million, because of, for example, a half-million dollar increase in the cost of energy. (We assume that competing colleges are not similarly affected by rising energy costs.) The effect is a jump in tuition, and a resultant decline in enrollments. This is shown in the first run in Figure 18.5. The trustees may respond to increasing costs by ''cost-cutting''. But we see that a reduction in the faculty makes matters worse! The slight reduction in tuition is outweighed by the worse student/faculty ratio. It helps to increase the faculty to 210. But we see that such a change is very ''touchy'', because 215 looks like a disaster. One would have to have a great deal of faith in the model to risk the 210 figure.

Next we explore the effect of a decline in the size of the `pool` from 1000 to 900, while retaining the pre-energy-crisis value of $7.8 million for the fixed costs. We also start with an initial faculty size of 200 and 2370 for the student body. The results are shown in Figure 18.6. We find that a faculty of 200 can no longer be sustained. This time an increase makes the problem worse. But a relatively modest decrease seems to correct the problem.

Let us now build a somewhat more realistic model. An important feature of many social science computer models is the delay between cause and effect. In `COLLEGE2`, two kinds of delays occur. First, we take into account that the increased tuition has a direct effect only on the entering class. Therefore, we must keep track of all four classes separately, in the list `st`, because they have varying sizes. (Once in college, we assume the students remain for four years.) Second, we build into the model the fact that news of a significant change in the student/faculty ratio does not reach the clientele immediately. While `ratio` represents the actual ratio, `perceived` represents applicants' perception. The perceived ratio moves only one-third of the way from the previous value toward the actual ratio. These changes are

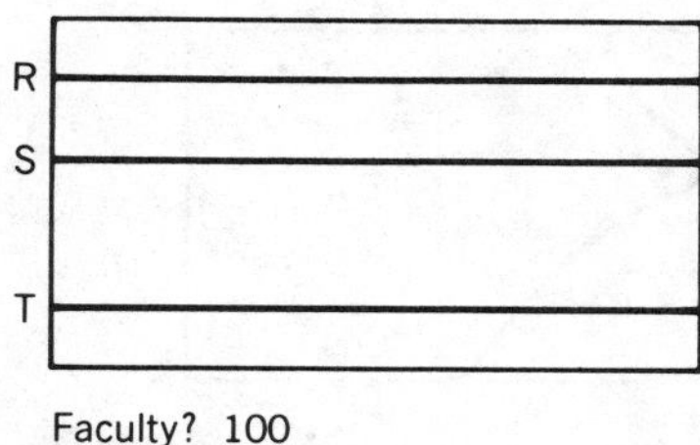

Faculty? 100
Students = 2000
Tuition = 4000
Ratio = 20

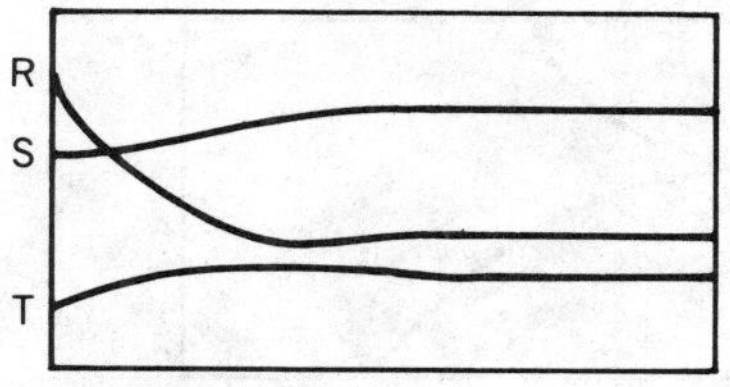

Faculty? 160
Students = 2330
Tuition = 4463
Ratio = 14.56

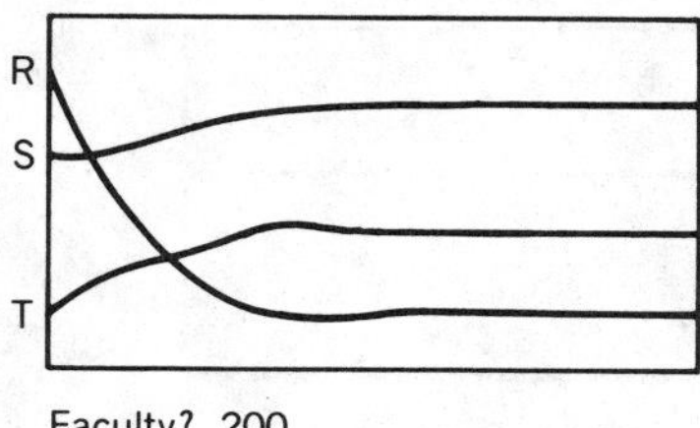

Faculty? 200
Students = 2370
Tuition = 5063
Ratio = 11.85

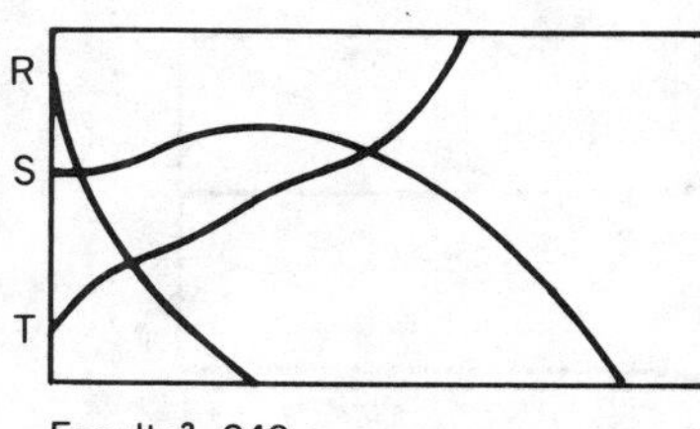

Faculty? 240
Students = 303
Tuition = 44962
Ratio = 1.26

FIGURE 18.4.
Output of COLLEGE, original assumptions.

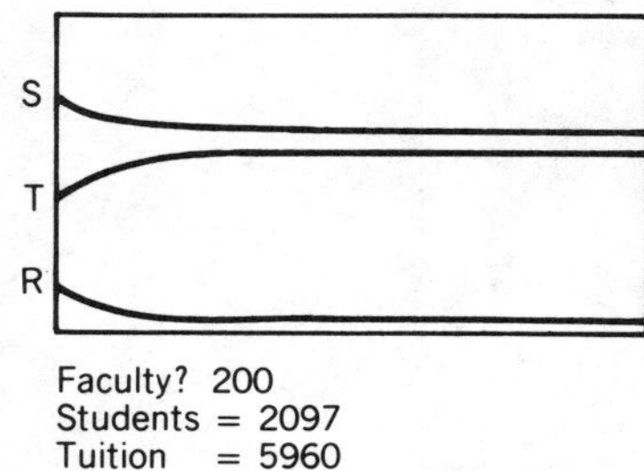

Faculty? 200
Students = 2097
Tuition = 5960
Ratio = 10.49

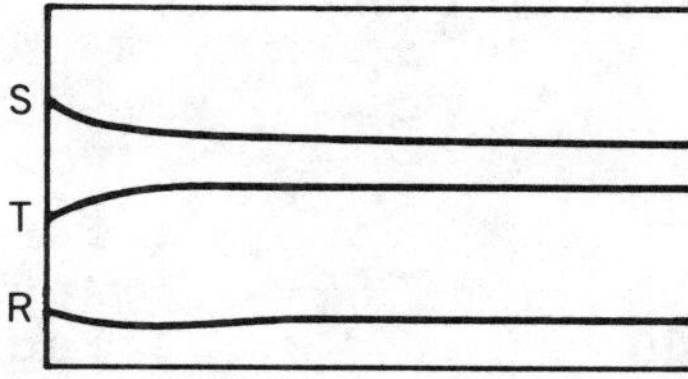

Faculty? 180
Students = 2072
Tuition = 5648
Ratio = 11.51

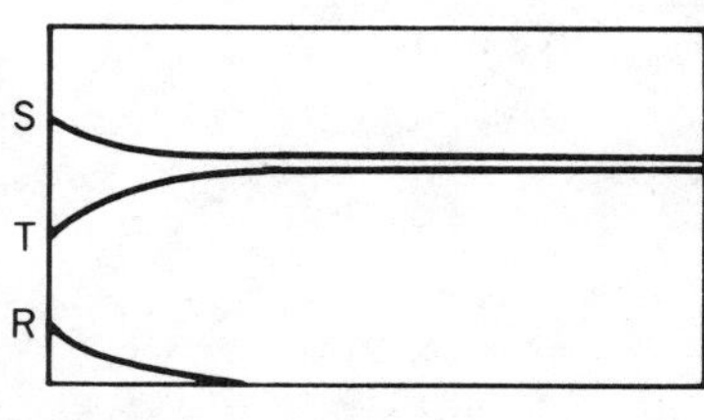

Faculty? 210
Students = 2104
Tuition = 6132
Ratio = 10.02

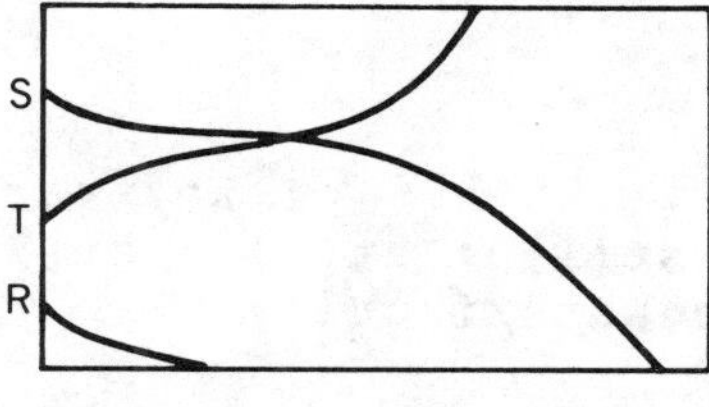

Faculty? 215
Students = 467
Tuition = 28074
Ratio = 2.17

FIGURE 18.5.
Output of COLLEGE, with energy inflation.

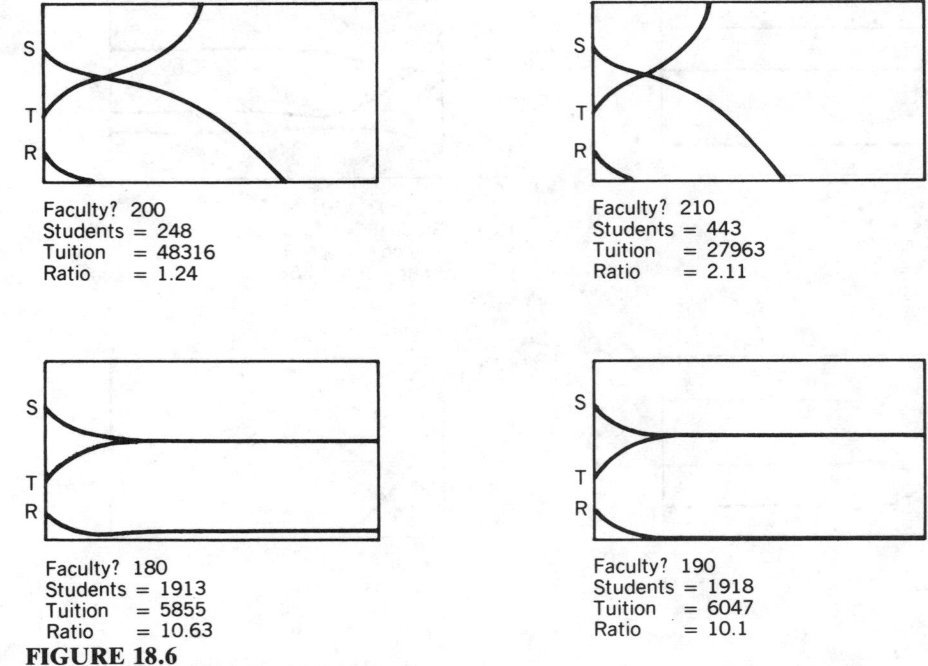

FIGURE 18.6
Output of COLLEGE, smaller applicant pool.

incorporated into the routines `initialize`, `factors`, and `attract`. Only these are shown.

A portion of program COLLEGE2 follows.

```
SUB initialize

    DIM st(4)                            ! Four classes
    LET pool = 1000                      ! Applicant pool
    LET faculty = 100                    ! Faculty size
    MAT st = 500 * con                   ! Class sizes

    WINDOW #2
    PRINT "Faculty";
    INPUT newfaculty                     ! New faculty size
    LET delta = (newfaculty-faculty)/nyears   ! Over five years

END SUB

SUB factors                          ! Key variables
    LET students = st(1) + st(2) + st(3) + st(4)
    LET ratio = students/faculty
    IF year=0 then
       LET perceived = ratio
    ELSE
    LET perceived = (2*perceived + ratio)/3    ! Move 1/3 way
    END IF
    LET tuition = (faculty*cost + fixed - endow)/students
END SUB
```

```
SUB attract                         ! Students next year
    LET a1 = max(perceived/ratiomin, 1)
    LET a2 = max(tuition/tuitmin, 1)
    FOR c = 4 to 2 step -1          ! Advance classes
        LET st(c) = st(c-1)
    NEXT c
    LET st(1) = pool/(a1 * a2^1.5)
END SUB
```

Runs of COLLEGE2 are shown in Figure 18.7. The first run shows the same equilibrium as for COLLEGE. But when we increase the faculty, the outcome is quite different. We find that although increases in the size of the faculty are still favorable in the long run, they have negative effects in the short run, owing to delays. Thus the reactions of students to an increase in tuition is much more immediate than to a decrease in the student/faculty ratio. One has to wait for the latter to catch up with the former before the favorable results show up. We therefore show projections for 40 years. A new equilibrium seems to occur, but the size of the student body oscillates. And, due to the delays, a faculty of 190 is already too large. The immediate effect of the tuition increase quickly reduces the student body, resulting in a very small ratio and, therefore, the increase in faculty is of no help.

The optimal decision will depend on the time scale in which the college does its long-range planning. For the long run an increase to 175 appears favorable. But this may be unacceptable because of lean years in the near future and the severe swings that occur. Increasing the faculty to 150 seems to be more prudent.

A faculty of 150 with 2304 students is the new equilibrium. We now explore the effects of a decrease in the pool to 900. Once again increased tuition

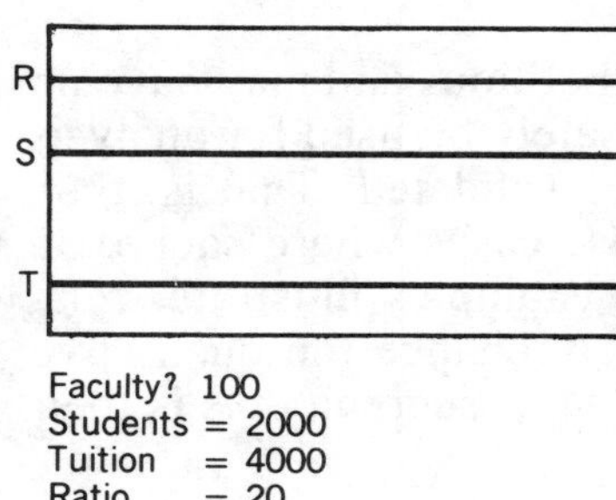

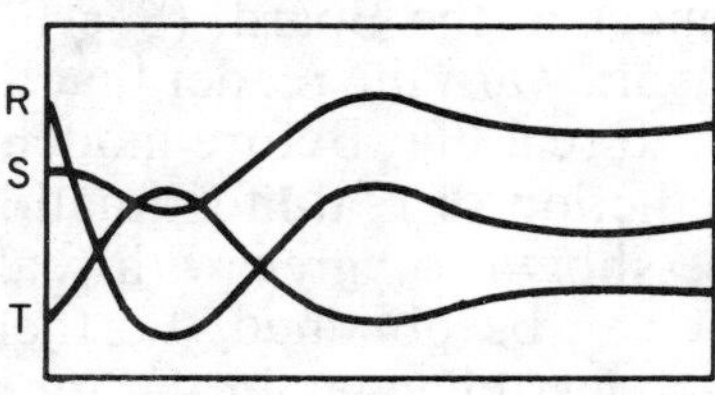

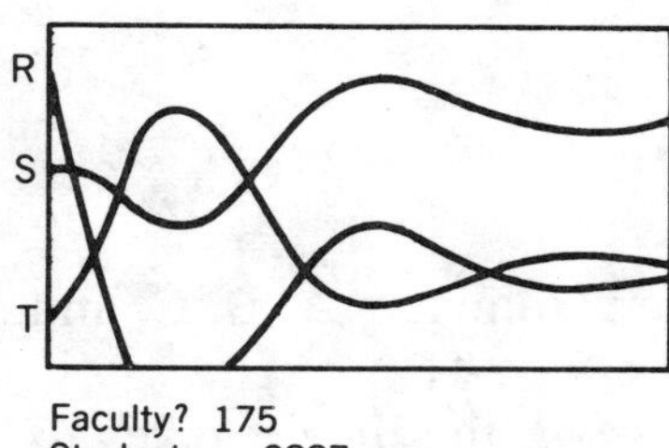

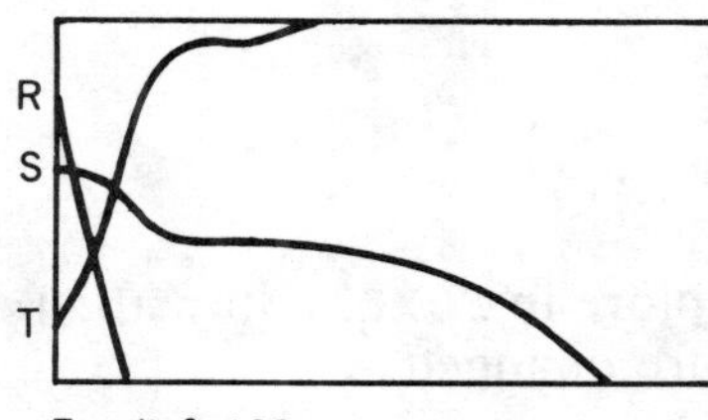

FIGURE 18.7
Output of COLLEGE2, original assumptions.

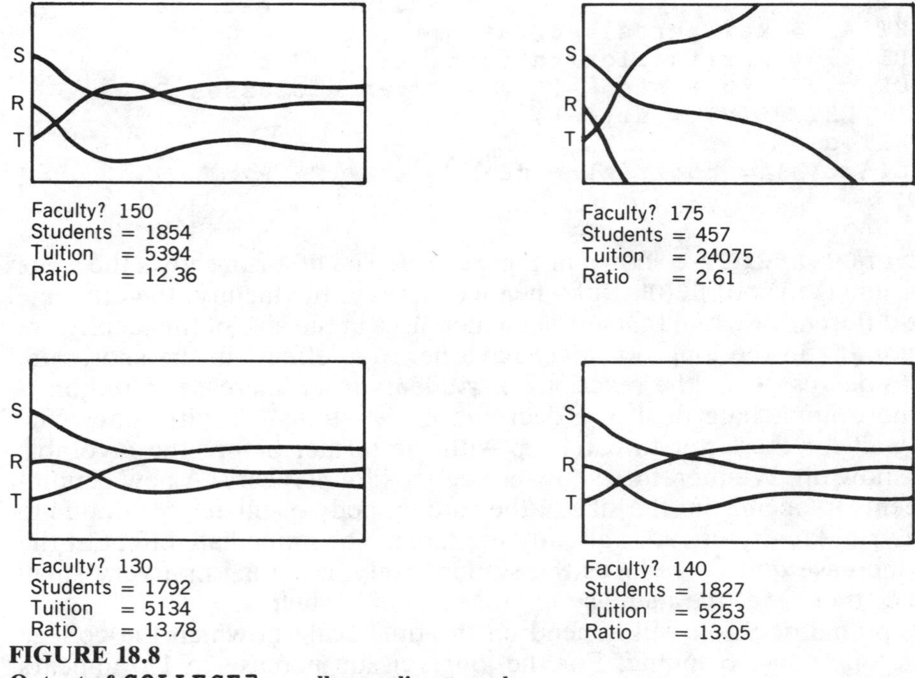

FIGURE 18.8
Output of COLLEGE2, smaller applicant pool.

reduces the number of students. But we see that once the equilibrium is disturbed, it takes a long time for the oscillations to settle down. An increase in the faculty again causes a disaster. But, although a decrease helps in the short run, it is less good in the long run. The decision will depend on the preferences of the Board. (See Figure 18.8.)

We again warn the reader that these models are fictitious and may have no relation to real life. Before models like these can safely be used for analysis and prediction of real-life situations, they must be validated. That is, they must be shown to agree with real-life data in those cases where such data exist or can be obtained. Furthermore, as these examples illustrate, relatively modest changes in the model can completely change the qualitative nature of the results. For that reason, a major value of such models is their assistance in probing for sensitive spots.

PROJECTS

1. Explore in **FOXRAB** how the results vary as the parameters A, B, C, and D are changed.
2. Modify **FOXRAB** so that it will discover the *period*, the time it takes to return to the starting position. (Allow for rounding errors and for not quite hitting the original position.) Study how the period depends on the parameters A, B, C, and D.

3. Starting with **FOXRAB**, explore the effects of a hunting season on foxes and on rabbits. Draw conclusions about the effects of scheduling the hunting season at different points in the ecological cycle.

4. Experiment with **POPULUS** as follows:

   a. Use trial and error to discover the birth rate that leads to ZPG. (A birth rate exactly equal to 2.00 is too small, because a fraction of the population dies prior to reaching reproductive age. The birth rate for couples having children would be even slightly higher, because not all couples of parent age choose to have children.)
   b. Change the subroutine `output` so that it shows the number of school-aged (14 - 17, inclusive) and college-aged (18 - 21, inclusive) persons. Project the numbers in these two groups for each year from 1980 to 2000.

5. The Statistical Abstract gives data by sex and by race (white and and black.) Expand **POPULUS** to allow separate treatment by sex and race. Also arrange to allow immigration and emigration, if you can obtain estimates of these. Make projections according to your special interest. (You should realize that projections beyond 10 or 20 years are suspect because changes that occur during that time will probably effect the birth and mortality rates.)
6. Make the model **COLLEGE2** more realistic by introducing the following additional factors:

   a. Add annual gifts as an item of income, which thus reduces tuition. Try to formulate a reasonable assumption on how the amount generated by gifts depends on the attractiveness of the college.
   b. The rather extreme fluctuations of tuition are unrealistic. Allow a modest `deficit` during a transition stage. These amounts are, in effect, borrowed. They must be repaid with interest in later years.
   c. Allow more sophisticated ways of modifying the faculty size. The user should be allowed to specify, year-by-year, what the change should be.

   Explore the properties of the improved model.

FURTHER READING

1. McCracken, Daniel B., and Dorn, William S., *Introductory Finite Mathematics with Computing*, John Wiley, New York, 1976. This text presents an extensive treatment of elementary ecological and population models.
2. Bennett, William A., *Introduction to Computer Appiications for Non-Science Students (BASIC)*, Prentice-Hall, Englewood Cliffs, N.J., 1976. This text treats a number of fascinating topics such as random text generation and cryptography.
3. Wetherell, Charles, *Etudes for Programmers*, Prentice-Hall, Englewood Cliffs, N.J., 1978. For the more advanced student, this book is a rich collection of projects. Languages other than BASIC are stressed.

PART FOUR

OTHER APPLICATIONS

CHAPTER 19

BUSINESS PROBLEMS

19.1 INTRODUCTION

Computer methods are used to solve many business problems. We have selected three applications that deal with three quite different topics. They also illustrate a variety of programming techniques.

The first is the projection of an institutional budget, using the current year as a base and specified escalation percentages for each expense and revenue category.

The second is a compound interest program that solves all the common cases. It also is designed to have a *manu-driven* user interface that makes the program very easy to use.

The third is the *critical path method*, or *CPM*, used to identify the bottlenecks in a project. We show it first with a small data set and then discuss the changes necessary for a large application.

19.2 BUDGET PROJECTION

We will start with a problem that any business must address. The present year's budget is known, and estimates are available as to how fast various expense and revenue items will grow. What can we expect for the future? This is the type of problem often handled by *spreadsheet* programs.

Our example will be a university budget. To keep the data of manageable size, we will project a ''high-level'' budget, as a board of trustees might see it. Thus, there will be few categories, with similar items lumped together. The same program could be used for a detailed budget. It would only require more data and larger arrays.

For the modest size budget we present the information could be provided in `DATA` statements. In a realistic application, however, such data is kept in a file, and we therefore use a datafile `BUDGETF`.

BUDGETF, data for BUDGET.

```
8
Instruction, 51.1, 7.2
Administration, 13.5, 7.2
Library, 5.8, 12
Computing, 4.2, 9
Athletics, 4.8, 7.9
Fin. Aid, 7.7, 10.1
Plant, 8.3, 8.5
Auxiliary, 15.6, 6.5
6
Tuition, 37.6, 9
Endowment, 16.4, 4.2
Gifts, 11, 8.1
Sponsored, 19.7, 5
Auxiliary, 15.6, 6.5
Direct, 11.8, 6.2
```

The first entry in the file is the number of expense categories. Then, for each expense category there is a line containing the name of the category, the size of the current budget (in millions of dollars), and the percentage by which this expense item is escalated. Next come the current budget and escalation factors for the revenue categories.

Before looking at the program, let us consider how growth rates are determined. There are two fundamentally different approaches. One may look at the recent past to see how expenses and revenues have escalated, and use the assumption that the near future will resemble these rates. Or, the trustees may suggest desirable growth rates, based on inflation, on what the institution's goals are, and on what it can afford. And, of course, a combination of the two approaches may also be employed.

In the program `BUDGET`, the array `E` will contain this year's budget in column 0, and projected budgets for future years in the other columns. Thus each column represents a year. The rows represent expense items, with row 0 containing the total of the year's expenses. Growth rates are stored in `Egrow` and the names of the expense categories (used only to print answers) are in `Ename$`. The arrays `R`, `Rgrow`, and `Rname$` contain the same information for revenues.

The arrays are dimensioned to allow up to 50 expense and 50 revenue categories, as well as projections up to 10 years. We specify in `years` that we will actually project five years, and `now` has the current year's date.

The program consists mostly of subroutine calls, with the budget subroutines collected into a library `BUDGLIB`. The structure chart is shown in Figure 19.1. This is a good illustration of the use of external subroutines. We repeatedly have to do the same task for both expenses and revenues. We can avoid duplication by using the same routine for both, first sending the E-arrays as parameters, and then sending the R-arrays.

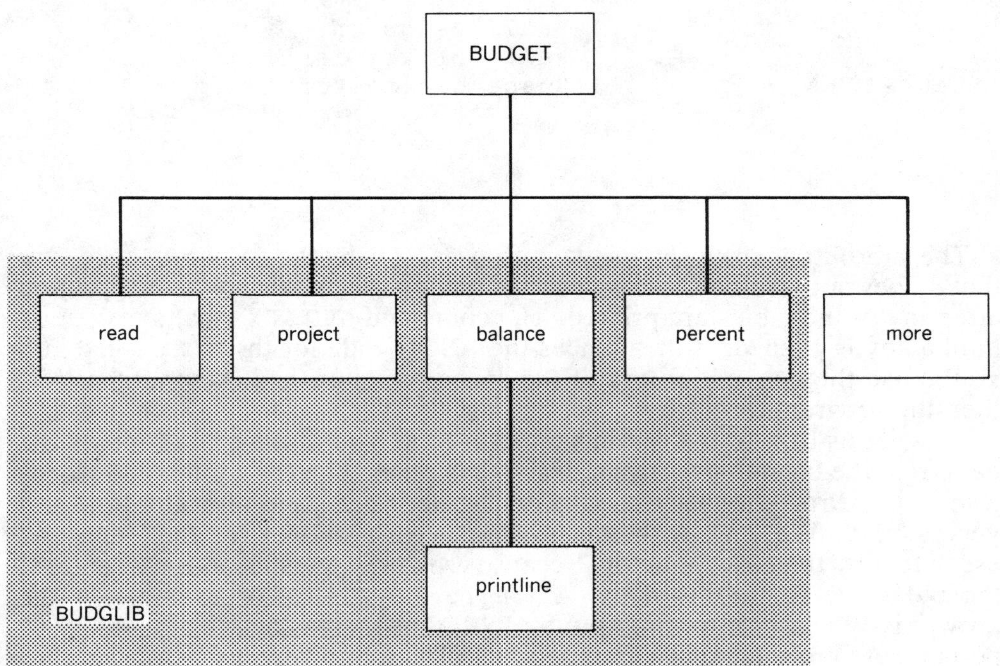

FIGURE 19.1
Structure chart for the program BUDGET.

```
REM  BUDGET
REM
REM  Budget projection

LIBRARY "BUDGLIB.trc"

DIM E(0 to 50, 0 to 10)              ! Expenses
DIM R(0 to 50, 0 to 10)              ! Revenues
! Rows are budget categories, row 0 is for total
! Columns are years, column 0 is the current year

DIM Ename$(50), Rname$(50)           ! Category names
DIM Egrow(50), Rgrow(50)             ! Percentage growth rates

LET years = 5                        ! Years to project
LET now = 1986                       ! Current year
CLEAR                                ! Full screen output

OPEN #1: name "BUDGETF"              ! Budget data file
CALL read (#1, E, emax, Ename$, Egrow) ! Read data
CALL read (#1, R, rmax, Rname$, Rgrow)
CALL project (E, emax, Egrow, years)   ! Projections
CALL project (R, rmax, Rgrow, years)

CALL balance (E,R,now,years)         ! Balance sheet
CALL more                            ! Pause, go on?
CALL percent ("Expenses", E, emax, Ename$, now, years)
CALL more
CALL percent ("Revenues", R, rmax, Rname$, now, years)
CALL more
```

```
SUB more                                  ! Shall we go on?
    GET KEY z                             ! Wait for key input
    IF z=32 then STOP                     ! Space bar to terminate
END SUB

END
```

The subroutine `more` serves two purposes. It halts the output to make sure that it does not scroll off the screen, and it allows us to terminate the program after any of the tables are printed. The command **GET KEY z** halts execution until a key is pushed. It then places the ASCII code for the key pushed into `z`. We use the convention that if the space bar is pushed (key number 32), then the program terminates.

Now let us turn to the routines in **BUDGLIB**. The routine `read` inputs the data from the file into the arrays. It also computes the year's total, and places it in row 0. Projections are carried out by `project`, one year at a time and very simply. We start with the previous year's budget for that item and escalate it by the growth factor. Because growth is specified as a percentage, the old value is multiplied by `1 + Bgrow(i)/100`. For example, if the growth is 12 percent, we multiply by 1.12, thus increasing the amount by 12 percent. Again, totals are computed and placed into row 0.

The routine `balance` prints a balance sheet. For each year it computes the difference between revenues and expenses. Thus a positive balance is favorable whereas a negative one represents a deficit. It prints annual totals for expenses, revenues, and the balance. To allow a sufficient number of columns for this table, it uses **SET ZONEWIDTH 8**, making each *column* or *zone* only eight characters wide. The actual printing is done by the routine `printline`, which produces a formatted output. (See Appendix 3.)

Although the projected balance sheet is the single most useful planning tool, we also present two useful supplementary tables. They show for each expense and revenue category what percent of the total it represents this year, and what it projects to be in the final year. This helps us pick up significant trends.

```
EXTERNAL

!  BUDGLIB
!  Library for BUDGET program
!
!       read            Reads data from file
!       project         Projects data using growth rates
!       balance         Prints the "balance" sheet
!       printline       Prints one formatted line
!       percent         Computes and prints percentages

SUB read (#1, B(,), bmax, Bname$(), Bgrow())       ! Read data

    INPUT #1: bmax                        ! No. of items
    LET total = 0                         ! Budget total
    FOR i = 1 to bmax
        INPUT #1: Bname$(i), B(i,0), Bgrow(i)
        LET total = total + B(i,0)
    NEXT i
    LET B(0,0) = total

END SUB
```

```
SUB project (B(,), bmax, Bgrow(), years)     ! Project by categories

    FOR j = 1 to years
        LET total = 0
        FOR i = 1 to bmax
            LET old = B(i,j-1)
            LET new = old * (1 + Bgrow(i)/100)
            LET B(i,j) = new
            LET total = total + new
        NEXT i
        LET B(0,j) = total
    NEXT j

END SUB

SUB balance (E(,), R(,), now, years)    ! Yearly balance sheet

    DIM Dif(0 to 0, 0 to 10)        ! Just row 0
    SET zonewidth 8

    FOR j = 0 to years              ! Revenue minus expenses
        LET Dif(0,j) = R(0,j) - E(0,j)
    NEXT j

    PRINT tab(16);                  ! Heading
    FOR j = 0 to years
        PRINT now+j,
    NEXT j
    PRINT

    CALL printline ("Expenses", E, years, "###.#")
    CALL printline ("Revenues", R, years, "###.#")
    CALL printline ("Balance", Dif, years, "++%.#")
    PRINT

END SUB

SUB printline (label$, B(,), years, f$)     ! Line of balance sheet

    PRINT label$; tab(16);
    FOR j = 0 to years
        PRINT using$(f$, B(0,j)),     ! Total to one decimal
    NEXT j
    PRINT

END SUB

SUB percent (label$, B(,), bmax, Bname$(), now, years)

    ! Computes income and expenses and percents of total

    DEF pc$(x) = using$("##.#",x*100) & "%" ! Percent, to one place

    PRINT label$; tab(16); now, now+years
    FOR i = 1 to bmax
        PRINT Bname$(i); tab(16);
        PRINT pc$(B(i,0)/B(0,0)), pc$(B(i,years)/B(0,years))
    NEXT i
    PRINT

END SUB
```

Our run shows a fairly typical budget problem. The university is showing a slight surplus for the present year (slight in that it is one percent of the total—and subject to errors), but if the present trend continues, there will be a sizable deficit by the end of the fifth year.

```
run

                  1986      1987      1988      1989      1990      1991
Expenses         111.0     119.6     128.9     138.9     149.8     161.5
Revenues         112.1     119.8     128.1     136.9     146.5     156.7
Balance           +1.1      +0.2      -0.8      -2.0      -3.3      -4.8

Expenses          1986      1991
Instruction      46.0%     44.8%
Administration   12.2%     11.8%
Library           5.2%      6.3%
Computing         3.8%      4.0%
Athletics         4.3%      4.3%
Fin. Aid          6.9%      7.7%
Plant             7.5%      7.7%
Auxiliary        14.1%     13.2%

Revenues          1986      1991
Tuition          33.5%     36.9%
Endowment        14.6%     12.9%
Gifts             9.8%     10.4%
Sponsored        17.6%     16.0%
Auxiliary        13.9%     13.6%
Direct           10.5%     10.2%
```

The balance sheet identifies the problem. The percentage tables may suggest possible solutions. Let us examine expenses first. Two categories are growing disproportionately: the Library and Financial Aid. The trustees may decide that they must increase the proportion designated for financial aid to compensate for federal cutbacks. But they may also decide, reluctantly, to reduce the growth rate of the Library budget to eight percent.

Looking at revenues, there is an alarming decline in the role played by endowment. If this cannot be corrected, other revenues have to grow faster. Let us assume that they do not want to increase tuition any faster. Auxiliary activities (dormitories, dining hall, and so forth) are budgeted to break even. And, they do not believe that Sponsored Activities (grants and contracts) can grow faster. So they make two policy changes. They note that ticket prices for athletic and cultural events have lagged behind, and decide to escalate "Direct Revenue" at nine percent. Additionally, they launch an all-out effort to have the in-flow of gifts grow at a 10 percent rate.

When they run **BUDGET** with the three modified growth rates, they find that they are projecting a quite stable future. This run was terminated after the balance sheet by pushing the space bar.

```
run

                  1986      1987      1988      1989      1990      1991
Expenses         111.0     119.4     128.4     138.1     148.5     159.8
Revenues         112.1     120.3     129.2     138.8     149.2     160.4
Balance           +1.1      +1.0      +0.8      +0.7      +0.7      +0.6
```

19.3 MENU-DRIVEN PROGRAMS

A common feature of user-friendly programs is that they are *menu-driven*. A *menu* displays a set of options and makes it simple for the user to choose among them. Choice may, depending on the computer, involve pushing a *function key* or pointing with a *mouse*. To demonstrate, we will construct a small menu library. The particular routines are hardware dependent, ours being for an IBM PC. We will also discuss what may have to be changed for a different computer. But the important fact is that, once the small menu library is appropriately changed, programs using the library need not be changed!

```
EXTERNAL

!  MENULIB
!
!       menuinit            Sets up the menu windows
!       menu                Shows the menu, gets the response

SUB menuinit (#1, #2)                   ! Set up menu windows

    CLEAR
    OPEN #2: screen 0,1,0,.15           ! Menu window
    OPEN #1: screen 0,1,.2,1            ! Working window

END SUB

SUB menu (M$(), prompt$, #1, #2, ans)  ! Show menu, get response

    WINDOW #2
    LET mn = ubound(M$)                 ! No. of items
    SET COLOR "black/white"
    SET CURSOR 1,1
    FOR i = 1 to mn
        PRINT i; M$(i),
        IF i=5 then PRINT               ! Leave blank line
    NEXT i

    DO                                  ! Force correct answer
       WINDOW #1
       PRINT prompt$;
       GET KEY z
       LET ans = z-314                  ! f-keys start with 315
       IF ans<1 or ans>mn then
          PRINT "Push f1-f"; str$(mn)
       ELSE
          PRINT M$(ans)                 ! Item selected
          EXIT DO
       END IF
    LOOP
    WINDOW #2
    SET BACK "black"
    CLEAR
    WINDOW #1

END SUB
```

The routine `menuinit` clears the entire screen and sets up two windows. Window #1 occupies most of the screen, available as working space for the calling program. Window #2 is a small slice of the bottom of the screen, reserved for showing menus. This routine is called once by the main program.

Every time the user is to be shown a choice, the program calls the routine `menu`. It passes the array `M$` containing the menu items, the prompt to be printed, and the two windows (so it can switch between them). Upon return, the number of the menu item chosen is `ans`. In a complex program the user may be presented by different choices at different times. The same routine handles all of these. The main program simply calls `menu` with different arrays `M$` and with different `prompt$`.

The first task of `menu` is to print the menu items. It switches to the menu window, chooses color "black/white" (black on white background) for a reverse video presentation, sets the cursor to the beginning of the window, and prints the items in an appropriately numbered format. We have chosen to print two lines of up to five items each, with a blank line in between. This will effectively display up to 10 items on the IBM PC.

Note that we did not have to pass the number of menu items as a parameter. The function `ubound` gives the largest component number of an array, and `menu` discovers the number of items (`mn`) for itself.

The `DO` loop obtains the user's choice. It is fashioned so that if the user makes an error (e.g. pushes the wrong key), he or she can try again. First the prompt is printed in the working window. Then, `GET key` waits for the user to push a key. On the IBM PC the function keys `F1` through `F10` correspond to numbers 315 - 324, so that subtracting 314 will yield the correct key number. If this number is out of range, we print an error message. This will happen, for example, if the user pushes "5" instead of "F5". Otherwise, the choice is printed (to remind the user of what was chosen), window #2 is cleared, and we return to the working window.

There are many easy variants of these routines. The menu window could be chosen in the right margin or on top. The size of the menu window may have to be adjusted for the computer and the font size. If color is available, we may prefer "red/yellow" in place of "black/white". Also, the numbering of function keys will differ from computer to computer. And, if available, we

```
Quantity to find: Final
Initial? 1000
Payment? 0
% Interest? 12.3
Years? 10
Times per? 4
Final = $3358.41

Quantity to find:
```

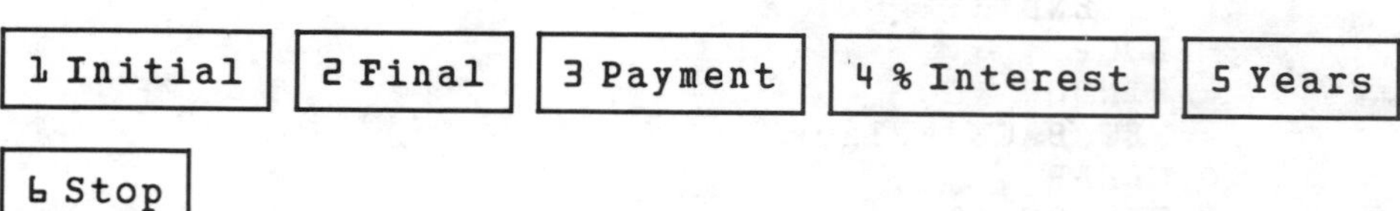

FIGURE 19.2
Typical menu for an IBM PC.

```
Quantity to find: Final
Initial? 1000
Payment? 0
% Interest? 12.3
Years? 10
Times per? 4
Final = $3358.41

Quantity to find:
```

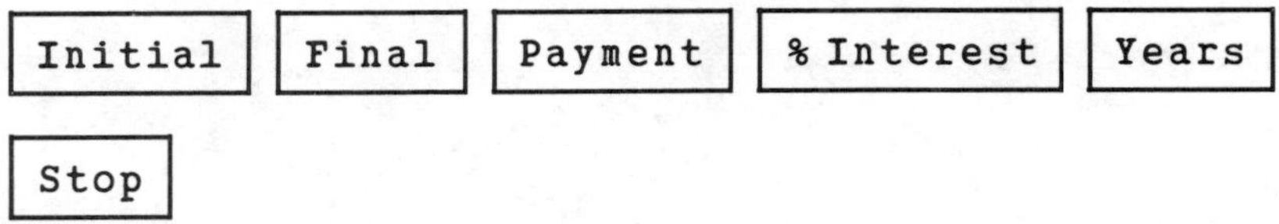

FIGURE 19.3
Typical menu for an Apple Macintosh.

may prefer `GET mouse` in place of `GET key`. In that case, we must infer the choice from the mouse position.

We wish to reiterate that the routines using the menu library are *not* affected by such changes. We will make use of the library in the next section. Figures 19.2 and 19.3 show a typical menu for the IBM PC and the Macintosh, respectively.

19.4 COMPOUND INTEREST

Many business and financial calculations involve compound interest. These were formerly solved by using large special numerical tables. Today they are easily solved on microcomputers.

We first consider the simplest case. An amount of money is placed in a bank and left there for a number of years. How large will the balance be at the end of the specified period?

In the program `COMP` the user is asked for the following four quantities necessary to carry out the computation:

a = original amount (dollars)
r = annual interest rate (%)
y = number of years
t = times per year (compounded)

The subroutine `basics` computes three auxiliary quantities:

n = number of interest periods
r1 = interest per period (as a fraction)
r2 = $(1+r1)^n$

The final balance is simply

$$b = a * r2$$

The answer is printed in a clean format, with a leading "$" sign and to two decimals (nearest cent).

```
REM  COMP
REM
REM  Simple compound interest program

INPUT prompt "Initial: ": a
INPUT prompt "Interest: ": r
INPUT prompt "Years: ": y
INPUT prompt "Times per: ": t

CALL basics
LET b = a*r2
LET f$ = "$$$$$$$.##"
PRINT "Final = ";
PRINT using f$: b

SUB basics                                  ! Intermediate quantities

    LET N = y*t
    LET r1 = r/100/t
    LET r2 = (1+r1)^N

END SUB

END
```

The following run shows that $1000 left for 10 years at 12.3 percent interest rate compounded quarterly yields $3358.41 .

```
run

Initial: 1000
Interest: 12.3
Years: 10
Times per: 4
Final =   $3358.41
```

We will now expand our simple program to a general purpose one that solves the five most common compound interest problems. It is call **COMP2** and its structure chart is shown in Figure 19.4.

COMP2 includes the possibility of periodic payments or withdrawals. For this purpose, we must introduce one more quantity:

$$p = \text{payment (dollars, + or −)}$$

A positive payment increases the balance, as when we keep adding to a savings account. A negative payment reduces the balance, as in repaying a loan. We will assume that fixed payments are made periodically, and that the period of the payments is the same as the compounding period. Thus, if we pay off a mortgage with fixed monthly payments, we assume that the bank also charges interest monthly, and hence, t = 12.

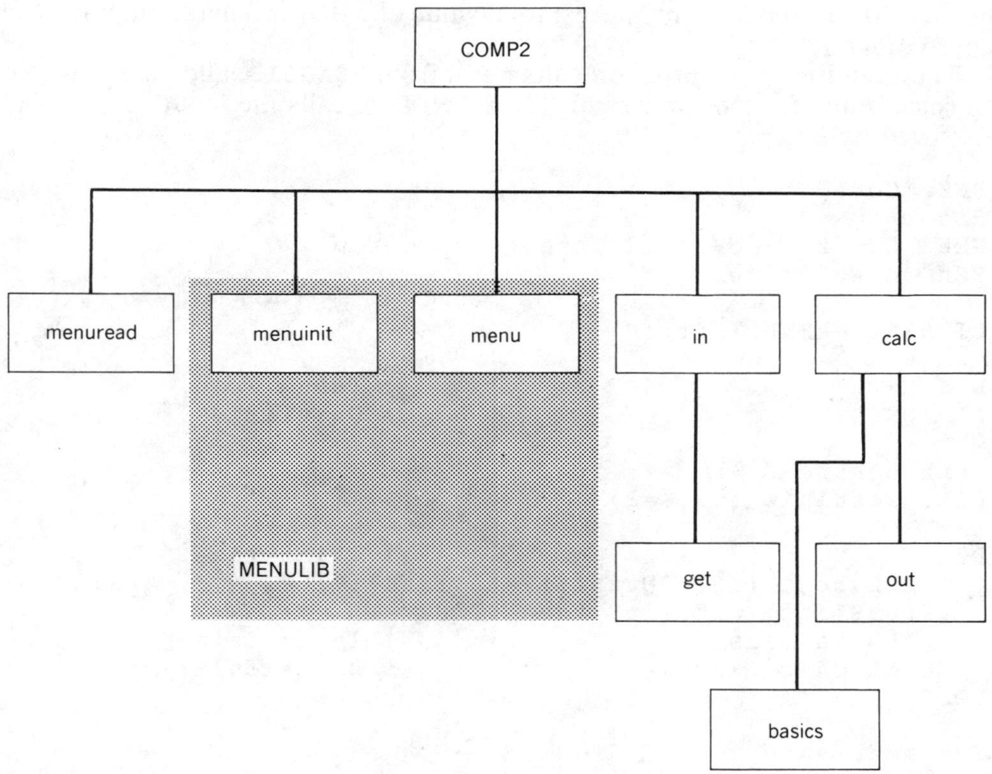

FIGURE 19.4
Structure chart for COMP2.

With payments included, the equation for the final balance becomes

$$b = a * r2 + p * r3 \qquad \text{(Equation *)}$$

where

$$r3 = (r2-1)/r1$$

Each problem is solved in `calc`. Therefore, we start with this routine. The five cases correspond to finding `a`, `b`, `p`, `r`, and `y`, respectively. Case 2 is a direct application of the equation (*). Cases 1 and 3 solve equation (*) for `a` and `p`, respectively. (The other two cases are harder.) Each case calls `basics` to do preliminary calculations, and then applies the appropriate formula. It sets up a formatting string and calls the simple routine `out` to print the answer. Note that Case 3 allows `p` to be negative. Cases 1 and 2 print an error message if the answer is negative.

To understand Case 5, we must point out that (*) yields

$$r2 = (b*r1 + p)/(a*r1 + p)$$

If the denominator is zero, there is no solution. And, if the quotient (called `q`) is less than 1, then it cannot be `(1+r1)` to a positive power. These are the impossible cases. Otherwise, we use logarithms to obtain `y` from `r2`.

There is no similar method to find `r`. This requires an iterative search, similar to finding the root of an equation. (See Section 16.3.) We search between 0 and 100 percent interest for a value of r that will make equation (*) approximately true.

The skeleton of the program calls menu from MENULIB, allowing the user to select one of the five cases or "Stop". It then calls the input routine in, followed by calc.

```
REM  COMP2
REM
REM  General compound interest program
REM  Menu driven

LIBRARY "MENULIB.trc"

DIM M$(6)                                    ! Menu
DIM Q$(6)                                    ! Quantities

CALL menuread
CALL menuinit (#1, #2)

DO                                           ! Which case?
   CALL menu (M$, "Quantity to find: ", #1, #2, ans)
   IF M$(ans) = "Stop" then STOP
   CALL in (ans)                             ! Input data
   CALL calc (ans)                           ! Do calculations
LOOP

SUB menuread

    MAT READ Q$
    DATA Initial, Final, Payment, % Interest
    DATA Years, Times per

    MAT M$ = Q$                              ! Almost same
    LET M$(6) = "Stop"

END SUB

SUB in (case)                                ! Get data

    FOR i = 1 to 6
       IF i<>case then                       ! Skip desired quantity
          SELECT CASE i
          CASE 1
               CALL get (a,1)
          CASE 2
               CALL get (b,1)
          CASE 3
               CALL get (p,0)
          CASE 4
               CALL get (r,2)
          CASE 5
               CALL get (y,2)
          CASE 6
               CALL get (t,2)
          END SELECT
       END IF
    NEXT i

END SUB
```

```
SUB get (x, c)                          ! Get input and check

    ! If c = 2, make sure x is positive
    ! If c = 1, make sure x is nonnegative
    ! If c = 0, accept any x

    DO
       PRINT Q$(i);
       INPUT x
       LET ok = 1
       IF c=1 and x<0 then
          PRINT "Cannot be negative"
          LET ok = 0
       ELSEIF c=2 and x<=0 then
          PRINT "Must be positive"
          LET ok = 0
       END IF
    LOOP until ok=1

END SUB

SUB calc (case)

    SELECT CASE case
    CASE 1                              ! Initial amount
         CALL basics
         LET a = (b - p*r3)/r2
         IF a<0 then
            PRINT "Not possible"
         ELSE
            LET f$ = "$$$$$$$.##"
            CALL out (1, f$, a)
         END IF
    CASE 2                              ! Final amount
         CALL basics
         LET b = a*r2 + p*r3
         IF b<0 then
            PRINT "Not possible"
         ELSE
            LET f$ = "$$$$$$$.##"
            CALL out (2, f$, b)
         END IF
    CASE 3                              ! Payment
         CALL basics
         LET p = (b - a*r2)/r3
         LET f$ = "$$$$$$-.##"
         CALL out (3, f$, p)
    CASE 4                              ! Interest
         LET s = sgn(b - (a + y*t*p))
         LET r = 100
         CALL basics
         LET s2 = sgn(b - (a*r2 + p*r3))
         IF s2 = s then
            PRINT "Can't solve"
         ELSE
            LET low = 0
            LET high = 100
            FOR times = 1 to 17   ! To three places
```

```
                LET r = (low+high)/2
                CALL basics
                LET s2 = sgn(b - (a*r2 + p*r3))
                IF s2 = s then LET low = r else LET high = r
            NEXT times
            LET f$ = "###.## percent"
            CALL out (4, f$, r)
        END IF
    CASE 5                              ! Years
        LET y = 0
        CALL basics
        IF a*r1+p = 0 then
           PRINT "Not possible"
        ELSE
           LET q = (b*r1 + p)/(a*r1 + p)
           IF q < 1 then
              PRINT "Not possible"
           ELSE
              LET y = log(q)/log(1+r1)/t
              LET f$ = "###.##"
              CALL out (5, f$, y)
           END IF
        END IF
    ! CASE 6 is impossible
    END SELECT
    PRINT
    PRINT

END SUB

SUB basics                              ! Intermediate quantities

    LET n = y*t
    LET r1 = r/100/t
    LET r2 = (1+r1)^n
    LET r3 = (r2 - 1)/r1

END SUB

SUB out (ans, f$, x)                    ! Formatted output

    PRINT M$(ans); " = ";
    PRINT using f$: x

END SUB

END
```

The input of data is handled by `get`, which asks for a number and may check its legality. The purpose of `in` is to cycle through the six quantities, skipping the quantity to be found, and calling for the appropriate check for each number. For example, `a` cannot be negative, hence check 1 is called for; `t` must be positive, hence check 2; and, `p` can be positive, negative, or zero, hence no check is required.

The array `Q$` is set up to contain the names of the six quantities that may have to inputted. The menu `M$` differs from this slightly. Because `t` is never the unknown, we replace it by the menu option "Stop".

```
run

Quantity to find: Final
Initial? 1000
Payment? 0
% Interest? 12.3
Years? 10
Times per? 4
Final =    $3358.41


Quantity to find: Payment
Initial? 50000
Final? 0
% Interest? 11.7
Years? 25
Times per? 12
Payment =    $-515.56


Quantity to find: % Interest
Initial? 50000
Final? 0
Payment? -515.56
Years? 25
Times per? 12
% Interest =  11.70 percent


Quantity to find: Years
Initial? 15000
Final? 0
Payment? -350
% Interest? 14.5
Times per? 12
Years =    5.06


Quantity to find: Stop
```

The run illustrates four cases. The first repeats the computation shown for COMP. The second shows that to pay off a mortgage of $50,000 at 11.7% interest in 25 years requires monthly payments of $515.56. The third case is applicable if the bank tells us what our monthly payments will be and we wish to find out how much interest is being charged. The final case finds out how long it will take us to repay a loan of $15,000 if we can afford monthly payments of $350. The fifth time we elect the menu option "Stop", and the program is terminated.

19.5 CRITICAL PATH METHOD

In carrying out any multi-stage project, there are certain *critical tasks* that are bottlenecks that can impede the early completion of the project. We will program a simple technique for the identification of the critical tasks.

A simple but typical multi-stage project is shown in Figure 19.5. A team of programmers is assigned the task of programming a complex algorithm (A) and a friendly user-interface (U). The boxes represent *tasks* (stages in the project) and the numbers in the boxes indicate the number of days required to complete a task. The paths indicate the order in which the tasks must be carried out. First there is a design stage, then coding (with the algorithm divided into three routines A1, A2, and A3), then debugging. Next the three pieces are combined, and integrated with the user interface. Finally, both internal and field testing is required.

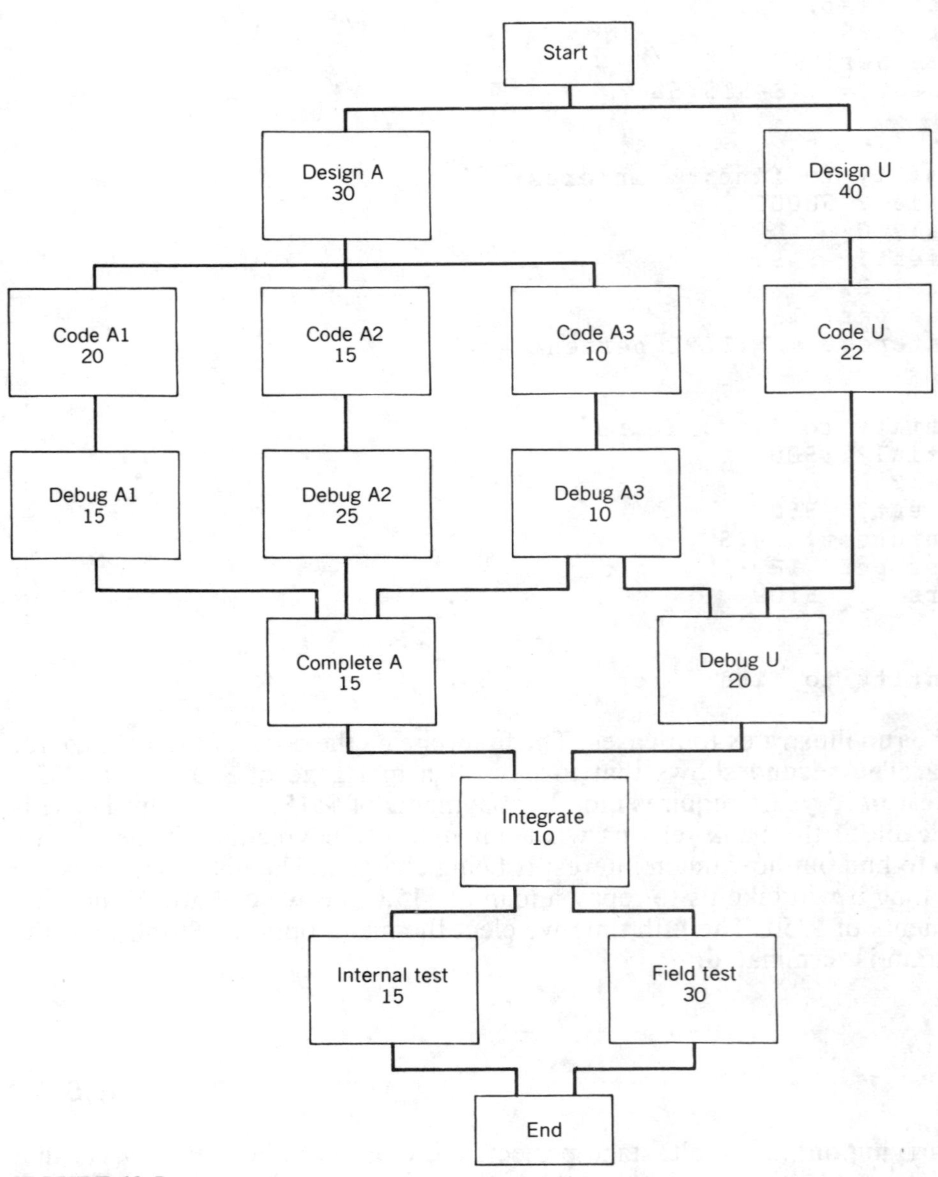

FIGURE 19.5
Programming project tasks, with times required.

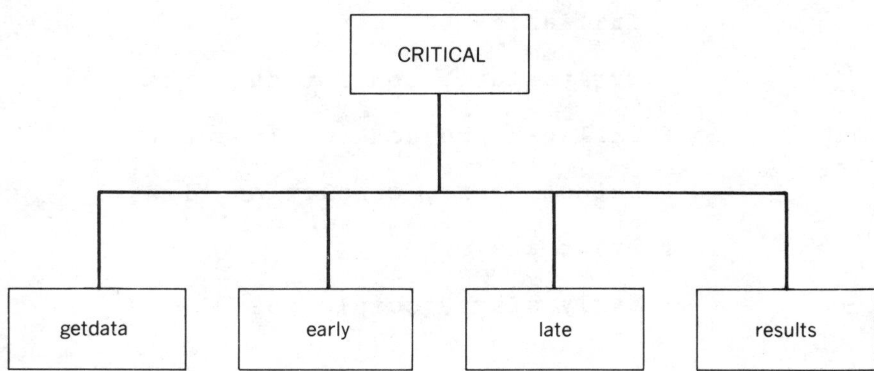

FIGURE 19.6
Structure chart for the program CRITIC.

In the program `CRITIC`, whose structure chart is shown in Figure 19.6, three arrays contain the necessary information. The names of the tasks go into `name$`. The table `T` has task times, with the time needed for completion in column 0. The other times are computed by the program `CRITIC`. The table `pred` makes it easy to find the immediate predecessors of a task, those tasks that must be completed just before the given task can begin. Specifically, `pred(i,j) = 1` if `i` is an immediate predecessor of `j`. Otherwise, `pred(i,j) = 0`.

The data start with the number of tasks. For each task we have its name, the number of its immediate predecessors, their names (if any), and the time for completion of the task. The data are read in the routine `getdata`. To construct `pred` properly, it is necessary that the data for all of a task's predecessors precede the data for the task in the `DATA` statements. We include a final task called "END" that signifies the completion of the project.

The skeleton then calls `early` for each task to find the earliest time that the task can be started (when all its immediate predecessors are completed) and the earliest it can be completed (the start time plus the time needed for completion). The completion time of "END", called `compl`, is the earliest that the project can be completed. We then reverse the order and call `late` for each task to find the latest time that it can be completed (without delaying the project) and the latest it can be started. The difference between the early and late start times of a task is known as the *slack*. Finally, `results` displays the answers.

```
REM  CRITIC
REM
REM  Critical path analysis

DIM name$(50)                      ! Task names
DIM T(50,0 to 4)                   ! Task times
!          0  time needed
!          1  early start
!          2  early completion
!          3  latest start
!          4  latest completion
DIM pred(50,50)                    ! Pred(i,j)=1 if j predec. of i
```

```
CALL getdata                        ! Initialize
FOR i = 1 to tasks
    CALL early                      ! Early start, completion times
NEXT i
LET compl = T(tasks,1)              ! Earliest project completion
FOR i = tasks to 1 step -1
    CALL late                       ! Latest start, completion times
NEXT i
CALL results                        ! Print answers

SUB early                           ! Early start, completion

    LET e = 0
    FOR j = 1 to i-1                ! Find predecessors
        IF pred(i,j)=1 then
           LET tj = T(j,2)
           LET e = max(e,tj)
        END IF
    NEXT j
    LET T(i,1) = e                  ! Early start
    LET T(i,2) = e + T(i,0)         ! Early completion

END SUB

SUB late                            ! Latest start, completion


    LET l = compl
    FOR j = i+1 to tasks            ! Find successors
        IF pred(j,i)=1 then
           LET tj = T(j,3)
           LET l = min(l,tj)
        END IF
    NEXT j
    LET T(i,4) = l                  ! Latest completion
    LET T(i,3) = l - T(i,0)         ! Latest start

END SUB

SUB results                         ! Print answers

    CLEAR
    PRINT "Completion time ="; compl
    PRINT
    PRINT "Task", "Needed", "Start", "Slack"
    PRINT
    FOR i = 1 to tasks-1
        LET slack = T(i,3) - T(i,1)
        PRINT name$(i), T(i,0), T(i,1), slack
    NEXT i
    GET KEY z                       ! Wait until user is ready


END SUB

SUB getdata                         ! Initialize

    READ tasks
    MAT pred = zer(tasks,tasks)
```

```
    FOR i = 1 to tasks
        READ name$(i), n        ! Name, number of
        FOR k = 1 to n          !       predecessors
            READ p$             ! Predecessor
            FOR j = 1 to i-1    ! Find its number
               IF name$(j)=p$ then EXIT FOR
            NEXT j
            IF j>i-1 then       ! Not found
               PRINT "Data out of order"
               STOP
            ELSE
               LET pred(i,j) = 1
            END IF
        NEXT k
        READ T(i,0)             ! Time needed
    NEXT i
END SUB
DATA 15
DATA Design A, 0, 30
DATA Design U, 0, 40
DATA Code A1, 1, Design A, 20
DATA Code A2, 1, Design A, 15
DATA Code A3, 1, Design A, 10
DATA Code U, 1, Design U, 22
DATA Debug A1, 1, Code A1, 15
DATA Debug A2, 1, Code A2, 25
DATA Debug A3, 1, Code A3, 10
DATA Debug U, 2, Code U, Debug A3, 20
DATA Complete A, 3, Debug A1, Debug A2, Debug A3, 15
DATA Integrate, 2, Complete A, Debug U, 10
DATA Internal test, 1, Integrate, 15
DATA Field test, 1, Integrate, 30
DATA End, 2, Internal test, Field test, 0
END
```

The first run shows the solution. It takes 125 days to complete the project. Six of the tasks have zero slack. These are the critical tasks.

```
run
Completion time = 125
Task            Needed          Start           Slack

Design A         30              0               0
Design U         40              0               3
Code A1          20              30              5
Code A2          15              30              0
Code A3          10              30              15
Code U           22              40              3
Debug A1         15              50              5
Debug A2         25              45              0
Debug A3         10              40              15
Debug U          20              62              3
Complete A       15              70              0
Integrate        10              85              0
Internal test    15              95              15
Field test       30              95              0
```

Figure 19.7 shows the tasks with the early starting and completion times included. The critical path is highlighted. The project can only be speeded up if one of the critical tasks is completed in less time than was originally scheduled.

In our attempt to speed up the project, we assume that "Debug A2" can be completed in 15 days rather than 25. As the second run shows, this does speed up completion, but only by 3 days, not 10. The reason is that now we have a different critical path and, as a result, tasks that previously had slack now become bottlenecks. The critical path now includes the user interface tasks.

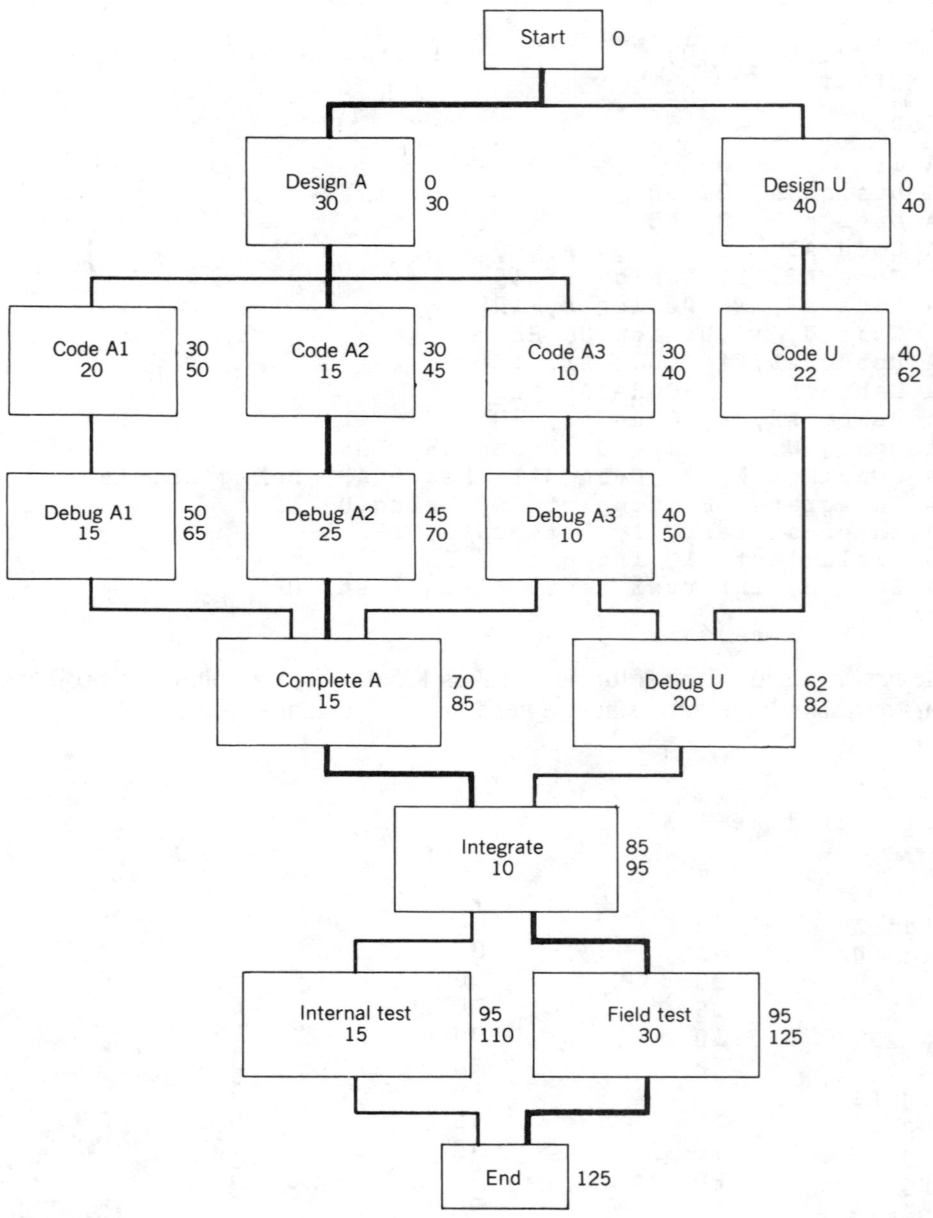

FIGURE 19.7.
Programming tasks showing critical path and earliest start and completion times.

```
run

Completion time = 122

Task             Needed         Start        Slack

Design A          30             0             2
Design U          40             0             0
Code A1           20            30             2
Code A2           15            30             7
Code A3           10            30            12
Code U            22            40             0
Debug A1          15            50             2
Debug A2          15            45             7
Debug A3          10            40            12
Debug U           20            62             0
Complete A        15            65             2
Integrate         10            82             0
Internal test     15            92            15
Field test        30            92             0
```

How should we modify the program to handle a project that requires 500 tasks? First we examine our data structures. Storing 500 names in `name$` and 2500 numbers in `T` is perfectly reasonable. But, then `pred` would become a table with 250,000 entries, which is not realistic. However, each entry contains only one bit of information, equivalent to "yes" or "no". If we let "1" stand for "yes" and "0" for "no", we can use *bit-packing*. The information can then be stored in a string of 250,000 bits, which is only 250,000/8 = 31,250 bytes. So we replace this table by the string `pred$`. For convenience we introduce `pred(i,j)` as a defined function that returns the "bit" in row i, column j.

Finally, it is not reasonable to have 500 lines of data in our program. Consequently, we create the following data file:

```
15
Design A, 0, 30
Design U, 0, 40
Code A1, 1, Design A, 20
Code A2, 1, Design A, 15
Code A3, 1, Design A, 10
Code U, 1, Design U, 22
Debug A1, 1, Code A1, 15
Debug A2, 1, Code A2, 25
Debug A3, 1, Code A3, 10
Debug U, 2, Code U, Debug A3, 20
Complete A, 3, Debug A1, Debug A2, Debug A3, 15
Integrate, 2, Complete A, Debug U, 10
Internal test, 1, Integrate, 15
Field test, 1, Integrate, 30
End, 2, Internal test, Field test, 0
```

Only small changes are needed to `CRITIC` to produce `CRITIC2`. We show two lines from the header and the new version of `getdata`.

CRITIC2, modifications from CRITIC only.

```
! pred$ has predecessor information bit-packed
DEF pred(i,j) = unpackb(pred$, (i-1)*tasks+j, 1)          ! (i,j) bit

SUB getdata                             ! Initialize

    PRINT "Data file";
    INPUT f$
    OPEN #1: name f$

    INPUT #1: tasks
    FOR i = 1 to tasks^2
        CALL packb (pred$, i, 1, 0)     ! All zeroes
    NEXT i

    FOR i = 1 to tasks
        INPUT #1: name$(i), n,          ! Name, number of
        FOR k = 1 to n                  !       predecessors
            INPUT #1: p$,               ! Predecessor
            FOR j = 1 to i-1            ! Find its number
                IF name$(j)=p$ then EXIT FOR
            NEXT j
            IF j>i-1 then               ! Not found
               PRINT "Data out of order"
               STOP
            ELSE
               CALL packb (pred$, (i-1)*tasks+j, 1, 1)    ! Set to 1
            END IF
        NEXT k
        INPUT #1: T(i,0)                ! Time needed
    NEXT i
    CLOSE #1

END SUB
```

We need to explain `packb` and `unpackb`, which are used for bit-packing. The statement

```
CALL packb (s$, i, bits, n)
```

packs the integer `n` into the string `s$` using `bits` bits and starting at bit position `i`. The value of the function

```
unpackb(s$, i, bits)
```

is the integer represented by `bits` bits in `s$` starting at bit position `i`. In our case we pack either 0 or 1. Hence, `bits` always equals 1 and `n` is limited to 0 or 1. We originally pack the string entirely with zeroes. Then we set some of the bits to 1. The function `pred` finds the bit corresponding to the ith row and jth column.

The output of `CRITIC2` is, of course, the same as that of `CRITIC`.

EXERCISES

1. Use `COMP2` to solve the following problems:
   a. We have $1000 in a savings account that bears five percent interest quarterly. Every quarter, for 10 years, we add $50. How much do we have at the end?
   b. A car dealer offers to finance a balance of $5750 on a car by monthly payments of $209 for three years. What interest is being charged?
   c. We mortgage our house for $52,500 and pay off $550 per month. If there is 11 percent interest on the mortgage, how long does it take to reduce the mortgage to $20,000? (With monthly payments, we assume that interest is also compounded monthly.)
   d. We take out a 25-year mortgage for $40,000 at 12.3 percent interest. What are our monthly payments?
   e. We wish to set up a trust fund that will provide $10,000 annual income for 20 years. If the interest rate stays at 7.5 percent, how large an amount must we put into trust?
2. Modify `COMP2` so that, after providing the answer requested, it offers to print a "mortgage table," showing the interest paid, the principal reduction, and the remaining principal for each time period.
3. Manhattan Island was purchased in 1626 for $24. If those early investors had decided to invest the same amount at six percent interest, compounded quarterly, how much would their investment be worth today? (You will need to add more "$" signs to `f$` for printing the final amount.)
4. Write down the tasks necessary to build a house, making reasonable assumptions of how long each task may take. Use `CRITIC2` to find the critical tasks. Make a significant reduction in the time needed for one critical task and compute the time saved in the total project.
5. Modify the program `CRITIC` so that the order in which tasks are given in the data is not important. That is, add a routine that will arrange the tasks in the desired order.
6. Modify `MENULIB` so that the menu is printed in a column on the right side of the screen. Rerun `COMP2` with the new style menu.
7. Modify the routine `primes` in `NUMLIB` (Chapter 16) to use a string in place of the list "slot" and use bit-packing. How much room do you save?

PROJECTS

1. If interest at rate `r` is compounded `t` times a year, and `t` > `1`, then the investment is worth more than it would be at the same rate compounded once a year. We may therefore ask what annual rate `rf` paid and compounded once a year, yields the same return as a rate `r` compounded `t` times a year. `rf` is known as the *effective interest rate*. Write a program that, given `r` and `t`, finds `rf`. Study how `rf` behaves as `t` increases for fixed `r`. Show that it tends to a limiting value as `t` becomes quite large; this corresponds to the *continuous compounding* advertised by many

banks. Find a formula in BASIC that yields the limiting value for any given `r`.

2. Expand the program **BUDGET** to allow the Trustees to specify
   a. Different growth rates for different years.
   b. Fixed increase (or decrease) in a budget item in a specified year, such as in the expansion or abolition of a program.

CHAPTER 20

GAMES

20.1 INTRODUCTION

This chapter discusses games, not games of pure chance such as craps, but games in which victory is achieved through intelligent play and experience. Good examples of these games having *complete information* are chess and checkers. Unfortunately, programs that play chess or checkers are long and complicated. Therefore, we choose to study three simple games: Tictactoe, Nim, and Pattern.

We start with three versions of that old favorite—Tictactoe. In the first version, the computer always has the first move and always takes the center square. From then on, all it must do is to check to make sure the human player blocks when necessary. The strategy thus reduces to nothing more than a single `IF` structure for each move.

In the second version, we allow the player to move first. The number of possible moves is now much greater than can be handled conveniently by a series of `IF - THEN` checks. So we introduce the notion of an *heuristic*. Here, the heuristic is a simple board evaluation scheme that gives weight to the markers in a row. This version plays the game fairly well. But for more complicated games, a board evaluation scheme, no matter how complex, is rarely sufficient.

In the third version of Tictactoe we introduce searching the *move tree* to a predetermined depth before employing the board evaluation scheme. This strategy, of looking ahead at all possible moves up to some limit, illustrates some of the sophisticated principles used in playing games such as checkers and chess.

We next discuss the game of Nim. For this game the computer can pre-compute the optimal moves at each stage, and can then play perfectly.

Our final game, Pattern, is one that the computer can play better than most humans, even when the humans know the strategy. The computer plays better because it can keep precise track of all combinations at all times, a tactic that would require slow and extensive paper work if it were used by a human player.

20.2 TICTACTOE: SIMPLE VERSION

People who play tictactoe know from experience that if one moves first, and moves into the center square, then a very simple strategy exists that will result in no worse than a tie. The strategy calls for choosing a side or corner square to produce two marks in a row. The human player is thus forced to block or lose.

Before discussing the program, we need to realize that programming any game requires devising a convenient way for the computer to keep track of the course of the game. For our simple tictactoe game, all we need is a way to number the squares. For a reason that will become apparent later, we choose the coding scheme shown in Figure 20.1. In other words, the outside squares are numbered clockwise from 1 to 8, and the center square is numbered 9. We note that the corner squares are odd numbered, and the side squares are even numbered.

Our program `TICTAC1` uses this coding scheme and carries out the simple stategy that we already discussed. Its structure chart is shown in Figure 20.2.

```
REM    TICTAC1
REM
REM    Tictactoe game
REM
REM    Game board is numbered
REM
REM         1   2   3
REM         8   9   4
REM         7   6   5
REM
REM    Machine moves first, forces game

DEF fnm(m) = mod(m-1, 8) + 1          ! Special modulo function

LET result = 0                        ! Game not over
CALL playgame (result)
IF result = 1 then                    ! Machine win
   PRINT "      and wins."
ELSE
   PRINT "The game ends in a draw."
END IF
PRINT
```

1	2	3
8	9	4
7	6	5

FIGURE 20.1
Coding scheme for the tictactoe squares.

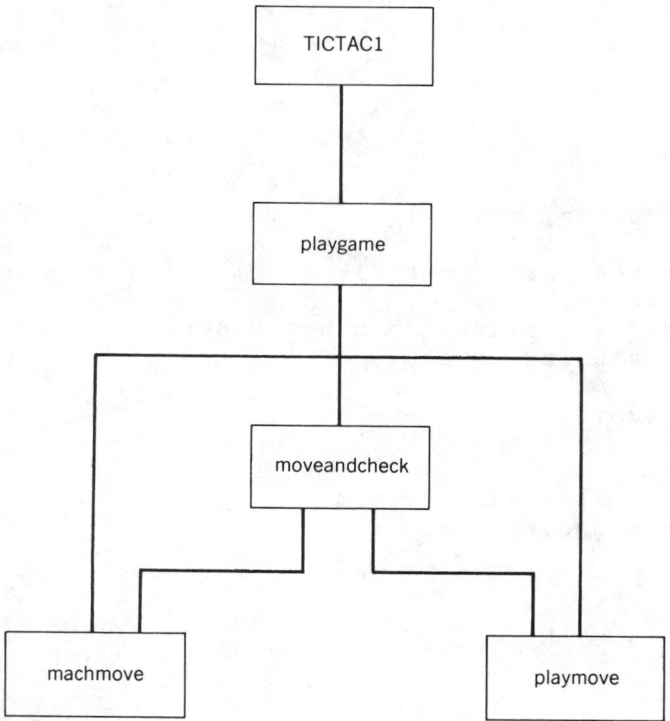

FIGURE 20.2
Structure chart for TICTAC1.

```
SUB playgame (result)                   ! Play one game

    CALL machmove (9, m1)               ! Machine's first move
    CALL playmove (p1)                  ! Player's first move
    CALL moveandcheck (p1+1, m2, p2, result)    ! 2nd move for both
    IF result = 1 then EXIT SUB
    CALL moveandcheck (m2+2, m3, p3, result)    ! 3rd move for both
    IF result = 1 then EXIT SUB
    IF mod(p1, 2) = 0 then                  ! Player's first move even
       CALL machmove (fnm(m3+7), m4)        ! Machine's 4th move
       LET result = 1                       ! A guaranteed win
    ELSE
       CALL moveandcheck (m3+3, m4, p4, result)  ! 4th move for both
       IF result = 1 then EXIT SUB
       CALL machmove (fnm(m4+6), m5)        ! Fill last cell
    END IF

END SUB

SUB machmove (next, mmove)

    LET mmove = next
    PRINT "The machine moves"; mmove

END SUB
```

```
SUB playmove (pmove)

    PRINT "Your move";
    INPUT pmove

END SUB

SUB moveandcheck (next, mmove, pmove, result)

    ! Makes machine's move "mmove" (from "next").
    ! Computes forced block move "block".
    ! Gets player's move "pmove"; if player does not block,
    !       computer makes that winning move.

    CALL machmove (fnm(next), mmove)
    LET block = fnm(mmove+4)
    CALL playmove (pmove)
    IF pmove <> block then            ! A machine win
       CALL machmove (block, nextmmove)
       LET result = 1
    END IF

END SUB

END
```

Once the player has made her first move, the rest of the game is a series of predetermined moves by the machine (m1, m2, ...), each one forcing the human player to defend. Because the player's proper move is always forced, and is opposite on the board to the computer's move, this logic is readily contained in the short subroutine `moveandcheck`. This subroutine makes the machine move supplied to it (`mmove`), determines the proper player move (`block`), receives the player's move (`pmove`), and then checks it. If the player has failed to make the proper move, the subroutine makes it and reports the win by setting `result` to 1.

The main routine `playgame` opens at square 9 and then keeps making forcing moves. At one point, the computer plays differently according to whether the player moved initially into a corner or a side square (the player's first move is `p1`). In the latter case the computer can win.

One other detail merits attention. To take advantage of the symmetry of the game, the computer's next move is usually determined as the computer's previous move plus a certain number. For example, if the computer's second move is "3", its third move is "5". By symmetry, if the computer's second move is "5", its third move is "7". However, if the computer's second move is "7", its third move is "1", not "9" (which is the center square). We therefore introduce a defined function `fnm` which produces 1 whenever 9 is supplied, 2 when 10 is supplied, and so forth. In other words, whenever a value greater than 8 is supplied, `fnm` subtracts 8 from it. This calculation is similar to the `mod` function, but differs in that 8 is not changed to 0.

Two typical runs are shown. The first shows a standard game, which must end in a draw. In the second run, the player erroneously plays his first move into a side square, and loses.

```
run

The machine moves 9
Your move? 3
The machine moves 4
Your move? 8
The machine moves 6
Your move? 2
The machine moves 1
Your move? 5
The machine moves 7
The game ends in a draw.

run

The machine moves 9
Your move? 2
The machine moves 3
Your move? 7
The machine moves 5
Your move? 1
The machine moves 4
      and wins.
```

20.3 TICTACTOE: HEURISTICS VERSION

The structure of **TICTAC1**, which uses a sequence of predetermined moves, does not lend itself to more complicated games, or even to tictactoe when the player is allowed to move first. There are just too many different possibilities, even if we take advantage of the rotational symmetry of the game board. We must therefore devise an approach to the game whereby the machine's move is based on the current board situation, and not on the preceding sequence of moves.

For **TICTAC1** the data structure was simply a scheme to number the squares. For **TICTAC2** we need additional data structures, one to represent the game board and the other to represent the status of each of the eight possible winning paths. It is not difficult to do so—many alternatives come to mind—but the trick is to devise ones that are easy for the computer to handle.

We will represent the game board by a list `board` with nine components to represent the nine squares. An entry of 0 will represent an unoccupied square, +1 a square occupied by the machine, and -1 a square occupied by the human. Thus,

```
board() = (0, 0, 1, 0, -1, 1, 0, 0, 0)
```

represents a board in which the machine occupies squares 3 and 6, and the human player occupies square 5.

It is possible, of course, to determine any fact about the game from the current entries in the list `board`. For instance, one can easily tell in the preceding example that neither player has yet won, just by drawing the game on paper and looking at it. But what is easy for humans to do is often hard for

TABLE 20.1

Winning path	Consists of squares
1	1, 2, 3
2	8, 9, 4
3	7, 6, 5
4	1, 8, 7
5	2, 9, 6
6	3, 4, 5
7	1, 9, 5
8	7, 9, 3

the computer to do. To help the computer keep track of things, we introduce the concept of a *winning path*. There are exactly eight different winning paths and they are shown Table 20.1. Paths 1 through 3 are the three rows, paths 4 through 6 are the three columns, and paths 7 and 8 are the diagonals. We keep track of the winning paths in the array `winners`, which we read once and never change. (`Winners` is in the form of an *incidence matrix*, whose entries consist of 0 and 1; it is discussed along with the subroutine `status`.)

The computer determines its move by using a strategy called an *heuristic*, basing its decision entirely on an *evaluation* of the current game board. This evaluation will not be perfect, and might even permit the human player to win. (Hence, we use the term *heuristic*, which generally leads to good moves, rather than *winning strategy*, which would always lead to the best possible move.)

Heuristics for tictactoe are simple because the game is simple. For more complicated games, such as chess, the heuristics are complicated. But in all cases, the heuristics are simple enough to allow the computer to try all available moves and choose the one for which the evaluation gives the highest value, all in a reasonable amount of time.

Here we use a simple heuristic that gives a high (positive) value to two marks in a row (with the third square open) for the computer, and a low (negative) value to the same for the human player. The evaluation formula we have selected (from the many that are possible) counts +4 for each winning path containing two "X" marks and one open square, and −4 for each winning path contain two "O" marks and one open square.

We will keep track of the status of the paths in the list `values`, whose entries will be the `sum` of the mark values on each path. Thus, if a certain path has two "X" marks (machine moves) and one blank, its path value is 1 + 1 + 0 = 2. For the preceding example, paths 1, 5, and 8 have values = 1; paths 2, 3, 4, and 6 have values = 0; and path 7 has value = −1.

Obviously, if any value = 3, the computer has already won and we don't bother to evaluate further; if any value = −3, thè human has won. If any value = 2 (or −2), that path is occupied by two marks of one kind and no marks of the other. There are, however, two ambiguous cases. If the value = 1 (or −1), the path could have either one mark and two blanks, or three marks that are not all of the same type. If the value = 0, then the path is either unoccupied or there is one mark of each type in the path. It turns out that these ambiguities will not be important, due to the fact that values of 2 and −2 are the important ones.

`TICTAC2` carries out this approach. Its structure chart is given in Figure 20.3.

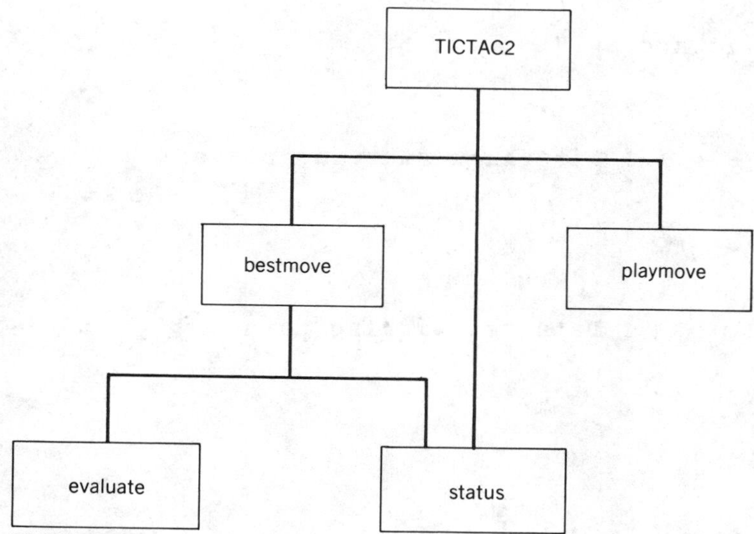

FIGURE 20.3
Structure chart for TICTAC2.

```
REM   TICTAC2
REM
REM   Tictactoe game
REM   Computer move determined by heuristics

DIM board(9)                          ! Game board
DIM values(8)                         ! Value of the eight paths
DIM winners(8,9)                      ! Incidence matrix

CALL init

LET player0 = 1                       ! Machine starts, first time
FOR game = 1 to 4                     ! Play four games
    MAT board = zer
    LET player = player0

    DO
       IF player = 1 then             ! Player is the machine
          CALL bestmove (board, winners, values, move)
          PRINT "Computer moves"; move
       ELSE                           ! Player is the human
          CALL playmove (board, move)
       END IF

       LET board(move) = player      ! Make the move
       CALL status (board, winners, values, result)
       LET player = -player          ! Alternate players
    LOOP while result = 0             ! Game still in progress

    SELECT CASE result
    CASE 3
        PRINT "     and wins."
    CASE -3
        PRINT "     and you win."
```

```
        CASE else
             PRINT "     and it is a draw."
        END SELECT
        PRINT

        LET player0 = -player0          ! Alternate starting player
    NEXT game

    SUB init

        MAT READ winners
        DATA 1,1,1,0,0,0,0,0,0          ! Data for winning paths
        DATA 0,0,0,1,0,0,0,1,1
        DATA 0,0,0,0,1,1,1,0,0
        DATA 1,0,0,0,0,0,1,1,0
        DATA 0,1,0,0,0,1,0,0,1
        DATA 0,0,1,1,1,0,0,0,0
        DATA 1,0,0,0,1,0,0,0,1
        DATA 0,0,1,0,0,0,1,0,1

    END SUB

    END

    !  The external subroutines follow

    SUB playmove (b(), m)

        DO
           PRINT "Your move";
           INPUT m
           IF m=int(m) and m>=1 and m<=9 and b(m)=0 then EXIT DO
           PRINT "Illegal move, try again."
        LOOP

    END SUB

    SUB bestmove (board(), winners(,), values(), move)

        ! Examines the board, and chooses the best move,
        ! based on the heuristics in the subroutine "evaluate"

        DIM boardtemp(9)                        ! Temporary workspace

        LET maxvalue = -1000                    ! Initial maximum value
        FOR trialmove = 1 to 9
            IF board(trialmove) = 0 then        ! Okay to try move
               MAT boardtemp = board
               LET boardtemp(trialmove) = 1         ! Trial move
               CALL status (boardtemp, winners, values, result)
               IF result = 0 then               ! Game still on
                  CALL evaluate (values, trialvalue)
               ELSEIF result = 1 then           ! A draw
                  LET trialvalue = 0            ! A neutral value
               ELSE                             ! Result = 3 or -3
                  LET trialvalue = 100*result     ! Win or loss
               END IF
```

```
            IF trialvalue > maxvalue then
               LET maxvalue = trialvalue
               LET move = trialmove
            END IF
         END IF
      NEXT trialmove

END SUB

SUB status (board(), winners(,), values(), result)

    ! Determines occupancy of the eight paths,
    ! and the result if the game is over

    MAT values = winners * board
    LET movecount = dot(board, board)

    LET result = 0                        ! Determine result
    FOR path = 1 to 8
        LET pv = values(path)
        IF abs(pv) = 3 then
           LET result = pv
           EXIT FOR
        END IF
    NEXT path
    IF result = 0 and movecount = 9 then LET result = 1

END SUB

SUB evaluate (values(), value)

    !  Board evaluation heuristic

    LET value = 0
    FOR path = 1 to 8
        LET x = values(path)
        LET value = value + sgn(x)*x^2
    NEXT path

END SUB
```

The skeleton is simple and straightforward, and plays four games. It initializes `board` and chooses the starting player, `player0`. Then a `DO` loop carries out the alternation of the moves. When the game is over, the result is printed and the starting player is switched. The convention that `player` is +1 for the computer and −1 for the human simplifies several features of the program.

The skeleton calls three external procedures (note that they follow `END`). It calls the subroutine `playmove` to obtain and check the player's move. The routine `bestmove` contains all the intelligence for determining the computer's move. The third, `status`, calculates `values` from the board situation, and also determines the result of the game, when the game is over.

The subroutine `bestmove` works by trying all available legal moves, computing a `value` for each move, and then choosing the move with the greatest value. It tries each legal move by actually making the move, in a temporary game board, so as not to modify the actual board. It then calls `status` to compute the values and result for the temporary board. If the game is not over, it calls the subroutine `evaluate` to compute a `trialvalue` for the temporary board, based on our simple heuristic. If the game is over, it assigns special values to the variable `trialvalue` depending on whether the game is a win, loss, or draw.

The subroutine `status` computes the path values from the board provided. One might think of several ways to compute path values from `board`. The simplest way is to use an *incidence matrix*. This matrix, called `winners`, has eight rows, one for each path, and nine columns, one for each square. If a certain square is on a given path, then the matrix has a "1" in that position; otherwise, it has a "0".

With this definition of the incidence matrix, computing path values is easily done with a matrix-by-vector multiplication. (The reader is advised to work out a numerical example.) It is hard to think of an easier, more succinct way of calculating path values. Matrix theory is also used to compute the number of moves that have occurred. Computing the *dot product* of the vector `board` with itself, using the vector function `dot`, yields exactly the number of moves that have occurred. Notice that it is not correct simply to add up the entries in `board`, because some of them are positive and some negative. But, adding the *squares* of the entries is correct, because $(-1)^2 = (1)^2 = 1$, and that is exactly what the dot product does. The entries are limited to +1, 0, and −1, so the dot product is identical to the sum of the absolute values.

The subroutine `status` also determines whether or not the game is over, and gives the correct value to `result` if it is. We use the coding scheme `result = 1` if a draw, `3` if a computer win, and `-3` if a player win.

Finally, the subroutine `evaluate` contains the heuristic for evaluating the *goodness* of the set of path values. Our evaluation formula is particularly simple. All it does is to compute the sum of squares (with signs) of the path values. This has the effect of drawing attention to paths that contain 2 or −2. If the computer has two in a row, the contribution to the sum is +4. If the human has two in a row, the contribution to the sum is −4. Paths that contain 0, +1, or −1 contribute negligibly.

In the following example games we note several weaknesses. But it must be remembered that the purpose of any heuristic is to come up with a good move, not necessarily the best move.

```
run

Computer moves 9
Your move? 1
Computer moves 3
Your move? 7
Computer moves 4
Your move? 8
     and you win.

Your move? 9
Computer moves 1
Your move? 2
Computer moves 7
Your move? 6
     and you win.
```

```
Computer moves 9
Your move? 2
Computer moves 1
Your move? 5
Computer moves 7
Your move? 3
Computer moves 8
     and wins.

Your move? 1
Computer moves 9
Your move? 3
Computer moves 2
Your move? 6
Computer moves 4
Your move? 8
Computer moves 7
Your move? 5
     and it is a draw.
```

We observe that if the human first responds in a corner, the computer does not play well, even when it starts. Nor does the computer play well if the human starts in the center. However, if the computer starts (and plays in the center) and the human starts on an edge, the computer plays correctly to obtain the guaranteed win (recall Section 20.2). Lastly, if the human starts and chooses a corner square, the computer may be able to force a draw. These sample games show that the heuristic is too crude to lead to optimal play. (See Exercise 2.)

It might be possible to improve the board evaluation heuristic, but it turns out that for more complicated games, and even for tictactoe, there is a better way. It is called *look ahead* and involves examining *several* future moves, not just one. This is discussed in the next section.

20.4 TICTACTOE: LOOK-AHEAD VERSION

In the first two example runs for **TICTAC2** (Section 20.3), if the computer could have examined even one move ahead it would have realized that the human could win on his or her next turn. The computer could then have chosen a different move and avoided the losses.

This look-ahead can be accomplished in a way that is both simple and profound. In the subroutine **bestmove**, where it calls **evaluate** to find the value of each of several board positions, it will instead *call itself* to estimate which move the opponent might make, and then evaluate on the basis of that! That is the basic idea—the rest is detail. A routine that calls itself is known as *recursive routine*; recursion is a powerful programming tool that renders certain complex problems remarkably simple.

Figure 20.4 illustrates how recursion is applied to the move look-ahead problem. We start with a game already in progress. It is the computer's turn to move. Its possible moves are into the squares 3, 4, 6, 7, or 8; these are shown as the first row of circle numbers. (We have already discussed how possible moves are generated in connection with the program **TICTAC2**.) The squares below the circles are the values associated with each move. How-

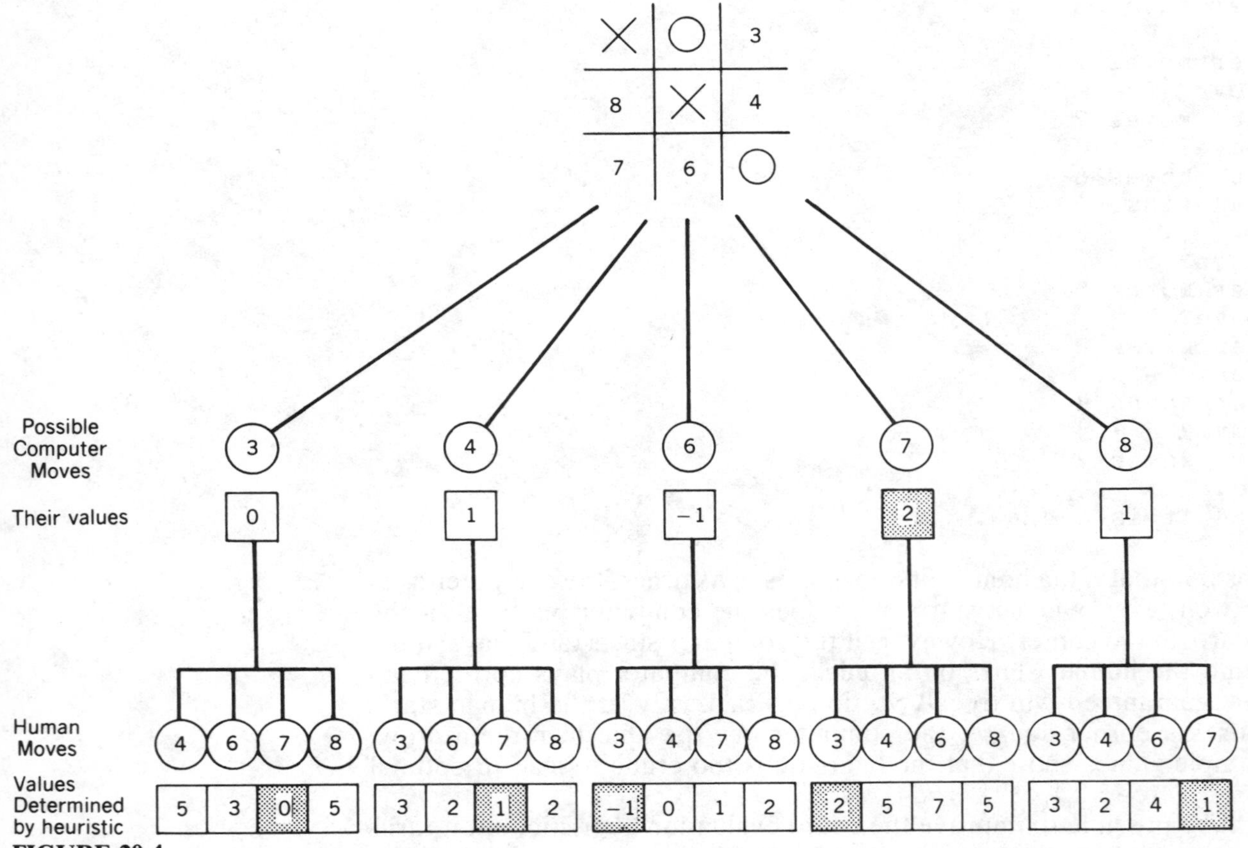

FIGURE 20.4
Move tree for TICTAC2–two move lookahead.

ever, and this is the key idea, these values are *not* obtained using the evaluation formula. Instead, the program (a) generates all possible human moves at the next level, (b) evaluates each of these using the evaluation formula, (c) assumes that the human chooses the move with the *smallest* value (shaded squares), and (d) that value becomes the value of the prior computer move. The computer naturally chooses the move with the largest value.

The entire program `TICTAC3` is not shown because the only changes involve the subroutine `bestmove`. Instead, we will show only the improved version of `bestmove`, and the correct call to it. The structure chart for `TICTAC3` (Figure 20.5) is the same as `TICTAC2's` except that the subroutine `bestmove` calls itself recursively.

TICTAC3, changes from TICTAC2 only.

```
CALL bestmove (board, winners, 2, player, values, dummyvalue, move)

SUB bestmove (board(),winners(,),depth,player,values(),value,move)

    ! Examines the board, and chooses the best move.
    ! Determined by recursively calling "bestmove", except if
    ! depth = 0, when it is based on the heuristics in "evaluate"
```

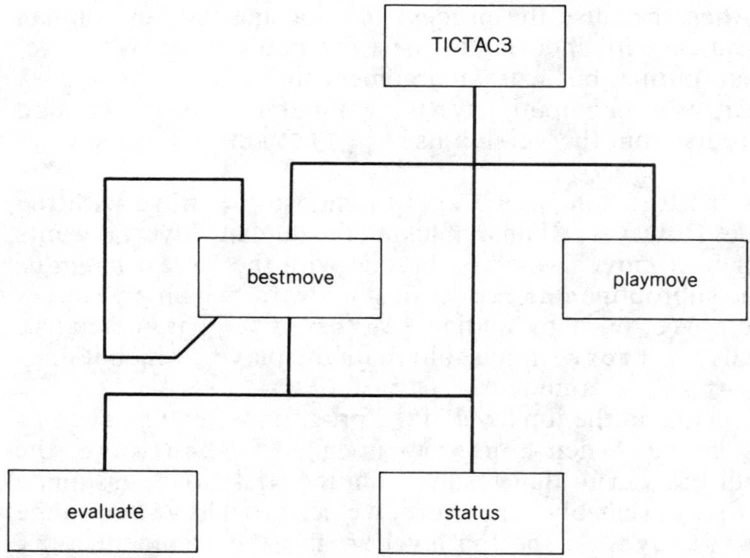

FIGURE 20.5
Structure chart for TICTAC3.

```
    DIM boardtemp(9)                        ! Temporary workspace

    LET maxvalue = -1000*player             ! Initial maximum value
    FOR trialmove = 1 to 9
        IF board(trialmove) = 0 then        ! Okay to try move
           MAT boardtemp = board
           LET boardtemp(trialmove) = player        ! Trial move made
           CALL status (boardtemp, winners, values, result)
           IF result = 0 then               ! Game still on

              IF depth > 1 then
 CALL bestmove (boardtemp,winners,depth-1,-player,values,tvalue,dummym)
              ELSE
                 CALL evaluate (values, tvalue)
              END IF

           ELSEIF result = 1 then           ! A draw
              LET tvalue = 0                ! A neutral value
           ELSE                             ! Result = 3 or -3
              LET tvalue = 100*result       ! A win or loss
           END IF

           IF player*tvalue > player*maxvalue then
              LET maxvalue = tvalue
              LET move = trialmove
           END IF
        END IF
    NEXT trialmove
    LET value = maxvalue

END SUB
```

Recursion works here because the process of choosing the best human move is virtually identical with choosing the best computer move. We therefore use the same subroutine, but with an argument that is either +1 or −1 according to whether we are computing for the computer or for the human. Thus, `bestmove` differs from the version used in `TICTAC2` only in several details.

The first detail is that the computer wants to choose the move with the largest possible value. However, when mimicking the human player, it wants to choose his or her best move, which is the one with the largest *negative* value. Therefore, the subroutine `bestmove` must know for which player it is doing the calculation. We tell it by adding `player` to the parameter list. When `bestmove` calls `bestmove`, it must alternate the player, which it does by supplying `-player` as the argument.

The second detail is that at the top level of the program we call `bestmove` to find out the best move. When `bestmove` is called by `bestmove`, the purpose is to find out the `value` that results from the trial move, assuming that the other player plays sensibly. Therefore, we need to add `value` to the parameter list for `bestmove`. At the top level we use the argument `dummyvalue` to suggest that we are not interested in the value, only the move. At the lower level we use `dmove` to suggest that we are not interested in the best move, only its value.

The final detail is that `bestmove` need not keep calling `bestmove` to the end of the game. That would be both unnecessary and inefficient, and would be impossible for games more complicated than tictactoe. Therefore, we must keep track of the *depth* of the search for the optimal move. We do this by introducing the argument `depth`, which indicates the number of moves to look ahead. It is decreased each time `bestmove` calls `bestmove`. As soon as `depth = 0`, further searching is halted and the heuristic evaluation routine is called.

If the starting depth is 1, then `TICTAC3` performs identically with `TICTAC2`—a trial move is made and then immediately evaluated. In our sample runs of `TICTAC3` we use a depth of 2; we make a trial move and then, for each such move, a trial move of the opponent. We describe this as a *two-move look-ahead*. The computer is now playing properly.

```
run

Computer moves 9
Your move? 1
Computer moves 2
Your move? 6
Computer moves 7
Your move? 3
Computer moves 5
Your move? 4
Computer moves 8
     and it is a draw.

Your move? 9
Computer moves 1
Your move? 5
Computer moves 3
Your move? 2
```

```
Computer moves 6
Your move? 4
Computer moves 8
Your move? 7
     and it is a draw.

Computer moves 9
Your move? 2
Computer moves 1
Your move? 5
Computer moves 7
Your move? 3
Computer moves 8
     and wins.

Your move? 1
Computer moves 9
Your move? 5
Computer moves 2
Your move? 6
Computer moves 7
Your move? 3
Computer moves 4
Your move? 8
     and it is a draw.
```

Other games, such as chess, require more look-ahead. In general, the deeper the look-ahead, the better the quality of play. The bad news is that greater depth in looking ahead requires more computer time, and the computer time increases very rapidly with the depth.

20.5 THE GAME OF NIM

Another game, and one that is often used in computer demonstrations, is Nim. Nim starts with several, usually three, piles of objects. Play involves removing one or more objects from any single pile. The player who takes the last piece wins. A player who does not know the strategy will find it difficult to win against one who does, and the number of possible combinations is much too large to remember.

There is a mathematical formulation that permits an easy determination of the best move. Instead of presenting this mathematical trick, which is not applicable to other games, we will instead show how the computer can discover an optimal strategy by and for itself.

We will play Nim with three piles, allowing up to nine pieces per pile. The state of the game is given by the list `Pile`. We will also need a compact representation of the state. The variable `s` will be a three-digit number

See Kemeny, J. G. and Kurtz, T. E., *BASIC Programming*, Third Edition, John Wiley and Sons, New York, 1979, see Section 11.4.

whose digits represent the piles. Thus, if `Pile(1) = 5`, `Pile(2) = 3`, and `Pile(3) = 8`, then `s = 538`. And, `s` takes on values from 0 to 999.

The key fact about Nim is that there are *good states* and *bad states*. From a good state an expert player can always win. From a bad state a player can win only if the other player makes a mistake.

An optimal move is one that leaves a bad state for the opponent. The preceding key fact may be restated by saying that there is at least one optimal move from a good state, but none from a bad state. (This technique is applicable to a number of different games, provided that the total number of possible states is a fairly small number. We just make a complete listing of all possible states, along with the best move for going from each good state to a bad state.)

A move will be described by specifying a pile "p" and the number of pieces to take "n". The program **NIMMAKE** constructs a *move table* that contains an optimal move for each good state. Column 1 of **Move** contains `p`, whereas column 2 contains `n`. If there is no optimal move, we let `p = 0`.

We construct the move table *from the bottom up*. A player presented with all piles empty (`s = 0`) has already lost. Hence, this is a bad state. For each other state we search for a move that will lead to a bad state, and enter this move into the table. If there is no such move, then we enter `p =0` to signal that the state being tested is also a bad state.

The skeleton of **NIMMAKE** runs through the states, from smallest `s` to largest possible (0 to 999). For each state it calls `find_move` and enters the move into the table **Move**. It also writes the table to a file **NIMTABLE**, so that this computation needs to be carried out only once.

The routine `find_move` is surprisingly simple. It tries each pile and all possible number of pieces. For each it carries out the move and checks whether the resulting state, `new_s`, is a bad state. If it is, the move is optimal and is preserved, and the routine is exited. If `find_move` runs through all possible moves without finding a resulting bad state, then the state being checked is itself bad.

To allow us to switch between the two representations of a state, the routines `code` and `decode` provide conversion.

```
REM    NIMMAKE
REM
REM    Create game table for NIM

OPEN #1: name "NIMTABLE"          ! File to save table
ERASE #1                          ! May have previous table

DIM Move(0 to 999, 2)             ! Col 1 = pile, Col 2 = pieces

LET nstates = 10^3                ! Number of states
LET t1 = time                     ! Time it
FOR s = 0 to nstates-1            ! States, from bottom up
    CALL find_move (Move, s, p, n)
    LET Move(s, 1) = p
    LET Move(s, 2) = n
    PRINT #1: p; ","; n
NEXT s
PRINT time-t1; "secs."
```

```
SUB find_move (Move(,), s, p, n)  ! Optimal move, or p = 0

    DIM Pile(3)                     ! No. in each pile
    CALL decode (s, Pile)
    FOR p = 1 to 3                  ! Try each pile
        LET temp = Pile(p)
        FOR n = Pile(p) to 1 step -1     ! Largest move first
            LET Pile(p) = temp - n       ! Make move
            CALL code (Pile, new_s)      ! New state
            IF Move(new_s,1)=0 then EXIT SUB      ! Found optimal
        NEXT n
        LET Pile(p) = temp          ! Restore
    NEXT p
    LET p, n = 0                    ! No good move

END SUB

SUB code (P(), s)                   ! Code piles

    LET s = P(1) * 10^2  +  P(2) * 10  +  P(3)

END SUB

SUB decode (s, P())                 ! Decode state

    LET P(3) = mod(s,10)
    LET s2   = int(s/10)
    LET P(2) = mod(s2,10)
    LET P(1) = int(s2/10)

END SUB

END
```

We included a timer in the skeleton. It shows that the computation and writing the table to a file takes about 135 seconds on an IBM PC. There is no other visible output.

We do not show what the file NIMTABLE now contains. But, for example,

Move(321,1) = 0	Move(321,2) = 0
Move(325,1) = 3	Move(325,2) = 4

Thus "321" is a bad state, and an optimal move from state "325" is to take 4 from pile 3, leading to the bad state "321".

We now examine the program **NIM** that plays the game. (See Figure 20.6 for its structure chart.) Its skeleton reads the move table from **NIMTABLE** and sets up the initial piles (randomly chosen to have from five to nine pieces). Then it alternately calls on the player and machine to move. The variable **total** keeps track of the total number of pieces left, hence **total = 0** signals the end of the game.

The routine **player_move** asks the player for a move and checks whether it is legal. It stays in a loop until a legal move is specified. The routine **machine_move** selects the computer's optimal move from the move table. If there is none, it calls **anymove** to take one piece from some pile.

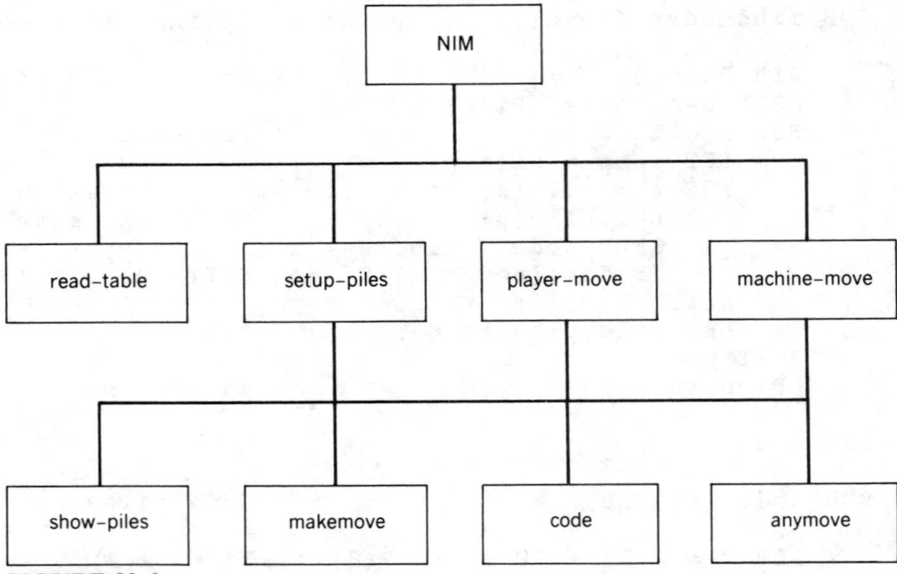

FIGURE 20.6
Structure chart for the program NIM.

The routines `player_move` and `machine_move` also call `makemove` to update both the piles and `total`. Before each player move, `show_piles` is used to print the state of the game. Finally, `code` is identical to the same routine in `NIMMAKE`.

```
REM   NIM
REM
REM   Game of NIM

DIM Move(0 to 999, 2)                       ! Optimal move table
DIM Pile(3)                                 ! Number in each pile

RANDOMIZE
CLEAR                                       ! Use entire screen

LET nstates = 10^3                          ! Number of states
CALL read_table                             ! Read into Move(,)
CALL setup_piles (total)
DO
   CALL show_piles
   CALL player_move (total)
   IF total=0 then
      PRINT "You win!"
      EXIT DO
   END IF
   CALL machine_move (total)
   IF total=0 then
      PRINT "I win!"
      EXIT DO
   END IF
LOOP
GET KEY z                                   ! Pause
```

```
SUB read_table                          ! Game table

    OPEN #1: name "NIMTABLE"
    FOR s = 0 to nstates-1
        INPUT #1: Move(s,1), Move(s,2)
    NEXT s
    CLOSE #1

END SUB

SUB setup_piles (total)

    LET total = 0
    FOR p = 1 to 3
        LET Pile(p) = int(5*rnd + 5)    ! five to nine
        LET total = total + Pile(p)
    NEXT p

END SUB

SUB player_move (total)

    DO
       LET ok = 1                       ! Check on move
       PRINT "Pile, Number taken";
       INPUT p, n
       IF p<>int(p) or p<1 or p>3 then
          LET ok = 0
       ELSEIF n<>int(n) or n<1 or n>Pile(p) then
          LET ok = 0
       END IF
       IF ok=1 then EXIT DO
       PRINT "Illegal move."
    LOOP
    CALL makemove (p, n, total)

END SUB

SUB machine_move (total)

    CALL code(Pile, s)
    LET p = Move(s,1)                   ! Look up optimal move
    LET n = Move(s,2)
    IF p=0 then CALL anymove (p, n)       ! No good move
    PRINT "My move: "; p; ","; n
    PRINT
    CALL makemove (p, n, total)

END SUB

SUB makemove (p, n, total)             ! Carry it out

    LET Pile(p) = Pile(p) - n
    LET total = total - n

END SUB
```

```
SUB show_piles

    PRINT "Piles: ";
    PRINT Pile(1); Pile(2); Pile(3)

END SUB

SUB anymove (p, n)                       ! Make a small move

    LET n = 1                            ! Take one
    FOR p = 1 to 3                       ! Find non-empty pile
        IF Pile(p)>0 then EXIT SUB
    NEXT p

END SUB

SUB code (P(), s)                        ! Code piles

    LET s = P(1) * 10^2  +  P(2) * 10  +  P(3)

END SUB

END
```

Two runs are shown. In the first, the player plays optimally and wins. In the second, the player makes a mistake on the opening move and hence, the machine wins.

```
run

Piles:  5  5  9
Pile, Number taken? 3, 9
My move:  1 , 1

Piles:  4  5  0
Pile, Number taken? 2, 1
My move:  1 , 1

Piles:  3  4  0
Pile, Number taken? 2, 1
My move:  1 , 1

Piles:  2  3  0
Pile, Number taken? 2, 1
My move:  1 , 1

Piles:  1  2  0
Pile, Number taken? 2, 1
My move:  1 , 1

Piles:  0  1  0
Pile, Number taken? 2, 1
You win!
```

```
run

Piles:  8  5  7
Pile, Number taken? 3, 1
My move:  1 , 5

Piles:  3  5  6
Pile, Number taken? 3, 2
My move:  1 , 2

Piles:  1  5  4
Pile, Number taken? 2, 2
My move:  3 , 2

Piles:  1  3  2
Pile, Number taken? 2, 2
My move:  3 , 2

Piles:  1  1  0
Pile, Number taken? 1, 1
My move:  2 , 1

I win!
```

20.6 A PATTERN MATCHING GAME

An example of a game that the computer plays well simply by being able to keep track of details is a pattern matching game. There are two players, who take turns. One player secretly thinks of a pattern of four digits, each one in the range 1 through 5, including duplications. There are 625 such patterns ($5^4 = 625$). The other player attempts to guess the pattern.

The first player gives information as to how close the guess was in the following way: he first reports the number of digits present in both the secret pattern and the guessed pattern, counting duplications. He then reports the number of digits that match exactly. Thus, if the secret pattern is *(1,1,2,3)* and the guessed pattern is *(4,1,1,1)*, the first player reports ''two digits in common'' (the two 1s in the secret pattern matching with two of the three 1s in the guess) and ''one exact match'' (the digit 1 in the second position).

It is easy to see that each guess provides additional information. For example, if the guess is *(1,1,2,3)* and the first player reports no digits in common, then the secret pattern must be composed entirely of 4s and 5s. Good human players can usually guess the pattern in five to eight guesses.

The computer can almost always guess the secret pattern in four guesses. The strategy is quite simple. Each time the computer makes a guess, the guess must be consistent with the responses given to all previous guesses. That is, if a previous guess *(1,1,2,3)* elicited the response ''two in common, none exact'', then the computer can eliminate many patterns and might choose next to guess *(2,4,1,5)*. The more previous guesses there are, the narrower the choice for the next guess.

After each guess and its response, the computer discards all patterns (originally, there are 625 patterns) that are inconsistent with that guess and response. It then chooses its next guess from the remaining patterns. Each guess serves to reduce the size of the set of remaining patterns until there is only one left.

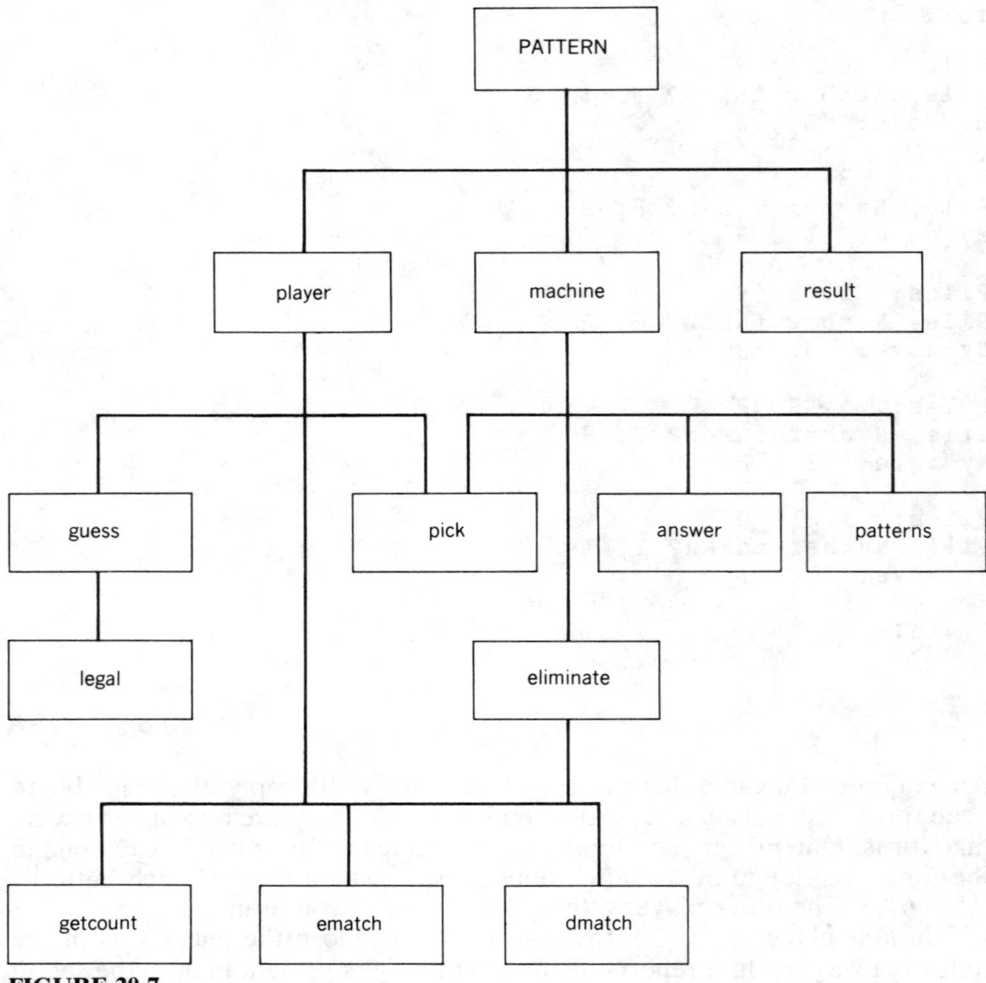

FIGURE 20.7
Structure chart for PATTERN.

We will have the computer choose a pattern randomly from the remaining set of consistent patterns. This simple strategy leads to a surprisingly good result. If there are 20 similar patterns left and a few isolated ones, it is better to guess one of the 20. And random choosing makes it much more likely that we will do so. There are, in fact, optimal strategies that can insure guessing the secret pattern in no more than four guesses. But random choice comes close, often resulting in guessing the pattern in four guesses, and usually in five.

The program **PATTERN**, whose structure chart appears in Figure 20.7, carries out two plays of the game, one by a human, and one by the computer.

```
REM   PATTERN
REM
REM   Pattern guessing game

DECLARE DEF legal

DIM patt$(625)                       ! All possible patterns
DIM count(5), mycount(5)             ! Frequencies
```

```
LET digits = 4
LET dmax = 5

RANDOMIZE
CLEAR                                ! Use entire screen

CALL patterns (n)                    ! Set up patterns
CALL player (p_guesses)              ! Player's turn
CALL machine (m_guesses)             ! Computer's turn
CALL who_won (p_guesses, m_guesses)
GET KEY zz                           ! Keep screen until key pressed

SUB player (p_guesses)               ! Player guesses

    CALL pick (secret$, n)           ! Pick a secret pattern
    CALL getcount (secret$, mycount)

    PRINT "I have picked a pattern."
    LET p_guesses = 0                ! No. of player guesses
    DO
       CALL guess (p$)
       LET p_guesses = p_guesses + 1
       CALL ematch (secret$, p$, e)
       IF e=digits then              ! Correct
          PRINT "That's right!"
          EXIT SUB
       ELSE
          CALL getcount (p$, count)
          CALL dmatch (count, mycount, d)
          PRINT d; "digits   "; e; "exact"
       END IF
    LOOP

END SUB

SUB guess (p$)                       ! Get player's guess

    DO
       PRINT "Guess";
       INPUT p$
       IF legal(p$)=1 then EXIT DO
       PRINT "Incorrect format"
    LOOP

END SUB

SUB machine (m_guesses)              ! Computer guesses

    DO
       PRINT
       PRINT "Think of a number"
       PRINT "Push 'return' when ready."
       GET KEY z
       LET m_guesses = 0
       DO
          CALL pick (myp$, n)        ! Next guess
          PRINT "My guess is: "; myp$
          LET m_guesses = m_guesses + 1
```

```
            CALL answer (d, e)
            IF e=digits then EXIT SUB    ! Got it!
            CALL eliminate (myp$, d, e, n)
         LOOP until n=0
         PRINT "Not possible. Let's try again."
         CALL patterns (n)            ! Set up for a new try
      LOOP

   END SUB

   SUB answer (d, e)

      DO
         LET ok = 1
         PRINT "Matches: digits, exact";
         INPUT d, e
         IF d<>int(d) or d<0 or d>digits then
            LET ok = 0
         ELSEIF e<>int(e) or e<0 or e>d then
            LET ok = 0
         END IF
         IF ok=1 then EXIT DO         ! Okay, so exit
         PRINT "Not possible."
      LOOP

   END SUB

   SUB who_won (p_guesses, m_guesses)

      PRINT
      PRINT "You needed"; p_guesses; "guesses."
      PRINT "I needed"; m_guesses; "guesses."
      IF p_guesses < m_guesses then
         PRINT "You win!"
      ELSEIF p_guesses > m_guesses then
         PRINT "I win!"
      ELSE
         PRINT "It is a tie."
      END IF

   END SUB

   SUB patterns (n)                   ! All possible patterns

      LET n = 0                       ! Number of them
      FOR d1 = 1 to dmax
          LET d1$ = str$(d1)
          FOR d2 = 1 to dmax
              LET d2$ = str$(d2)
              FOR d3 = 1 to dmax
                  LET d3$ = str$(d3)
                  FOR d4 = 1 to dmax
                      LET d4$ = str$(d4)
                      LET n = n+1
                      LET d$ = d1$ & d2$ & d3$ & d4$
                      LET patt$(n) = d$
```

```
                NEXT d4
            NEXT d3
        NEXT d2
    NEXT d1

END SUB

SUB pick (myp$, n)                      ! Pick a pattern from first n

    LET r = int(n*rnd + 1)
    LET myp$ = patt$(r)

END SUB

SUB eliminate (p$, d, e, n)             ! Patterns not matching d,e

    CALL getcount (p$, mycount)
    LET k = 0                           ! Number remaining
    FOR p = 1 to n
        LET p2$ = patt$(p)
        CALL ematch (p$, p2$, e2)
        IF e=e2 then                    ! Okay so far
           CALL getcount (p2$, count)
           CALL dmatch (count, mycount, d2)
           IF d=d2 then                 ! Consistent, so keep pattern
              LET k = k+1               ! by moving it up
              LET patt$(k) = p2$
           END IF
        END IF
    NEXT p
    LET n = k                           ! Reduced number

END SUB

SUB getcount (p$, count())              ! Frequency of digits

    MAT count = zer
    FOR c = 1 to digits
        LET i = val(p$[c:c])
        LET count(i) = count(i) + 1
    NEXT c

END SUB

SUB dmatch (count(), count2(), d)           ! Digit matches

    LET d = 0
    FOR i = 1 to dmax
        LET match = min(count(i),count2(i))
        LET d = d + match
    NEXT i

END SUB

SUB ematch (p$, p2$, e)                 ! Exact matches

    LET e = 0
    FOR c = 1 to digits
```

```
        IF p$[c:c]=p2$[c:c] then LET e = e+1
    NEXT c

END SUB

DEF legal(p$)                               ! legal = 1 if p$ is okay

    LET legal = 1
    IF len(p$)<>digits then
       LET legal = 0
       EXIT DEF
    END IF
    LET dmax$ = str$(dmax)
    FOR c = 1 to digits
        LET c$ = p$[c:c]
        IF c$<"1" or c$>dmax$ then LET legal = 0
    NEXT c

END DEF

END
```

Because the computer plays by choosing a pattern at random from among the set of remaining consistent patterns, it must have a list of all the patterns. The list `patt$` holds all possible patterns, each represented by a four-character string. The patterns are set up in the routine `patterns`.

We now examine several of the subroutines. The subroutine `player` starts by having the computer choose a secret pattern, using `pick` to select randomly one of the 625 available patterns `secret$`. Then the subroutine asks the player for a guess, which is `p$`. The function `legal` makes sure the guess is a legal one, and returns the value "1" if it is.

Additionally, the routine `ematch` counts the exact matches between `p$` and `secret$`.

To help get the number of matches on digits, we want a count of how many times each of the digits 1 through 5 occurs. The subroutine `getcount` computes these frequencies for both `p$` and `secret$`, and stores them in the lists `count` and `mycount`. The routine `dmatch` uses the two counts to find the number of digit matches.

The digit and exact matches are reported to the player. Eventually, the player will guess the pattern, the loop will be exited, and the subroutine will return `p_guesses`, the number of guesses needed by the player.

The subroutine `machine` starts by allowing time for the player to think up a secret pattern. The machine then embarks on a series of guesses, each one of which is provided by the subroutine `pick`. For each guess, the human responds with the number of digits in common and the number of exact matches. If there are four exact matches, then the secret pattern has been guessed, and the loop is exited. Otherwise, the subroutine `eliminate` further reduces the size of the remaining consistent patterns, and the loop continues. If the human makes a mistake, thus providing inconsistent information, this eventually leads to having no remaining patterns. In that case, the computer notifies the human and arranges to start over.

```
run

I have picked a pattern.
Guess? 1123
 1 digits    0 exact
Guess? 4451
 3 digits    3 exact
Guess? 4551
 2 digits    2 exact
Guess? 4441
That's right!

Think of a number
Push 'return' when ready.
My guess is: 3241
Matches: digits, exact? 3, 0
My guess is: 2412
Matches: digits, exact? 2, 0
My guess is: 5123
Matches: digits, exact? 3, 3
My guess is: 1123
Matches: digits, exact? 4, 4

You needed 4 guesses.
I needed 4 guesses.
It is a tie.

run

I have picked a pattern.
Guess? 1123
 2 digits    1 exact
Guess? 1244
 2 digits    1 exact
Guess? 1552
 2 digits    0 exact
Guess? 2221
 1 digits    1 exact
Guess? 5324
That's right!

Think of a number
Push 'return' when ready.
My guess is: 5351
Matches: digits, exact? 1, 1
My guess is: 4343
Matches: digits, exact? 4, 2
My guess is: 3344
Matches: digits, exact? 4, 4

You needed 5 guesses.
I needed 3 guesses.
I win!
```

We show two plays of the game. In both the human plays very well (or is lucky!) and yet one ends in a tie and the other is won by the computer.

EXERCISES

1. For TICTAC2 or TICTAC3, write a subroutine to print a picture of the game board after the computer's move.
2. The trouble with TICTAC2 is that evaluate fails to take into account the *tempo*, that is, whose turn it is. For instance, if the computer and the human have two in a row, the evaluation routine treats these as equal in importance but of opposite sign, so they cancel. Obviously, if, after the computer makes its trial move, the human has two in row, then the human can win on the next play. Modify evaluate to take tempo into account.
3. Modify TICTAC3 to allow the user to specify the maximum depth of the move look-ahead, instead of always using 2. Experiment to determine if there are cases where the computer does not play optimally with a depth of 2. Determine the minimum additional depth needed for the computer to play optimally.
4. There is always a trade-off between heuristic evaluation complexity and the depth of look-ahead. For instance, in TICTAC2, which used a depth of 1, the heuristic provided was seen to have serious flaws and it was suggested (in Exercise 2) that improvements could be made by devising a more complicated heuristic. On the other hand, if a greater search depth is allowed, the heuristic can be simpler and still give good results. To illustrate this idea, replace the calculation in the subroutine evaluate in TICTAC3 with something simpler, such as

   ```
   LET value = value + x
   ```

   Conduct experiments to determine the additional depth necessary to play correctly.
5. If the depth starts out at 9, then the evaluation formula is ignored. The only evaluation is then "win" or "lose". Explore the optimal moves in this case. (This will take a long time on a personal computer.) Does this version play any better than TICTAC3?
6. How many possible tictactoe games are there? Each game is a sequence of the integers from 1 to 9, but some games end before all nine squares are filled. (Hint: The number is less than 9!, which equals 362,880.)
7. The subroutine bestmove selects the move that has the maximum value. In case of ties, it selects the first such move it encounters. Make things exciting by randomly choosing the best move from several moves having the same maximum value.
8. Modify NIM to allow playing several games. The player should be asked whether to play another game when one is concluded. (Be sure that the move table is read only once.)
9. For NIM, find out how many "bad" or safe positions there are. Can you discern a pattern?
10. Modify the program NIMMAKE to allow up through 11 objects per pile. The variable s will still be a three-digit number, but "10" and "11" will now be allowable digits. In effect, we will use a number system to the base 12. Modify NIM to play with the new table. (Only small changes are needed in each program.)

11. Modify **NIM** to display the number of items in each pile graphically.
12. In Misere, a game similar to Nim, the player who takes the last piece loses. Modify **NIMMAKE** to compute a move table for Misere.
13. Modify **PATTERN** so that when the machine guesses, the number of patterns remaining is printed. Observe how various reports decrease this number.
14. What changes are necessary in **PATTERN** to allow each digit to be 1 through 7? What changes are necessary to allow five-digit patterns?

CHAPTER 21

ADVANCED GRAPHICS

21.1 INTRODUCTION

We introduced elementary graphics commands in Chapter 7, and suggest that you review them before reading this chapter.

Just as a large program can be divided into subroutines, a complex graphical construct can be devided into units called *pictures*. In BASIC a *picture* is a subroutine that can be subjected to transformations, such as shifts and rotations. Pictures may be collected into libraries, and complex pictures may be built from simpler ones.

Besides **PLOT** commands, which we have already discussed, BASIC has **BOX** commands for graphics in rectangular regions. These commands are easier to use and draw much faster. Two special **BOX** commands permit the program to memorize a rectangular region and display it elsewhere. These allow simple animation in BASIC. One of the animation programs we shall show you provides an interesting use of recursion.

For each **SET** command there is a corresponding **ASK** command that allows the program to discover what values had been set. We will show that asking about screen and window coordinates is useful for certain graphics routines. Finally, we will build a library for graphing functions, and will explain the library **PLOTLIB** used in Section 18.4.

If you have an IBM PC or similar computer, pictures not requiring color will look better if a **SET MODE "hires"** statement is inserted near the beginning of the program.

21.2 PICTURES

A *picture* is a special graphics subroutine. It is invoked by a **DRAW** command. In its simplest use, it serves to store the instructions for drawing a particular shape that may be used by many programs.

To begin, the library `PICLIB` contains several pictures. The first constructs a five-pointed star within a unit circle.

PICLIB (first part).

```
PICTURE star                              ! Star in -1,1,-1,1

    OPTION ANGLE degrees
    LET a = 90                            ! Starting angle
    FOR i = 1 to 6
        PLOT LINES: cos(a), sin(a);
        LET a = a + 144                   ! Next angle
    NEXT i
    PLOT                                  ! Stop connecting

END PICTURE
```

The points of the star start on the top (at 90 degrees) and are separated by 1/5 of the circle (72 degrees). What distinguishes a star from a pentagon is that we connect a point not to the next one but to the one after that (144 degrees away). The only other information we need is that the point

$$x = \cos(a) \qquad y = \sin(a)$$

is on the unit circle, an angle of *a* degrees counterclockwise from the rightmost point.

The program `STAR1` simply draws a star in the middle of the screen. We will not show the output because we will show a more interesting use of `star`.

```
REM   STAR1
REM
REM   Draws picture "star"

LIBRARY "PICLIB.trc"

SET WINDOW -5, 5, -3, 3
DRAW star

END
```

What distinguishes pictures from ordinary subroutines is that one can apply geometric transformations to pictures. The simplest such is a `shift`, which moves the picture to a different part of the screen. For instance, the statement

```
DRAW star with shift(c,d)
```

will add `c` to the x-coordinates and `d` to the y-coordinates. Thus, the point (0,0), the center of the star, is shifted to the point (c,d). This is illustrated in the next program, which draws 15 stars. The output is shown in Figure 21.1.

```
REM   STAR2
REM
REM   Draws fifteen stars

LIBRARY "PICLIB.trc"
```

FIGURE 21.1
Fifteen stars; drawn with the picture `star`.

```
SET WINDOW 0, 10, 0, 6
FOR x = 1 to 9 step 2                    ! Need 2x2 squares
    FOR y = 1 to 5 step 2
        DRAW star with shift(x,y)             ! Center at (x,y)
    NEXT y
NEXT x

END
```

More complex pictures can be constructed from simpler ones. This is illustrated in the rest of `PICLIB`. We start with a simple picture that draws a rectangular area. It is used to draw a window for a house. And both routines (`rectangle` and `window`) are used to construct the picture of a house.

The routine `rectangle` shows that pictures, like subroutines, can have parameters. In `window`, setting color "background" allows us to draw in the background color, which is equivalent to *erasing*.

PICLIB (last part).

```
PICTURE rectangle (x1, x2, y1, y2)

    PLOT AREA: x1,y1; x2,y1; x2,y2; x1,y2

END PICTURE

PICTURE window

    SET COLOR "background"
    DRAW rectangle (-.1, .1, -.2, .2)  ! The window
    SET COLOR "yellow"
    PLOT -.1,0; .1,0                   ! And its sills
    PLOT 0,-.2; 0,.2

END PICTURE
```

```
PICTURE house

    SET COLOR "green"
    DRAW rectangle (-1 ,1, -1, 1)       ! The house itself

    SET COLOR "red"
    PLOT AREA: -1,1; 0,1.5; 1,1    ! Its roof
    DRAW rectangle (-1, -.8, 1, 1.4)    ! And chimney

    SET COLOR "yellow"               ! A door
    DRAW rectangle (-.15, .15, -1, -.3)
    SET color "background"
    PLOT 0,-1; 0,-.3

    DRAW window with shift(-.5,-.5)     ! And four windows
    DRAW window with shift(-.5,.5)
    DRAW window with shift(.5,.5)
    DRAW window with shift(.5,-.5)

END PICTURE
```

We can now write a very simple program for drawing a house. The result is shown in Figure 21.2.

```
REM   HOUSE1
REM
REM   Illustrates pictures

LIBRARY "PICLIB.trc"

SET WINDOW -2, 2, -2, 2
DRAW house                          ! Uses picture "house"

END
```

The program **HOUSE2** makes use of all the transformations available in BASIC. (For a description of what each one does see the Summary.) It first draws the house in the lower left corner. Then it draws a larger house. The

FIGURE 21.2.
A single house.

transformation `scale(1.5,2)` increases the x-dimension by 50 percent and doubles the y-dimension. Therefore, the new house will be wider and much taller than the one produced with **HOUSE1**. Because we do not want to overlay the first house, we shift the larger house to the upper right of the screen. Note that we can apply more than one transformation; we separate them by the symbol *.

Next the program draws a house that has been rotated 45 degrees. This is shown in the lower center. Finally, we apply `shear(30)`, which tilts vertical lines by 30 degrees. This is shown in the upper left of the screen. Note that horizontal lines remain horizontal after a shear. The output is in Figure 21.3.

```
REM    HOUSE2
REM
REM    Illustrates picture transformations

LIBRARY "PICLIB.trc"

SET WINDOW 0, 10, 0, 10

DRAW house with shift(1,1)                        ! Regular house
DRAW house with scale(1.5,2) * shift(7,6)         ! Larger, taller
OPTION ANGLE degrees                              ! For rotate
DRAW house with rotate(45) * shift(5,2)           ! Tilt
DRAW house with shear(30) * shift(2,5)            ! Shear

END
```

Transformations are applied from left to right. The order is important because reversing the order may result in a different picture. This is illustrated in **PIC**. We start with a unit square in the first quadrant. Then we show the difference between a rotation followed by a shift, and a shift followed by a rotation. A rotation always rotates the plane around the origin. Here the

FIGURE 21.3
Houses after various transformations.

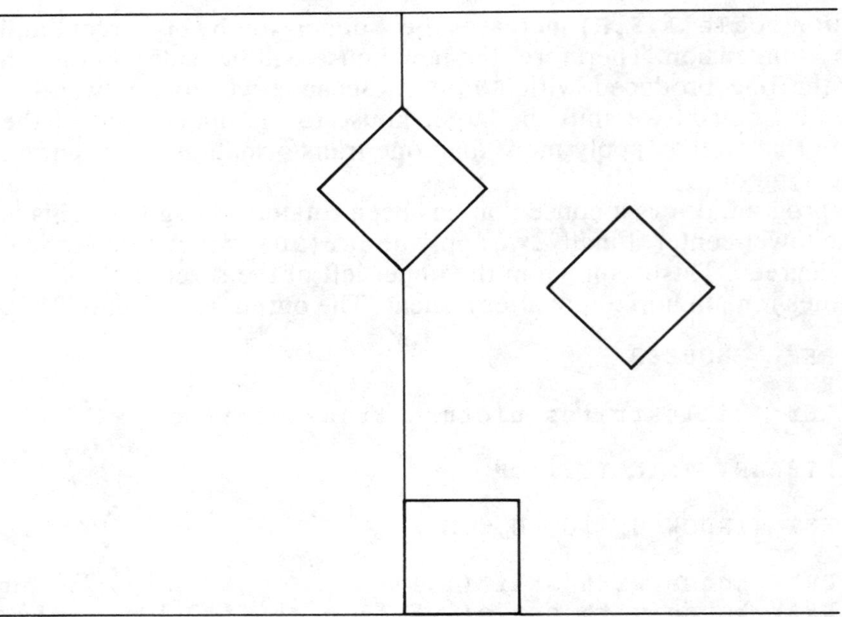

FIGURE 21.4
Multiple transformations in different orders.

origin is the lower left corner of our square. Thus, if we rotate around this by 45 degrees, the corner stays at the origin but the main diagonal becomes vertical. We then move the *origin* to the point (2,2).

If we shift first and then rotate, the lower left corner goes to (2,2), but the rotation is still around the origin. Hence, the square swings in a large circle. The main diagonal ends up high on the y-axis. The results are shown in Figure 21.4.

Normally, we carry out scaling, rotations, or shearing before we shift the result to the position we want.

```
REM   PIC
REM
REM   Illustrates order of transformations

LIBRARY "PICLIB.trc"

OPTION ANGLE degrees
SET window -4, 4, 0, 5
PLOT -4, 0; 4, 0                        ! Axes
PLOT 0, 0; 0, 5

DRAW square                             ! Original picture
DRAW square with rotate(45) * shift(2,2) ! Rotate, then shift
DRAW square with shift(2,2) * rotate(45) ! Shift, then rotate

PICTURE square

    DRAW rectangle (0, 1, 0, 1)

END PICTURE

END
```

21.3 BOX COMMANDS

Although the **PLOT** commands are very useful, they are unnecessarily complicated for certain simple situations. For example, if we wish to draw a rectangle whose x-coordinates go from 1 to 4 and whose y-coordinates go from 3 to 7, we need to write

```
PLOT LINES: 1,3; 4,3; 4,7; 1,7; 1,3
```

BASIC provides shortcuts for drawing rectangular regions whose sides are horizontal and vertical. These are the **BOX** commands, and their arguments are just like the arguments of the **SET WINDOW** statement. For example, the preceding rectangle can be drawn with a **BOX LINES** command.

```
BOX LINES 1, 4, 3, 7
```

Corresponding to **PLOT AREA** we have **BOX AREA**, which fills in the area. Finally, **BOX CLEAR** erases a rectangular area. If the picture is in color, **BOX CLEAR** fills the rectangle with the background color.

These three statements are used in the program **BOX1**, which is easy to read. Note in particular that a **BOX LINES** statement whose four numbers happen to be the four numbers of the window coordinates draws a frame around the window! The result is shown in Figure 21.5.

```
REM   BOX1
REM
REM   Illustrate BOX commands

OPEN #1: screen .25, .75, .1, .9
SET WINDOW -5, 5, -5, 5

BOX LINES -5, 5, -5, 5                 ! Frame around window
BOX AREA   -3, 3, -3, 3                ! Solid square
BOX CLEAR -1, 1, -1, 1                 ! Cut hole

END
```

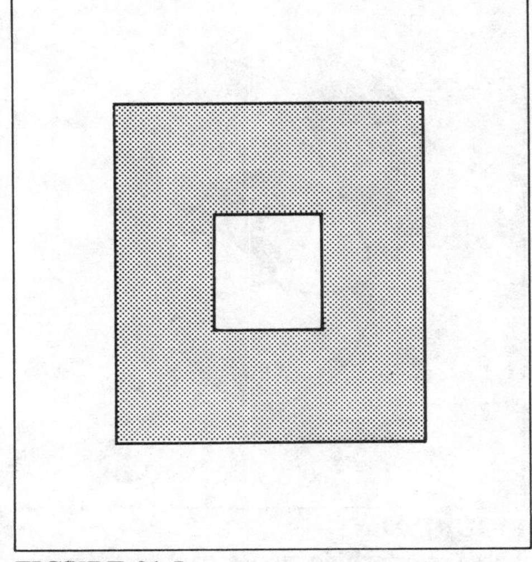

FIGURE 21.5
A square with a square hole.

Not only are the **BOX** commands simpler to use, they are also faster. We will need this speed when we do animation in the next section.

The **BOX CIRCLE** command provides a fast and accurate circle drawing routine. It draws a circle inscribed in the rectangle specified by the arguments, but will look like a circle only if the specified coordinates describe a square region as seen on the screen. Otherwise, the *circle* will really be an *ellipse*. **BOX2** draws three circles and floods regions in various colors. (See Figure 21.6.) When color is available, the output is spectacular.

```
REM   BOX2
REM
REM   Illustrate BOX CIRCLE

OPEN #1: screen .25, .75, .1, .9      ! Window
SET WINDOW 0, 10, 0, 10               ! Cordinates
SET back "blue"                       ! Background color
BOX LINES 0, 10, 0, 10                ! Frame

BOX CIRCLE 2, 6, 4, 8                 ! Three circles
BOX CIRCLE 4, 8, 4, 8
BOX CIRCLE 3, 7, 2, 6

SET color "red"                       ! Color segments
FLOOD 3,6
FLOOD 7,6
FLOOD 5,3
SET color "green"
FLOOD 5,5
SET color "yellow"
FLOOD 9,9

END
```

BOX statements may be incorporated into pictures, but if a transformation is applied it will only affect the **PLOT** statements, and have no effect on **BOX** statements.

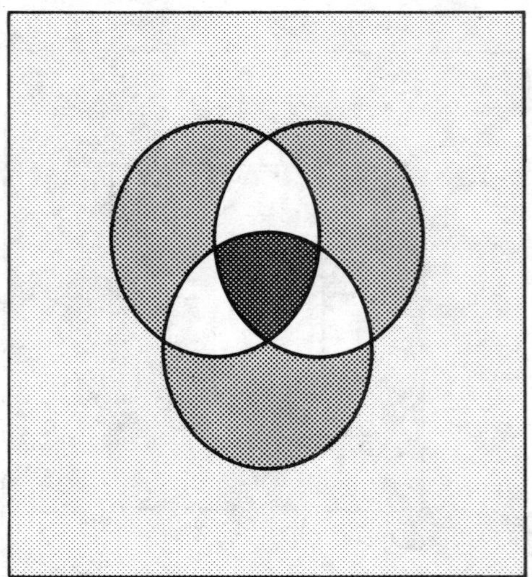

FIGURE 21.6
Three overlapping circles.

21.4 ANIMATION

We will write a program to show a *shooting star*. The process is simple. First, we draw a star in the upper left corner. Then, in a loop, we erase the star and redraw it further to the right and lower. If we tried to do this with ordinary DRAW commands, we would not get the illusion of motion. The drawing would be too slow. (See Exercise 10.)

The command BOX KEEP allows the program to memorize a rectangular portion of the screen. The result is stored in a string variable in a special coded form. Then BOX SHOW allows us to display the same picture in another rectangular region. This can be done fast enough to give the illusion of motion.

STAR3 carries out this program. It draws a star in the upper left and memorizes it in the string star$. It pauses for a second before the motion starts. The animation is carried out in a simple FOR loop. Each time through the loop we erase the old star (BOX CLEAR) and redisplay it a unit further to the right and lower. We will not show the output here because the program must be run to experience the animation. (For a more realistic shooting star, see Exercise 9.)

```
REM   STAR3
REM
REM   Shooting star

LIBRARY "PICLIB.trc"

SET WINDOW 0, 20, 0, 12

LET x = 1                               ! Original star
LET y = 11
DRAW star with shift(x,y)
BOX KEEP 0, 2, 10, 12 in star$          ! Memorize
PAUSE 1                                 ! Delay

FOR n = 0 to 12                         ! Movement
    BOX CLEAR x-1, x+1, y-1, y+1        ! Erase old star
    LET x = x+1                         ! Next position
    LET y = y-1
    BOX SHOW star$ at x-1, y-1          ! Star has moved
NEXT n

END
```

We now turn to a famous chess problem that requires us to place eight queens on a chess board so that no two attack each other. That is, no two are allowed to be on the same horizontal or vertical line, or on the same diagonal. QUEENS not only solves the problem, but it uses animation to demonstrate the method of solution.

Let us first discuss the method of solution. We will work one column at a time, working from left to right. First, we place a queen in the column. The list row remembers which rows the queens occupy; for instance, row(c) is the row in which the queen in column c was placed. We then check whether this is a legal position—i.e., there is no earlier queen in the same row or on one of the two diagonals. If it is legal, then we go on to try to place the remaining queens. If it is not a legal position, or we do not succeed in placing the rest, we must choose a different row for our queen.

The program is simplified by using recursion. The subroutine `solve` is a recursive routine incorporating the strategy. It loops through all possible rows. For each, it displays the queen and then checks legality. If it is legal (`ok = 1`) and there are more queens to place (`c < n`), then it calls itself with the next higher value of `c`. If that succeeds, the routine is exited. If not, the queen is erased and a new row is tried.

Five routines handle the graphics. `Keep_queen` draws the queen by using `DRAW queen`, and them memorizes it using a `BOX KEEP` followed by a call to `wipe`. The picture `queen` is somewhat messy because it must draw a complicated figure. But, note the simplicity of `grid` and `show`, used to draw the chessboard and display a queen, respectively. The routine `wipe` clears an area larger than was used by `BOX SHOW` to make certain that all parts of the queen are erased.

The main portion of the program consists mostly of subroutine calls. Note that we use a variable `nqueens` for the number of queens. Changing its value allows trying the puzzle on a smaller or larger chessboard. (See Exercise 11.)

```
REM   QUEENS
REM
REM   Eight queens problem
REM   For a different number change "nqueens"

OPEN #1: screen .25, .75, .1, .9  ! Square window (roughly)
DIM row(10)                       ! Position in column

LET nqueens = 8                   ! Number of queens
SET window 0, nqueens, 0, nqueens     ! Coordinates for board
DRAW grid (nqueens)               ! Draw board
MAT row  = zer(nqueens)           ! Empty board
CALL keep_queen (q$)              ! Memorize figure

CALL solve (nqueens, 1, row, q$, ok)    ! Ask for solution
IF not ok=1 then PRINT "Not possible"

END

SUB solve (n, c, row(), q$, ok)   ! Solve, starting at column c

    FOR r = 1 to n                ! Possible positions
        LET row(c) = r            ! Row r in column c
        CALL show (q$, c, r)      ! Display queen
        CALL check (row, c, ok)   ! Is it legal?
        IF ok=1 and c<n then
           CALL solve (n, c+1, row, q$, ok)      ! Solve later columns
        END IF
        IF ok=1 then EXIT SUB     ! Solved this piece
        CALL wipe (c, r)          ! Erase old queen
    NEXT r                        ! Try another position

END SUB
```

```
SUB check (row(), c, ok)             ! Is it legal?

    LET ok = 0                       ! Assume not okay
    LET r = row(c)                   ! New position
    FOR c1 = 1 to c-1                ! Check against earlier queens
        LET k = c - c1               ! Distance
        LET r1 = row(c1)
        ! Check horizontal, two diagonals
        IF r=r1 or r=r1+k or r=r1-k then EXIT SUB
    NEXT c1
    LET ok = 1                       ! Passed all tests

END SUB

SUB show (q$, c, r)                  ! Display queen

    BOX SHOW q$ at c-.8, r-.8

END SUB

SUB wipe (c, r)                      ! Erase queen

    BOX CLEAR c-.9, c-.1, r-.9, r-.1

END SUB

SUB keep_queen (q$)                  ! Draw and memorize queen

    DRAW queen
    BOX KEEP .2,.8,.2,.8 in q$
    CALL wipe (1, 1)

END SUB

PICTURE grid (n)                     ! Draw board

    FOR i = 0 to n
        PLOT i,0; i,n
        PLOT 0,i; n,i
    NEXT i

END PICTURE

PICTURE queen                        ! Draws a queen

    PLOT .2,.8; .3,.2; .7,.2; .8,.8
    PLOT .2,.8; .3,.5; .4,.8; .5,.5; .6,.8; .7,.5; .8,.8
    FLOOD .5,.4

END PICTURE
```

We show a solution for eight queens in Figure 21.7. But the program needs to be run to observe the animation.

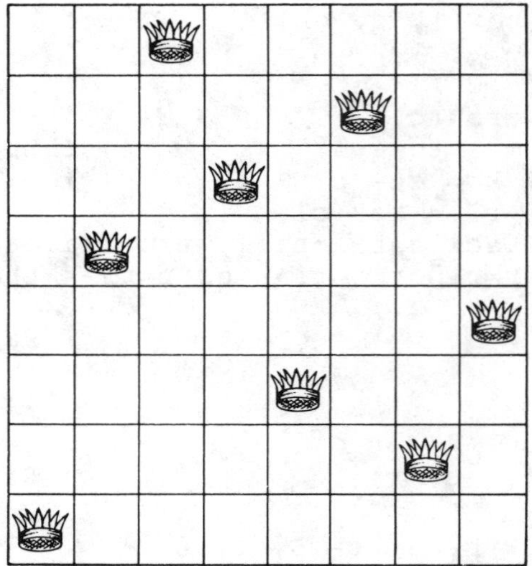

FIGURE 21.7.
A solution to the eight queens problem.

21.5 ASK COMMANDS

SET commands allow the adjustment of certain parameters that are built into BASIC. For example, the *margin* is normally set at 80 characters for printing. But a **SET MARGIN** statement may be used to change this. Corresponding to each **SET** statement there is an **ASK** statement so that the program may discover the current value of the parameter. Thus,

```
ASK MARGIN m
```

assigns to m the current size of the margin.

One use of **ASK** is for a subroutine that needs to change one of the language parameters temporarily. It uses **ASK** to discover the current value, then changes it using **SET** and, at the end, changes it back to the old value. We illustrate this with the very simple program **ASK**, which has a subroutine that prints an array in narrow columns.

```
REM   ASK
REM
REM   Illustrate an ASK command

DIM x(10), y(10)

FOR i = 1 to 10                       ! Sample array
    LET x(i) = i
NEXT i
MAT PRINT x                           ! Normal zonewidth

MAT y = 2*x
CALL special (y)                      ! Special format

MAT y = 3*x
MAT PRINT y                           ! Check that format restored

END
```

```
SUB special (y())                     ! Print in narrow zones

    ASK zonewidth zw                  ! Old value
    SET zonewidth 5                   ! Change it
    MAT PRINT y
    SET zonewidth zw                  ! Restore it

END SUB
```

In the following run we see that the first and third arrays are printed in normal format (with five numbers per line), while the second array is printed—by the routine `special`—using a narrow zonewidth.

```
run

 1              2              3              4              5
 6              7              8              9              10

 2    4    6    8    10   12   14   16   18   20

 3              6              9              12             15
 18             21             24             27             30
```

21.6 TWO GRAPHICS LIBRARIES

We will now construct a library that is useful for drawing graphs. The first picture, **frame**, is trivial but useful. It draws lines around the boundaries of our window. We have seen that this can be accomplished by a single **BOX LINES** statement. But we need to know the window coordinates. It would appear that a library routine would have to receive **x1**, **x2**, **y1**, and **y2** as parameters. That is an awful lot of trouble for so simple a routine. In fact, this is not necessary because the routine can use **ASK WINDOW**.

The second picture, **axes**, does two tasks. It draws the x-axis and y-axis, which is very simple. Then it marks units on the axes with small tick marks, which is surprisingly tricky. The problem is the size of the ticks. One is tempted to pick an arbitrary size, say .1, for the height of the x-axis tick. This may look very good if y goes from 0 to 10. But, if y goes from 0 to 100, the tick will be 1/1000 of the screen size and will be invisible. Or, if y goes from 0 to 2, the tick will be enormous. We would like *standard size* ticks, and would like roughly the same size on both axes.

Therefore, **axes** must use **ASK WINDOW**. But that is not enough. It must also use **ASK SCREEN** to discover whether we are drawing on the entire screen, or on a tiny portion of the screen, or something in between. The two **LET** statements in **axes** are designed to achieve these goals. The height of the x-tick is 1/60 of the height of the entire physical screen, while the width of the y-tick is 1/100 the width of the screen. This makes them a reasonable size. And, on a typical screen, they will be the same size.

```
EXTERNAL

!   GRAPHLIB
!
!     frame           Draws a frame around window
!     axes            Draws axes with tick marks
!     fplot           Plots an external function

PICTURE frame                           ! Draw frame around window

    ASK WINDOW x1, x2, y1, y2
    BOX LINES  x1, x2, y1, y2

END PICTURE

PICTURE axes                            ! Draw axes with ticks

    ASK SCREEN a1, a2, b1, b2           ! For size of ticks
    ASK WINDOW x1, x2, y1, y2
    LET xtick = (y2-y1)/60/(b2-b1)
    LET ytick = (x2-x1)/100/(a2-a1)

    PLOT x1, 0;  x2, 0                  ! Axes
    PLOT 0, y1;  0, y2

    FOR x = int(x1) to int(x2)          ! Ticks
        PLOT x, -xtick; x, +xtick
    NEXT x

    FOR y = int(y1) to int(y2)
        PLOT -ytick, y; +ytick, y
    NEXT y

END PICTURE

PICTURE fplot (x1, x2, nsteps)          ! Plot external function f

    DECLARE DEF f

    LET h = (x2-x1)/nsteps              ! Step size
    FOR n = 0 to nsteps                 ! Loop through points
        LET x = x1 + n*h
        LET x = round(x,8)              ! Watch for round-off error
        WHEN exception in               ! Protect bad function valu
             PLOT x, f(x);
        USE
             PLOT                       ! Break in graph
        END WHEN
    NEXT n
    PLOT                                ! Don't connect to next poi

END PICTURE
```

The routine `fplot` is similar to those we saw in Chapter 7 for graphing a function. Because it is a library routine, it must graph a function `f` that is external to it. It also takes certain precautions. The simplest loop would be

```
FOR x = x1 to x2 step h
```

but, due to round-off errors, the last point may never be drawn. Hence, we loop on the number of steps. We also protect the plotting with a **WHEN** structure in case `f(x)` is not well-defined at some point.

The program **FPLOT1** uses all three pictures to draw a sine curve. The result is shown in Figure 21.8.

```
REM    FPLOT1
REM
REM    Demonstrate GRAPHLIB

LIBRARY "graphlib.trc"

SET mode "hires"
OPEN #1: screen .2, .8, .1, .9
DRAW frame

SET WINDOW -pi, pi, -4, 4
DRAW axes
DRAW fplot (-pi, pi, 40)

END

! The function definition must be external
DEF f(x) = 3*sin(x)
```

To illustrate the need for **WHEN**, **FPLOT2** plots `f(x) = 1/x`. Without the protection the program would give an exception when $x = 0$. The reason for the **PLOT** statement is that in case of an exception we want to cause a break

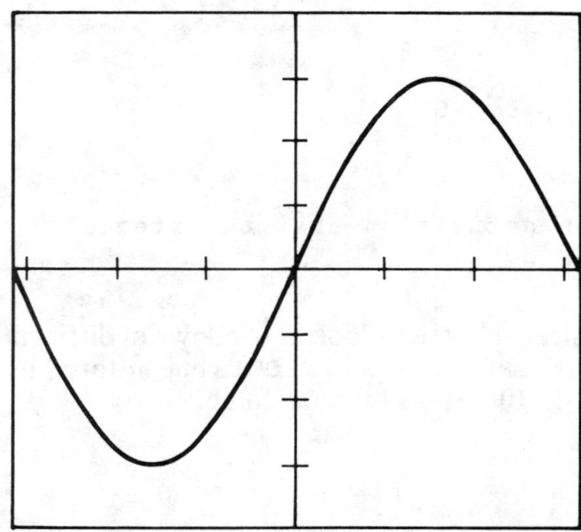

FIGURE 21.8
Showing use of the picture `fplot`.

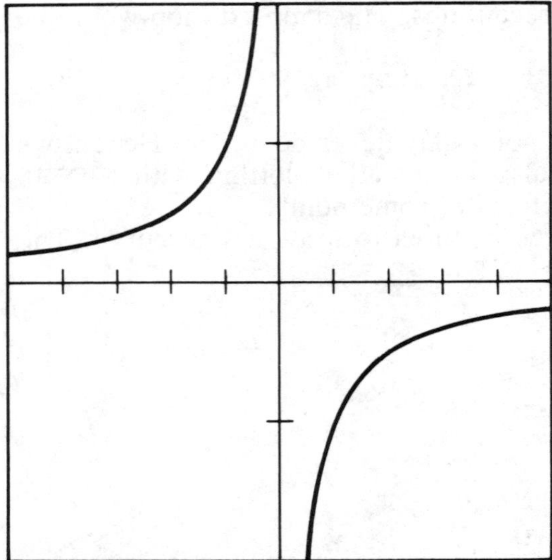

FIGURE 21.9
Plotting f(x) = 1/x, which has a discontinuity.

in the curve. We do not want the left-side curve to be connected to the right-side curve. Figure 21.9 shows the result.

```
REM   FPLOT2
REM
REM   Demonstrate GRAPHLIB

LIBRARY "graphlib.trc"

SET mode "hires"
OPEN #1: screen .2, .8, .1, .9
DRAW frame

SET WINDOW -2, 2, -5, 5
DRAW axes
DRAW fplot (-2, 2, 40)

END

! The function definition must be external
DEF f(x) = 1/x
```

Finally we illustrate how ticks look in windows of different size and shape. **FPLOT3** draws the same curve as **FPLOT1**, but in three differently shaped windows. Figure 21.10 displays the outcome.

```
REM   FPLOT3
REM
REM   Demonstrate GRAPHLIB

LIBRARY "graphlib.trc"
```

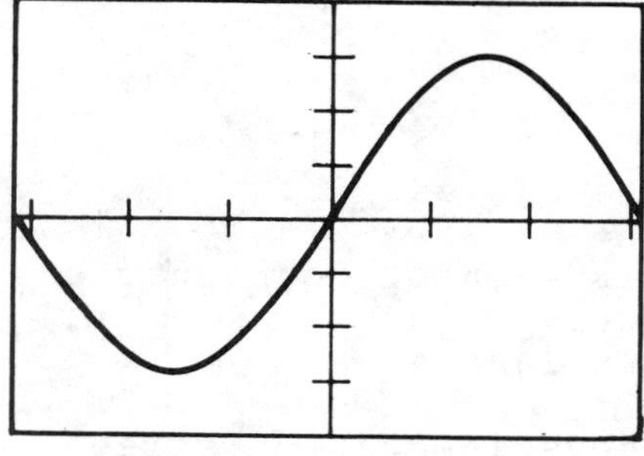

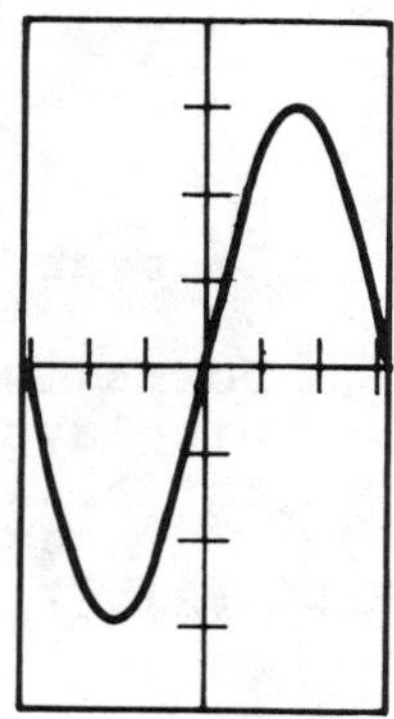

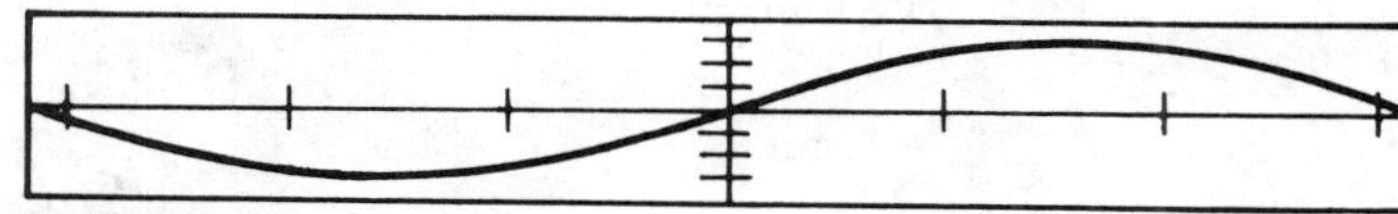

FIGURE 21.10
Three sine curves in differently shaped windows.

```
SET mode "hires"
OPEN #1: screen 0, .5, .5, 1
OPEN #2: screen 0, .8, 0, .2
OPEN #3: screen .7, .9, .4, 1

FOR w = 1 to 3                          ! Cycle through windows
    WINDOW #w
    DRAW frame
    SET WINDOW -pi, pi, -4, 4
    DRAW axes
    DRAW fplot (-pi, pi, 40)
NEXT w

END

! The function definition must be external
DEF f(x) = 3*sin(x)
```

We conclude this section with a discussion of the library **PLOTLIB** that was used in Chapters 17 and 18. It contains three routines.

The routine `split_screen` allows the user to display the results of four different cases on the same screen, by splitting the screen into four quarters. In each quarter screen we open one graphics window (#1) and one text window (#2). The parameter `ex` is the example or case number, and the first three lines adjust `a` and `b` for the particular quarter screen.

The other two routines are used to display graphs of several variables. The values of variables over time are stored in the table `data`, with one column for each variable. The array `range` has minimum and maximum values for each variable, while `label$` contains one-letter labels identifying the variables. The routine `data_setup` draws the axes and ticks with labels, while `display` draws the graphs. The techniques used are similar to those in **GRAPHLIB**.

```
EXTERNAL

!  PLOTLIB
!
!       Library for split-screen and multiple curves
!
!       split_screen      Forms two windows in each of four quarters
!       display           Displays multiple curves
!       data_setup        Establishes axes and labels

SUB split_screen (ex, #1, #2)       ! Two windows in quarter screen

    LET a, b = 0                    ! Lower left
    IF ex=2 or ex=4 then LET a = .5     ! Right side
    IF ex=1 or ex=2 then LET b = .48    ! Upper half

    CLOSE #1                        ! For graphics
    OPEN #1: screen a+.1, a+.4, b+.24, b+.48
    BOX LINES 0, 1, 0, 1            ! Frame

    CLOSE #2                        ! For text
    OPEN #2: screen a+.1, a+.4, b, b+.2

END SUB

SUB display (#1, data(,), range(,), tmax, tlast, label$())

    ! Graph data array, one graph for each column
    ! Use range for y-axis, 0 to tmax for x-axis
    ! Use label$ to identify graphs

    LET n = ubound(data, 2)         ! Number of columns
    WINDOW #1
    FOR i = 1 to n
        LET y1 = range(i,1)
        LET y2 = range(i,2)
        SET WINDOW 0, tmax, y1, y2
        LET place = data(0,i) - (y2-y1)/10
        PLOT TEXT, at -tmax/10, place: label$(i)
        FOR t = 0 to tlast
            PLOT t, data(t,i);
        NEXT t
        PLOT
    NEXT i

END SUB

SUB data_setup (xmax, ymax, unit)       ! For graphic display of data

    SET MODE "hires"
    SET WINDOW -xmax/10, xmax, 0, 1.1*ymax  ! With margins
    PLOT 0,ymax; 0,0; xmax,0        ! Plot axes
    LET tick = xmax/100
    FOR y = 0 to ymax step unit     ! Mark y-axis
        PLOT -tick,y; tick,y
        PLOT TEXT, at -xmax/15, y-10: str$(y)
    NEXT y

END SUB
```

21.7 SUMMARY

A *picture* is a graphics subroutine, with or without parameters, that is invoked by a DRAW command. Pictures may use other pictures to build complex figures from simple building blocks. As with subroutines, pictures may be collected into libraries that can be separately compiled.

The special feature of a picture is that it can be transformed geometrically, as with

```
DRAW picture WITH one or more transformations
```

The picture tranformations of BASIC

Transformation	Action
shift(x1, y1)	Moves origin to x1, y1
scale(k)	Multiplies coordinates by factor k
scale(k1, k2)	Mutiplies x- and y-coordinates separately
rotate(a)	Rotates counter-clockwise by angle a
shear(a)	Tilts y-coordinates to right by angle a

The angle a is measured in radians unless an OPTION ANGLE degrees statement is included.

Several transformations may be applied to the same picture. They are separated by asterisks, and are applied from left to right.

BOX commands are available for figures in rectangles with horizontal and vertical sides. The convention on coordinates for BOX commands is the same as for the SET WINDOW command.

```
BOX LINES x1, x2, y1, y2            ! Draws rectangle
BOX AREA x1, x2, y1, y2             ! Draws solid rectangle
BOX CLEAR x1, x2, y1, y2            ! Erases rectangle
BOX CIRCLE x1, x2, y1, y2           ! Inscribed circle or ellipse
BOX KEEP x1, x2, y1, y2 in k$       ! Memorizes rectangular region
BOX SHOW k$ at x1, x2, y1, y2       ! Displays rectangular region
```

BOX commands are simpler to use and faster than PLOT. BOX KEEP and SHOW make animation possible. BOX commands occurring within pictures are not affected by transformations.

Corresponding to each SET statement is an ASK statement. For example,

```
SET ZONEWIDTH zw            ! Sets width of zone to zw
ASK ZONEWIDTH zw            ! zw is set equal to current zonewidth
```

ASK commands enable graphics routines to discover the size of the current window and the window coordinates.

EXERCISES

1. Write a picture hexagon that draws a regular hexagon. (It is similar to stars.) Modify STAR2 to draw hexagons.
2. Modify the picture of Exercise 1 to have a parameter n and draw a regular n-sided polygon.

3. Create a picture of your own choice and display several copies on the screen, each rotated by a different angle.
4. Modify Exercise 3 to display shears by different angles.
5. Rewrite `BOX1` without using `BOX` commands. Note how much messier the code is!
6. Use the `BOX` commands to construct an interesting pattern of rectangles.
7. Use the `BOX` commands to construct an interesting pattern of circles.
8. Draw a simple picture of an airplane and have it fly across the screen.
9. Modify `STAR3` to have the star follow a circular path. For the new position use

   $$x = 12 * sin(n/7) - 1$$
   $$y = 12 * cos(n/7) + 1$$

10. Modify `STAR3` to draw each star from scratch, without using `BOX KEEP` and `SHOW`. Does it still look like a shooting star?
11. Run `QUEENS` for 2 to 10 queens. For what values is there no solution?
12. Modify `solve` in `QUEENS` by adding an extra parameter `count` that counts the number of queens drawn—i.e., the number of steps in the solution. Run it for 4 to 10 queens. Note the difference in difficulty in solving for an odd and even number.

PROJECTS

1. Random Art

   Divide the screen into a number of small squares. Construct several simple patterns of the size of one small square. (They should be very simple, say, a square divided into four parts, with two parts flooded.) If color is available, use color. Memorize these patterns in a string array.

   The main part of the program does a `BOX SHOW` for each square of a pattern picked at random from your memorized patterns. It should allow the user to push a key to obtain a different arrangement.

   You can add some regularity to the picture by preselecting a few of your patterns (say seven) and displaying these patterns in a cyclic order.

2. Moving picture

   Use `BOX KEEP` and `BOX SHOW` to make your own movie.

CHAPTER 22

SOUND AND MUSIC

22.1 INTRODUCTION

Most personal computers are equipped with a small loudspeaker. BASIC provides two simple ways to produce sounds, and even music, using this loudspeaker. The **SOUND** statement produces single notes. The **PLAY** statement plays tunes that are "written" into strings.

Graphics pictures and transformations, described in Section 21.2, are used by the BASIC program **SCORE** to draw sheet music in the standard notation using staffs and notes.

Harmony (i.e. chords) in music generally follows certain rules. Some of these rules have been built into a BASIC program **HARMONY**, which writes four-part harmony for a given tune.

22.2 SOUND

The **SOUND** statement in BASIC plays a single note for a given length of time. For example,

```
SOUND 256, .5
SOUND 400, .2
```

plays a note having a frequency of 256 hertz, which is middle-C, for .5 seconds. One use for the **SOUND** statement is to signal an error to the user of a computer program. A typical such "beep" might be done with **SOUND 400, .2**.

One can play simple tunes using only the **SOUND** statement. For example, the program **SCALE1** plays the C-scale.

```
REM  SCALE1

REM  Sounds the C scale

SOUND 256, .5
SOUND 287, .5
SOUND 323, .5
SOUND 342, .5
SOUND 384, .5
SOUND 431, .5
SOUND 483, .5
SOUND 512, 2

END
```

Using only the **SOUND** statement to generate tunes requires one to know the frequencies of the notes of the scale. And, it is not possible to include pauses or *rests* between notes. For playing tunes, BASIC has the **PLAY** statement, which is discussed in the next section.

22.3 PLAY

The **PLAY** statement has the form

```
PLAY tune$
```

where the characters in the string `tune$` indicate the notes to be played. The notes are represented by the letters *a* through *g*, which may be lowercase or uppercase. The notes *c - d - e - f - g - a - b* constitute one octave, as in ordinary musical notation. The octave that begins with middle-C is called *octave 4*. Thus, a C scale starting at middle-C ends with c above middle-C, which is in octave 5. Octave 4 is indicated by `o4`, and octave 5 is given by `o5`. Finally, the letters *a - g* alone represent quarter notes, which are played at a tempo of 120 to the minute. Other durations are given by a digit following the letter. For example, `c2` is a half note, `c1` is a whole note, and `c4` is a quarter note. Thus, `c` and `c4` both represent a quarter note. An eighth note would be `c8`, and so on.

The program **SCALE2** uses the **PLAY** statement to render a C scale for us.

```
REM  SCALE2

REM  Plays the C scale

READ scale$
PLAY scale$

DATA o4 c d e f g a b o5 c1

END
```

Notice that the entire scale is read in as a single string. Notice also that we separate the notes and other commands with spaces, though this is not necessary. Finally, note that we start the scale in octave 4 and end it in octave 5, and that the final note is a whole note.

The key of C is fine, but what if we prefer another key or have a tune with *incidental* sharps or flats? And what about rests, tempo, and dynamics?

Sharps and flats are indicated by a `+` or `-`, respectively, following the letter representing the note. Thus, `c+` indicates C-sharp, while `b-8` indicates B-flat played as an eighth note. Dotted quarters, eighths, and so forth, are indicated by a period. Thus, `g.` is G played as a dotted quarter note, while `f+2.` is F-sharp played as a dotted half note. Rests are indicated by the letter *r*. Thus, `r` is a quarter note rest, whereas `r2.` is a rest of length equal to a dotted half note.

Overall tempo is given by the letter *t* followed by the number of quarter notes to be played in one minute. Thus, `t120` gives a tempo in which quarter notes are played 120 to the minute. This notation corresponds to standard usage.

BASIC allows tunes to be played normally, with legato, or with staccato. The notations are, respectively, `mn`, `ml`, and `ms`. Most of these options are used in a rendition of one of the all-time favorites, Brahm's Waltz in A-flat. The program **BRAHMS** entertains us with the first sixteen bars.

```
REM  BRAHMS

REM  Reads and plays Brahm's waltz in A-flat
REM  First sixteen bars only

DO while more data
   READ music$
   PLAY music$
LOOP

! Each data line is one measure
DATA t116 ml o5 c. mn o4 a-8 ml a-8 mn o5 c8
DATA ml c4. mn o4 a-8 ml a-8 o5 mn c8
DATA ml d-8 e-16 d-16 ms c o4 b-
DATA ml o5 c4. o4 mn a-8 ml a-8 mn o5 e-8
DATA ml f. mn c8 ml c8 mn e-8
DATA ml f. mn c8 ml c8 mn e-8
DATA ml g8 f8 ms e- d
DATA ml e-. mn o4 g8 ml g8 mn o5 c8
DATA ml c. mn o4 a-8 ml a-8 mn o5 c8
DATA ml c4. mn o4 a-8 ml a-8 o5 mn c8
DATA ml d-8 e-16 d-16 ms c o4 b-
DATA ml o5 c4. o4 mn a-8 ml a-8 mn o5 e-8
DATA ml f. mn c8 ml c8 mn e-8
DATA ml f. mn c8 ml c8 mn e-8
DATA ml g8 f8 ms e- d
DATA ml e-1

END
```

22.4 PLOTTING MUSIC

The notation used in Section 22.3 for playing music in BASIC would not be recognized by most musicians. But, through plotting, we can ask BASIC to convert that notation into standard notation. The program **SCORE**, along with a library of external routines, **SCORELIB**, accepts music in the notation of

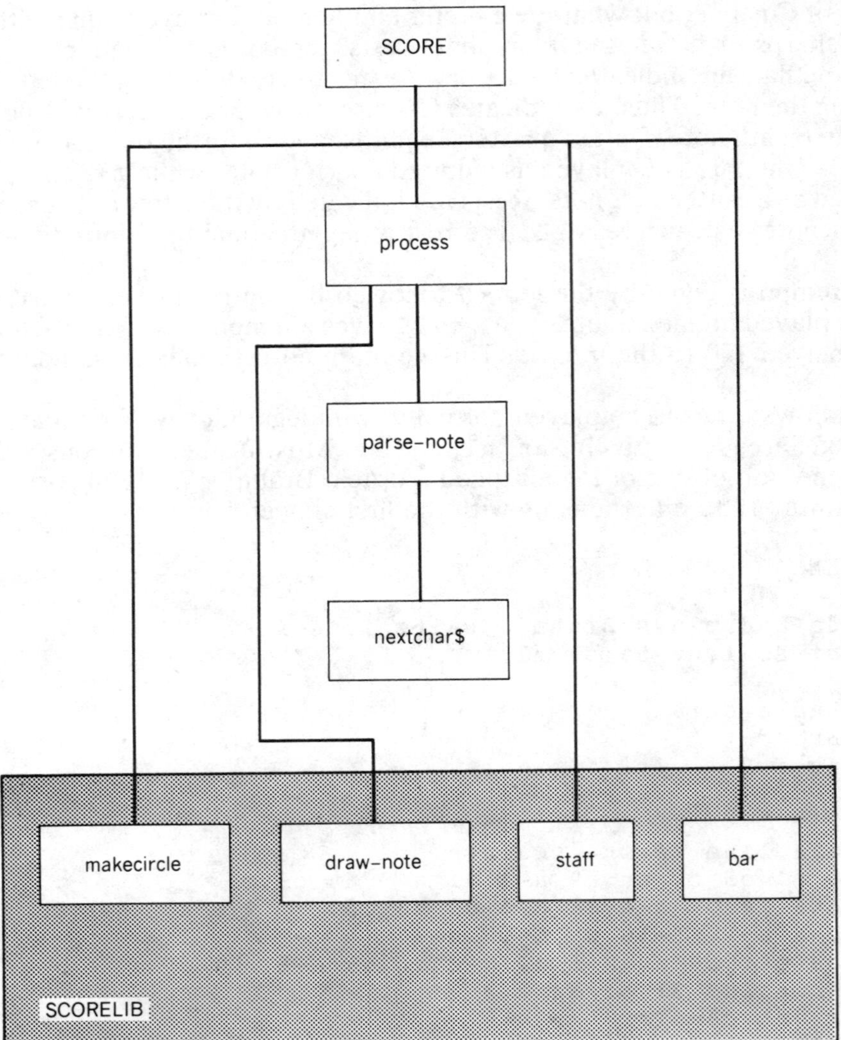

FIGURE 22.1
Structure chart for the program SCORE.

Section 22.3 and produces a *score* in standard notation. Its structure chart is shown in Figure 22.1.

The key ideas used here are *pictures* and *transformations*, which were described in detail in Section 21.2. For example, in **SCORELIB** we will see that a whole note is simply a circle, properly placed on the staff. A half note is merely a whole note with a vertical tail. A quarter note is a half note where the circle is filled in, i.e., a disk. Other notes are constructed in the same fashion.

The program **SCORE** performs two major tasks: *parsing* the items in the music string, and then *drawing* the corresponding note in the right place. The subroutines for parsing the items are included as internal routines in **SCORE**. All the drawing subroutines and pictures are contained in the library **SCORELIB**.

As an example, the string "A-4." represents the dotted quarter note *A-flat* in the current octave. The routine **parse_note** examines the characters of the string, and sets indicators that will be used later to plot the note.

The program SCORE, parsing routines.

```
DEF nextchar$                                ! Gives next char of item$

    LET nextchar$ = ucase$(item$[1:1])
    LET item$ = item$[2:maxnum]

END DEF

SUB parse_note (item$, octave, pitch, duration, sf, dotted)

    LET pitch = ord (nextchar$) - 67    ! "C" = 0
    IF pitch < 0 then LET pitch = pitch + 7
    LET pitch = pitch + 7*(octave-4)

    LET sf = 0                               ! Sharp (+1) or flat (-1)
    LET nc$ = nextchar$
    IF nc$ = "+" then
       LET sf = +1
       LET nc$ = nextchar$
    ELSE IF nc$ = "-" then
       LET sf = -1
       LET nc$ = nextchar$
    END IF

    SELECT CASE nc$
    CASE "1"
         LET nc$ = nextchar$
         IF nc$ = "6" then
            LET duration = 16
            LET nc$ = nextchar$
         ELSE
            LET duration = 1
         END IF
    CASE "2"
         LET duration = 2
         LET nc$ = nextchar$
    CASE "4"
         LET duration = 4
         LET nc$ = nextchar$
    CASE "8"
         LET duration = 8
         LET nc$ = nextchar$
    CASE else
         LET duration = 4                    ! The default
    END SELECT

    LET dotted = 0
    IF nc$ = "." then LET dotted = 1

END SUB

END
```

`Parse_note` takes the string in `item$`, already know to represent a note, and the current octave. It then computes the `pitch` as the combination of the note and the octave. Notice that we take "C" to be note number 0 in the current octave, and that the number assigned to "A" and "B" are, respectively, 5 and 6, not -2 and -1. This is because "A" and "B" in the current octave are *above* "C".

The variable `duration` is equal to 1 for a *whole note*, 2 for a *half note*, 4 for a *quarter note*, and so on. The indicator `sharp_flat` is equal to +1 for a *sharp*, -1 to a *flat*, and 0 otherwise. The indicator `dotted` equals 1 if the note is a *dotted note*, and is 0 otherwise.

The defined function `nextchar$` *picks off* the leading character in the string `item$`, and shortens `item$`.

```
REM   SCORE
REM
REM   Plots a score and draws notes
REM   for a single voice

LIBRARY "Scorelib.trc"

SET mode "hires"
CLEAR

DIM circle (0 to 18, 2)              ! Used to draw a note
CALL makecircle (circle)

LET length = 60                      ! Length of the score
SET window 0, length, -15, 30

DRAW staff

LET place = 2                        ! Place in the score
LET octave = 4                       ! Default octave
DO while more data
   READ music$
   DO                                ! Process items (notes, etc.)
      LET music$ = ltrim$(music$)
      IF len(music$) = 0 then EXIT DO
      LET p = pos(music$, " ")       ! End of an item
      IF p = 0 then LET p = len(music$) + 1
      LET item$ = music$[1:p-1]      ! Extract item
      CALL process (item$)
      LET music$ = music$[p+1:maxnum]
   LOOP
   DRAW bar with shift (place, 0)        ! End of measure bar
   LET place = place + 1.5
LOOP

DATA t116 ml o5 c. mn o4 a-8 ml a-8 mn o5 c8
DATA ml c4. mn o4 a-8 ml a-8 o5 mn c8
DATA ml d-8 e-16 d-16 ms c o4 b-
DATA ml o5 c2.

SUB process (item$)

    SELECT CASE ucase$(item$[1:1])
    CASE "M"                         ! Legato, staccato
    CASE "O"                         ! Change octave
         LET octave = ord(item$[2:2]) - 48
    CASE "R"                         ! Rest
```

```
        CASE "T"                          ! Tempo
        CASE else                         ! Must be a note
             CALL parse_note (item$, octave, pitch, duration, sf, dotted)
             CALL draw_note (pitch, duration, sf, dotted, place, circle)
        END SELECT

   END SUB
```

The main part of SCORE reads music just as BRAHMS did in Section 22.3. Each DATA line corresponds to one measure. There are two DO loops in SCORE—one to loop through the lines of the data (i.e., the measures), and one to loop through the items in the measure. Notice that the items may be notes or may be rests, octave setters, tempo setters, or dynamic indicators (legato or staccato). (The items in the music string are assumed to be separated by one space.) The routine process determines the type of the item. If a note, it calls parse_note to determine the particulars and then draw_note to draw the note according to those particulars.

The variable place determines the horizantal position on the staff. Its initial value is 2, which is close to the left end of the staff. Each time an element (note, dot, and so on) is drawn, place is increased by an appropriate amount.

We now examine the library SCORELIB, which we shall divide into three parts for convenience. The first part follows.

SCORELIB (first part).

```
   SUB draw_note (pitch, duration, sharp_flat, dotted, place, c(,))

        OPTION ANGLE degrees

        IF sharp_flat = 1 then
           DRAW sharp_sign with shift (place, pitch)
           LET place = place + 1.5
        ELSE if sharp_flat = -1 then
           DRAW flat_sign with shift (place, pitch)
           LET place = place + 1.5
        END IF

        LET up_down = 0                   ! Tail of note is up
        IF pitch >= 7 then LET up_down = 180    ! Tail of note is down

        DRAW note (duration,c) with rotate (up_down) * shift (place,pitch)
        LET place = place + 1.5
        IF dotted = 1 then
           DRAW dot (c) with shift (place, pitch)
           LET place = place + .5
        END IF
        LET place = place + 1

   END SUB

   PICTURE note (duration, c(,))

        SELECT CASE duration
        CASE 1
             DRAW whole_note (c)
```

```
        CASE 2
             DRAW half_note (c)
        CASE 4
             DRAW quarter_note (c)
        CASE 8
             DRAW eighth_note (c)
        CASE 16
             DRAW sixteenth_note (c)
        CASE else
             PRINT "Error: invalid duration"
        END SELECT
    END PICTURE
```

The routine draw_note is the workhorse of the library. It uses picture routines, which it invokes with the command DRAW. The placement and orientation of the pictures is controlled with transformations. The transformation shift(place,pitch) causes the picture to be drawn after moving it to horizontal position place and vertical position pitch. This tactic for placing the pictures depends on the pictures themselves being drawn as if they were at position (0,0), the origin.

The picture note selects the particular kind of note to be drawn according to the duration. The pictures that draw the various kinds of notes are found in the next part of SCORELIB.

SCORELIB (middle part).

```
PICTURE whole_note (c(,))

    MAT PLOT LINES: c

END PICTURE

PICTURE half_note (c(,))

    DRAW whole_note (c)
    PLOT LINES: .7,0; .7,7

END PICTURE

PICTURE quarter_note (c(,))

    DRAW disk (c)
    PLOT LINES: .7,0; .7,7

END PICTURE

PICTURE eighth_note (c(,))

    DRAW quarter_note (c)
    PLOT LINES: .7,7; 1.7,6

END PICTURE
```

```
PICTURE sixteenth_note (c(,))

    DRAW eighth_note (c)
    PLOT LINES: .7,6; 1.7,5

END PICTURE
```

Here is where the simplicity of using pictures is revealed. A complicated picture can be constructed from several simple pictures, just as a complicated program can be constructed from simple subroutines. A whole note is simply a circle; see the picture `whole_note`. `Half_note` works by drawing

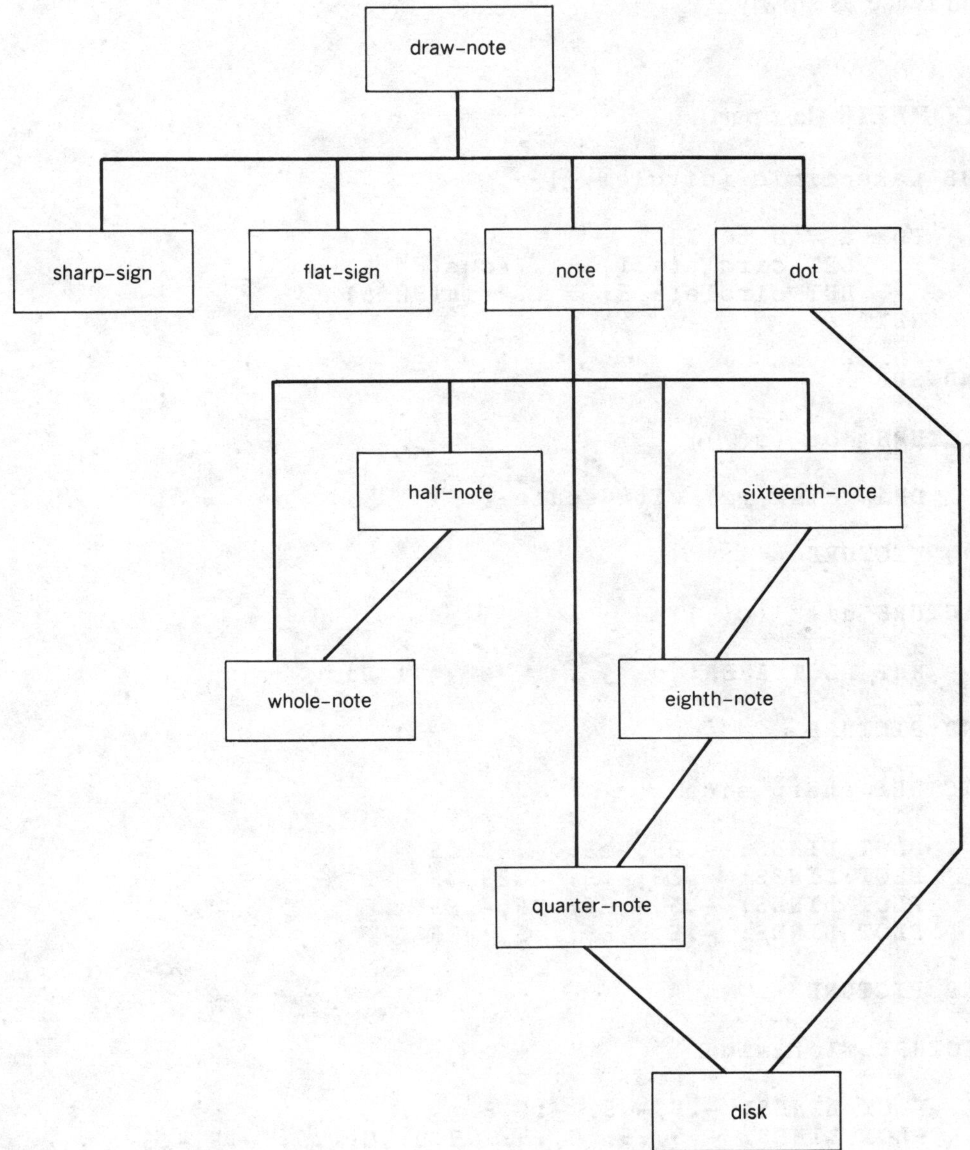

FIGURE 22.2
Structure chart for most of SCORELIB.

a whole note and attaching a vertical tail. `Quarter_note` draws a disk (filled circle) and attaches a vertical tail. `Eighth_note` draws `quarter_note` and attaches a small flag to the end of the tail. And, `sixteenth_note` draws `eighth_note` and attaches a second flag to the tail. The use of one picture by another is shown in the structure chart of `draw_note` and all the pictures it uses.

The two-dimensional array `c`, constructed when the program starts by the subroutine `makecirle`, contains coordinates of the circumference of a circle. `c` is passed as a parameter to all external routines that either draw a circle or call other routines that draw circles. While having this nuisance parameter is not ideal, the alternative would be to compute afresh the values in `c` each time a circle-drawing routine was called. The program would then run twice as slowly.

SCORELIB (last part).

```
SUB makecircle (circle(,))

    FOR a = 0 to 18
        LET circle(a,1) = .7*cos(20*a)
        LET circle(a,2) = .7*sin(20*a)
    NEXT a

END SUB

PICTURE dot (c(,))

    DRAW disk (c) with scale (.2)

END PICTURE

PICTURE disk (c(,))

    MAT PLOT AREA: c                 ! Disk drawn

END PICTURE

PICTURE sharp_sign

    PLOT LINES: -.25,-.5; -.25,.5
    PLOT LINES:  .25,-.5;  .25,.5
    PLOT LINES: -.5,-.25; .5,-.25
    PLOT LINES: -.5, .25; .5, .25

END PICTURE

PICTURE flat_sign

    PLOT LINES: -.5,-.5; -.5,2
    PLOT LINES: -.5,.5; 0,.5; .3,0; 0,-.5; -.5,-.5

END PICTURE
```

```
PICTURE staff

    ASK window x0, x1, y0, y1
    FOR h = 2 to 10 step 2
        PLOT LINES: x0,h; x1,h
    NEXT h
    DRAW bar with shift(x0,0)        ! Close at the left
    DRAW bar with shift(x1,0)        ! Close at the right

END PICTURE

PICTURE bar

    PLOT LINES: 0,2; 0,10

END PICTURE
```

Finally, we describe the remaining routines in `SCORELIB`. The first is `makecircle`, which constructs the array `c` and to which we referred earlier. The circle can then be drawn efficiently with

```
MAT PLOT LINES: c
```

This works like a `PLOT LINES` statement except that the successive points are in the rows of `c`. The first column of `c` contains the x-coordinates of the points, and the second column contains the y-coordinates. A disk (i.e., a filled circle) can be drawn with

```
MAT PLOT AREA: c
```

The picture `dot` draws the dot that appears in *dotted* notes by drawing a small disk. (A full-sized disk is used to draw a quarter note.) The picture `disk` simply invokes the `MAT PLOT AREA` command.

The picture `sharp_sign` draws a sharp sign, and the picture `flat_sign` draws a flat sign.

The picture `score` simply draws the five lines of a normal staff and places vertical bars at the two ends. Because "C" is note 0, the lines of the staff are at 2, 4, 6, 8, and 10. The `FOR` loop uses a step size of 2 to generate these values.

Finally, the picture `bar` draws a vertical bar that is used to mark the start or end of a measure.

Just the first four measures of *Brahm's Waltz in A-flat* are plotted; `SCORE` makes no provision for plotting longer portions. In fact, `SCORE` is only a

FIGURE 22.3
First four measures of Brahm's Waltz in A-flat.

bare-bones program. It does not plot rests or dynamic markings (legato and staccato). It also incorrectly draws the flags on the tails of eighth notes when the tail points down. And, it requires one space between the items of the music string.

22.5 HARMONY IN MUSIC

In the previous section we showed how the computer can *play* music written by human composers. It is also possible for the computer to *compose* music, which is then played by human musicians. As one might imagine, composing by computer is quite complicated. We will be content to explore one aspect of composition—that of teaching the computer to write four-part harmony for a given melody.

As a student of music theory knows, four-part harmony follows simple rules. Where choices are possible, the theory tells which choices are preferred. We shall not attempt to teach the computer all the rules usually given in a book on harmony, just the most important ones. Our BASIC program will combine these rules with a trial-and-error method to produce some surprisingly good results.

The four voices (soprano, alto, tenor, and bass) always sing a chord. Because there are only three notes in a chord, the root (lowest note) of the chord is doubled by another voice. We will agree that the soprano always carries the given melody and the bass always sings the root of the chord. This still leaves a number of choices: Which chord should we choose? Because we assume a two-octave range for the bass, in which octave should the root be placed for the bass? And how are the two remaining notes divided between alto and tenor, and in which octave?

Our trial-and-error method works like this. We start from the final note of the melody and work backwards. Although the music would never by played backwards, it is actually easier for our program to work in this manner. The reason is this: For simple melodies we want the final chord to be the tonic chord; therefore, the program *starts* with this chord and works backwards.

We have arbitrarily decided to work in the key of C, so the last note is normally a C and the final chord is the tonic chord. Working backward from this chord, we try the various preceding chords, according to an order of preference that depends on comparing them with the following chord (which the computer has just chosen because it is working backward), until we find a suitable one.

For the chord currently being tested, we pick out the note in the melody and assign the root to the bass (picking the octave), and then we consider all possible assignments to the two middle voices. Most of these are eliminated on the basis of a variety of requirements. If there is no possibility left, we move on to the next most desirable chord. If more than one possibility is left, we pick the *smoothest transition*.

If, at a given time, all the chords are eliminated, the computer is instructed to *back up* and try to change some of the music already written. We shall clarify our procedure further as we explain the program **HARMONY**.

We must first explain the notation used. Notes are numbered as follows: middle C is denoted by 0, notes above this are positive integers, and notes

---

Walter Piston, *Harmony*, 3rd edition, W. W. Norton, New York, 1962.

TABLE 22.1
The Chords and Their Notes

Chord Number	Notes	Note Numbers
1	C, E, G	0, 2, 4
2	D, F, A	1, 3, 5
3	E, G, B	2, 4, 6
4	F, A, C	3, 5, 7
5	G, B, D	4, 6, 8
6	A, C, E	5, 7, 9

below are negative integers. Thus G above middle C is note 4, while C below middle C is -7. We work in the key of C, so there are no sharps or flats. The score will be recorded in the table `score`, which has a row for every chord. The chords are numbered as shown in Table 22.1. Chord 1 is the tonic chord C - E - G, chord 2 is D - F - A, and so on. We do not use chord 7, which plays a special role in harmony.

The number of the chord is recorded in the 0th column of `score`, while the notes assigned to the four voices are recorded in the next four columns. The

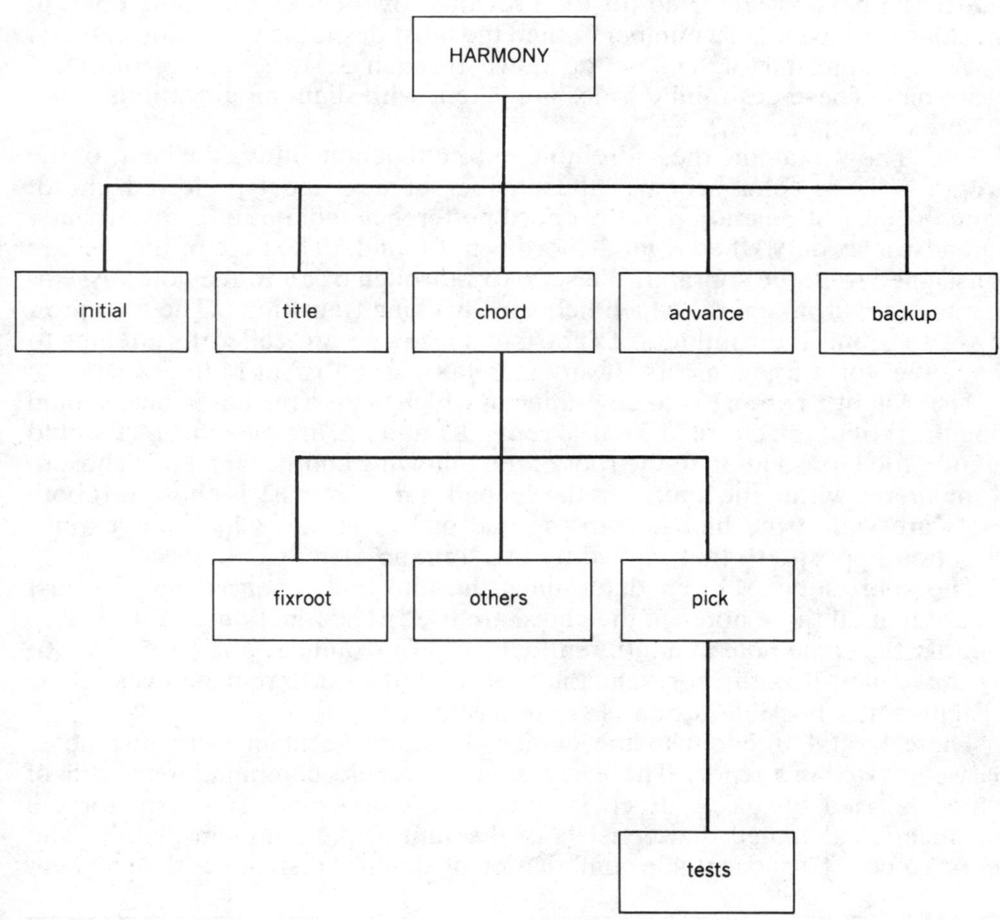

FIGURE 22.4
Structure chart for the program HARMONY.

variable `v` (for *voice*) identifies a column of `score`. Thus, `v = 0` is the chord number, `v = 1` is soprano, `v = 2` is alto, `v = 3` is tenor, and `v = 4` is bass. We are always comparing a chord just written, whose number is `oldchn`, with a trial preceding chord about to be written, whose number is `chn`.

The program `HARMONY` is organized *top down*, and the main part of the program is quite short, just 10 lines long. It calls the routines `initial`, `title`, `advance`, `backup`, and `chord`. `chord` is similarly broken down into constituent parts, and so on.

The initialization is performed by a subroutine `initial`, which sets up the chord preference table `pref`, reads the melody into the list `melody`, and sets up a standard tonic chord as the final chord. We then call `title` to print a heading.

The routine `advance` prints the chord and moves to the *preceding* note (because we are working backward through the melody). The main `DO` loop tries chords in order of preference, calling `chord`, until a good chord is found. If it succeeds, it advances; if no chord is satisfactory, it calls `backup`. The latter moves to the note previously examined and searches for a chord different from the one tried earlier. If the note number `n` becomes less than 1, we are done; if `n` ever again becomes equal to `nmax`, we are stuck and cannot generate a harmony that meets the established conditions.

In the table `pref` we have one row for each chord. The entries are the chord numbers as preferred for the previous row. Thus, if at some point in the song we have chord number 3, then the most desirable preceding chord is 6, the next most is 4, and so on down through 3, 1, 2, and 5, the least desirable. (These desirability rules are taken, with slight modifications, from Piston's book, *op. cit.*)

Let us now examine the subroutine `chord` that constitutes the heart of the program. Here, `chn` becomes the number of next most preferred chord, which occurs at position `p` in the chord preference table `pref`. (`p` starts at 1 and advances only when a good chord is not found.) The note of the melody is assigned to `S`, the soprano. We set `oldS` through `oldB` to the voice assignments in this trial chord, which helps in checking transitions. The flag `good` is set to 1 and the routines `fixroot` and `others` are called to attempt to make the voice assignments. If any step fails, `good` is set to 0.

The task of `fixroot` is to determine in which octave the bass voice should sing the root of the chord. Two trial roots, `B1` and `B2`, are picked. If `B1` would require too large a jump to the root of the following chord, then `B2` is chosen. If the first is within the limits but the second is not, then `B1` is chosen. If both roots are within the limits, then the one picked is that which moves in a direction opposite to that moved by the soprano melody.

The subroutine `others` determines the alto and tenor voices. It must assure that all three notes of the chord are used. The function `mod` is used to identify the same note in a different octave. For example, `mod(2-9,7) = 0`, so that 2 and 9 both represent the note *E*, but in different octaves. If no assignment is possible, `good` is set to 0.

There is still freedom in the choice of octaves and in switching notes between alto and tenor. There are seven possible combinations, each of which is tried by `pick`. Each is tested by `tests` and, if satisfactory, a distance is calculated that consists of the sum of the jumps in the alto and tenor voices. The acceptable combination of smallest distance is then picked.

If you have knowledge about musical harmony, you might wish to study these criteria carefully and compare them with the theory.

The routine `tests` applies a series of checks to each of the seven candidate chords. By packaging these messy details in a subroutine, we avoid being confused by them while we examined the higher level structure of the program. Now we are ready to face those details. The first check makes sure that the alto note is within the allowable range (−3 to 9, inclusive) and that the jump to the following note does not exceed five steps. The tenor note is then similarly checked. Another two conditions are that the soprano and alto voices must not *cross*, and the tenor and bass voices must not *cross*. The next check, for parallel octaves and fifths, is not made if the two chord numbers are the same. Otherwise, the program examines all pairs of notes at the following stage. Any pair that lies an octave or fifth apart is subjected to the further test that the jumps must not be equal. If any of the preceding tests fail, the flag `ok` becomes equal to 0.

The resulting harmony is surprisingly good. In all fairness, we should point out that the program does not do equally well on all melodies. But the fact that it frequently produces reasonable harmonies is pleasing, especially because it takes only a few seconds of computer time.

There is, of course, much room for improvement. For example, we have not tried to avoid octaves or fifths approached by similar motion, nor have we tried to prevent a lower voice from crossing above the previous note of a higher voice. We have also limited the freedom of choice by not allowing the seventh chord, by insisting that the bass must sing the root, and by our fixed order of preference for picking chords. (See Project 5 at the end of this chapter.)

```
REM  HARMONY

REM  Generates harmony for a given melody
REM  Uses rules found in
REM     Walter Piston, "Harmony," 3rd edition
REM     W. W. Norton, New York, 1962

DIM score(100, 0 to 4)              ! Note number by voice
DIM pref(6,6)                       ! Transition preference
DIM melody(100)                     ! Notes in melody
DIM jump(4)                         ! Voice transition

CALL initial                        ! Set up arrays

CALL title
CALL advance                        ! n = note number
DO while 0 < n and n < nmax         ! Main loop
   FOR p = p0 to 6                  ! In order of preference
       CALL chord (p, good)             ! Try chord
       IF good=1 then EXIT FOR      ! Found one
   NEXT p
   IF good=1 then CALL advance else CALL backup
LOOP
IF n=0 then PRINT "Done" else PRINT "Stuck"

SUB initial                         ! Set up arrays

    MAT READ pref                   ! Preference table
    DATA 5, 4, 1, 6, 2, 3
    DATA 6, 4, 2, 1, 5, 3
```

```
    DATA 6, 4, 3, 1, 2, 5
    DATA 1, 5, 4, 6, 3, 2
    DATA 2, 6, 5, 4, 1, 3
    DATA 1, 5, 3, 6, 2, 4

    READ nmax                           ! Melody
    MAT READ melody(nmax)
    DATA 28                             ! 28 notes
    DATA 2,1,0,2,1,0,7,5,7,4,2,0,1
    DATA 2,1,0,2,1,0,7,5,7,4,2,0,1,1,0

    FOR v = 0 to 4                      ! Last chord
        READ score(nmax,v)
    NEXT v
    DATA 1, 0, -3, -5, -7               ! Tonic chord
    LET chn = 1
    LET n = nmax                        ! Start from end

END SUB

SUB title

    PRINT "Note    Chord     S     A     T     B"
    PRINT

END SUB

SUB advance                             ! Print, go to previous note

    PRINT n; tab(8); score(n,0); tab(16);   ! Note number, chord
    PRINT using " -## ": score(n,1), score(n,2);       ! Voices
    PRINT using " -## ": score(n,3), score(n,4)

    LET n = n - 1
    LET oldchn = chn                    ! Chord number
    LET p0 = 1                          ! Start with first preference

END SUB

SUB backup                              ! Back to following chord

    LET n = n + 1
    IF n >= nmax then EXIT SUB          ! No place to go
    LET chn = oldchn                    ! Back up the chord number
    LET oldchn = score(n+1,0)           !     and the old chord number
    FOR p = 1 to 6                      ! What preference was it?
        IF chn = pref(oldchn,p) then EXIT FOR
    NEXT p
    LET p0 = p + 1                      ! Try next best chord

END SUB

SUB chord (p, good)                     ! Try chord of preference p

    LET chn = pref(oldchn,p)            ! New chord number
    LET S = melody(n)                   ! Soprano
    LET oldS = score(n+1,1)             ! Previous voices
```

```
    LET oldA = score(n+1,2)
    LET oldT = score(n+1,3)
    LET oldB = score(n+1,4)

    LET good = 1                        ! Assume okay
    CALL fixroot                        ! Bass
    CALL others (good)                  ! Alto and tenor
    IF good=1 then CALL pick (good)        ! Best combination
    IF good=1 then                      ! Accept chord
       LET score(n,0) = chn
       LET score(n,1) = S
       LET score(n,2) = A
       LET score(n,3) = T
       LET score(n,4) = B
    END IF

END SUB

SUB fixroot                             ! Bass sings root of chord

    LET B1 = chn - 8                    ! Root in two octaves
    LET B2 = B1 - 7
    IF     abs(B1-oldB) > 5 then        ! Select one of two
       LET B = B2
    ELSEIF abs(B2-oldB) > 5 then
       LET B = B1
    ELSEIF S <= oldS then
       LET B = B1
    ELSE
       LET B = B2
    END IF

END SUB

SUB others (good)                       ! Try to choose alto and tenor

    IF mod(B-S,7)=0 then                ! Same note but for octave
       LET A = B + 4                    ! Assign other two in chord
       LET T = B + 2
    ELSEIF mod(B+2-S,7)=0 then
       LET A = B + 4
       LET T = B
    ELSEIF mod(B+4-S,7)=0 then
       LET A = B + 2
       LET T = B
    ELSE
       LET good = 0                     ! Can't use chord
    END IF

END SUB

SUB pick (good)                         ! Best combination of voices

    LET dist = 1000                     ! For minimum distance calculation
    LET jump(1) = S - oldS
    LET jump(4) = B - oldB
```

```
    FOR k = 1 to 7                          ! Various combinations of A and T
        LET jump(2) = A - oldA
        LET jump(3) = T - oldT
        CALL tests (ok)                     ! Various criteria
        IF ok=1 then                        ! Acceptable combination
           LET d = abs(jump(2)) + abs(jump(3))    ! Distance
           IF d < dist then                 ! Best yet
              LET dist = d
              LET bestA = A
              LET bestT = T
           END IF
        END IF
        LET temp = A                        ! Next higher
        LET A = T + 7
        LET T = temp
    NEXT k

    IF dist < 1000 then                     ! Found one
       LET A = bestA
       LET T = bestT
    ELSE                                    ! None work
       LET good = 0
    END IF

END SUB

SUB tests (ok)                              ! Various criteria

    LET ok = 0                              ! Assume bad till passes all tests
    ! Test alto and tenor ranges
    IF A < -3 or A > 9 or abs(jump(2)) > 5 then EXIT SUB    ! Alto bad
    IF T < -7 or T > 5 or abs(jump(3)) > 5 then EXIT SUB    ! Tenor bad
    ! Test for crossing voices
    IF S <= A or T <= B then EXIT SUB
    ! Test for parallel octaves, fifths
    IF chn <> oldchn then
       FOR v1 = 1 to 3                      ! Pair of voices
           FOR v2 = v1+1 to 4
               LET olddist = score(n+1,v1) - score(n+1,v2)
               LET d = mod(olddist,7)
               IF d=0 or d=4 then           ! Octave or fifth
                  IF jump(v1) = jump(v2) then EXIT SUB     ! Parallel
               END IF
           NEXT v2
       NEXT v1
    END IF
    LET ok = 1                              ! Passed all tests

END SUB

END
```

We show the results of a run where eight bars of *Swanee River* were used as the melody. We note that the program had to back up only once. It first chose a 2-chord for note number 26, which is the first choice before a 5-chord. However, it was then unable to proceed. Thus, it replaced the 2-chord

FIGURE 22.5
Computer-produced harmony, standard notation.

with a repetition of the 5-chord and had no more difficulty in completing the score. We also show the score in its usual form in Figure 22.5.

```
run

Note      Chord         S     A     T     B

 28        1            0  -  3  -  5  -  7
 27        5            1  -  1  -  3  -10
 26        2            1  -  2  -  4  -  6
 26        5            1  -  1  -  3  -10
 25        6            0  -  2  -  5  -  9
 24        1            2  -  3  -  7  -14
 23        5            4  -  1  -  6  -10
 22        6            7     2  -  2  -  9
 21        6            5     2     0  -  9
 20        1            7     2  -  3  -14
 19        4            0  -  2  -  4  -11
 18        2            1  -  2  -  4  -13
 17        6            2  -  2  -  7  -  9
 16        1            0  -  3  -  5  -  7
 15        5            1  -  1  -  3  -10
 14        1            2     0  -  3  -14
 13        5            1  -  1  -  3  -10
 12        6            0  -  2  -  5  -  9
 11        1            2  -  3  -  7  -14
 10        5            4  -  1  -  6  -10
 9         6            7     2  -  2  -  9
 8         6            5     2     0  -  9
 7         1            7     2  -  3  -14
 6         4            0  -  2  -  4  -11
 5         2            1  -  2  -  4  -13
 4         6            2  -  2  -  7  -  9
 3         1            0  -  3  -  5  -  7
 2         5            1  -  1  -  3  -10
 1         1            2     0  -  3  -14
Done
```

EXERCISES

1. Using the **SOUND** statement, write a program that will produce the wail of a siren.
2. Transcribe the melody (soprano part) of *Swanee River* (Figure 22.1) to the notation of the **PLAY** statement, and then play it.
3. Transcribe a tune of your choice to the notation of the **PLAY** statement. Use dynamics (legato, etc.,) as shown on the original sheet music.
4. Prepare several tunes but store them as display-format files. Then, write a very short program that first asks for the name of the tune and then plays it.
5. Feed a tune (other than *Swanee River*) to the program **HARMONY** and see what harmonics are produced. You will have to play the result on a piano to hear what it sounds like.
6. Write a program that will convert the tune in one of the files you prepared in Exercise 4 to the form required by the program **HARMONY**. Only simple tunes can be used, and all timing and dynamic information will be lost.
7. Transpose *Brahm's Waltz* to the key of C, supply this tune as the melody to the program **HARMONY**, and see what harmony results.

PROJECTS

1. Expand **SCORE** to allow rests and dynamic information. Arrange to draw the clef symbols (bass or treble). For example, you may want to extend the language of the **PLAY** statement to allow specifying the key. The individual flat signs that appear in Figure 22.3 will not then be needed.
2. Write a program that will transpose a melody, in the format of the **PLAY** statement, from one key to another. Use the language extension (to specify the key signature) mentioned in Project 1.
3. Modify **HARMONY** so that it accepts input and produces output in a form compatible with the **PLAY** statement. If your computer allows four-part or more music to be played, play the result. If not, arrange to play each part separately.
4. Combine **HARMONY** with the expanded **SCORE** (see Project 1) to produce graphical output in the standard form. See how closely you can duplicate Figure 22.5.
5. Improve the program **HARMONY** by introducing additional tests, such as rejecting fifths and octaves approached by similar motion. Apply other tests suggested by musical theory. Soften the chord rejection scheme so that unattractive chords are not discarded but rather are given a score in proportion to their unattractiveness. Evaluate the results by actually playing the resulting music.

APPENDIX 1

ASCII CHARACTER SET

ASCII characters are numbered 0 through 127. In the following list, this number appears in the first column. It also is the argument for the `chr$` function that generates the corresponding character. If the ASCII character is printable (i.e., visible), it is shown in the second column. The third column contains the abbreviations that can be used as arguments for the `ord` function. In addition, any printable character can be used in the `ord` function. Thus, `ord("lca") = ord("a") = 97`. These special `ord` abbreviations can be in either lowercase, uppercase, or mixed case.

CHR$ Number	Graphic	ORD Argument	Name
0		NUL	Null
1		SOH	Start of heading
2		STX	Start of text
3		ETX	End of text
4		EOT	End of transmission
5		ENQ	Enquiry
6		ACK	Acknowledge
7		BEL	Bell
8		BS	Backspace
9		HT	Horizontal tab
10		LF	Line feed
11		VT	Vertical tab
12		FF	Form feed
13		CR	Carriage return
14		SO	Shift out
15		SI	Shift in
16		DLE	Data link escape
17		DC1	Device control 1
18		DC2	Device control 2

CHR$ Number	Graphic	ORD Argument	Name
19		DC3	Device control 3
20		DC4	Device control 4
21		NAK	Negative acknowledge
22		SYN	Synchronous idle
23		ETB	End of trans block
24		CAN	Cancel
25		EM	End of medium
26		SUB	Substitute
27		ESC	Escape
28		FS	File separator
29		GS	Group separator
30		RS	Record separator
31		US	Unit separator
32		SP	Space
33	!		Exclamation mark
34	”		Question mark
35	‰		Number sign
36	$		Dollar sign
37	%		Percent sign
38	&		Ampersand
39	’		Apostrophe
40	(		Left parenthesis
41	)		Right parenthesis
42	*		Asterisk
43	+		Plus sign
44	,		Comma
45	-		Minus sign
46	.		Period
47	/		Slant
48	0		Zero
49	1		One
50	2		Two
51	3		Three
52	4		Four
53	5		Five
54	6		Six
55	7		Seven
56	8		Eight
57	9		Nine
58	:		Colon
59	;		Semicolon
60	<		Less than sign
61	=		Equals sign
62	>		Greater than sign
63	?		Question mark
64	¶		Commercial at
65	A		Uppercase A
66	B		Uppercase B
67	C		Uppercase C
68	D		Uppercase D
69	E		Uppercase E
70	F		Uppercase F
71	G		Uppercase G
72	H		Uppercase H
73	I		Uppercase I

CHR$ Number	Graphic	ORD Argument	Name
74	J		Uppercase J
75	K		Uppercase K
76	L		Uppercase L
77	M		Uppercase M
78	N		Uppercase N
79	O		Uppercase O
80	P		Uppercase P
81	Q		Uppercase Q
82	R		Uppercase R
83	S		Uppercase S
84	T		Uppercase T
85	U		Uppercase U
86	V		Uppercase V
87	W		Uppercase W
88	X		Uppercase X
89	Y		Uppercase Y
90	Z		Uppercase Z
91	[		Left bracket
92	\		Reverse slant
93	]		Right bracket
94	^		Circumflex accent
95	_		UND Underline
96	‘	GRA	Grave accent
97	a	LCA	Lowercase a
98	b	LCB	Lowercase b
99	c	LCC	Lowercase c
100	d	LCD	Lowercase d
101	e	LCE	Lowercase e
102	f	LCF	Lowercase f
103	g	LCG	Lowercase g
104	h	LCH	Lowercase h
105	i	LCI	Lowercase i
106	j	LCJ	Lowercase j
107	k	LCK	Lowercase k
108	l	LCL	Lowercase l
109	m	LCM	Lowercase m
110	n	LCN	Lowercase n
111	o	LCO	Lowercase o
112	p	LCP	Lowercase p
113	q	LCQ	Lowercase q
114	r	LCR	Lowercase r
115	s	LCS	Lowercase s
116	t	LCT	Lowercase t
117	u	LCU	Lowercase u
118	v	LCV	Lowercase v
119	w	LCW	Lowercase w
120	x	LCX	Lowercase x
121	y	LCY	Lowercase y
122	z	LCZ	Lowercase z
123	{	LBR	Left brace
124	|	VLN	Vertical line
125	}	RBR	Right brace
126	~	TIL	Tilde
127		DEL	Delete

APPENDIX 2

GLOSSARY

Array	A multi-dimensional quantity. Arrays may contain either numbers or strings. One-dimensional arrays are also called Lists or Vectors. Two-dimensional arrays are also called Tables or Matrices.
Assignment	The placing of a value into a variable. It is accomplished with the LET statement.
BASIC	The name of the computer language used in this text. (There are actually many different versions of BASIC in the world.)
Built-in Function	A function (such as SQR, EXP, LOG, UCASE$, INV, and so forth) provided by BASIC. These functions may be numeric-, string-, or matrix-valued.
Choice	A statement structure that permits two or more alternatives in BASIC. There are three kinds, the IF THEN statement, the IF THEN - ELSEIF - ELSE structure, and the SELECT CASE structure.
Constant	A fixed value. Numeric constants are digits, decimal points, and so forth, formed according to common usage. String constants are strings of characters surrounded by quotation marks.
Defined Function	A function provided by the user. These functions may be numeric- or string-valued, and may be internal or external.

Error	A condition that can arise during the running of a program and that causes the program to stop. Errors are also called Fatal Errors or Exceptions. (In addition, there are typographical errors, which are easily corrected, and design errors, which are sometimes called Bugs.)
Expression	A combination of constants, variables, parentheses, and so forth, formed according to the rules of BASIC. Expressions can be numeric, string, or logical. Numeric expressions are also called formulas.
External	Describes a defined function, subroutine, or picture that is not contained within a program unit.
Internal	Describes a defined function, subroutine, or picture that is contained within a program unit.
Keyword	A word in BASIC (such as LET, PRINT, TO, STEP, and so forth) that has a special meaning.
Library	A file containing any number of external defined functions, subroutines, or pictures.
Line	A part of a BASIC program. A line may contain a BASIC statement, part of a BASIC structure, a comment, or be blank.
List	A one-dimensional array, also called a Vector.
Loop	An iterative structure in BASIC. There are two kinds, the FOR - NEXT and the DO - LOOP.
Parameter	The name given to an argument of a subroutine, function, or picture.
Picture	A separate piece of a BASIC program that is invoked with a DRAW statement. Pictures may be internal or external.
Program	A collection of BASIC statements and structures that conform to the rules of BASIC.
Program Unit	The main program, or any external defined function, subroutine, or picture.
Reserved word	A BASIC keyword or built-in function name that may not be used for other purposes. There are only a few reserved words. They include PRINT, ELSE, TIME, and so forth. Other keywords, such as LET, END, and so forth, are not reserved, and may be used for variable names. Consult your reference manual for details.
Statement	A simple BASIC command that can fit onto one line. Examples are the LET, PRINT, and END statements.
Structure	A grouping of BASIC statements treated as a single entity and occupying more than one line. Examples are the IF THEN - ELSE and the FOR - NEXT structures.
Structure chart	A diagram showing which subroutines call which other subroutines.

Subroutine	A separate piece of a BASIC program that is invoked with a CALL statement. Subroutines may be internal or external.
Table	A two-dimensional array, also called a Matrix.
Transformation	A modification to a picture (such as SHIFT or SCALE) that is applied to the picture in a DRAW statement.
True BASIC	The particular version of BASIC used in this text.
Variable	A place to store a number, string, or matrix. String variables have names that end with a $.

APPENDIX 3

DETAILS OF PRINT USING

BASIC normally prints numbers in a form that is convenient for most purposes. But on occasion we prefer a different form. For example, we might want to print financial quantities with two decimal places (for cents) and, possibly, with commas inserted every three digits to the left of the decimal point. **PRINT USING** provides a way to print numbers in almost any desired form.

The **PRINT USING** statement has the form

```
PRINT USING format$: x, y, z
```

Format$ is a string of characters that contains the instructions to **PRINT USING** for "formatting" the printing of **x**, **y**, and **z**. This string is called a *format string*. It may be a string variable (as shown), a string constant (in quotes), or a more general string expression.

PRINT USING also allows one to print strings centered or right-justified, as well as left-justified, which is what the normal **PRINT** statement does.

There is also a function **using$** that duplicates the **PRINT USING** statement exactly, but that returns the result as a string rather than printing it on the screen. For example, the following two statements yield the same output as the preceding **PRINT USING** statement.

```
LET outstring$ = using$(format$, x, y, z)
PRINT outstring$
```

The advantage is that you can modify or save the string **outstring$** before printing it.

We will first examine how to format numerical output.

Formatting Numbers

The basic idea of a format string is that the symbol "#" stands for a digit position. For example, let us compare the output resulting from two similar PRINT statements, one of them with USING.

```
PRINT x
PRINT USING "###": x
```

In the following table, the symbol "|" is used to denote the left margin and does not actually appear on the screen.

```
x         PRINT           PRINT USING "###"
-         -----           -----------------
1         | 1                           |  1
12        | 12                          | 12
123       | 123                         |123
1234      | 1234                        |***
```

We notice several things. Without USING, the number is printed left-justified with a leading space for a possible minus sign. And, as much space is used as needed. With USING, the format string "###" specifies a *field length* of exactly three characters. The number is printed right-justified in this *field*. If the field is not long enough to print the number properly, asterisks are printed instead. If all you need to do is to print integer numbers in a column but with right-justification, then the preceding example will suffice.

Printing financial quantities so that the decimal points are aligned is important. Also, we want to print two decimal places (for the cents) even when they are "0". The following example shows how this is done.

```
x         PRINT           PRINT USING "###.##"
-         -----           --------------------
1         | 1                      |  1.00
1.2       | 1.2                    |  1.20
-3.57     |-3.57                   |- 3.57
1.238     | 1.238                  |  1.24
123       | 123                    |123.00
-123      |-123                    |******
```

Notice that two decimal places are always printed, even when they consist of zeroes. Also, the result is rounded to two decimals if necessary. If the number is negative, it occupies the leading digit position. Additionally, if the number is too long to be printed properly (because of the minus sign), asterisks are printed instead.

Financial quantities are often printed with a leading dollar sign "$", and with commas for every three digits to the left of the decimal point. The following example shows how to do this with PRINT USING.

```
x                   PRINT USING "$#,###,###.##"
-                   ---------------------------
1                             |$         1.00
1234                          |$     1,234.00
1234567.89                    |$1,234,567.89
1e6                           |$1,000,000.00
1e7                           |*************
```

Notice that the dollar sign is always printed and is in the same position (first) in the field. Also, the separating commas are printed only when needed.

The format string can also allow leading zeroes to be printed, or to be replaced by asterisks, "*". The latter might be useful for check-writing programs.

```
x                   PRINT USING "$%,%%%,%%%.##"
-                   ---------------------------
1                                |$0,000,001.00
1234                             |$0,001,234.00
1234567.89                       |$1,234,567.89

x                   PRINT USING "$*,***,***.**"
-                   ---------------------------
1                                |$*,***,**1.00
1234                             |$*,**1,234.00
1234567.89                       |$1,234,567.89
```

We can also format numbers using scientific notation. Because scientific notation has two parts, the decimal part and the exponent part, the format string must also have two parts. The decimal part follows the rules already illustrated. The exponent part consists of from three to five *carets,* "^", that must immediately follow the decimal format. The following example shows how.

```
x                   PRINT USING "+#.#####^^^^"
-                   --------------------------
123.456                         |+1.23456e+02
-.001324379                     |-1.32438e-02
7e30                            |+7.00000e+30
.5e100                          |+5.00000e+99
5e100                           |************
```

We notice that a leading plus sign "+" in the format string forces the printing of the sign of the number, even when it is positive. Notice also that the last number cannot be formatted because the exponent part would have been "e+100", which requires an exponent field of *five* characters. Finally, notice that trailing zeroes in the decimal part are printed.

Formatting Strings

Strings can also be formatted through `PRINT USING` or the function `using$`, although there are fewer options for strings than for numbers. Basically, strings can be printed in the formatted field either left-justified, centered, or right-justified. As with numbers, if the string is too long to fit, then asterisks are printed. The following example shows several cases.

```
USING           String to be Printed
string          "Ok"        "Hello"       "Goodbye"
--              ----        -------       ---------
"<####"         |Ok         |Hello        |*******
"#####"         |  Ok       |Hello        |*******
">####"         |    Ok     |Hello        |*******
```

Notice that if centering cannot be exact, the extra space is placed to the right.

Any numeric field can be used to "format" a string, in which case the string is centered. This is especially valuable for printing "headers" for a numeric table. For instance, consider the following table.

```
s$                              PRINT USING "$#,###,###.##"
-                               ----------------------------
"Cash"                                    |     Cash
"Liabilities"                             |  Liabilities
"Accounts Receivable"                     | *************
```

Multiple Fields and Other Rules

A **PRINT USING** format string can contain several format items. For example, to print a table of, say, sines and cosines, we may want to use

```
PRINT USING "#.###    #.######    #.######": x, sin(x), cos(x)
```

The value of **x** will then be printed to three decimals, while the values of the sine and cosine will be printed to six decimals. Notice also that there are four spaces between the format items; there will also be four spaces between the columns in the printed result.

If there are more format items than there are values (numbers or strings) to be printed, the usused format items are ignored. If there are *fewer* format items than values to be printed, then the format string is reused. For example,

```
PRINT USING "    #.#####": 1.2, 2.3, 3.4
```

will yield

```
1.20000    2.30000    3.40000
```

Literals in Format Strings

We have just seen that spaces between format items in a format string are printed. That is, if there are four spaces, these four spaces are printed. The same is true for more general characters that may appear between format items. The rule is simple: You can use any sequence of characters between format items *except* the special formatting characters. The characters you use will then be printed.

The special formatting characters are

```
#   %   *   <   >   ^   .   +   -   ,   $
```

The following example illustrates this use.

```
PRINT USING "#.## plus #.## equals #.##": x, y, x+y
```

will yield

```
1.20 plus 2.30 equals 3.50
```

For additional information, consult your BASIC Reference Manual.

APPENDIX 4

DIRECTORY OF PROGRAMS

This appendix lists the names of the programs and support files used in this text. Along with each name is a brief description of the program or file and, in parentheses, the BASIC features and programming principles illustrated by the program. These programs and files are available on the program diskette.

Part One INTRODUCTION TO BASIC

Chapter 1

DIVIDE — Divides two numbers. (Illustrates the LET, PRINT, and END statements.)

DIVIDE2 — Same program as DIVIDE, but with different variable names.

DIVIDE3 — Divides two numbers inputted by the user. (Illustrates the INPUT statement.)

CELSIUS — Computes from Celsius to Fahrenheit degrees. (Illustrates the REM statement and more complicated formulas.)

CELSIUS1 — Same as CELSIUS but with prompted input and labelled output. (Illustrates quoted strings, and the semicolon separator in PRINT statements.)

Chapter 2

CELSIUS2 — Same as CELSIUS but in a loop to allow repeated conversions. (Illustrates the DO loop.)

CELSIUS3 — Same as CELSIUS2 but allows a termination condition. (Illustrates an UNTIL condition on the LOOP statement.)

SQR	Calculates the square root by approximation. (Illustrates looping until some condition is met, and the ABS function.)
SQR2	Same as SQR but with a PRINT statement to show that the guesses converge rapidly to the answer.
SQR3	Same as SQR, but inside a loop to allow repeated calculations. (Illustrates nested DO loops and on-line comments starting with an "!".)

Chapter 3

PERCENT	Computes sales commission with differential rates. (Illustrates IF THEN - ELSE - END IF structure.)
HONORS	Determines graduation honors. (Illustrates IF THEN - ELSEIF - ELSE - END IF structure, and compound logical expressions using AND and OR.)
QUAD	Quadratic equation solver. (Illustrates raising to a power and the SQR function.)
QUAD2	Like QUAD but recognizes the special case of a single root.
GUESS	Number-guessing game. (Illustrates the INT and RND functions, and the RANDOMIZE statement.)
SQR4	Like SQR3 but with a more civilized termination condition. (Illustrates the EXIT DO statement.)
QUAD3	Like QUAD2 but inside a loop to allow several solutions.

Chapter 4

FOR1	Prints Happy Birthday 10 times. (Illustrates the FOR loop.)
FOR2	Prints numbers from 1 to 5 and their squares. (Illustrates use of the FOR variable inside the loop.)
SUM	Sums the numbers from 1 to 100.
SUM2	Sums the numbers from a to b. (Illustrates the use of variables in a FOR statement.)
SUM3	Sums the odd numbers from 1 to b. (Illustrates a step size other than 1.)
FOR3	Prints the numbers from 1 to 2 in steps of 1/8th, and their square roots. (Illustrates fractional step size and the use of the comma in the PRINT statement.)
FOR4	Same as FOR3 but with narrower print zones. (Illustrates the SET ZONEWIDTH statement.)
CUBE	Finds the first integer whose cube is greater than 5000. (Illustrates exiting from a FOR loop with an EXIT FOR statement.)
SUM2DO	Same as SUM2 but in a loop to allow repeated calculations. (Illustrates a FOR loop nested within a DO loop.)
POWERS	Prints the numbers from 1 to 3 in steps of 1/8th, and their squares cubes, and fourth powers. (Illustrates nested FOR loops.)
POWERS2	Same as POWERS but prints the numbers in reverse order. (Illustrates negative step in a FOR loop.)

Chapter 5

SMALL	Computes the smallest of five numbers. (Illustrates the one-line IF THEN statement.)
SMALL2	Same as SMALL. (Illustrates numeric lists and the DIM statement.)
SMALL3	Same as SMALL2. (Illustrates the MAT INPUT statement and the use of a list quantity in a loop.)
SMALL4	Computes the smallest of an arbitrary number of numbers. (Illustrates the MAT INPUT statement with redimensioning.)
SMALL5	Computes the smallest number and its place in the list.
READ	Reads and prints several numbers. (Illustrates the READ and DATA statements.)
SUM4	Computes the sum of several numbers taken from DATA statements. (Illustrates the MAT READ statement with redimensioning.)
BUY	Computes total sales for a customer. (Illustrates the use of two lists in a program.)
BUY2	Like BUY, but for several customers. (The price list is used repeatedly.)

Chapter 6

STRING	Inputs and prints two words in various ways. (Illustrates string variables in INPUT and PRINT statements.)
LETTER	For letter writing.
STRING2	Simple manipulations on strings. (Illustrates the LEN, UCASE$, and LCASE$ functions, and concatenation.)
STRING3	More manipulations on strings. (Illustrates substring expressions.)
REVERSE	Reverses the spelling of a word.
STRING4	Compares two strings. (Illustrates string comparison.)
STRING5	Like STRING4 but ignores case. (Illustrates the use of the UCASE$ function to produce dictionary-like order.)
ALPHA	Like SMALL5 but prints the "smallest" string, in the sense of alphabetical order. (Illustrates string lists.)
LONG	Finds the longest of several words.
DRILL	Simple state capital drill program.

Chapter 7

GRAPH1	Plots three points. (Illustrates the PLOT POINTS statement.)
GRAPH2A	Plots a triangle. (Illustrates the PLOT LINES statement and the trailing semicolon.)
GRAPH2	Same as GRAPH2A. (Illustrates plotting several lines in a single PLOT LINES statement.)
GRAPH3	Same as GRAPH2 but in a window. (Illustrates the SET WINDOW statement.)

SQRP1	Plots the square root function.
SQRP2	Same as SQRP1 but with axes and label. (Illustrates the PLOT TEXT statement.)
SPIRAL1	Draws a spiral. (Illustrates the SIN and COS functions.)
SPIRAL2	Same as SPIRAL1 but in a window. (Illustrates the OPEN SCREEN statement.)
SQUARES1	Draws several nested squares with alternate shading. (Illustrates the FLOOD statement.)
SQUARES2	Same as SQUARES1 but in color. (Illustrates the SET COLOR and SET BACKGROUND COLOR statements.)
BOARD	Draws a checkerboard. (Illustrates the MOD function.)
WINDOWS	Establishes several windows. (Illustrates the ASK WINDOW and the WINDOW # statements.)
BARS	Draws a simple bar chart.

Chapter 8

GRADES	File of grades for use by AVERAGE.
AVERAGE	Computes grade averages using data from a file. (Illustrates the OPEN # and INPUT # statements with files, and the more #1 condition.)
LISTER	Lists a file. (Illustrates the LINE INPUT # statement.)
SALES	Like BUY from Chapter 5, but keeps its data in a table. (Illustrates a table quantity, and the MAT READ statement with redimensioning.)
SALEDATA	File of sales data for use by SALES2.
SALES2	Like SALES, but obtains its data from a file. (Illustrates the MAT INPUT # statement with redimensioning.)
POWERS3	Like POWERS2 but puts the table into a file. (Illustrates the PRINT # and SET # ZONEWIDTH statements.)
TABLE	The file that POWERS3 produces.

Chapter 9

TRIG1	Prints a small table of sines and cosines. (Illustrates the OPTION ANGLE DEGREES declaration.)
TRIG2	Same as TRIG1. (Illustrates the constant pi and the OPTION ANGLE RADIANS declaration.)
ASCII	Demonstrates simple facts about the ASCII character set. (Illustrates the CHR$ and ORD functions.)
CELSIUS4	Converts from Celsius to Fahrenheit degrees. (Illustrates the single-line DEF statement.)
EUCLID	Euclidean algorithm. (Illustrates multiline numeric defined functions, and the DEF and END DEF statements.)
DOUBLE	Doubles spacing between letters. (Illustrates multiline string defined functions, and the null string.)
EUCLID2	Like EUCLID but with the defined function later in the program. (Illustrates the DECLARE DEF statement.)

Chapter 10

SUB0	Obtains three positive numbers. (Illustrates poorly organized repeated code.)
SUB1	Same as SUB0. (Illustrates SUB and END SUB statements, and the use of internal subroutines.)
SALES3	Like SALES2 from Chapter 8, but organized using internal subroutines.
SALESLIB	External library of subroutines for SALES4. (Illustrates the EXTERNAL statement and external subroutine libraries.)
SALES4	Like SALES3, but using external subroutines. (Illustrates external subroutines with parameters.)
SUBADD	Adds numbers. (Illustrates external subroutines that follow the END statement, and parameter-naming conventions.)
SUB2	Same as SUB1. (Illustrates internal subroutines with parameters.)

Chapter 11

There are no programs in Chapter 11.

Part Two TEXT APPLICATIONS

Chapter 12

STROPS	Demonstrates several string operations. (Reviews string operations from Chapter 6, and illustrates the POS function.)
NAME	Reverses a person's name.
STRLET	Demonstrates string insertion. (Illustrates string insertion using the LET statement.)
WHEN1	Demonstrates what happens when attempting to take the square root of a negative number.
WHEN2	Demonstrates prechecking to avoid the fatal SQR error.
WHEN3	Demonstrates what happens when attempting to take the VAL of an invalid string. (Illustrates the VAL and STR$ functions.)
WHEN4	Demonstrates protecting from the effects of a fatal VAL error. (Illustrates the WHEN - USE structure.)
PARSE0	Parses words from a line. (Illustrates the use of NEXTWORD from the library TEXTLIB.)
PARSE1	Parses 10 words from one or more lines. (Illustrates obtaining new lines as a subsidiary operation to obtaining new words.)
PARSE2	Sames as PARSE1. (Illustrates use of the subroutine INPUT to obtain new lines as needed.)
TEXTLIB	Library of external routines to facilitate inputting from the user.
CALENDAR	Perpetual Gregorian calendar. (Illustrates sequential error checking and the EXIT SUB statement.)

Chapter 13

SCORES — Data file to be used with AVERAGE and AVUPDATE.

AVERAGE2 — Prints players' averages. (Illustrates inputting from a display-format file, and the use of a sentinel to signal the end of a file block.)

AVUPDATE — Adds new scores to the file. (Illustrates printing to a display-format file, and the SET # POINTER END statement.)

FILLTEXT — *Fills* text so that each line is about the same length. (Illustrates the ERASE statement, and the REPEAT$ function.)

TEXT1 — Short text to be used with FILLTEXT.

UPDATE — Updates a sequential master file. (Illustrates the use of *high values* to signal the end of a file, and the CREATE option on the OPEN file statement.)

MFILE — Initial master file, to be used with UPDATE.

TFILE — Initial transaction file, to be used with UPDATE.

NMFILE — Final master file, produced by UPDATE.

Chapter 14

SORTSLIB — Library of external string searching and sorting routines.

SORTNLIB — Library of external numeric searching and sorting routines.

TESTSORT — Tests numeric sorting routines. (Illustrates the MAT PRINT statement.)

TIMER — Times numeric sorting routines. (Illustrates the TIME function.)

INDEX — Constructs an index of a line-numbered program. (Illustrates the use of an indexed sort and the TAB operation.)

TIMERLN — Line-numbered version of TIMER, example file for indexing.

Chapter 15

FIND — Data base retrieval system. (Illustrates the construction of a large program and the use of multiple libraries of external subroutines. Also illustrates the SELECT CASE structure.)

DBLIB — Library of external support routines for FIND.

STATLIB — Library of external statistical utility routines.

CLASS — Directory file for sample data base.

DATA1 — Data files for sample data base.

.....

DATA8

Part Three MATHEMATICAL APPLICATIONS

Chapter 16

TRIG — Solves triangles. (Illustrates the ATN function.)

ZERO — Finds one zero of f(x) in an interval. (Illustrates the SGN function.)

ZERO2	Finds all zeros of f(x) in an interval.
PRIMES	Finds prime numbers using a sieve.
NUMLIB	Library of external subroutines to support number theory applications.
PRIMES2	Like PRIMES but uses SIEVE from NUMLIB.
FACTOR	Factors an integer into its prime factors; uses FACTOR from NUMLIB.
EQU	Solves linear equations. (Illustrates the MAT INV function, and matrix multiplication.)
LEONTIEF	Demonstrates the Open Leontief input–output model of the economy. (Illustrates the IDN and CON MAT functions, the DOT function, and matrix subtraction.)

Chapter 17

RANDOM	Generates random numbers. (Reviews the RND function.)
COIN	Simulates coin flipping.
DICE	Simulates dice rolling and the game of Craps.
CARDLIB	Library of external subroutines for simulating card games.
DEAL1	Deals and prints a bridge hand of 13 cards.
DEAL2	Deals and prints four bridge hands, each sorted.
POKER	Deals 100 five-card poker hand and checks each for pairs.
GENES	Simulates spread of a gene mutation.
CIRCLE	Estimates π by Monte Carlo.
CIRCLE2	Like CIRCLE but includes graphical results.
DODGER	Simulates one side of a nine-inning baseball game. (Illustrates *state transition table*, and random selection from events with unequal probabilities.)
MEMORY	Simulates use of disk memory by multiple users.

Chapter 18

FOXRAB	Classic predator–prey model.
POPULUS	Population model of the United States. (Illustrates the MAT ZER function.)
POPDATA	File of initial data for POPULUS.
COLLEGE	Model of a small college, simple version.
COLLEGE2	Model of a small college, with delays.

Part Four OTHER APPLICATIONS

Chapter 19

BUDGETF	File of data for the program BUDGET.
BUDGET	Prepares budget projections.
BUDGLIB	Library of external subroutines for BUDGET. (Illustrates formatted output using the USING$ function.)
MENULIB	Library of external subroutines for supporting menu-driven applications.

COMP	Calculates final balance using compound interest.
COMP2	Compound interest, five cases. (Illustrates use of menus.)
CRITIC	Demonstrates the Critical Path Method.
CRITFILE	File of initial data for CRITIC2.
CRITIC2	Same as CRITIC but obtains data from a file. (Illustrates bit-packing.)

Chapter 20

TICTAC1	Plays tictactoe game: simpler version.
TICTAC2	Plays tictactoe game: heuristic version. (Illustrates the use of a simple evaluation function.)
TICTAC3	Plays tictactoe game: lookahead version. (Illustrates move tree search using recursion.)
NIMMAKE	Constructs winning move file for NIM.
NIM	Plays the game of NIM, choosing moves from the file of winning moves.
PATTERN	Plays the pattern guessing game.

Chapter 21

PICLIB	Library of external pictures.
STAR1	Draws a single star. (Illustrates use of DRAW statement and picture routines.)
STAR2	Draws 15 stars. (Illustrates the SHIFT transformation.)
HOUSE1	Draws a picture of a house. (Illustrates subdividing large pictures into smaller pictures.)
HOUSE2	Draws several houses. (Illustrates the SCALE, ROTATE, and SHEAR transformations, and the use of multiple transformations.)
PIC	Demonstrates the effects of the order of applying multiple transformations.
BOX1	Draws a square within a square. (Illustrates the BOX LINES, AREA, and CLEAR statements.)
BOX2	Draws three circles. (Illustrates the BOX CIRCLE statement.)
STAR3	Imitates a shooting star. (Illustrates BOX KEEP and SHOW statements.)
QUEENS	Solves the eight queens problem. (Illustrates BOX instructions and recursive use of pictures.)
ASK	Prints a simple list. (Illustrates ASK and SET instructions, using zonewidth as an example.)
GRAPHLIB	Library of external pictures for drawing frames, axes, and plotting functions.
FPLOT1	Plots a simple function. (Illustrates use of GRAPHLIB.)
FPLOT2	Plots a function with a singularity. (Illustrates use of the WHEN - USE structure with plotting.)
FPLOT3	Plots the same function in several windows.
PLOTLIB	Library of external subroutines for plotting multiple functions in several windows; used in Chapters 17 and 18.

Chapter 22

SCALE1	Plays the C-scale. (Illustrates the SOUND statement.)
SCALE2	Plays the C-scale. (Illustrates the PLAY statement.)
BRAHMS	Plays 16 bars of Brahm's Waltz in A-flat. (Illustrates additional options with the PLAY statement.)
SCORE	Plots a score in standard notation. (Illustrates the use of pictures and transformations.)
SCORELIB	Library of external pictures for drawing notes and staffs.
HARMONY	Generates four-part harmony for simple tunes.

Index